The Revolution in Time

Tony Claydon is emeritus professor of early modern history at Bangor University in Wales.

The Revolution in Time

Chronology, Modernity, and 1688–1689 in England

TONY CLAYDON

Great Clarendon Street, Oxford, OX2 6DP,
United Kingdom

Oxford University Press is a department of the University of Oxford.
It furthers the University's objective of excellence in research, scholarship,
and education by publishing worldwide. Oxford is a registered trade mark of
Oxford University Press in the UK and in certain other countries

Published in the United States of America by Oxford University Press
546 Fifth Avenue, New York, NY 10036, United States of America

British Library Cataloguing in Publication Data
Data available

Library of Congress Control Number: 2019946153

ISBN 9780198817239 (hbk)
ISBN 9780197904831 (pbk)

DOI: 10.1093/oso/9780198817239.001.0001

The manufacturer's authorized representative in the EU for product safety is
Oxford University Press España S.A. of Parque Empresarial San Fernando de Henares,
Avenida de Castilla, 2 – 28830 Madrid (www.oup.es/en or product.safety@oup.com).
OUP España S.A. also acts as importer into Spain of products made by the manufacturer.

Acknowledgements

This book has been many years in writing. Over that time, I have benefitted hugely from conversations with colleagues across the world; from the insight of students I have taught, supervised, and examined; and from the helpfulness and professionalism of numerous library and archive staff. I hope I thanked each one of these as they contributed. I have also benefitted from the care and professionalism of everyone at Oxford University Press, including two anonymous readers, and I thank all these people now. My greatest debt, as ever, is to my husband.

Contents

List of Illustrations

List of Abbreviations

CUP	Cambridge University Press
HMC	Historic Manuscripts Commission
HMSO	His/Her Majesty's Stationary Office
OUP	Oxford University Press
MUP	Manchester University Press
UP	University Press

Notes on Style

Dates are given old style: that is, according to the Julian calendar; but the year is assumed to have started on 1 January.

Place of publication of works printed before 1900 is London, unless otherwise stated.

Introduction

Time, Revolution, and Modernity

There was, it seems, a silence. The lower house of the convention that had been elected over the winter of 1688–9 to settle the constitutional future of England had just formed itself into a grand committee to consider the state of the nation. This would allow freer discussion of an extraordinary situation in which the country's king, James II, had fled in the face of rebellion and order was being kept by the invading Dutch forces of his son-in-law, William, prince of Orange. But though the rules of a grand committee would facilitate debate (permitting people to speak more than once and so admitting full exchange of opinion), notes taken by a member of the house suggest that the men gathered at Westminster on 28 January 1689 were reluctant to exploit this liberty. They may well have been stunned by the circumstances in which they found themselves, and daunted by any attempt to explain, describe, or resolve them. Finally, however, 'after a great pause', a brash young member of the convention, Gilbert Dolben, found the courage to speak.[1] When he did, he used history to comprehend the political revolution. He suggested James might be treated legally as if he had died, even though he was still alive in French exile, because other kings had been deposed in the past. In particular, he cited the examples of Edward II in 1327; of Richard II in 1399; and of Edward IV, who had been driven into temporary exile in 1470, and had ceased to be recognized as ruler until he had fought his way back to throne.[2]

Dolben's speech set a fashion. In the convention debates that followed over the next fortnight—and in a host of pamphlets that soon joined in attempts to explain what had happened—people returned repeatedly to the depositions of the fourteenth century, and to the Wars of the Roses of which Edward IV's adventures had formed a part.[3] These instances were joined by other moments from distant history, especially as attempts to understand the revolution spread beyond the immediate legal and constitutional discussion. As preachers reflected on what 1688–9 might say about God's purposes for man; as personal and public historians wove narratives of James's fall; and as William's arrival was commemorated,

---

[1] 'A jornall of the convention at Westminster', reprinted in David Lewis Jones, ed., *A Parliamentary History of the Glorious Revolution* (London, HMSO, 1988), 233.

[2] Anchitell Grey, *Debates in the House of Commons from 1667 to 1694*, 10 vols, (1769), x: 7–9.

[3] See below, ch. 2.1.

The Revolution in Time: Chronology, Modernity, and 1688–1689 in England. Tony Claydon, Oxford University Press (2020). © Tony Claydon.
DOI: 10.1093/oso/9780198817239.001.0001

analyzed, and disputed over the course of the next two decades, a whole range of historical events—from the Stuart and Tudor ages, back through the medieval period, and on to the deepest pre-Roman history—were cited to classify and comprehend the revolution.[4] Through the political and conceptual turmoil, the nation clung to precedents, from no matter how long ago. The most distant past was brought into the present as the most certain guide to how to think and act.

To twenty-first-century eyes, such a direct, uncontextualized, and unproblematic application of distant events to current affairs, seems strange. Of course, politicians, journalists, and commentators still cite supposed 'lessons of history' to bolster their argument. Similarly, common lawyers seek precedents from the past; and some schools of American constitutional interpretation try to follow the intentions of long-dead founders in particular legal cases. But they do not behave quite as Dolben and his contemporaries did. They do not assume the relevance of long-bygone events to complex political situations so systematically, and with so little sense, or so little caution, that change over centuries might limit their applicability. From a contemporary perspective, what the people of the late seventeenth century did with the past was so strange that they seem themselves to belong to a very distant age. We therefore view them with a sense of alienation, and with an assumption that much has changed in the intervening years, that they seemed *not* to have had as they looked back to their own predecessors. This book is about that gap in perceptions. It will explore the frequently unfamiliar appreciations of time and history among the generation that faced the great crisis of late Stuart monarchy. It will do this partly to investigate how the subjects of those late Stuart monarchs understood the revolution, but also to explore the chronological framework in which they understood it. In particular, it will ask if their conception of time equipped them to see 1688–9 as a leap ahead into a novel state of politics, society, and culture, and thus if it may have helped them to accept and to shape the change of regime as a transformative step towards a new world. These are important goals. For it has been argued that this late Stuart generation was the first anywhere to achieve 'modernity' (to a large extent because of the effects of 1688–9); and also that it lived towards the end of a process in which 'modern' understandings of time emerged. Examining if these interpretations are true, and if they can be made to relate to one another, will flood light on how and whether William's reign (1689–1702) might be seen as the first 'modern' decade.

The case for the modernizing power of the revolution itself has been strengthening since the late twentieth century. The events of 1688–9 had traditionally been celebrated as progressive, or at the very least as a defeat for reactionary forces that would have denied England its liberal future. The revolution involved the removal of the last English monarch who had claimed a divine right to

---

[4] See below, chs. 2–3.

suspend law without parliamentary approval. It also imposed clear limitations on the power of rulers, and clear statements on the rights and role of Parliament in the polity. The final settlement—agreed in mid February 1689—deposed James from the throne and offered it to William, but accompanied it with a 'declaration of rights' of the legislature, and of subjects. Within a few weeks of this, the 'toleration' act had passed. This was seen as a major step towards freedom of religion since it allowed some significant groups to worship outside the hitherto monopolistic Church of England. All this made a traditional case for 1688–9 as a stride towards the modern world—at least in the sense that England had become more like the open society of the Victorian epoch and of the twentieth century.[5]

Yet over recent decades, a series of even more radical suggestions have been made about the nature and effects of the revolution. It was, according to some scholars, a revolt by a mass population that had come to see itself as the source of political legitimacy (a set of beliefs at least one scholar has been happy to label English 'nationalism').[6] The folk who had resisted James, and caused him to flee, had been drawn into politics by an emerging 'public sphere', which had allowed a mass population to learn about, and discuss, the mysteries of policy for the first time.[7] The effects of 1688–9 have also been painted in radical colours. In this view, the revolution aggravated the fracture in the English elite that institutionalized party politics, and so ensured a far more competitive conduct of public affairs. Press censorship ended in 1695, ensuring an explosion of information and opinion; general elections became frequent and hotly contested; partisanship reached far down into society, and became so passionate that the very nature of truth itself came into question; but at the same time, shifting relationships between the monarchy and politicians channelled these energies into a functioning two party system.[8] The revolution also allowed the triumph of an economic theory that

---

[5] Such a progressive view has been labelled 'Whiggish', but—though some strands of Georgian Whig thought saw 1688–9 as an advance—classic 'Whig' scholarship such as Thomas Babington Macaulay, *The history of England from the accession of James II*, 5 vols, (1848–56) or G.M. Trevelyan, *The English revolution, 1688–89* (London, 1938) tended to stress moderation rather than radicalism. Celebration of 1688–9 as a triumph of progressive liberalism was clearer in popular history: witness the school text book used by my mother in the late 1940s—George Townsend Warner, C. Henry K. Marten, and D Erskine Muir, *The New Groundwork of British History* (London: Blackie and Son, 1948), sect. 4, 537–40—or even Trevelyan writing in shorter summary: G.M. Trevelyan, *England under the Stuarts* (London: Methuen, 1904), 371–4.

[6] Steve Pincus, '"To protect English liberties": The English Nationalist Revolution of 1688–1689', in Tony Claydon and Ian McBride, eds, *Protestantism and National Identity: Britain and Ireland, c.1650–c.1850* (Cambridge: CUP. 1998), 75–104.

[7] Steve Pincus, '"Coffee politicians does create": Coffeehouses and Restoration Political Culture', *Journal of Modern History* 67 (1995), 807–34; Jürgen Habermas, *Structurwandel der Öffentlichkeit*, trans. Thaoms Burger and Frederick Lawrence as *The Structural Transformation of the Public Sphere* (Cambridge MA: Harvard UP, 1989); Joad Raymond, *Pamphlets and Pamphleteering in Early Modern Britain* (Cambridge: CUP, 2003)—a subtle work, that comes closest to claiming an emerging public sphere at pp. 25–6.

[8] Mark Knights, *Representation and Misrepresentation in Later Stuart Britain: Partisanship and Political Culture* (Oxford: OUP, 2005); Tony Claydon, 'Daily News and the Construction of Time in Late Stuart England, 1695–1713', *Journal of British Studies*, 53 (2013), 55–7; J.P. Kenyon, *Revolution*

assumed enterprise and labour were the source of wealth; and, crucially, it led to a massive expansion of the state as England began a long struggle with France. This remodelled government's role in society: as an employer (in the navy, in the army, and in the bureaucracies of the military and revenue departments); as a tax burden; and as a customer for the nation's goods. The war also altered relations between rulers and ruled by ensuring constant meetings of the people's representatives in Parliament, and by instituting large-scale and long-term public credit, which created new forms of wealth in the form of calls on government interest.[9] In short, this was a transformative political event with a transformative effect on the entire national community. People were far freer to worship, read, debate, and invest. Their fears for the future came to centre on a large and indebted state rather than popery and an ambitious monarchy.[10]

The English of this interpretation were 'moderns' in comparison to the generations before; and in one of the most recent readings of 1688–9, by Steve Pincus, this modernization was conscious and deliberate. The people who supported William had a set of clear plans to advance the sort of parliamentary liberty, of religious toleration, and of credit and enterprise-based economics, which would be the hallmarks of Britain in more recent ages. By calling William's triumph 'the first modern revolution', Pincus also suggested it represented a new kind of process. Comparing 1688–9 to the French, Russian, and other later upheavals, he claimed that—like them—it was driven by dissatisfactions sparked by a preceding and deliberate modernization of the state. In this theory, regimes allow opposition to form by bringing mass populations into national politics as they centralize and bureaucratize their organization; and they permit people to imagine different futures by taking radical action themselves. According to Pincus, James II was doing this as he built the military infrastructure of his government and as he promoted religious liberty; but his actions generated an alternative vision of the future, one that was ultimately to overthrow him.[11] This analysis distinguished 1688–9 from the reactionary, and often elite, protest against change that had characterized rebellious action in earlier times; and it supported interpretations that saw the late Stuart era as the age of England's true revolution, downgrading the claims

Principles: The Politics of Party, 1689–1720 (Cambridge: CUP, 1977); Gary Stuart de Krey, *A Fractured Society: The Politics of London in the First Age of Party, 1688–1715* (Oxford: OUP, 1985); Tim Harris, *Politics Under the Later Stuarts: Party Conflict in a Divided Society* (Harlow, Longman, 1993); Tony Claydon, *William III: Profiles in Power* (Harlow: Longman, 2002), ch. 4.

[9] As well as the works in n. 10 below, see John Brewer, *The Sinews of Power: War, Money and the English State, 1688–1783* (London: Unwin, 1989); Patrick O'Brien and Philip Hunt, 'The Rise of a Fiscal State in England, 1485–1815', *Historical Research*, 66 (1993), 129–76.

[10] Works that have put large parts of this case are Tim Harris, *Revolution: The Great Crisis of the British Monarchy, 1685–1720* (London: Allen Lane, 2006); Partick Dillon, *The Last Revolution: 1688 and the Creation of the Modern World* (London: Jonathan Cape, 2006); Steve Pincus, *1688: The First Modern Revolution* (New Haven: Yale UP, 2009).

[11] Pincus, *1688, passim*, but esp. ch. 2.

of the civil war and republic of the mid Stuart era.[12] In sum, recent scholarship has identified the advent of William III as one of the most significant moments in English history, and his reign as the very dawn of the modern age.

And William's subjects have been claimed to have been moving towards 'modernity' in a rather different way. They have been supposed to have lived towards the end of a modernizing transformation in concepts of time that may have begun in the later Middle Ages, and was well on its way to completion by the late seventeenth century. Here the strands of argument have been numerous. In fact, the plethora of suggestions has led one scholar, Robert Poole, to remark there seen to be as many forms of time as there are of love (paraphrasing Jane Austen), and to doubt that summarizing all proposals made by the researchers in this area would clarify very much for readers.[13] Yet whilst it is true that the arguments for shifts in temporal awareness have been bewilderingly diverse, the proposed changes have overlapped and intertwined, so it is possible to describe a broadly coherent theory of what happened. We can get some bearings, first, by noting there has been a broad pattern to the supposed transformations. All of them would have facilitated a 'progressive' model of chronology, in which the forward flow of time alters human conditions. Second, we can isolate a number of key ideas around which much scholarship has coalesced. What follows is a survey of seven conceptual changes that are supposed to have occurred after the medieval centuries, and which are thought to have modernized temporal awareness.

The first shift concerned how events were placed in time. Before the early modern era, it has been claimed, people had used a 'relative' chronology that dated things with reference to other happenings. So things were placed within the year by talking about the days or weeks that had lapsed from an earlier moment (for example, the church counted Sundays in Trinity); by using anniversaries of other events, or annually repeating festivals; or with reference to changing astronomical and meteorological seasons.[14] Similarly, instead of using a universal numerical

---

[12] One of the classic statements of this case was Angus McInnes, 'When Was the English Revolution?', *History*, 67 (1982), 377–92.

[13] Robert Poole, *Time's Alteration: Calendar Reform in Early Modern England* (London: UCL Press,1998), 19

[14] Donald J. Wilcox, *The Measure of Times Past: Pre-Newtonian Chronologies and the Rhetoric of Relative Time* (Chicago: Chicago UP, 1987); Philip Turetzky, *Time* (London: Routledge, 1988), ch. 6; Poole, *Time's Alteration*, 19–24; David Vincent, *Literacy and Popular Culture* (Cambridge: CUP, 1989), 181; Diana Greenway, 'Dates in History: Chronology and Memory', *Historical Research*, 71 (1999), 127–39. There is a fine case study of the effects of relative time in James McConnel, 'The 1688 Landing of William III at Torbay: Numerical Dates and Temporal Understanding in Early Modern England', *Journal of Modern History*, 84:3 (2012), 539–71. Relative time also resulted in local, customary, calendars and non-numeric dating—see Bob Bushaway, *By Rite: Custom, Ceremony and Community in England, 1700–1880* (London: Breviary Stuff, 1982); Ronald Hutton, *The Rise and Fall of Merry England* (Oxford: OUP, 1994); Andy Wood, *The Memory of the People: Custom and Popular Sense of the Past in Early Modern England* (Cambridge: CUP, 2013); Keith Wrightson, 'Popular Senses of Times Past: Dating Events in the North Country, 1615–1630', in Michael J. Braddick and Phil Wilthington, eds, *Popular Culture and Political Agency in Early Modern England* (Woodbridge: Boydell, 2017), 91–108.

system to signify the year or period in which something had happened, events were located from a start date, or by describing what was also going on simultaneously with them. So, for example, government worked in regnal years (the period since a monarch had come to the throne) rather than using the Anno Domini system; and the wider society set narratives 'in the time of the late wars', or 'in the days of our fathers', rather than referring to decades or precise dates.[15] By the late seventeenth century, however, people are thought to have moved from thinking in such 'relative' terms, to adopt an 'absolute' time. Now, folk imagined a sort of abstract and universal clock. This measured out the minutes, days, and years of a chronology that moved forward at an even—so regularly countable—pace. It was unaffected by particular occurrences, and flowed without account of them, so it became the most efficient way of describing when they had happened. In the new worldview, one simply needed to set an event in its proper position in the onward movement of absolute time: there was no need to know when any other particular thing had taken place. Such thinking was encouraged by the growing availability of real clocks and watches that seemed to indicate the point reached within a universal time; by print forms such as newspapers, that put numerical dates on their appearance; by the triumph of a Newtonian mechanics that depended on abstract time to calculate its explanation of how the physical world worked; and by increasing contact between geographically distant communities that needed to coordinate activities with reference to a universal standard.[16]

A second shift was the secularization of time. Before the early modern centuries, Christian thought is supposed to have dominated perceptions of history; and people had structured their years and days through cycles of religious ritual. Thus all of the past was believed to be organized by God's divine plan for the universe. Everything happened in order to advance the drama of salvation, after the opening tragedy of man's fall from grace. Whatever slippage there may have been in applying the doctrine (clergy in particular implied that godly behaviour would reap divine

---

[15] The first phrase, perhaps unsurprisingly, yields multiple hits in an electronic search of early modern publication; the second was used in Samuel Bradford, *A sermon preach'd before the right honourable Lord-Mayor, the aldermen, and citizens of London, at St. Mary Le Bow, on Thursday, November 5, 1696* (1697), 2.

[16] Daniel R. Woolf, 'From Histories to the Historical: Five Transitions in Thinking About the Past, 1500–1700', *Huntington Library Quarterly*, 68 (2005), 33–70, esp. 47–9; Stuart Sherman, *Telling Time: Clocks, Diaries and the English Diurnal Form, 1660–1785* (Chicago: Chicago UP, 1996); Arno Borst, *The Ordering of Time*, trans. Andrew Winnard (Cambridge: CUP, 1993), esp. ch. 12; Rudolf Dekker, *Family, Culture and Society in the Diary of Constantijn Huygens jnr* (Leiden: Brill, 2013), ch. 2; D.S. Landes, *Revolution in Time: Clocks and the Making of the Modern World* (rev. and enlarged edn, Cambridge, MA: Harvard UP, 2000); Eviator Zerubavel, 'The Standardisation of Time: A Sociohistorical Perspective', *American Journal of Sociology*, 88 (1982), 1–23; Wilcox, *Measure of Times Past*, chs 1–2—though for a more ambiguous assessment of the role of clocks, see Ronald Bedford, Lloyd Davis, and Phillipa Kelly, *Early Modern English Lives: Autobiography and Self-Representation, 1500–1660* (Aldershot: Ashgate, 2007), 21–8; and Gerhard Dohrn-van Rossum, *History of the Hour: Clocks and Modern Temporal Orders*, trans. Thomas Dunlap (Chicago: Chicago UP, 1996). For stress on the constructed nature of absolute time, see Elizabeth Deeds Ermarth, *Realism and Consensus in the English Novel* (Princeton: Princeton UP, 1983).

reward), there was technically little room for human initiative, since providence had fixed the course of human affairs.[17] At the more mundane level, people structured their activities according to rhythms set by the church. Liturgical seasons such as Advent and Lent gave a sense of where one was in a year; annual festivals such Christmas, Easter, Pentecost, and saints' days provided a repeating framework for community life; and days were built around the regular offices of prayer—either attended in person, or perhaps marked by the bells that summoned the religious to services performed on behalf of the absent.[18] By the later seventeenth century, however, the Protestant Reformation, the rise of Renaissance humanism, the scientific revolution, and a number of other cultural changes, are thought to have begun to empty chronology of divinity. Days and years were now structured, not by the rituals of the church, but rather by the demands of the state and an emerging capitalist economy. Such duties as arriving at work on time, or paying taxes or rents on a set date, replaced spiritual festivals as temporal markers. At the same time, far more faith was placed in the possibilities of human action to affect history. Providence withdrew, at least from the direction of the ordinary run of affairs. History was now largely driven by individual initiative, and by social, technological, or environmental processes that belonged to this world rather than the next.[19]

The two shifts just surveyed combined to create a third: the move from 'full' to 'empty' time.[20] 'Full' time was already replete with divinely determined events and religious meaning.[21] In fact, it was so full that it had a curiously frozen quality. According to theologians such as St Augustine, everything that would happen was so fixed and foreseen by God that time's forward flow was in a fact an illusion.[22] But with secularization, and once time was perceived as an absolute phenomenon

[17] Alexandra Walsham, *Providence in Early Modern England* (Oxford: OUP, 1991), ch. 1.

[18] Hutton, *Rise and Fall*, ch. 1; Eamon Duffy, *The Stripping of the Altars* (New Haven: Yale UP, 1992), ch. 1; Keith Thomas, *Religion and the Decline of Magic* (London: Wiedenfield and Nicolson,1971), 738–45.

[19] C. John Sommerville, *The Secularisation of Early Modern England* (Oxford: OUP, 1992); C. John Sommerville, 'The Secularisation Puzzle', *History Today*, 44 (1994), 14–19; Charles Taylor, *A Secular Age* (Cambridge, MA: Harvard UP, 2007), 58–61; C.A. Patrides, *The Grand Design of God: The Literary Form of the Christian View of History* (London: Routledge, 1972), 58–9; James William Johnson, 'Chronological Writing: Its Concepts and Development', *History and Theory*, 2 (1962), 124–45; Thomas, *Religion*, 785–94; Walsham, *Providence*, 28–9, 333–4; Etinenne Bourdon, 'Temporalities and History in the Renaissance', *Journal of Early Modern Studies*, 6 (2017), 39–60. For growing anxieties caused by natural philosophers' concentration on ordinary, or secondary, causes, rather than providence, see Micheal Hunter, *Science and Society in Restoration England* (Cambridge,: CUP, 1981), chs 6–7.

[20] Most clearly outlined in Benedict Anderson, *Imagined Communities* (rev. edn, London: Verso, 1991), ch. 2—though for a critique relating more closely to the early modern period, see Kevin Birth, 'Calendars: Representational Homogeneity and Heterogeneous Time', *Time and Society*, 22 (2013), 216–36.

[21] Related points about a time dominated by religious meaning are made in C. Taylor, *Secular Age*, 54–8: his formulation of 'higher' time disrupting secular time is useful—but not all conceptions of temporal shifts can be given full weight here, or any thread will be lost.

[22] St Augustine, *Confessions*, trans. Henry Chadwick (Oxford: OUP, 1991), book xi, ch. xxxi, and see below ch. 3.4.

that advanced without reference to the things that occurred within it, chronology emptied. The new time was a void, waiting to be filled with events. Analogous to empty space, it offered a new range of possibilities, because different narratives might occupy any given span, according to how human enterprise worked within the world. In this way, time also became a resource. It could used, spent, or wasted, and, to avoid the worst consequences of this, folk needed to exercise time discipline. The keeping of diaries to audit personal endeavour, and insistence that workers concentrate on particular tasks for particular periods, were characteristic of this 'empty' view of chronology, as was the stress in Renaissance literature on the heroic battle that an individual must wage against the decaying and destroying effects of time, especially by concentration on progeny, self-improvement, and the pursuit of fame.[23]

The changes covered so far also facilitated a fourth transformation in the early modern centuries. This was the destabilization of the 'present'. Before the transformation in chronological perspective, the present had been little remarked upon. It was just an inert moment between a past (which was now unchangeable), and a future which was either unknowable, or which would simply unfold according to its preset design. Yet once time had become an absolute, secular, and empty resource, the present became far more interesting. If time were being shaped by human action, it became the point at which the future was being actively created: the point at which it might even be being planned and constructed, in Reinhart Kosellick's formulation.[24] The present was therefore seen as progressive, and fluid; and it was further destabilized because of a new sense of 'contemporaneity'.[25] The universal nature of abstract time meant the present must be occurring all over the world, at the same moment—including in places so far away that people did not know what it looked like there, but would know it must look like something. As a result, the present became a source of anxiety and fascination. One needed to gain as much information about it as possible in order to react to its constantly

[23] E.P. Thompson, 'Time, Work Discipline, and Industrial Capitalism', *Past and Present*, 38:1 (1967), 56–97; Barbara Adam, *Time and Social Theory* (Cambridge: CUP, 1990), ch. 5; Ricardo J. Quinones, *The Renaissance Discovery of Time* (Cambridge, MA: Harvard UP, 1972); Max Engammare, *On Time, Punctuality and Discipline in Early Modern Calvinism*, trans K. Maag (Cambridge: CUP, 2010); C. Taylor, *Secular Age*, 58–9; Lynn Hunt, *Measuring Time, Making History* (Budapest: Central European UP, 2007), 14–15; G.J. Whitrow, *Time in History: The Evolution of Our General Awareness of Time* (Oxford: OUP, 1988) 107–14. For suggestions that a shift to a sense of time as a resource predated the early modern period, see Nigel Thrift, 'Vivos Voco: Ringing the Changes in the Historical Geography of Time Consciousness', in Michael Young and Tom Schuller, eds, *The Rhythms of Society* (London: Routledge, 1988), 53–94.

[24] Reinhart Koselleck, 'Historia Magistra Vitae: The Dissolution of the Topos Into the Perspective of a Modernized Historical Process', in his *Futures Past: On the Semantics of Historical Time*, trans. Keith Tribe (New York: Colombia UP, 2004), 26–42, esp. 39. Koselleck was supported by Lucian Hölscher, *Die entdeckung der zukunft* (Frankfurt: Suhrkampf, 1999), which argued the premodern world lacked a strong sense of the future that might be shaped.

[25] Anderson, *Imagined Communities*; Brendan Dooley, ed., *The Dissemination of News and the Emergence of Contemporaneity in Early Modern Europe* (Farnham: Ashgate, 2010); Andrew Pettegree, *The Invention of News: How the World Came to Know About Itself* (New Haven: Yale UP, 2014).

evolving demands. This feeling explained, but it was also created by, such things as the thirst for news, and the popularity of emerging literary forms such as the novel that focused upon an endlessly updating 'now'.[26]

The remaining suggested shifts in chronological conception are perhaps the ones that do most to argue for a new progressive temporality. The fifth was the replacement of cyclical with linear time. Before this change, it has been argued, people had assumed that the world's affairs were arranged in repeating patterns, which brought things back, inevitably, to a starting point; and they understood their chronological position by seeing themselves at stages in these cycles. Key examples included the rhythm of the seasons; the wheel of fortune that governed individuals' lives; the replacement of each successive generation by its children; and the rise and fall of empires that appeared to be dictated by inescapable forces within civilization.[27] By the end of the early modern era, however, people began to think that time could, and had, moved in a much more linear fashion. It rarely, if ever, returned to exactly the same starting point or simply covered the same old ground. Rather it moved in clear directions—even if these might reverse, or veer off course, temporarily.[28] A significant dimension of this was a new 'periodized' view of history. Societies had moved through different states of being, which had had different, non-repeating, characteristics. It was therefore worth thinking about the conditions peculiar to each of these periods, analysing the turning points that had ushered in new epochs, and perhaps to begin to label these successive ages. The early Renaissance humanists' division of time into 'ancient', 'modern', and 'middle' ages could be argued to be the start of the process.[29] This

---

[26] Daniel Woolf, 'News, History and the Construction of the Present in Early Modern England', in Brendan Dooley and Sabrina. A Baron, eds, *The Politics of Information in Early Modern Europe* (London: Routledge, 2002), 80-118; Dooley, *Dissemination of News*; Ian Watt, *The Rise of the Novel* (London: Chatto and Windus, 1957); Lennard J. Davis, *Factual Fictions: The Origins of the English Novel* (New York: Colombia UP, 1983); J. Paul Hunter, *Before Novels* (New York: W.W. Norton, 1990); C. John Sommerville, *The News Revolution in England* (Oxford: OUP, 1996). Tony Claydon, 'Daily News', is partly supportive of the suggested transition; Peter Burke, 'Foreword: The History of the Future', in Andrea Brady and Emily Butterworth, eds, *The Uses of the Future in Early Modern Europe* (New York: Routledge, 2010), listed practical ways people began to act to shape the future in the early modern world; much of J.G.A. Pocock's work has explored the early modern centuries as a period when assumptions about politics as coping with change replaced assumptions about perpetuating ancient practice: see particularly *The Machiavellian Moment* (Princeton: Princeton UP, 1975), and *Virtue, Commerce and History* (Cambridge: CUP, 1985).

[27] For the natural rhythms that created a cyclical view of time, see Vincent, *Literacy and Popular Culture*, 181-3; Poole, *Time's Alteration*; Reinhart Koselleck, 'History, Histories and Formal Time Structures', in his *Futures Past*, 93-104, esp. 96. For cyclical historical views, see Achsah Guibbory, *The Map of Time: Seventeenth-Century English Literature and Ideas of Pattern in History* (Urbana, IL: Illinois UP, 1986), 8-17; Frank E. Manuel, *Shapes of Philosophical History* (Stanford: Stanford UP, 1965), 59-65.

[28] Mahlin Dahlstrom, review of Malin Dahlstrom, review of Nicklas Olsen, History in the Plural: An Introduction to the Work of Reinhart Koselleck,, Reviews in History, http://www.history.ac.uk/reviews/review/1276, accessed 9 June, 2015; John Walter, 'The Commons and Their Mental Worlds', in John Morrill, ed., *The Oxford Illustrated History of Tudor and Stuart Britain*' (Oxford: OUP, 1996), 215-17.

[29] Theodore E. Mommsen, 'Petrach's Conception of the Dark Ages', *Speculum*, 17 (1942), 226-42; François Hartog, *Régimes d'historicité: présentisme et experience du temps* (Paris: Seuil, 2003), 227-8.

periodized view easily tripped into suggestions of 'progress' in human history, particularly, at first, in material prosperity. Ultimately, it generated the stadial theory which saw humanity moving through different stages of development—each with its particular, and steadily more sophisticated, way of life. It also created a sense of a most recent 'modern' era, superior to past ages because it had access to the most up-to-date and advanced thinking and technologies.[30]

The sixth claimed change in time was its acceleration. Not only was an empty—and so fluid—future being created in an unstable present, this was occurring at a rapidly increasing rate. Before the early modern centuries, there had been few dramatic turning points in history, these had been widely spaced, and they had often taken a long time. The result had been a sense of deep continuity: grandchildren had lived in very much the same world as their grandparents, and history seemed to move slowly, if at all. From the Renaissance, however, social, cultural, political, economic, and technological change came more quickly. A series of geographical, scientific, religious, and administrative revolutions meant people were richer, more knowledgeable, governed more intensively, confronted by a greater variety of spiritual choice, and so on. As a result, generations felt they lived in a different cosmos to those who preceded them, and individuals found they had to keep adapting their worldview within their lifetime.[31] Meanwhile, improvements in communication and news media packed experience with an ever greater density of events. Knowledge of these events changed the conditions in which people felt they existed, and this placed greater urgency on their response to situations.[32]

---

[30] Whitrow, *Time in History*, 134; F Smith Fussner, *The Historical Revolution: English Historical Writing and Thought, 1580–1640* (London: Routledge,1962), 299. On the modern, see Hunt, *Measuring Time*, 19–20; Paul Hazard, *The Crisis of the European Mind, 1680–1715* (New York: New York Review of Books, 2013); Bourdon, 'Temporalities and History', 51; Joan DeJean, *Ancients against Moderns: Culture Wars and the Making of a Fin de Siècle* (Chicago: Chicago UP, 1997)—though see Joseph M. Levine, *Humanism and History: The Origins of English Historiography* (Ithaca: Cornell UP, 1987), ch. 6. For the stadial theory, see Karen O'Brien, *Narratives of Enlightenment: Cosmopolitan History from Voltaire to Gibbon* (Cambridge: CUP, 1997), 132–6; for progress, see Robert Nisbet, *The History of the Idea of Progress* (New York: Basic Books, 1980); David Spadafora, *The Idea of Progress in Eighteenth-Century Britain* (New Haven: Yale UP, 1990); Paul Slack, *The Invention of Improvement: Information and Material Progress in Seventeenth Century England* (Oxford: OUP, 2015), and Andrea Brady and Emily Butterworth's introduction to their *Uses of the Future in Early Modern Europe* (London: Routledge, 2009), 1–18, which suggests the Renaissance and Reformation instilled a sense that recent times had been an improvement on the Middle Ages in the early modern centuries. See also, Peter Fritzche, *Stranded in the Present: Modern Time and the Melancholy of History* (Cambridge, MA: Harvard UP, 2004), 200–1, which suggests the modern era has seen the past as a series of radical discontinuities. It is possible that linear conceptions of time may have been fostered by the development of 'timeline' depictions of history: for these, see Daniel Rosenberg and Anthony Grafton, *Cartographies of Time: A History of the Timeline* (Princeton: Princeton UP, 2010). In the late seventeenth century, the 'battle of books' (a dispute about whether modern authors could ever surpass classical models) may also have promoted a sense of a current age superior to the past: Joseph M. Levine, *The Battle of the Books: History and Literature in the Augustan Age* (Ithaca Cornell UP, 1991).

[31] See Koselleck, *Futures Past*, esp. 'Space of Experience and Horizon of Expectation: Two Historical Categories', 255–78

[32] Sommerville, *News Revolution*, 8–13; Woolf, 'News, History'; Peter Lake and Steven Pincus, eds, *The Politics of the Public Sphere in Early Modern England* (Manchester: MUP, 2007), 10.

Put simply, they had to do things quickly, before their perception of the situation changed. Taken together, these accelerations resulted in a 'contraction of the present'.[33] As time speeded up, the period available for meaningful comprehension of the world, and for relevant action within it, shrank: and people felt an ever greater pressure of time upon them.

The seventh and final suggested shift, and perhaps the most important for understanding thinking about 1688–9, was that time ceased to be typological in the centuries before the revolution. In many ways this change summarized all the others. Back when time was relative, religious, full, cyclical, and had an inert and unaccelerated, present, it was easy to link events to other moments from long before. Widely separated happenings could be seen as sharing moral, political, or divine meanings. This mental habit was facilitated by the sense of repeating patterns; by belief in God's unchanging purposes for creation; and by telling time with reference to things in the past. In this mode of thinking, earlier events became 'types'. They were prefigurings of, or rule-setting precedents for, later happenings. Thus people would draw constant analogies between their current situation and narratives from the Bible or from classical or later history; they would study the past for lessons that it could teach about present conduct; and they would be more interested in the supposed meanings of stories than where they fitted into any unfolding historical narrative. This was why, for example, instances from the past would be abstracted from their period by the compilers of commonplace books, and categorized with other occurrences from very different epochs.[34] Those who put such books together were using them to illustrate unchanging axioms of politics or ethics, not to understand historical development. Yet once conceptions of time and history shifted, the narrative of human existence was seen flowing away from past moments. Moving in its linear fashion through absolute, empty time, and driven through changing periods by the secular processes of an unstable present, it steadily transformed the mental, social, and cultural contexts in which things happened. Ancient events lost meaning as guides to current situations as circumstances altered, so using them as lessons for today became anachronistic.[35] Within this 'atypological' chronology, the point of

---

[33] The phrase is from Hartmut Rosa, *Social Acceleration: A New Theory of Modernity* (New York: Columbia UP, 2013), 76.

[34] Daniel R. Woolf, *Reading History in Early Modern England* (Cambridge: CUP, 2000), 96–102; Zachary Sayre Schiffman, *The Birth of the Past* (Baltimore: Johns Hopkins UP, 2011), 172–82.

[35] Guibbory, *Map of Time*, 1–5; Woolf, 'From Histories to the Historical', esp. 41–5; Noelle Gallagher, *Historical Literatures: Writing About the Past, 1660–1760* (Manchester: MUP, 2012), 11; Peter Burke, 'The Sense of Anachronism from Petrach to Poussin', in Chris Humphrey and W.M. Ormrod, eds, *Time in the Medieval World* (York: York Medieval Press 2001), 157–74; Timothy Hampton, *Writing from History: The Rhetoric of Exemplarity in Renaissance Literature* (Ithaca: Cornell UP, 1990), ch. 7; Schiffman, *Birth of the Past*; Reinhart Koselleck, 'Modernity and the Planes of Historicity', and 'Historia Magistra Vitae', in his *Futures Past*, 1–25, 26–42. Arthur B. Ferguson, *Clio Unbound: Perception of the Social and Cultural Past in Renaissance England* (Durham, NC: Duke UP), 1979, conclusion; Fritzche, *Stranded in the Present*, introduction.

examining history altered. Now, individual moments could not be abstracted from the unfolding narrative around them. Instead, history had to be examined as whole. It was a complete story, which, if analysed in its entirety, might give insights into the processes that had brought about the contemporary world—or at the mundane level might simply entertain with its narrative arcs—but it could not be used as a random access storehouse of models for behaviour.[36]

As was stressed, the scholars who have posited these seven shifts in mental habits have put a great variety of arguments in their favour. Not all have placed emphasis on the same changes; very different kinds of evidence have been deployed to try to prove the theories; and there has been no agreement on the crucial era in which the shifts occurred. Old habits of thought have been seen collapsing in everything from the fourteenth to the nineteenth centuries.[37] Nevertheless, the ideas that have been posited have enough in common to leave the impression that a major and broadly coherent transformation in temporal perceptions had occurred, and that it was largely complete by the later seventeenth century. Indeed, there has been focus on the last Stuart decades as the key moment in the change, in England at least. At numerous points in the literature cited in footnotes here, and throughout the scholarship on time, these years have been presented as ones that saw the acceptance of Newtonian mechanics, newly confident assertions of the superiority of 'modern' to 'ancient' scholarship and literature, the first widespread availability of personal timepieces, the increasing density of periodic and constantly updating news, a religious toleration that weakened authoritative sacralized ideologies, the publication of histories that treated the past as a unified and developing narrative, and a commercial boom that fed notions of economic improvement.

From all this one could conclude that, by this point, English people had arrived at a new and dynamic view of time. And from the claims made about such a worldview characterizing later centuries, one could label the new chronology 'modern'. As Peter Fritzche has said (summarizing quite a bit of commentary), 'modern' mentalities assume novel circumstances are constantly being created which have no parallels in earlier ages; and the 'the conceit of modernity is that history is the relentless iteration of new'.[38] The new chronology we have outlined

---

[36] Woolf, 'From Histories to the Historical', esp. 44–9; Gallagher, *Historical Literature*, introduction; Woolf, *Reading History*, 125–31; Hampton, *Writing from History*, ch. 7; A. Ferguson, *Clio Unbound*, conclusion.

[37] Key moments have been suggested around the time of the French Revolution (for example, Hunt, *Measuring Time*; Koselleck, *Futures Past*), the high-eighteenth-century Enlightenment (for example, Schiffman, *Birth of the Past*), the late seventeenth century (as summarized in the rest of this paragraph), and various points in a Renaissance that stretched from the late Middle Ages to around 1650 (for example, Woolf, 'From Histories to the Historical'). Poole, *Time's Alteration*, p. 22, summarizes disputes about timing in the shift from natural/cyclical to absolute/linear time.

[38] Fritzche, *Stranded in the Present*, 8. For more on modernity as endlessly transformative, see Marshall Berman, *All That Is Solid Melts into Air: The Experience of Modernity* (New York: Simon and Schuster, 1982).

fitted this definition: in it time flowed; it moved situations on; it periodized history; it accelerated; it create anachronism; and it cut people off from their past—even as it encouraged more rounded study to understand the human processes that drove it. More specifically, this 'modern' time created a grand chronological pattern. Within it, the human story had been a linear narrative, played out at increasingly rapid pace, in which people's actions had transformed and improved the world until it had reached its present state; and could be expected to continue to do so in the future—challenging and replacing old structures, probably at an ever faster rate. Such modernity was perhaps more evident after 1800—in Whiggish and Marxist historiographies; in scientific and technological optimism; and in movements for political and social reform. But in the scholarship we have just surveyed, the foundations of such a worldview had been firmly laid by the time of William's arrival in England.

And if modern time had arrived by 1688–9, it might have helped to underpin the 'modernizing' interpretation of this crisis. If the people who witnessed James II's fall had adopted the new chronology, they might have used it to understand, and even to mould, the revolution as a radical event that could usher in a 'modern' world. Convinced that things were always changing, and perhaps marching towards a better tomorrow, they would have been able to embrace the change of political regime, and its far-reaching consequences. They may even have been emboldened by a sense that history was made by ordinary humans like them, so that they could see William's arrival as an opportunity to initiate a wholly novel, and greatly improved, period of human existence. This was certainly the interpretation of what had happened that was held by the commentators from the later eighteenth century quoted by Steve Pincus as he argued the people of that era had thought 1688–9 had been a radical and modernizing event. For these more distant children of the revolution, it had led to 'a new epoch', a 'new era', and 'a new order of things'; it allowed England to stand 'upon another and better bottom'; and it introduced a novel age 'of light and liberty' that inspired the self-consciously progressive revolutions in America and France.[39]

This book will examine how far 'modern' chronology did, in fact, shape the thought of those who lived through the collapse of James II's government, as they tried to make sense of it in the decade or so after it had occurred. As a thought experiment to test the extent and nature of any 'modernity' in 1688–9, it will ask how the generation that lived through those events placed what they had witnessed in history; and it will examine the model and experience of time that lay behind their understanding. The results will be mixed. Sometimes, the people of the revolution did incorporate their recent past into a new and dynamic chronology. As they reflected on William's triumph, they saw linear patterns of history; or

---

[39] Pincus, *1688*, 12.

tried to explain events in terms of human processes that altered society; or remarked how rapidly the events of their day were moving. This allowed them to suggest that 1688–9 might have sprung from a present with an open-ended future, and that it may have initiated a new era. But at least as commonly, and as Dolben's speech in the convention suggested, they did not present things like this. In a variety of ways, the concepts of time and history that they used looked more like the ones that are supposed to have been replaced during the early modern epoch; or sometimes they seemed to have fallen into perceptions that are impossible to place on any spectrum running neatly from the 'pre-modern' to the 'modern'.

This diversity of response will have two main consequences for the issues discussed in this introduction. First, it will suggest that any changes in temporal understanding were more complex than the impression of a grand transformation that has been left by the general scholarship on time. If a 'modern' progressive chronology had emerged by the time William invaded England, we will see repeatedly that its adoption by English people as they discussed 1688–9 was patchy. They did not always talk as if human-directed events were constantly remodelling society—though some did, sometimes. If only for polemical or partisan purposes (and often their commitment to their interpretation will appear to go far deeper than this), William's subjects presented an essentially static world. Sometimes they even reversed the supposed direction of conceptual travel: people at the end of the seventeenth century could deploy ideas that froze any flow of time far more completely than had been common in earlier decades. Elsewhere, witnesses to the revolution failed to construct any coherent understanding of time; or they created 'hybrid' or self-contradictory chronologies that seemed to want to accept change and *stasis* simultaneously; or they disagreed profoundly which chronological model best fitted the circumstances they faced. In sum, the people studied here will be far less easy to categorize in their understanding of time, and in many ways far more interesting, than theories of a great chronological shift would suggest.

Second, the variety of chronologies we shall discover will question how far the revolution can be understood as a 'modernizing' phenomenon. 1688–9 may, in its concrete consequences, have transformed the nation, and created a novel state and society. But the revolution was surprisingly rarely defended, or perhaps even understood, in these terms. And it could not be, because of the failure of the new views of time to dominate patterns of thought. As we shall see in chapter one, those who lived through the prince of Orange's invasion were often so bewildered by what was happening that they could not perceive any progressive pattern of events. As explored in chapters two and three, the very folk who accepted and implemented change under William constructed a constitutional universe in which it was very hard for change to occur; and they justified what they were doing using a Protestant language which—whilst seeing a role for dramatic providential interventions in time—was hobbled in describing historical development by its insistence on the constant and eternal purposes of God. People might be reconciled to political and social transformations by such discourses, but within these worldviews they could not advocate those transformations, and perhaps could not even recognize that they were happening. To add to the complexity, we will see in chapter four that, whilst there were some coherent interpretations of 1688–9 which saw it as an advance into a new state of affairs, these initially came from people who opposed William's capture of the throne, and who wished to reverse its effects. As chapter five relates, the challenge of such opposition ideology eventually elicited more progressive views of time among the king's advocates, but this happened slowly, partially, and ambiguously. All this must cast doubt on 1688–9 as a 'modern' revolution. Upheavals of that particular kind are not brought about by people who do not advocate, who appear not to believe in, and perhaps cannot even conceptualize, change. Thus if modernity happened at the end of the seventeenth century, it cannot have been brought about by self-conscious modernizers. At best it was the paradoxical consequence of quite other views of time and how history worked; this has profound consequences for models of changes in chronological perception, and how those changes might have spurred on real events.

1

The Experience of Time During William's Invasion

1.1 A Distant Witness

If any set of events was likely to reveal that a new sense of time was possible by the late seventeenth century in England, the story of the autumn of 1688 would be such a narrative. The developments between harvest and Christmas that year were so rapid, and the alterations that they wrought so astonishing, that it was almost inevitable that some elements of a 'modern' chronological awareness would become apparent. It took only a very short period from the first reports that William was preparing to invade for an extraordinary tale of change to unfold. Within only a few weeks, the prince of Orange landed his army in Devon, marched on London, caused the entire unravelling of King James II's regime, occupied London, and frightened the king from his realm. At each point in these processes, news tumbled over itself as people were forced to update and reappraise their understanding of their world. This was not the first time events had moved this quickly in the crisis-ridden seventeenth century, but it was one of the most dramatic points at which a 'modern' sense of time should have emerged. In the circumstances surrounding James's fall, it would have been hard for those who recorded their reactions not to betray a sense of a fluid and progressive present, creating a future whose nature had not been scripted, and sense that time was racing forward to an unfamiliar tomorrow.

And yet, some people could not place William's arrival in 'modern' time frames—even some who belonged to families in the middle of the breakneck revolution. The Harleys of Brampton Bryant were an old parliamentarian clan who had mobilized their Worcestershire heartlands against Charles I, and now did the same against his Catholic son. As Dutch forces advanced, they raised a troop of horse and secured the county town for the Orange cause; and they voraciously sought news of the galloping progress of William's invasion. Friends, relations, and newsletter authors in London wrote to provide what information they could, and so tried to help the family respond to the swiftly evolving political universe.[1] But one son of Brampton, Nathaniel Harley, was far away, in the Levant

---

[1] See the run of communications in HMC, *The manuscripts of the Duke of Portland preserved at Welbeck Abbey*, iii (1893), 417–20.

The Revolution in Time: Chronology, Modernity, and 1688–1689 in England. Tony Claydon, Oxford University Press (2020). © Tony Claydon.
DOI: 10.1093/oso/9780198817239.001.0001

at Aleppo. Months after the excitement, he wrote back home to complain 'I have not heard from anyone since the alteration in England, and therefore could not credit it, were it not confirmed from all parts'. For him, the revolution only existed in its distant and delayed effects. French privateers were turning up to disrupt trade in the eastern Mediterranean, as part of a war between England and France that Nathaniel assumed was starting, but whose full meaning and significance he could not reliably assess. The seamen Nathaniel talked to boasted that King Louis had already captured Amsterdam. He clearly doubted this, but without correspondence, or more facts, he did 'not know how you in England may like' the conflict. In this reaction, Nathaniel certainly revealed astonishment at the scale of the transformation that had occurred. But in an exaggerated form, he also illustrated ways in which many English people failed to match the 'modern' chronological paradigm as revolution broke over them. Distance, disruptions of communications, rumour, uncertainty, and bewilderment at what seemed to be happening prevented witnesses experiencing William's triumph as a progressive and constantly updating narrative, or comprehending it as the dawn of a clear new era.[2]

1.2 Acceleration, the Destabilized Present, and the Revolution as Turning Point

Yet—whatever things looked like from the Levant—for those living in England and Wales in the autumn of 1688, a sense of progressive time was palpable. A rapidly evolving political narrative was related in an impressive variety of media, so people kept hearing updates about William, and were hungry for information about a contemporaneous present. Each new thing moved the story to a dramatic new phase. Witnesses sensed that a radically different future was being made at this critical point, and their actions in this moment might shape that future it in vital ways. There was a real sense that a cavernously empty time was being filled now, by an evolving story; and people began to wonder if they were living through a turning point that would usher in a new period of history. And the most strik-ing feature of this temporal modernity—indeed the one that underpinned all the others—was acceleration. As the prince of Orange invaded, people perceived the world at a pace that they noted was far faster than their usual experience. Not only did a lot happen in a few weeks, but the density of reporting increased dramatically. Means of communication intensified in number, frequency, and focus upon Dutch progress, and ensured that exponentially more news about a single story was crammed into each set span of time. Bombarded by information, the

[2] Ibid., 242.

people of 1688 saw a world changing hour by hour, and felt time rush forward as their understanding of the situation struggled to keep up.

The most quantifiable evidence for this acceleration comes from the frequency of newspaper publication. Although printed journals were not the only source of updates about the world, they did play an important role in conveying information about William's progress, and the autumn of 1688 saw a dramatic increase in published journalism. There were two reasons for this. First, James II tried to counter Orange propaganda with his own publicity material.[3] This included use of the government's paper—the *London Gazette*—which had enjoyed a virtual monopoly of printed news after the reintroduction of controls on the press at the start of the 1680s. Through October and November, the *Gazette* kept its readers up to date with the Dutch expedition by reproducing loyal addresses from towns and counties across the kingdom, covering royal statements denouncing William, and claiming that only a limited number of Englishmen had rallied to the prince. Then, from 15 November, the *Gazette* expanded the space for such material by enlarging its number of issues from two to three a week.[4] It was true that the expedient lasted little more than a fortnight. The lack of good tidings for James's cause meant there was not much to fill the *Gazette*'s extra columns, and it reverted to two issues each seven days in December. Yet, by the middle of that new month, a second factor had more than compensated for the reversal in coverage. The collapse of James's regime included the collapse of its control of the press: as a result, the *Gazette* lost its monopoly, and other newspapers appeared. A *Universal Intelligence* had its first edition on 11 December. This was joined three days later by an *English Current*, and the day after that by a *London Mercury*. All three works survived to the end of the year and came out twice a week. This, of course, magnified the rate at which current affairs were described in print, especially since there was only limited overlap in the reports the different titles carried. A randomly selected fortnight in the summer of 1688 would have seen only the four scheduled issues of the *Gazette*, but the last two weeks of the year saw sixteen new issues of papers.

The effect of the increasing frequency of publication was enhanced because the new titles carried domestic news. The *Gazette* had always concentrated on Europe. This, its editors had thought, was less likely to be controversial than covering England, and so less likely to stir opposition to the regime. There was an important shift in the autumn of 1688, as the paper carried the court's response to William's invasion (as Sam Garland has shown, this was an unprecedented density of domestic coverage of English news: from almost nothing, it rose to over 40 per cent of the paper's column inches)—but the real turn to local information came with the new

---

[3] See Tony Claydon, 'William III's *Declaration of Reasons* and the Glorious Revolution', *Historical Journal*, 39:1 (1996), 87–108.

[4] The increase in the frequency of publication was announced in the *London Gazette*, 2150 (15–17 December 1688).

papers.[5] The first of these to appear, the 11 December issue of the *Universal Intelligence*, began with reports from Italy, Germany, France, and Holland—but within half a column, a black Gothic heading announced 'The Domestic News'. Under this, there were short sections on Ireland and Scotland before 'The news of England' took up the remaining three quarters of the issue.[6] Such a concentration on local occurrences marked the other papers: as the *English Current*'s title suggested, that work contained only English news; and its example was followed by the *London Mercury*.

This sudden reopening of domestic reporting has been noted in histories of journalism.[7] It was at least comparable to the few earlier eras of intense news production, such as the early months of the exclusion crisis in 1679. What interests us here, though, is its impact on perceptions of the passage of time. An increase in the number of issues accelerated the sense of chronological flow because so much more was reported, and so inevitably seemed to be occurring, each week. And the concentration on English affairs enlivened this impression, because the events formed part of a single political narrative. The *Gazette* had always been full of happenings. But as these had been scattered over a wide continent, they had often seemed unconnected. A particular story in the *Gazette* had never advanced very much in each issue, because the journal covered it in a brief paragraph before moving somewhere else. By contrast, the *Intelligence*, *Current*, and *Mercury* reported the tight-packed turns of a single tale: the final dissolution of James's authority. The first issue of the *Mercury*, for example, told of riots against Catholic targets in London; arrests of ministers of the old government; the disbanding of regiments of the king's army; the arrest of the monarch at Feversham (he was detained having tried to flee, and would be brought back to Whitehall before finally making his escape later in December); the movements of the Princess Anne back towards the south-east of England (she had slipped north to join Williamite rebels when her father had left to confront the invasion); the rallying of Norfolk to the prince of Orange's cause; an assassination attempt on one of William's commanders; the arrival of the prince himself at Windsor; and his intention to enter the capital the next Monday. The impression was of dizzying forward rush.[8]

Of course, it is difficult to judge the popularity and influence of the newspapers. Although the sudden appearance and survival of the titles suggests a market, these journals were new and may have taken time to build up an audience. We also cannot be sure how many people saw the whole genre of papers, rather than concentrating on just one title, though the social milieu in which many of them

---

[5] Samuel Garland, 'News in Late Seventeenth-Century Britain', PhD Dissertation, Bangor University, 2016, 195.

[6] *Universal Intelligence*, 1 (11 December 1688).

[7] Garland, 'News', ch. 8; Sommerville, *News Revolution* 96–9.

[8] *London Mercury or Moderate Intelligencer*, 1 (15 December 1688).

would have been read (often picked up from tables in coffeehouses) suggests many people may have looked at them all. Yet whatever the truth about journalism, an acceleration of news was attested well beyond these sources. For decades before a diverse periodical press became a feature of English life, information had spread through a dense web of printed, handwritten, and oral media, which included pamphlets, manuscript newsletters, personal letters, and face-to-face conversation. Evidence of all these communications tells of an increased rush of data as William invaded.

Two news genres were quite close to newspapers in purpose and form, and they shared in the concentration of information. The first were individual pamphlets carrying reports of William's arrival. Publications dealing with domestic and politically controversial events had been suppressed by the regime for most of the period since 1660, but they appeared in full vigour as the Dutch advanced. Not only did James issue proclamations and rebuttals of Orange propaganda that informed as well as tried to persuade, but pro-Dutch printers began to exploit the breakdown of the old regime's authority.[9] They got out pieces that provided encouraging coverage of how William's military advance was progressing, and were joined by the printing press the prince himself had brought with him on the expedition.[10] Other pamphlets took the form of stand-alone summaries of events. For example *Great news from Nottingham* told not only of the gathering of Williamite forces in that town at the start of December, but also reported the taking of Hull by the prince's supporters and the shutting down of papist chapels in Newcastle. *An account of the proceedings at Whitehall* informed Londoners of the flight of James on 11 December, and the constitution of a provisional government of peers.[11]

Moving from print to handwriting, a second medium was even closer to the emerging press journalism. These were the handwritten newsletters sent from London to inform recipients across the kingdom of events in the capital. Since the early seventeenth century, a gaggle of newsgatherers had performed this service for folk in the provinces—sometimes paid a retainer to keep their clients up to date.[12] This type of communication had long compensated for the dearth of domestic news in printed sheets: and at points in the past, such as during the

---

[9] For early Jacobite material, see Claydon, 'William III's *Declaration*', esp. 91–7.

[10] See, for example, *A true and exact relation of the prince of Orange his publick entrance into Exeter* (1688); *An account of last Sunday's engagement between His Majesty's and the Prince of Orange's forces* (1688); *True news from Reading* (1688); *News from White-Hall, being an account of the arrival of … Prince William Henry of Orange* (1688); *An account of the reasons of the nobility and genty's invitation* (1688); *An enquiry into the present state of affairs* (1688).

[11] *Great news from Nottingham the fifth of December 1688* (1688); *An account of the proceedings at Whitehall, Guildhall and the Tower of London* (1688).

[12] Ian Atherton, 'The Itch Grown a Disease: Manuscript Transmission of News in the Seventeenth Century', in Joad Raymond, ed., *News, Newspapers and Society in Early Modern Britain* (London: Routledge, 1999), 39–65.

Popish Plot of 1678, had become breathless outpourings of aspects of a single story—just as the new newspapers did in December 1688.[13] For the period of William's invasion, several series of newsletters have come down to us, and they echoed the press's sense of rapid narrative. One particularly interesting collection survives in North Wales. Originally written to the powerful Mostyn family, this cache provided several updates a week, from at least three different scribes (it is not clear whether these were writing independently or were part of a coordinated team).[14]

The Mostyn newsletters underlined the acceleration of events, and so of time, in a number of ways. First, like the newspapers, they came to focus on one set of developments. The information in such letters had always been dense—but it had not usually created a fast-paced story because it had been so disparate. For instance, the epistle sent on 18 September, just before the invasion scare began, was a jumble. It mixed crime stories with court manoeuvrings, appointments to official posts, and updates on foreign wars. From early October, however, the Dutch expedition dominated. The Mostyn scribes talked of little but William's gathering force, and James's response. Second, the language of the newsletters stressed how fast things were changing. This was partly a response to the underlying pace of events since the last letter had been sent. For instance, note the example dispatched on 6 November, which reported that the Dutch fleet had been seen off Dover, and then off the Isle of Wight, and then had turned landwards towards Dorset or Devon. Moreover, the newsletters explicitly commented that things were happening quickly. On 2 October, the news was that Dutch preparations 'go vigorously forward'; and two days later, they had 'not slackened'. Finally, the letter writers were obviously sensitive to flows of information and hinted that these had increased during the crisis. The Mostyn correspondents talked repeatedly of messages flooding in to London (arriving daily, even every few hours), especially from the cutting edge of William's invasion. On October 16 'three posts together' came from Holland, updating the court on Dutch preparations; after the first report of William's landing in Brixham, messages poured in from the West Country detailing how far his disembarkation had got and how the local population had responded.[15]

Other caches of newsletters confirm this density of information. A series sent to Stockholm was dispatched weekly and found a great deal to report of the collapse in James's authority in each missive. The one sent on 19 October spoke of suspicious ship movements; James's publication of prayers for use during any invasion; the king's concessions to the Church of England to try to win back

---

[13] Garland, 'News', chs. 2–4; Mark Goldie, *Roger Morrice and the Puritan Whigs* (Woodbridge: Boyell, 2007), 569–71, provides a list of surviving newsletter collections.

[14] For the most in-depth study of this material, see Garland 'News'.

[15] Bangor University Archives, Mostyn MSS 9094, newsletters for 16 October, and the series from 9 November.

support; his general pardon to subjects; and the restoring of the City of London's charter. The letter written seven days later sent news of the king's surrender in his dispute with Magdalen College, Oxford; appointments of lord lieutenants in preparation for the Dutch arrival; reports that William was ready to depart from Holland; English troop movements to try to repel him; James's attempts to gain support by convincing his subjects of the legitimacy of his young son; Irish soldiers arriving in England via Chester; and so on.[16] Another set of newsletters sent to the Countess of Suffolk at Audley End was as replete. Again sent weekly, these gabbled out varied dimensions of the revolution: especially through November as they relayed details of James's advance to Salisbury and of the medical problems, the Dutch successes, the regional rebellions, and the defections from his army and family that broke his nerve and had him to retreating to London by start of the next month.[17]

Beyond newsletters, other kinds of epistle created work for the Royal Post Office, which had—albeit intermittently—allowed communication at a distance since the Tudor era and which had blossomed under Charles II into a 'primary vehicle' of information exchange.[18] We have surviving records of the vast quantities of ordinary, personal correspondence which must have passed between people as they came to terms with the rapid changes of the revolution—and these confirm the temporal impression left by more formal news media. As friends, family, and colleagues wrote letters in the last months of 1688, they produced breathless accounts of happenings, and they explicitly remarked how quickly events were moving. There are excellent examples in the cache of letters that were written to the admiral Lord Dartmouth in late November and December. In one missive, Sir Henry Shere talked of a racing tsunami of misfortune for James. 'Yesterday', he said, Lord Churchill, the duke of Grafton, and their regiments had deserted to William, and 'just now, while I am writing this', news had come that the Prince of Denmark, Duke of Ormonde, and Lord Rochester had gone too. Shere expected this pace to continue: 'every day' more would be added to the list and 'heap up new calamities' upon the king's head.[19] Colonel Richard Norton lamented the rapid dissolution of the old regime, which had left him with no income, and told Dartmouth he expected new developments would follow along very quickly. 'What further issue of these affairs', he remarked in mid December, 'little time will show'.[20] Sir Edward Sherburne reported that things were moving so fast that even his furious letter writing could not keep up. He wrote on 13 December, begging Dartmouth to intervene to prevent him being evicted from

<hr>

[16]   British Library, Add MSS 45731, ff. 29, 35.

[17]   British Library, Add MSS 34487, ff. 33, 35, 37, 38, 42.

[18]   Steven Pincus, 'The State and Civil Society in Early Modern England', in Peter Lake and Steven Pincus, eds, *The Politics of the Public Sphere in Early Modern England* (Manchester: MUP, 2007), quote at p. 217; G.R. Robinson, *The British Post Office* (Princeton: Princeton UP, 1948); Susan E Whyman, *The Pen and the People: English Letter Writers, 1660–1800* (Oxford: OUP, 2009), 46–53.

[19]   HMC, *The manuscripts of the Earl of Dartmouth*, vol III (1896), 133.

[20]   Col. Richard Norton to Lord Dartmouth, 11 December 1688, HMC, *Dartmouth*, vol III, 135.

the apartment James had given him in the Tower of London. Later that same day, however, he had to add a postscript recording that the new authorities in the capital had already forced him to quit the rooms.[21]

Beyond this basic acceleration of reported events, there are two points to make about private correspondence during William's invasion. First, it became distorted into the genre of newsletter we just surveyed. Public events held such interest that they tended to displace other sorts of content in the epistles of the era. Business arrangements, family developments, the doings of friends, health issues, concern about obtaining provisions—the usual weft of human experience—were barged aside by the need to relate the great story of the Dutch expedition. This was evident in the corpus of letters that we have, and it was remarked upon at the time. Charles Bertie, writing to the Earl of Danby, who was off in Yorkshire, had some concerns about the noble's health in his letter of 27 October, but the public situation proved overwhelming, and the epistle rapidly became the sort of jumble of political and military news that was being sent by the professional news scribes.[22] Edward Wilson, writing from the north of England in October, said the letters he was getting were 'full of news'—much of it filling gaps in newsletter coverage; and Katherine Powlett, a correspondent of Lady Margeret Russell, who was away from London at Woburn in Bedfordshire, told her of a dispute about the personal effects of relatives in an inheritance battle, and a society wedding—but only after a much longer section giving the latest on politics and military preparations. Bridging the two parts of the letter was the reflection that the marriage didn't have the same sort of 'fame' that such events usually carried because 'we can here think nor talk of nothing but the Dutch'.[23] One apparent exception was the note sent by Lady Rachel Russell from Woburn back to the capital on 30 November. This avoided giving the usual breathless catalogue of happenings, but then admitted it did so simply because it was impossible to include everything. 'One hears every day so much', sighed Russell, that without penning a whole volume ''tis not easy to enter on the subject of news'.[24]

The second notable feature of letters in the autumn of 1688 was how frequently they were written. Correspondence had always been dense in the seventeenth century. People had long been keen to provide frequent updates to others, and many spent much of their days maintaining networks with closely spaced messages. However, this intensified in the autumn of 1688. Most concretely, the Post Office sent daily mails from London to areas closest to William's advancing army. This was more frequent than the thrice weekly standard for dispatches from the capital to provinces, and would have allowed private individuals as well as the court to

---

[21] Edward Sherburne to Lord Dartmouth, 13 December 1688, HMC, *Dartmouth*, vol III, 137.

[22] HMC, *The manuscripts of the Earl of Buckingham, the Earl of Lindsey etc.* (1895), 447.

[23] E. Wilson to D.F., HMC, *The manuscripts of S.H. Le Fleming* (1890), 215; HMC, *The manuscripts of the Duke of Rutland preserved at Belvoir Castle* (1889), 123.

[24] *The letters of Lady Rachel Russell* (7th edn, 1809), 186.

contact others more often.[25] A little more impressionistically, there is evidence that people were writing unusually often. On 17 November, the Countess of Huntingdon reassured her husband—who was on campaign for King James in the West Country—that she had not missed writing by every post for a fortnight. She wanted to explain that any gaps in her correspondence were the result of letters going astray in the current chaos, rather than epistolatory negligence.[26] This, however, was a pale shadow of the letters sent the other way. The earl had written to his wife every few hours on his ride out of London. He wrote at three in the morning from Andover on 6 November, and then again at six in the morning from Salisbury. There was then a longer gap, because, as he explained, he had covered seventy miles since his last letter, and was feeling sick. But the next letter was dispatched as soon as he reached Honiton in Devon in the early afternoon of the seventh.[27] The Huntingdons were not alone. John Ellis, the secretary to the Irish revenue commission in Dublin, was receiving extremely frequent briefings from a number of correspondents in London, which meant he could receive as many as four updates a day; and in late November, William Fleming was reporting that the mail had been overwhelmed in the north-west of England. 'They so throng in the post office here', he grumbled, 'one cannot get the newsletters'.[28]

Oral media, of course, leaves no direct impression on the historical record—but its shadows in written sources suggest that face-to-face conversation had the same quality of breakneck, forward-speeding narrative in 1688. Witnesses suggested a nation so obsessed by developments that it could discourse of little else. A correspondent writing from Yorkshire on 12 October, promised the recipient 'some of the talk of these talkative times', and Lady Rachel Russell reported that all of London had been 'talking of the same matter' (that is, William's preparations) when she visited the capital earlier that month.[29] Of course, complaint about the hunger of people for news and gossip had long been a staple of social commentary, but there does seem to have been a particular intensity in reports of what people were saying about the collapse of James's power. For example, as Sam Garland has argued, the newsletter writers—whose own reports were becoming focused on the single and fast-moving narrative of the Dutch expedition—were gaining a good deal of material from oral sources. Writers frequently introduced items with acknowledgement of such originals. 'We hear', they said, or 'they say', or 'it is talked this evening'; and the material that followed was overwhelmingly information, or at least speculation, about where William's great project had got to.[30]

---

[25] *London Gazette*, 2399 (12–15 November 1688) and 2405 (26–9 November 1688).

[26] HMC, *The manuscripts of the late Reginald Rawden Hastings* (London: HMSO, 1930), 190.

[27] Ibid., 187–9.

[28] George Agar Ellis, ed., *The Ellis Correspondence* 2 vols (1892), II, 196–287—see letters for 2 October, 229–34; HMC, *Fleming*, 223.

[29] E. Wilson to D.F., HMC, *Fleming*, 215; *Letters of Lady Rachel Russell*, 174.

[30] Garland, 'News', 215–6.

Thus, a multiplicity of media crowded events into the consciousness of witnesses. People were living with a sense of an accelerated chronological flow that was perhaps best captured by their recurring use of the word 'hurry' to describe their world.[31] This term was probably being used partly in its older sense of commotion, but the *Oxford English Dictionary* suggests the modern meaning of a rush occasioned by a shortage of time was emerging in the later seventeenth century, and was clearly meant by most witnesses. And this sense of a packed present was magnified by a further feature of temporal awareness in 1688 that has been seen as an element of modern chronology. This was contemporaneity. Because people were curious about what was happening in a variety of theatres in such a significant situation, they thought in terms of a geographically extended moment. They conceived of events happening in a 'now' that stretched far beyond their immediate locality, and the news that was available there. Developments across northwest Europe were seen as part of a unified narrative, which had reached the same temporal point in the various locations. There was, therefore, a contemporaneous point of time that united the spatially diverse strands, and so created an even greater impression that a huge number of happenings were unfolding at once.

Some sense of contemporaneity was generated by the telling of a spatially dispersed narrative, which we noted in the sudden opening up of domestic news. For instance, the first issue of the *Universal Intelligence* had stories connected to William's gambit from Norfolk, Hull, Dover, and Nottingham, as well as London; and it also reported that popish chapels had been burned in 'divers parts of this kingdom', including York, Bristol, Gloucester, Worcester, Shrewsbury, and Stafford.[32] Manuscript newsletters followed the trend. One sent on 11 October to a recipient in Westmorland told of rioting in Portsmouth, Irish troops arriving in Chester, royal instructions to the justices of Middlesex and Westminster, the City of London's trained bands going through drill routines, and the Duke of Beaufort's efforts to raise soldiers in Wales.[33] Private correspondence often had a similar structure. A letter to the Earl of Derby from London on 13 November talked of troops being sent to Salisbury, of a riot in London, and of the state of the prince's army around Exeter; whilst an unsigned letter to a 'Mr Norton' on 28 November, talked of James's nose bleeds (on Salisbury Plain), the desertion of Grafton and Churchill (to the prince's camp to the west of the king's), and the escape of the Princess Anne (from London).[34]

This awareness of a packed and expansive current moment was even demonstrated in the absence of concrete news from elsewhere. Because of the delays in conveying information (which will be examined in more detail later), people had to speculate what was happening in other places. As they did this, they created a

---

[31] See, for example, Ellis, *Ellis Correspondence*, II, 218, 229, 278; British Library, Add MSS 45731, ff. 3, 57; *Letters of Lady Rachel Russell*, 280.

[32] *Universal Intelligence*, 1 (11 December 1688).   [33] HMC, *Fleming*, 213.

[34] British Library, Add MSS 34487, f.40; HMC, *The manuscripts of Lord Kenyon* (1894), 207.

vivid imaginary present—their consciousness skipping over space to complement their 'here and now' of direct experience with a mentally constructed 'there and now'. The fact that the Dutch took so long to set off after assembling their fleet generated a good deal of illustrative evidence. For weeks, the English assumed the invasion was coming, and so let their minds wander to a contemporaneous mid-Channel or North Sea. The letters written to John Ellis provide a series of typical examples. On 18 September Ellis was told 'The Dutch fleet is said, and believed by most people, to be between Dunkirk and England, about sixty or seventy sail strong'.[35] On 2 October, a correspondent wrote that it was 'off of Gore, and is three or four hundred sail strong'.[36] The next day the same force was supposed to have sailed northwards towards Yorkshire or Scotland; though by 9 October it was believed, in fact, to be still in port—the winds having been unfavourable to its designs.[37] The longer the delay went on, the more Ellis' contacts constructed images of contemporaneous conditions in the enemy forces to explain why the blow against James had still not been struck. On 23 October there were reports of 'a mighty sickness amongst men and horses, and the Prince of Orange very melancholy'.[38] On 27 October the Dutch were recovering from a tempest that had driven them back on the coast 'in shattered condition'; and only on 3 November was Ellis sent news that they had set sail from Maze.[39] Of course, many of these reports had proved inaccurate, and the temporal impact of this will be considered soon. What is important here is the extended, indeed transmarine present. The people of 1688 were living in a moment that spread far from their own location; that included mental constructions of what was happening elsewhere, as well as concrete reports of this; and that packed their sense of how much was going on with imagination as much as definite facts.

All the evidence so far surveyed confirms that the autumn of 1688 created a key feature of the 'modern' sense of time. People were living with a sense of an extremely rapid flow of events. Yet this sense of acceleration was enhanced because witnesses projected their fast-paced narrative into the near future. They not only said what had just happened, but speculated, imagined, or predicted what would happen next. This produced a still more packed present as it crowded the consciousness with things that were believed to be in the offing, as well as things that had just occurred; and it pulled the future back towards the current moment, squeezing time as people began to consider that future as if it had already begun to unfold. There are a vast series of examples of such anticipation (as one might expect in a situation where things had been moving quickly and people assumed that the profound changes they were witnessing would have pro-found consequences): here we only have space for brief illustration of this fairly obvious phenomenon.

---

[35] Ellis, *Ellis Correspondence*, ii, 196.   [36] Ibid., ii, 232.   [37] Ibid., ii, 237, 240.
[38] Ibid., ii, 256   [39] Ibid., ii, 266, 274.

Much of this sort of expectation concerned English troop movements. Witnesses endlessly reported that regiments were about to march out of London to respond to the Dutch invasion, that the king's fleet was going to sail to intercept William's navy, or that the capital was preparing to defend itself against attack.[40] Some concerned the king's whereabouts: people wrote of the royal intention to advance to Salisbury, and then of his decision to return to Whitehall.[41] The most telling type of anticipation, however, was of the prince's arrival in England itself. Given the stakes involved in William's possible landing, the idea that it might happen soon created a palpable tension that threw people's awareness forward in time, and it generated a particularly rich vein of evidence because it was spread across a long period. Because confirmation that a huge fleet had assembled in Holland's ports reached England in the late summer, but the arrival did not actually take place until early November, James's subjects suffered months in which they might be invaded and believed through all those weeks that the prince's forces were about to land. As early as 16 October Owen Wynne shared Londoners' expectation that 'the Dutch Armada will appear every minute upon the coast'.[42] On 26 October John Cooke predicted that the Dutch would come the approaching weekend, because of favourable high tides and full moon, and that this had put the administration for which he worked 'in crisis'.[43] A day later Charles Bertie told the Earl of Danby that 'his Majesty expects them on our coast with the first fair wind'.[44] Three days further on, Wynne was back to report that the wind was fair for the Netherlands, so 'we expect to hear of them every moment'.[45] The tension, in fact, went on so long that witnesses themselves began to comment upon it. Even by 19 October, nearly three weeks before William actually arrived, John Cooke observed that the Dutch had 'been so long talked of as ready to pay us a visit', but they had still not 'made a descent anywhere, nor ....appeared on our coast'.[46]

In such anticipation, the present was loaded with events that were still to come, and this occurred in another element of the modern sense of time that emerged in 1688. This was the belief, not only that the future was rapidly emerging from the present, but that individual human action in that present would affect and create that future. There was, palpably, a sense that time was 'empty'. For all that some might have hoped history was being guided by providence (a dimension we shall explore in chapter 3), many also wrote as if the future might be filled with alternative scenarios and as if people's responses in their particular moment

---

[40] To take random examples from a mass of material: anon to John Ellis, 2 October 1688, Ellis, *Ellis correspondence*, ii 234,; newsletter of 1 November 1688, HMC, *Fleming*, 218; newsletter of 16 October 1688, Bangor University Archives, Mostyn MSS 9094.

[41] See, for example, Ellis, *Ellis correspondence*, 234; HMC, *Portland*, 417; newsletter, 27 November 1688, HMC, *Fleming, 223,*.

[42] Ellis, *Ellis corrpesondence*, ii, 253   [43] British Library, Add MSS 45731, f. 33.

[44] HMC, *Buckingham*, 448.   [45] Ellis, *Ellis correspondence*, ii, 271.

[46] British Library, Add MSS, 45731, f. 20.

would determine what it would look like. Much of this sense stemmed from the scale of the political choices presented as William advanced. If people rallied to the prince's support, they would be in a state of treasonous rebellion which would have consequences if the expedition failed. If they did not, however, they might be complicit in the survival of a popish and oppressive regime. So much is obvious. Yet contemporary commentary underlined this sense of crucial decision in two interesting ways. It focused sharply on the notion of a critical juncture, and so heightened that sense of an unstable present in which a fluid future was being set. It also stressed that the need to act went well beyond the political elites who had traditionally claimed a role in steering the ship of state. This vital moment was for everyone.

Some of the clearest indications of this present-critical time sense came as Englishmen rallied for William. Those who explained their defiance of James's authority, and who called on others to join them, appealed to an urgent moral duty, pressing upon everyone, to act. The nation's destiny was in the balance, and everyone had to do something, and at this very time, to ensure the best outcome. One of the earliest to make a move was Lord Delamere in the north-west. Within a week of William's landing at Torbay, he raised his estates around Warrington for the prince, and sent out a widely publicized letter to his tenants and neighbours.[47] Informing them that he planned to rendezvous at Bowden Downs, just outside Manchester, he urged them to come in person with arms, or to send money with a substitute if they were incapable of fighting. As he made this broad appeal to the population, he used phrases that constructed his present as the crucible in which the future would be forged. He was sure his audience would think that England and the Protestant religion were 'now' in terrible danger, but that there would be no 'better occasion to root out popery and slavery'. He, and by implication his audience, would think himself 'false to my country if I sat still at this time'. Anyone 'that is passive all this time', Delamere was sure, would come to regret this if James's survived because of their indifference. 'All lies at stake' he warned, so even though he longed 'to spend my days in peace', the immediate choice between freedom and bondage was too pressing to ignore.

The mood of other gatherings varied in attitude to James. Some openly endorsed the prince of Orange; some urged the king to resolve the crisis by calling a free Parliament. Yet all had that sense of universal urgency seen in Delamer's appeal, producing rhetoric that emphasized the insistent immediacy of its present tense. William himself conveyed his feeling that actions by English people in this precise time would be key. Speaking to men joining his camp at Exeter on 15 November, he expressed disappointment that some had not come sooner, but reassured them it was 'not now too late' since he still very much needed local assistance and

---

[47] *Lord Del—r's speech* [1688?]; this was circulated widely enough to find an answer in *The Lord Delamere's letter to his tenants in Warrington, in Lancashire, answered* (1688).

goodwill.[48] Two days later, a gathering of gentry at York noted alarm at the conflict 'now breaking forth' and appealed to James to redress 'present grievances'; five days after that, Lord Devonshire told the mayor of Derby, whose town he had occupied with a force of supporters, that he was doing what he must for 'the healing of our present distractions'.[49] In the same month, rallies at Exeter and Nottingham expressed quite how important their current action was. A gathering of Devon gentlemen was clear that the cause which 'we now undertake' was to save the country; a similar meeting of local elites in the East Midlands was sure the nation's liberties and properties were at risk and that their 'present undertaking' was essential to prevent this.[50] Early in December, the fashion for mass demonstration had reached East Anglia. In Norwich, the Duke of Norfolk told citizens they must fight for a free Parliament as it was the only option 'in this present unhappy juncture of affairs'; later, at Kings Lynn, he told a crowd that had expressed fears of rapidly approaching danger that he would lead the men of the locality to defend against it—and that this was the key moment to do so, as 'the coming of the Prince of Orange hath given us opportunity'.[51]

People in 1688 thus felt that their actions in an unstable present would shape a fluid future. But of course, this sense of extensive possibility might lead to one further element of a modern chronology. Responses to the revolution could be periodized: some people believed they were witnessing a turning point that might usher in a new era. It is true that there were factors that told against any such conceptualization, at least in the immediate weeks after William landed at Torbay. Although events moved very rapidly towards a collapse in James's power, it took rather longer to reach the post-revolution settlement, so it was difficult for people to know how different the world would actually be. Yet despite this political fog, some sense of the significance of what had happened emerged very early and could go further than simple amazement at the removal of a king. From the first, James's collapse was read as a reversal of a long-term Catholic plot against England's faith and liberties, and as an opportunity to strengthen the constitution and the Protestant religion against future attack. It could therefore be the start of some sort of new era of freedom and security. Once it was clear that the old regime had disintegrated, there were widespread and prominent expressions of relief—and, more significantly, hints that 1688 meant not only defeat for the nation's enemies, but a chance to make good defences against them. Such a mood

---

[48] 'Speech by the prince of Orange to some principle gentlemen of Somersetshire and Dorsetshire', in *A fourth collection of papers relating the present juncture of affairs in England* (1688), 18.

[49] *Declaration of the nobility and gentry in this county of York* (1688); 'True copy of a paper delivered by the Lord Devonshire', in *Fourth collection of papers*, 19.

[50] *General association of the gentlemen of Devon* (1688); *Declaration of the nobility, gentry, and commonality at the rendez-vous at Nottingham* (1688).

[51] 'His grace the duke of Norfolk's speech to the mayor of Norwich on the first of December', in *A second collection of papers relating to the present juncture of affairs* (1688), 32; 'A letter from a gentleman at Kings Lyn, December 7', in *Fourth collection of papers*, 20.

emerged clearly in London in mid December. With the old king gone, city authorities invited William to come to the capital—but they invited him not only as the instrument of a blessed deliverance from James's evil, but because he had a further role to play in securing the kingdom. The lieutenancy of the city acknowledged the 'happy relief you have brought us' and urged the prince of Orange to come as fast as he could to 'perfect that great work which your highness has happily begun'. The Lord Mayor, aldermen, and common council also urged the prince to come, 'to carry on and perfect your glorious design to rescue England', and 'in a free parliament to establish the religion, the laws, and the liberties of these kingdoms upon a sure and lasting foundation'.[52] Very soon after William accepted the invitation to London, and called the convention, a print debate began about what that body should do to complete the recent political reversal; and at a perhaps more visceral level, doggerel verse began to look forward to a new golden age now that the evils of popery were vanquished.[53]

Other signs that people soon came to think of 1688–9 as a turning point will be examined later (for example, it was soon interpreted in apocalyptic terms as a key stage in the final defeat of the Roman Antichrist), but it is clear that many expected William's arrival to result in rather more than a change in who wore the crown.[54] And the possible scale of the shift was underlined by the rapid emergence of the term 'revolution' to describe it. Here of course, historians have to be highly sensitive to the contemporary meanings of words. 'Revolution' in English has certainly meant something epocally significant since the wholesale and deliberate transformations of the French and Russian versions. But in the early modern era, as scholars often point out, a 'revolution' might not require such novelty. As the word itself implied, it could mean a return to a starting point within a cyclical model of history; and it could be used without suggesting any inevitable pattern to the changes a 'revolution' wrought.[55] For example, people could call William's triumph a revolution even if they believed it was an unsustainable perversion of the natural course of events, or if they thought it might be short-lived. Those who opposed the change of regime were as happy to talk of a revolution as William's supporters, and writers were soon warning that a lack of morality or zeal might

---

[52] *Fourth collection of papers*, 31; *To his highness the prince of Orange, the humble address of the lord mayor* (1688).

[53] For the start of the constitutional debate, see below ch. 2.1; for verse see 'To haters of popery' in *The muses farewell to popery and slavery* (1688), 97–9; *A full description of these times* (1688).

[54] See below, ch.3.

[55] The OED's entry on 'revolution' shows transformative and cyclical meanings coexisting from the late Middle Ages, and Anna-Karina Rühl's analysis of the word in the seventeenth century suggested rotation and alteration inflected one another in its deployment: Anna-Karina Rühl, 'Zwischen göttlicher Vorsehung und Common Law', Magister thesis, Leibniz Universität, Hannover, 2007, esp. 24–9. The most common use of the word in pamphlet titles before 1688 was to describe the yearly orbit of the earth in astronomical guides: for example *Vox uraniae* (1686), *Apollo anglicus* (1688).

rapidly forfeit any advantages the revolution had brought.[56] Others clearly meant simply a change of ruler. The word had been used in this way to describe the dizzying—and ultimately directionless—changes of government in mid seventeenth century, and John Evelyn seemed to think that a change in the personnel of government was its key characteristic when he first applied the description to 1688.[57] His diary entry for 2 December listed a series of declarations for the prince from up and down the country, and so implied a great social movement against James, but it was only after he had talked about the great favourites at court fleeing, and the papists in office laying down their commissions, that he said 'it looks like a Revolution'.[58]

Despite all this, there can be no doubting the magnitude of change suggested by the term in the winter of 1688–9. It was used to highlight how complete and striking William's success had been, and within this, there was inevitably some sense that a significantly different situation had been created by the victory. This was especially the case as 'revolution' was coming to have transformative, as well as cyclical, meanings by the later seventeenth century.[59] Indeed, it is arguable that application of the term to William's victory eased this shift. 1688–9 marked a dramatic upturn in the use of the 'revolution' in printed literature, as evidenced by a term search on the standard electronic database of publications. This upsurge was almost entirely fuelled by debate over what might have changed in that year.[60] So, when the recorder of Bristol praised the prince of Orange in the early days of January 1689, and used a language of long-term significance when describing recent events, he may have been at the forefront of an important linguistic change. For the recorder, the 'revolution' that William had brought about was not only 'a joy and comfort to the present', but would be a 'wonder to all succeeding ages'.[61] Other early commentators talked of a revolution to argue that the Dutch expedition must have been guided by heaven, since only God could have brought about such

---

[56] For Jacobite uses see *The ballance adjusted, or the interest of church and state weighed and considered upon the revolution* (1689); *Observations upon the late revolution in England* (1689); [William Sherlock], *A letter to a member of the convention* (1689), 3. For an early warning about the reversibility of the revolution from its supporters, see Edward Stephens, *Reflections on the occurences of the last year* (1689).

[57] For example in R. Fitzbrian, *The good old cause…being a short and sober narrative of the great revolutions of affairs in these later times* (1659); David Lloyd, *Modern policy compleated, or the publick actions…of his excellency the lord general Monck under the revolutions since 1639 to 1660* (1660); *A lively portrait of our new cavaliers…in a compendious narrative of our late revolutions* (1661); James Howell, *Twelve several treatises of the late revolutions in these three kingdoms* (1661).

[58] E.S. De Beer, ed., *The Diary of John Evelyn*, 6 vols (Oxford: OUP, 1955), iv, 609.

[59] For the variety of meanings of the term, see Tim Harris, *Restoration: Charles II and His Kingdoms, 1660–1685* (London: Allen Lane, 2005), 32–7.

[60] All-term search for 'revolution' 1600–1750, in Jisc Historical texts: https://historicaltexts-jisc-ac-uk. ezproxy.bangor.ac.uk/results?terms=revolution&date=1600-1750&undated=exclude, search made 27 September 2018. This reveals rare usage of the word before 1688, exploding in that year, and climbing through the next decades.

[61] 'Speech of the recorder of Bristol to his highness the prince of Orange, January 7th', in *Fourth collection of papers*.

sudden alteration. This, of course, implied a divine plan, and so some radical purpose behind the old king's fall. The pamphleteer James Welwood talked of 'a revolution wherein the finger of God was so visible'; and a writer offering advice to the gathering convention thought the remarkable progress of 'the present revolution' was the clearest evidence that providence was at work.[62] Elsewhere, the potential significance of recent events was highlighted by an adjective larded onto the basic term. For many, this was not just any revolution, but a 'great' one.[63] This not only set it apart from other revolutions that had simply changed rulers, but may have initiated the process by which 1688–9 became known, uniquely, as 'The Revolution' in the political discourse of the eighteenth century.[64] Adorned by a capital letter and the definite article, it came to be recognized as a clear turning point: a foundational moment in the constitution.[65]

1.3 Unmodern Time: Lacunae, Multiplicities, Reversals, and Localizations

So far we have seen that the experience of time over the autumn of 1688 resembled the accelerated and progressive chronological sense, along with its awareness of a critically important present, which has been posited as the 'modern' condition. Yet we need to pause before we laud such evidence as proof of a new mentality. The revolution might have been an extraordinarily fast-paced and perhaps transformative adventure, but it did not unequivocally invent modern time. Most obviously, and as we have mentioned, there had been earlier points in history when dense news had created chronologies similar to 1688–9. The politics and conflicts of the civil war in the 1640s had been hungrily consumed by a public informed by a vigorous print industry and had been discussed in a variety of cultural spaces.[66] Scholarship on the years of the Exclusion Crisis (1679–83) has similarly demonstrated a ferment of information, rumour, speculation, and appetite for updates in a national community benefitting from a lapse in regulation of print.[67] So the autumn of 1688 might be a development or particularly dramatic

---

[62] James Welwood, *A vindication of the present great revolution* (1689), 25; 'Proposals humbly offered to the Lords and Commons in the present convention', in *Fourth collection of papers*, p. 6.

[63] [Daniel Defoe], *Reflections upon the late great revolution* (1689); Welwood, *Vindication*; [Edmund Bohun], *History of the desertion* (1689), epistle dedicatory; *History of the late great revolution in England and Scotland* (1689).

[64] See, for example, the note on the use of 'The Revolution' in Ephraim Chambers, *Cyclopaedia*, 2 vols (1728), ii, 1014.

[65] The was particularly the case among Whigs—see Kenyon, *Revolution Principles*, esp. ch. 8.

[66] For good summaries, see Michael Braddick, ed., *The Oxford Handbook of the English Revolution* (Oxford: OUP, 2015), chs 16–19; Kevin Sharpe, *Image Wars: Promoting Kings and Commonwealths in England, 1603–1660* (New Haven: Yale UP, 2010), ch. 3.

[67] Garland, 'News', chs 1–3; Mark Knights, *Politics and Opinion in Crisis, 1678–81* (Cambridge: CUP, 1994), part II; Tim Harris, *London Crowds in the Reign of Charles II* (Cambridge: CUP, 1987), chs 5–7.

resurgence of existing trends, but it was not the first manifestation of them. More interestingly, closer inspection of 1688 reveals problems with the flows of information that are supposed to have constructed a modern sense of time. News was dense, and it was fast moving, but there were significant gaps, delays, and misdirections, which meant that experience could not always stream forward smoothly. This created a more complex and ambiguous chronological awareness than the breathless narrative we have described.

One dimension of the revolution that has received too little attention was the deliberate suppression of information. Press and public may have been exchanging news vigorously, but governments were attempting to stop people finding things out, and may have been more effective than scholars have acknowledged. The prince of Orange did not advertise the details of his military build-up, and this left people in England scrabbling for the truth about its size, capabilities, and purpose. Even as the Dutch prepared to leave port, William's ambassadors in London were denying any invasion was intended, and the king in London was relying on reports from scout ships that had accidentally sailed into the path of part of the prince's gathering fleet.[68] For his part, James tried to stop talk about William's invasion. He issued a proclamation against the spread of 'false news' on 26 October, and attempted to suppress the manifesto the prince published to explain his action.[69] A new proclamation on 2 November threatened punishment for anyone who distributed, published, read, or kept the document.[70] Traditionally historians have dismissed these efforts as ineffective, but they may have to be taken more seriously.[71] There was contemporary comment that nobody seemed to know what the prince had actually said in his propaganda—so it was not making its way to all corners of the land as some historians (including this one) have suggested; coffeehouses appear to have ceased their practice of providing printed newsheets for their customers; and some correspondents said they must be circumspect in relating current affairs, in deference to James's orders.[72]

Much more significantly, information was interrupted by limitations in communications technology. The events of the autumn of 1688 may have coalesced into a single news story, providing a sense of chronological pace, but some of the

[68]   Anon to Sir Thomas Mostyn, 4 October 1688, and anon to Sir Thomas Mostyn, 18 October 1688, Bangor University Archives, Mostyn MSS 9094,.

[69]   *A proclamation to restrain the spreading of false news* (1688). The manifesto was *The declaration of his highness William Henry, prince of Orange, of the reasons inducing him to appear in arms* (1688).

[70]   *A proclamation… whereas the prince of Orange* (1688).

[71]   For optimistic assessments, see Lois Schwoerer, *The Declaration of Rights, 1689* (Baltimore: Johns Hopkins UP, 1981), ch. 5; Lois Schwoerer, 'Propaganda in the Revolution of 1688–9', *American Historical Review*, 82 (1997), 843–74; Jonathan Israel, 'General Introduction' and 'The Dutch Role in the Glorious Revolution', in Jonathan Israel, ed., *The Anglo-Dutch Moment* (Cambridge: CUP, 1991), 1–46, 105–62.

[72]   Anon to Sir Thomas Mostyn, 30 October 1688, Bangor University Archives, Mostyn MSS 9094; newsletter of 11 October 1688, HMC, *Fleming*, 214; HMC, *Rutland*, 122; Russell J. Kerr and Ida Coffin Duncan, eds. *The Portledge Papers* (London: Cape, 1928), 51.

individual elements happened a long way from audiences. The ports of the Netherlands where the prince assembled his fleet; the West Country where the Dutch landed; the counties of Cheshire, Nottinghamshire, and Yorkshire where the English rebelled against James; Ireland, where tensions between Catholics and Protestants flared; and London, where the king tried to coordinate a response were hundreds of miles from each other and could be far from those trying to make sense of what was going on. Such distances mattered, because they delayed the reception of news. Whilst travel across water could be quite swift (it was possible to cross the Irish Sea, the Channel, or the southern parts of the North Sea in a day or so), it was also unreliable. Storms and contrary winds often prevented boats powered by sail from making the crossing, and this resulted in lacunae in the regular stream of 'posts' bringing details of events on the continent or in Ireland: newspaper editors often lamented that they had no news from abroad.[73] Travel by land was less subject to total disruption, but was slower. Roads, particularly in England, were frequently in very poor condition (as Constantjin Huygens, travelling with the prince's expedition complained), and horses (the fastest means of getting about the country) tired.[74] Evidence from newspapers (when London journals published a dated story from another part of the country) and correspondence (when recipients said they got a letter) suggests it usually took two to three days for messages to get from the far west or north of England to London; and one, perhaps tragic, instance provides us with an absolute upper speed limit. When William arrived in Torbay, a local customs officer rode non-stop to the court in Whitehall with a dispatch. Commentators in the capital reported their astonishment that he had covered the distance (they claimed 160 miles, though in fact it is closer to 200) in twenty hours—but also expressed their concern for his health.[75] It seems the effort and fatigue of such a rapid journey left the man in a serious condition, and the king's physicians were ordered to take particular care of him. It is unclear if he recovered.[76]

Censorship and slow communication thus created gaps in people's knowledge and inevitably affected their experience of time. First, and most obviously, the progressive narrative that has been charted for 1688 was frequently paused by delay in news. The records of witnesses are full of frustration that the unfolding experience of the invasion had been halted by problems in receiving information. For example, Robert Harley, touring the Welsh Marches in late October, complained that 'here is no good account of news'; and around the same time, the Mostyn newsletter writers shared the court's lament that nothing new could be

<hr>

[73] For example, *London Gazette*, 2404 (24–6 November 1688); 2410 (12–14 December 1688).

[74] Rudolf Dekker, ed., *The Diary of Constantijn Huygens Jr* (Amsterdam: Panchaud, 2015), 61–5.

[75] Stephen Taylor, ed., *The entring book of Roger Morrice*, iv: *1687–1689* (Woodbridge: Boydell, 2007), 331; Anon to Sir Thomas Mostyn, 9 November, 1688, Bangor University Archives, Mostyn MSS 9094.

[76] Newsletter of 10 November 1688, HMC, *Fleming*, 218.

discovered about what William was up to, even when communications were flowing.[77] On the 9th, a correspondent reported that 'his Majesty had an express from Holland, but it brought little news being of old date'. On the 11th the same agent moaned that 'contrary winds hinders the coming of foreign mails', so everyone 'would continue in the dark'. On the 16th another writer sighed that 'this day came in three Dutch posts together, but they give not so large an account of matters as was expected'.[78] Similarly, the Earl of Dunmore told the Earl of Derby on 4 October that 'We hear no more news of the Dutch, the wind being contrary'; and even once William was close to occupying London, the Princess Anne could complain there was no reliable information in Nottingham, the town to which she had fled.[79] Those waiting for fresh tidings complained they had been thrust into a sort of dead time in which progressive narrative ceased.

Perhaps more interestingly, gaps in news created a far more complex present than the simple 'modern' model. There was no single, contemporaneous moment creating, and moving forward into, the future. Unlike people in the twenty-first century (who not only believe things are happening now in other parts of the world, but can usually watch them live), those of the late Stuart era could not find out what the distant events of their moment were until quite a period after that moment had passed. This meant their present was polychronic; and that evolving timelines were experienced out of sequence. An observer at one location would know what was happening there, but this updating of the situation had to be mixed with information from further away that that person knew was from some period ago. The nature of the present thus became ambiguous, and consciousness of the unfolding of time was jumbled. In a very real sense, in fact, the people of 1688 were like astronomers observing events elsewhere in the universe. Watching, say, a supernova in another part of the galaxy, scientists know that technically this occurred hundreds or thousands of years ago, because the light from the explosion takes so long to arrive at earth. Yet it is hard not to experience the cataclysm as if it were happening now, and to think and talk as if it were unfolding at this very moment. Astronomers are thus aware of a choice of presents in which to frame the supernova (does one talk about the event itself in the present tense, or constantly remind one's audience that it is only information about the event that is manifest now?); and they inevitably tell its story out of order. The explosion may, in actual fact, have occurred during Earth's most recent Ice Ages, but it cannot be related, and so woven into history, until a much later point. Such temporal dislocation is unusual in our world of instant communication, but it was the lot of everyone in the late Stuart period, even for some quite local events.

<hr>

[77] HMC, *Portland*, 420.

[78] Anon to Sir Thomas Mostyn, 9 and 11 October, 1688; anon to Sir Thomas Mostyn, 16 October, 1688, Bangor University Archives, Mostyn MSS 9094.

[79] HMC, *Kenyon*, 197; Beatrice Curtis Brown, ed., *The Letters and Domestic Instructions of Queen Anne* (London: Cassell, 1935).

To make these sorts of displacement and multiplicity more concrete, we can take two examples. First, we can think about another important theatre of action in 1688. Most of the events covered in this chapter so far took place in the Netherlands or England. But there was a crucial context for William's expedition in Louis XIV's invasion of Germany. The French had sent troops into the Rhineland in the late summer, and if these had been victorious, they would have posed such a threat to the Netherlands that the Dutch would have to defend themselves rather than intervening in England. However, if German forces could stop Louis's armies, William would have a freer hand. What was happening along the Rhine was therefore vital information for the English, but it took well over a week to arrive in London, and longer to get to the provinces—and once there it had the same complex temporal status as sightings of supernovae. The *Gazette* for 4 October carried James's restoration of the charter of the City of London, which was part of his attempts to regain support in the face of the Dutch threat.[80] But it also carried details of Louis's siege of Philipsburg. The latter story was highly material to the former (the need for concessions by James would be determined by French military fortunes on the Rhine), so, for the newspaper's readers, both partook in a single rapidly progressing present. But the readers also knew that they were not in the present in the same way. As the date on the Philipsburg report showed prominently, it was, in fact, a fortnight old. It was dated 30 September, but this was using the new Gregorian calendar, standard on the continent—a system that was ten days ahead of the Julian one still used in England, including to date the *Gazette's* issue. The present of the reader's understanding was thus fractured and ambiguous. Facts of various age were contained within it; and this was underlined by other stories within the issue. There was a report from Vienna of progress in the Emperor's fight against the Turk (important because it might determine how much help he could be to the Dutch). This was three weeks old. There were, additionally, updates on fleet movements from Cadiz that might give information on how Spain might intervene. These were stale by over a month.

Communication delays thus created a temporally complex present, but—as a second example shows—they could also disrupt the experience of evolving narrative. On 10 November, a newsletter writer was attempting to piece together where William had got to in the first days in England. This was difficult because of the number of conflicting dispatches arriving in London—'the reports are as various as those who report'—but also because of delays and variations in those communications. The correspondent began his account by saying it was clear that the Dutch had disembarked. However, he then provided a disordered picture of whether the prince had got to Exeter: an account that couldn't decide whether to sequence material in the order that things had happened, or that news was

---

[80] *London Gazette*, 2388 (4–8 October 1688).

received. The writer started by stating that 'William was not come to that city when the post came on Wednesday'. This seemed to assert a matter of present fact, but really it was only a matter of present report. The moment at which the prince had not arrived was not a moment in Devon, but one in London—the point when the post came in. This became clear instantly, because the writer then said that an express had been sent after the mail, which had overtaken it, and gave an—albeit very basic—account of William's coming into Exeter. The writer had therefore known that the prince had arrived before being told by the post that he had not yet done so, but still seemed to want to express the temporal muddling of the current crisis by conveying the disordering processes of news distribution. What had happened in Exeter was simple and progressive. The prince had taken a few days to march to Exeter, but had eventually got there. The experience of this story in London, however, had been nowhere near as straightforward. News of the arrival had arrived before news of the earlier delay, and the resulting narrative confusion was reflected as the newsletter started with a report that had actually arrived later.[81] Such temporal dislocations were common. To take another example: another newsletter scribe declared on 21 November that 'this last hath produced a great deal of important news which I will tell you according to the order of time it was brought hither' (not the order in which things had happened). The result was a comprehensive, but chronologically jumbled, account of the risings in the north, the king's return from Salisbury, the departure of the Dutch fleet from Torbay, and desertions from the army to William's cause.[82]

Interruptions in the flow of news thus stopped and disordered time for people in 1688. But the responses to this created still more complex and ambiguous chronological patterns. We have already begun to discuss one obvious reaction to not knowing what was going to happen next. When events were moving quickly, people anticipated the next stage of the story. But when such anticipation was about events at a distance, the chronological effect was not simple acceleration. To predict events in one's own locality was to talk about the future and to pull it closer to the present. But the 'present' at a distance was in the past. So to speculate forward from this past present was not to talk about the future, but rather to construct a speculative contemporaneous present, and to weave a narrative leading to it from the most recent information one had. In simpler terms, people were not guessing what might happen, they were guessing what had happened. This again destroyed any simple or unified present moving forward in time.

All this might seem like abstract theorizing. But for people facing William's invasion, thinking about what might have happened elsewhere was a pressing challenge, because distant events might be so significant. Consequently, the autumn was filled with speculations, many of which turned out to be wrong.

---

[81] HMC, *Fleming*, 219.   [82] British Library, Add MSS 72569, f. 46.

To illustrate this, one can take a single newsletter. The message sent to Sir Thomas Mostyn in Caernarfonshire on 18 October contained some solid facts about events in the capital, but much was a tissue of contradicting rumours about things beyond London. 'We have had uncertain posts of the movement of the Dutch fleet for the past two days', the writer lamented. They had been discovered off Sole Bay and other places, but the reports 'proved mistaken'. The last certain advice was that William had not sailed, but it was reported that a fast had been held among the invaders 'yesterday' in preparation for them sailing north 'this day'. Again, however, a 'flying express' from the continent suggested (falsely, it would turn out), that the French had amassed thirty thousand troops on the borders of the United Provinces to prevent the prince of Orange's design, and that this 'if confirmed will certainly break their invasion'.[83]

This sort of desperate attempt to fill in narrative from other places had two important chronological effects, illustrated in the newsletter just quoted. First, it created a plurality of alternative presents. At the simplest level, this was because people rapidly learned to be cautious in accepting news. Because so much of what they heard turned out to be erroneous, they became aware that much of it was likely to be false, and put caveats on their reaction. As Mostyn's correspondent admitted, one could only draw conclusions from the amassing of French troops *if* that was confirmed, and his scepticism was characteristic of these vital weeks. Many witnesses noted the abundance of unreliable information. Alexander Farington, reporting the mood in London back home to Westmorland, said that 'many rumours are spread abroad'; whilst Richard Lapthorne noted that 'false rumours never more abounded in the nation'.[84] Others placed warnings on their reports, noting that their sources were plebeians or coffee-house gossips, or stressing that there was no certainty in what they relayed.[85] Such speculation created alternate presents because of the possibility of mistakes, and the effect was compounded when there was directly contradictory information. Mostyn's correspondent had talked of the Dutch being in Sole Bay 'and other places'; and twelve days later, the same writer was still facing variant versions of the world. 'We have no uncertain advice of the Dutch fleet. Some have reported that they have sailed northwards and others that they are still on the coasts'.[86] Such exasperation was widespread. On 1 November, John Evelyn noted that there were 'continual alarms of the Prince of Orange's landing but no certainty; reports of his great losses.... but without any assurance'; whilst in late September, someone writing to Abigail Harley revealed that the court had just had two contradictory

---

[83] Anon to Sir Thomas Mostyn, 18 October 1688, Bangor University Archives, Mostyn MSS 9094.

[84] HMC, *Fleming*, 216; Kerr and Duncan, *Portledge Papers*, 51.

[85] For example, Andrew Clark, ed., *The life and times of Anthony Wood* (Oxford, 1894), 278, diary entry for 27 September; British Library Add. MSS, 45731, ff. 24, 61; Ellis, *Ellis Correspondence*, ii, 202, 210–11.

[86] Anon to Sir Thomas Mostyn, 30 October 1688, Bangor University Archives, Mostyn MSS 9094.

expresses from Holland.[87] One said that the prince was ready to embark, but the other held that his forces were far from being gathered and that he had had to delay for at least four days.[88]

At one level, this kind of uncertainty is compatible with the idea of a rapidly evolving, and so 'modern', present. Things were moving so fast that they destabilized the current moment. But the process was also creating alternate timelines in ways that perhaps fit less well with the supposed modern experience. The people of 1688 were repeatedly being asked to choose between differing realities. It was difficult for contemporaries to have a sense of an evolving current moment because they were not sure which of the moments on offer was real. Moreover, the point at which people made the choice between alternative presents could involve a reversal of narrative, and so of time's flow, that was the second chronological effect of having to speculate about events at a distance.

To make this clearer we can examine a passage in Roger Morrice's *Entring Book* (a comprehensive chronicle of events written from 1677, and by 1688 weekly, by a London Presbyterian, for a purpose not entirely clear to historians).[89] On 10 November, Morrice sat down to record his experience of the seven-day period in which news of William's landing at Torbay had arrived in London. This might have been a moment when all the uncertainty about the prince's movements was resolved, but instead there had been multiple errors of information. On 3 November, Morrice recalled, there had been a 'universal report' that the Dutch had landed at Portsmouth. This had seemed to have been confirmed when the Duke of Berwick's regiment marched westward from Brentwood, but the story lost steam by the evening of the next day, and it was 'suddenly after contradicted'. The anticlimax seemed to have bred the opposite kind of rumour: this time that there was to be no invasion at all. Talk in Morrice's circle had been that the Dutch were feinting. They had, it was suggested, built up an expeditionary force to panic the English regime, but had had no intention of actually using it immediately. Yet by the end of Morrice's entry for the week, this talk too was exposed as a canard. The diarist provided details of what had actually happened (the Dutch had sailed on the first of the month and arrived off the Devon coast on the fourth)—though even this definitive account hinted at another alternative reality when it suggested William had at first been thought to have been sailing to the North of England.[90]

If we pause to think what sort of chronology was involved here, we find one that kept leaping back in time. Each successive false story created a forward narrative about what was happening elsewhere, but at the point at which it proved false, those who had entertained it were forced to adopt a different present. This meant they had to unpick the account they had had in their minds, return to the

---

[87] De Beer, *Diary of John Evelyn*, iv, 603.   [88] HMC, *Portland*, 417.
[89] Goldie, *Roger Morrice*, esp. 98–116.   [90] Taylor, *Entring book*, iv, 329–32.

last certain information they had, and tell a new story to get them where they now thought they were. So, Morrice began with the knowledge that the Dutch has massed an invasion fleet in their ports. He came to believe this had sailed and landed at Portsmouth. But when all this turned out to be nonsense, he doubled back to the Dutch in their ports. From then, a new (if less eventful) narrative evolved. This one had the Netherlanders staying in their homeland and using the fleet as a bluff in English politics. But then news of the actual landing of William in Devon arrived. This in turn unravelled the 'bluff' narrative and pulled Morrice back to his original moment (when he had thought the Dutch were about to sail), so he could use it as a starting point for a yet another, and finally accurate, story. But even now, false narrative was nested with the true. Some English observers had thought the Dutch had sailed north. But they had then had to return the enemy in their imaginations to an earlier point in the voyage, from which they had actually progressed along the Channel. All of this involved dizzying changes in temporal direction. The same span of time had been palimpsestically traversed by four different narratives.

Morrice's case was particularly rich, but it was not unusual. The Mostyn news-letter's reversal of time when the Sole Bay story was discredited was but one supporting example; other instances among a great many included repeated reappraisals of how badly the Dutch fleet had been damaged by a storm that had struck it when it first tried to sail for England. Anne Pye in London, writing to Abigail Harley at Brampton a week after the tempest—but only as news of it was arriving—demonstrated the typical substitution of narratives. 'An express came on Thursday', she began, 'that said the Dutch fleet had suffered greatly', but she immediately undid this by stating 'three expresses are come in to-day not confirming this news, which is now looked upon as false'.[91] Morrice similarly corrected himself within a few sentences. He first stated that the damage was probably severe if the weather 'was as violent at sea as it was by land', but then said the Dutch had in fact made an accurate meteorological forecast and had been able to get back to port in reasonably good order.[92] The disorientating effect of these kinds of retellings had been nicely summarized a few days earlier by a correspondent of John Ellis. On 16 October this writer revealed that people had been subjected to a series of widely differing accounts of William's progress, and that as a result, the 'Dutch have ebbed and flowed these three days in the report of the vulgar'.[93]

Clearly, rumour was unsettling people throughout the autumn, but at one point false narrative had a truly terrifying impact. From the end of the second week in December, tales began to circulate that an army of wild Irish was marching through the country and massacring Protestants, and that they were now only a

---

[91] HMC, *Portland*, 420.   [92] Taylor, *Entring book*, iv, 324–5.
[93] Ellis, *Ellis correspondence*, ii, 253.

few miles from whoever was reporting the fears. Perhaps initially sparked by James's attempts to import troops from Ireland, these anxieties convulsed the nation. The panic started in London in the early hours of 13 December. News circulated that an Irish force had burnt Uxbridge and killed its inhabitants and was now advancing on the city. The populace spent the night arming itself, thronging the streets, and illuminating the windows of all buildings, and concern only subsided when an emergency session of the provisional government of peers that had set itself up on James's initial flight resolved to check if the reports were true. When messengers returned with the information that the people of Uxbridge were all alive, and asleep, this reassurance—along, no doubt, with the effects of exhaustion—helped the authorities restore greater calm.[94] This only, however, resolved the situation in the capital. Posts from London stirred very many other places over the next few days. As Morrice put it, terror 'circulated so generally…that it's in vain to name particular countys.…the universal cry was their throats should be cut'.[95]

The Irish panic familiar to historians, but it is worth stressing here because of the power of its abortive narrative. Before they discovered the baselessness of their fears, people's actions were controlled by a story that had no actual existence and had to be untold later. The English were immersed in a timeline that had to be wrenchingly unwound when its assumptions were discredited. Thus the behaviour of the London mob forced the provisional government to make extensive military preparations to protect the city in case the Irish really were at Uxbridge, and to calm the citizens even if they were not—and it took a highly visible defence of the London with artillery to finally convince its inhabitants they were safe.[96] Similarly, the duchess of Beaufort, based at Badminton in Wiltshire, was sucked into the 'Irish fright' timeline, despite her initial attempts to resist it. When she first heard that Andover had been burnt, she 'thought it was but a story' and 'was pretty quiet'. Soon, however, the duchess was unnerved by news that Reading and Newbury were also burnt, and that a great body of Irish had got as close as Marlborough (only forty miles away). She got involved in a consuming argument with a troop of men who refused to march out to confront the enemy unless they could take the weapons stored in her house, which she insisted were her only security. It was only when a letter arrived from the duke, who wrote from an unburned Reading and had travelled through an undamaged Newbury, that she could escape the fantasy. Two days later she was complaining how hard it was to disabuse others. Writing to the duke on the 17 December, she suggested rumours of Irish arson and massacre were being deliberately fanned to do mischief, and

---

[94] 'The proceedings of the lords spiritual and temporal from their first meeting in the Guildhall, London', reproduced in Robert Beddard, *A Kingdom Without a King* (Oxford: Phaidon, 1988), 84.

[95] Taylor, *Entring book*, iv, 391.

[96] Beddard, *Kingdom Without a King*, 45; G.H. Jones, 'The Irish Fright', *Bulletin of the Institute of Historical Research*, 55 (1982), 148–53.

reported continuing disturbances born of the 'fibs'.[97] The false narrative thus consumed people, and sometimes for long periods, a fact acknowledged in regrets about the time that had been wasted or misspent within that imagined world. Charles Bertie, for example, writing to the Earl of Danby on 20 December, and urging him to bring the English troops he had raised in Yorkshire to London, lamented a delay caused by tackling a non-existent Irish insurgency. 'The same groundless fears that distracted us last week', he complained, 'have conjured up again such a body of Irish in our parts to prevent your lordship's journey southwards'.[98]

1.4 Pre-modern Postmodernity, and Early Modern Pre-modernity, in Time Perception

So, some features of 1688 point towards a modern experience of time, but some are far more ambiguous. It is clear that witnesses to William's invasion felt an onward rush of events. A rich density of connected happenings, and of their reporting, crafted an accelerated narrative that demanded knowledge of a contemporaneous present, and generated a sense that actions in the moment would determine a fluid future, and perhaps lead to a turning point in history. For these people time was filling at breakneck rapidity, but it was not full. And yet, this very acceleration of events also disrupted a 'modern' sense of time. Because news could not travel as fast as the precipitously changing story demanded, any progressive chronology became fragmented. The flow of events had gaps. It got out of order. It had to be reversed and unpicked. It created multiple presents, forcing everyone to choose between different temporal realities. Describing such a situation poses challenges. People's sense of time fitted the idea of a new chronology to some extent, but how best to label the rest of their experience is debateable. Ironically for a period which was supposed to be emerging into the modern, the concept of *post*-modernity may offer fruitful ways to think about what happened. The sort of chronological fragmentation we have explored is at the heart of a 'postmodern' condition developed by scholars to describe the experience of life since the later twentieth century—at least in the capitalist West—and which is supposedly marked by lack of grand pattern, incoherence, and fracture.

The idea of postmodernity starts from the argument that the progressive 'grand narratives' that were constructed from the eighteenth century—and that gave people sense of their place in an unfolding human story—have collapsed. Notions such as scientific advance, or a steady liberal emancipation of politics and society, have been questioned, and this has created a 'post-history' where the past can no longer explain the present because there is no pattern of development over time.

---

[97] HMC, *The manuscripts of the Duke of Beaufort* (1891), 92–3.   [98] HMC, *Buckingham*, 456.

This has trapped people in an isolated present; but the present itself has shattered. As sources of information and opinion have multiplied—and as a huge diversity of political, cultural, and social discourses have circulated—vast numbers of competing descriptions of the current moment are offered. These replace one another with dizzying rapidity because of the speed of information flow and the rapid spread of new philosophies. As one commentator has put it, people in the postmodern world are 'scattered across temporal universes that can no longer be reconciled'; according to another, confusion at over-rapid change means any sense of direction evaporates, and this leaves a 'frantic standstill'.[99] In such a situation, chronological bearings disappear. People are left with nothing but the uncertainty, ambiguity, and disorientation which are at the heart of postmodernism generally.[100]

Of course, not everyone would accept this description of the twenty-first century. Many would also object that 'postmodernism' has been used to describe so many different phenomena in different disciplines that it is too imprecise to be useful; and some have preferred to see it as a manifestation of the modern itself—hence the alternative notion of 'late' modernity.[101] Again, if there are any parallels between postmodernity and the experience of people in 1688, they were not caused by the same processes. The grand narratives of modernity that are supposed to have collapsed in recent decades were not fully constructed, let alone destroyed, by the seventeenth century; and whatever advances in media there had been by the late Stuart epoch, they were far from the information overload and diversity of our new millennium. Yet despite these obvious and important caveats, thinking about 1688 in 'postmodern' terms may catch important parts of its essence and explain some of people's reactions to the chronological chaos they faced.

As we have seen, the situation during William's invasion presented people with a hyper-accelerated series of events that was difficult to assimilate and created multiple presents. Partly this was because false stories were circulating, and partly because large elements of everyone's present were out of date, so nobody knew what scenarios had played themselves out in distant locations. This meant people had to make choices between possible presents, in a way that has some similarity

---

[99] Ursula K. Heise, *Chronochisms: Time, Narrative and Postmodernism* (Cambridge: CUP, 1997), 6–7; Hartmut Rosa, 'The acceleration of social change, and the transformation of history', Cambridge Lecture, 27 May 2016.

[100] For some explorations of these ideas, see Jean-Francois Lyotard, *La condition postmoderne: rapport sur le savoir* (Paris: Editions de Minuit, 1979); Frederic Jameson, 'Postmodernism and Consumer Society', in Hal Foster, ed., *The Anti-Aesthetic: Essays in Postmodern Culture* (Port Townsend, WA: Bay Press, 1983) 111–25; Frederic Jameson, *Postmodernism, or the Cultural Logic of Late Capitalism* (Durham, NC: Duke UP, 1997); Hans Bertens, *The Idea of the Post-Modern: A History* (London: Routledge,1995), 163–4; also Hiese, *Chronochism*, but the literature is vast.

[101] For some of the problems with conceptualizing postmodernity, see Mike Featherstone, *Consumer Culture and Postmodernism* (London: Sage, 2007), ch. 1, and Penelope Corfield, *Time and the Shape of History* (New Haven, CT: Yale UP, 2007), ch. 5. Berman, *All That Is Solid*, introduction, sees disorientation as a feature of a third stage of modernity.

to the twenty-first-century diversity of constructions of the world. The rapidity of turnover in these realities may also have had parallels. As we saw, anticipation and speculation created many false timelines that had to be quickly unpicked. Though different in precise origin to the 'postmodern' churn of worldviews, this may have added to a comparable sense of conditionality. No credit could be put on one's current understanding of the world, because it might soon be upended. Certainly, descriptions of a 'modern' present included an important element of uncertainty. Once time was empty, the future was fluid, and this bred anxiety about current actions. But the lack of confidence described for the postmodern condition is of a different order. It verges on an inability to make any sense of one's situation, and it seems to come closer to what witnesses of William's invasion were going through. There were responses to the Dutch expedition that suggest the people of 1688 were suffering the sort of psychological trauma that commentators on today's world have outlined.

The most important was simple bewilderment. There was clear confusion and uncertainty in witness accounts of William's invasion—and sometimes people seemed to have been rendered literally speechless by this. Unable to make out a clear progressing story in their world, they were unable to recount one. Philip Musgrave tried to keep his correspondents up to date with events in London in mid December, but found the swirl of news and rumour (which included the Irish panic) overwhelming. 'Since the king's departure', he sighed, 'the distractions have been so great here, that till this moment I know not what to write to your lordship'.[102] There was a similar lapse into silence by Lady Scott around the same time. She had been hoping for advice from her correspondent, but James's flight had prevented even that. 'This sudden unhappy news', she admitted, had been the occasion for her delay in writing: she had been caught 'not knowing whether it were my best *way to go thither or farther*'.[103]

Such bewilderment might be understandable during the uncertainty of William's actual invasion—but it survived into the weeks after the prince had gained control, when the political situation seemed more stable. Comment in the early weeks after the Dutch arrived in London expressed confusion at what had just happened: though now it was the enormity and surprise of the change, as much as its speed, which confounded people. Welcoming William to London on 20 December, Sir George Treby admitted people were 'astonished', and thought recent events 'miraculous'.[104] Preaching on 23 December 1688, the prince's chaplain, Gilbert Burnet, talked of 'amazing' occurrences: ones so 'extraordinary' they seemed a 'dream'.[105] By the thanksgiving days which were called in late January to

---

[102] HMC, *Dartmouth*, iii, 135.   [103] HMC, *Dartmouth*, iii, 137.
[104] *The speech of Sir George Treby* (1688), 2.
[105] Gilbert Burnet, *A sermon preached in the chappel of St James before the prince of Orange, the 23rd December, 1688* (1688), 1.

celebrate William's deliverance of the kingdom, such sentiment was in full spate. For Simon Patrick, preaching at St Paul's, Covent Garden, William's arrival was 'unlikely', 'unexpected and unlook'd for'. It was a 'strange change', 'beyond all Humane Expectation'.[106] For the reverend Thomas Watts it was 'strange', 'miraculous', 'extraordinary', and 'wonderfull'.[107] And the bewilderment went beyond preachers. For James Welwood, a pamphleteer who tried to justify the change of regime almost as soon as it had occurred, the revolution was 'unfathomably stupendous'; for one of the first contributors to the convention that was assembled to debate the future of crown in January 1689, recent history was so extraordinary he 'was not able to comprehend' it.[108]

And at the heart of this confusion was how to place such bizarre events in time. There were, some witnesses to the revolution insisted, no earlier occurrences that could help make sense of it; and future historians would find it hard to integrate William's success into any credible account of its epoch. As early as October 1688, John Evelyn thought the public mood was so 'strange', it was 'unheard of in any former age'; and, slightly later, those commentating on the change of regime were similarly stuck for precedents.[109] For the pamphleteer White Kennett, the revolution was 'unexampl'd in the Records of Time.'[110] For the preacher John Tillotson, 'we know not how to compare it with any thing but itself.'[111] For another cleric, John Oakes, the recent change was 'unparalled'; whilst for a country clergyman in Dorset, the recent change was so vast and sudden, it looked like 'a great Romance', that no one would believe was 'modern History' had not 'all the nation of sensible Witnesses' vouched for its veracity.[112] Some commentators did attempt to fit the revolution into a temporal framework, but it was not that of any normal human past. For the cleric William Wilson, reflecting in mid January, the last few weeks belonged to the distant era of supernatural wonders.[113] Similarly, Simon Patrick thought geology rather than history was the best way to think about recent events. For him, William's triumph was like an earthquake that swallowed mountains.[114] Among such befuddled witnesses, the speed and scale of change had done something quite other than create a chronology in which a linear narrative unfolded through progressive events. Rather, it tore events out of time. They were so extraordinary that they could not be woven into any coherent story

---

[106] Simon Patrick, *A sermon preached at St Paul's Covent Garden on the day of thanksgiving* (1689), 1, 7.

[107] Thomas Watts, *A sermon preached upon February 14th* (1689), 9–10.

[108] Welwood, *Vindication*, preface; Grey, *Debates*, x, 26.

[109] De Beer, *Diary of John Evelyn*, vi, 600.

[110] [White Kennet], *A dialogue between two friends* occasioned by the late revolution of affairs (1689), 1.

[111] John Tilloston, *A sermon preach'd at Lincolns-Inn-Chappel on the 31st of January, 1688* (1689), 25.

[112] John Oakes, *The last sermon and sayings* (1689), 3; *A sermon preach'd in a country church, February 14, 1688* (1689), 9–10.

[113] William Wilson, *A sermon preached before the mayor, aldermen and common-council of Nottingham…14th of Febr. 1688/9* (1689), 8–11.

[114] Patrick, *Sermon preached at St Paul's*, 19.

and had to be contemplated as self-sufficient particularities, with no clearly discernable meaning.

Such reaction to 1688–9 has parallels with postmodernity's fragmentation of temporal experience, particularly its disorientating isolation of the present moment from any clear pattern of history. And it had cultural and psychological effects that at least appear to mirror descriptions of the postmodern condition. First, and most obviously, it prevented the construction of advancing patterns of history which might periodize the human past into clear stages of development. For all that some labelled James's fall a 'revolution', and hinted at a turning point that might usher in a golden new age, the kinds of incomprehension we have just charted prevented any such conception for many more. William's triumph was so unexpected and extraordinary, that it was severed from any meaningful flow of time. There were no earthly causes that might explain such an astonishing turn of events, and there were no comparators in the past that might guide predictions about what was going to happen next. It was therefore hard to know or imagine what the significance of 1688–9 might be, how it might serve as a hinge between eras, what periodization it might suggest, or how it could possible fit into a great unfolding story. In postmodernity, the collapse of grand narratives is supposed to have left a sense of directionless (if rather manic) stasis. The situation for people as William triumphed was different, but potentially comparable. The revolution was too strange to fit into any overarching plan of history, and as the next chapter of this book explores, a mental response may have been to deny that it had actually changed anything fundamental at all.

Another response to temporal bewilderment during William's invasion was to retreat from contemporaneity. If trying to cope with multiple possible presents was overwhelming, one might respond by removing what was perhaps their prime cause. Confusion was usually produced by trying to think about what was going on in places too far away to allow instant communication; but there was always the option of refusing to engage with such hypothetical 'nows'. Abandoning the modern sense of a universal present that applied everywhere, actors could retreat into a geographically localized time. At one level, practicalities forced this response. If slow communications meant people had no idea what conditions were beyond their immediate surroundings, they had no choice but to surrender mental involvement with distant places. The records of William's invasion are full of instructions to others that they would have to try to shape the course of events where they were, whilst the writer looked after their own locality. Such reactions ran the gamut from great issues of state, through military tactics, to domestic arrangements. So the court had to tell the commissioners who had been sent to treat with William at Hungerford, that 'His Majesty, not knowing how matters go with you' was leaving it 'wholly to your lordships prudence' to judge matters and to decide whether to continue in negotiations or break them off 'as you think his service requires'.[115] The Earl of Danby explained to William that he was staying at York because he could not take further action until he had further orders from him.[116] Danby had also told his wife that she needed to do what she could at the family seat to secure the house and make everything as safe as she could in her part of the world.[117]

These examples may seem banal: unavoidable responses to the logistics of communication. But they remind us that the people of 1688–9 could not be fully chronologically modern, and sometimes the conscious creation of a geographically limited present went beyond practical necessity. People not only acknowledged that the present had limited meaning beyond their immediate surroundings, but could deliberately create this situation as a way of coping— politically or psychologically—with their predicament. A very obvious case here is people counselling relatives not to worry about them—as the Earl of Huntington did, telling his wife to conclude 'all things are well here till you hear from me to the contrary'.[118] As was mentioned, he was writing very frequently, but he never- theless encouraged the assumption that no news from him would be good news, thinking it best to insulate his spouse in her own local time for her own mental well-being. Perhaps the most calculated creation of spatially limited chronology, however, came in a letter to the Earl of Dartmouth from his friend Sir Henry Shere on 25 November. At this point Shere was marching back from Salisbury Plain with the king, and Dartmouth was at sea, having been dispatched as a com- mander of James's fleet. Unhelpful winds had prevented Dartmouth challenging the prince, and now Shere worried about the predicament in which this failure left his friend. There seemed to be no course of action which would not surrender the admiral's life, his reputation, or both. Fighting the Dutch would now be pointless and hopeless; aiding them would be disloyal and dishonourable; surrendering command would be a cowardly dereliction of duty. In these circum stances, Shere advised Dartmouth to cut himself off from communication until the crisis had resolved itself. He could remain at sea for a while: 'for this fermen- tation cannot last ten days'. Shere told his friend that 'by that means' he would 'put it out of your power to obey or refuse [requests from either side for help], while you have made it impossible for you to receive, or they to send, you orders'. This was hard-nosed advice (for which Shere apologized), but it was also a recom- mendation to withdraw from a fluid and contemporaneous present. Dartmouth could save himself by stopping time—in the sense of new information to which he might have to react—within the immediate location of his ship. Shere wanted his friend to seal himself within a chronological bubble, bobbing on the surf of the Channel. In this instance at least, temporal acceleration did not demand

<hr>

[115] HMC, *Report on the manuscripts of the late Allan George Finch*, ii (London: HMSO, 1922), 193.
[116] HMC, *Buckingham*, 450.   [117] HMC, *Buckingham*, 447.   [118] HMC, *Hastings*, ii, 193.

close, news-hungry engagement, but rather an urgent need to retreat to somewhere where nothing could happen.[119] Such isolation from the flow of history underlines the scale of the temporal challenge people faced in 1688 and, like their basic bewilderment, has parallels in reactions to the postmodern condition. A desire to escape the hecticness of life into a more limited and manageable zone of experience has become a noted craving in contemporary society since the 1960s. Alvin Tofler suggested that the success of the musical 'Stop the World I Want To Get Off' in that decade had as much to do with its title as its plot or songs, and charted the psychological damage the acceleration of life was starting to create; David Harvey has argued the rise of sealed subcultures since the sixties was a reaction to the unprocessable speed of contemporary change.[120]

Another parallel between 1688 and the contemporary world is becoming more resonant as the twenty-first century matures. This is the tendency to respond to the lack of clear narrative in events themselves by imposing a clarifying script upon them. This script may have rather little substantiating evidence in those events, but it provides some order by arranging them into a familiar, and usually simple story. This, for example, may be the root of the populist nationalisms that have become a feature of Western democracies (chaos is made comprehensible by weaving it into a tale of a national destiny threatened by hostile alien forces); it may lie behind meta-analyses such as 'privilege' that can simplify the (in truth messy) reasons for inequality in society; and it surely explains the huge variety of conspiracy theories that circulate in new media (pattern is imposed on disorder by assuming it is the consequence of a master plan of subversion). Similar scripts emerged in 1688 to cope with fractured narrative. People assumed events were playing out according to familiar stories. This allowed them to believe they understood what was happening (even if the stories themselves were not always reassuring), but it meant time was not perceived within a 'modern' model, where an active present creates a flexible future.

The narratives most commonly used to structure experience in 1688 were drawn from previous examples of political chaos in the seventeenth century. Two domestic histories were used; indeed they offered a choice of constructions according to whether one was optimistic or pessimistic about the outcome of William's invasion. The pessimistic version was that the revolution could be seen as a replay of the rebellion and civil war of the 1640s. Just as many commentators had structured understanding of the exclusion crisis of 1679–83 by exclaiming that ''41 is come again', people facing William's invasion warned that the murder and mayhem would be repeated because people were once more casting off the

---

[119] HMC, *Dartmouth*, iii, 134.
[120] Alvin Tofler, *Future Shock* (London: Bodley Head, 1970), chs. 15–16; David Harvey, *The Condition of Postmodernity* (Oxford: Blackwell, 1989).

authority of their legitimate king.[121] Thus print materials warning of the dangers of William's invasion spoke of 'effusions of Christian blood' and of plots against the king by people who had 'no sense of former intestine distractions'.[122] Much of this material came from James's spokesmen, so had obvious reason to channel people's perceptions in this direction, but there are glimpses that minds were running that way naturally. The Duchess of Beaufort reported to her husband on 17 December that 'the Presbyterians had been wonderfully busy', and that the talk of the streets was whether there was going to be a new commonwealth.[123] Her first observation reflected belief in an ongoing Puritan plot to destroy monarchy that had brought it down in 1649, and that must therefore be active again as a king's power wobbled; her second reveals how long a shadow the English republic cast over later periods of political instability. No substantial political grouping was calling for the abolition of monarchy in the winter of 1688–9, but the scripting of turmoil as radical revolution brought the idea to the fore.

The more optimistic narrative, and one that gained increasing currency as it became clear that the Dutch expedition would not lead to widespread conflict in England, was that God was again protecting a good Protestant kingdom by direct interventions in history, as he had done on several occasions since the reign of Elizabeth. We will explore the temporal effects of this more fully later.[124] For now, though, we should note that comparing the revolution to victory over the Armada in 1588, the discovery of the Gunpowder Plot in 1605, or the restoration of a good Protestant monarch in 1660 (all common rhetorical tropes, as we shall see) provided reassuring storylines that filtered the disorienting rush of events and slotted the comprehensible elements of it into known frameworks. Thus the astonishing success of William's fleet in slipping past James's navy in the Channel was more understandable if it was told as a repeat of God's Armada-like orchestration of the wind to favour godly ships. The closeness of total Catholic victory (which might have occurred if James had ordered his numerically superior army to attack William on Salisbury Plain) seemed less traumatizing if this was simply a new telling of a Gunpowder-like thriller, in which heaven allowed papists to come near to success only to humiliate them more totally. The potential shame of accepting a new king from abroad was transformed if God did sometimes send saviours from the Continent, as he had in 1660.

A third scripting of events in 1688 was usually less explicit, and relied on a story that had first played outside England, but it was the most powerful. This was a response to uncertainty we have already explored: the Irish panics of mid December. Above, these were examined as false timelines that had to be unpicked,

<hr>

[121] Harris, *London Crowds*, 134–5.
[122] 1688 prayers against William, reproduced in [Bohun], *History of the desertion*, 18; *By the king, a proclamation given…20 October* (1688).
[123] HMC, *Beaufort*, 93.   [124] See below, ch. 3.

but there was little analysis of exactly why they had proved so convincing. The reason was probably that they were fantastical replays of the Irish rebellion of 1641. This uprising by Catholics had escalated into brutality (though their Protestant targets had not been entirely innocent), and it had been exaggerated by anti-popish English propaganda, so that it rapidly became an epitome how far unchecked cruelty could go. Text and pictures had spread images of pornographic inhumanity, from people forced to jump to their deaths from bridges, to unborn babies ripped from mother's wombs.[125] In 1688, fear of what might happen as order broke down, combined with speculative and disturbing stories from Ireland itself (where James's Catholic viceroy had seized control, and the Protestant population seemed to be fleeing in panic), coalesced into terror that the horrors of 1641 were being replayed. The English believed a truly ghastly massacre of Protestants had occurred fifty years before. Now, in comparable conditions, the wild Irish must be on the move again. In itself, of course, this narrative was dreadful. Yet it contained a strange sort of comfort because it provided certainty. It imposed a pattern on disorder and partial knowledge, and left no choice about action. Whatever doubts one had about William's invasion, one's duty now must be to rally with neighbours to save the Reformation, and everyone's skins.

In some ways, this scripting of events into familiar discourses aided a 'modern' sense of progressive chronological flow. Things, the scripts suggested, were moving in a particular—linear—direction; people should (and did) anticipate the next stage in the drama, and they must prepare urgently for the approaching part of the story. But such scripts also filled time in a way at odds with a 'modern' chronological sense. If one was convinced the autumn of 1688 was a replay of the civil war, the defeat of the Armada, or the Irish rebellion, the future was not a fluid entity to be fixed only by actions in the present, and that present was not unstable, because it was clear what would happen next. The world would inevitably descend into bloodshed; or God would assuredly defend a godly monarchy; or the Irish must arrive from the town forty miles away where they had already, surely, wrought such destruction. The difficulty people had disabusing neighbours of their Irish delusion, even as evidence piled up against it, attests to the absolute fullness of the time it had created. Arguably, the willingness of many to accept a foreign invasion once they had conceptualized it as a Protestant salvation, or the stubborn rejection by Jacobite opponents of a revolution they were convinced had brought in a new Cromwell (whose regime must, eventually, fall), are evidence of the same phenomenon. Once locked within a prevailing script, events could not take a different course. The tale must, and would, be read to its end.

---

[125] For consideration of the Irish material, see Ethan Shagan, 'Constructing Discord: Ideology, Propaganda and English Responses to the Irish Rebellion of 1641', *Journal of British Studies*, 36 (1997), 4–34.

The parallels with postmodernity we have been examining are meant to be illustrative, not systematic. Differences between the late Stuart era and the twenty-first century are obviously too stark to deliver close truths about reactions to the revolution, even if postmodernity is coherent enough a concept to serve as an analytical tool. But the echoes that are there underline that the experience of people in the autumn and winter of 1688 were not unequivocally 'modern'. They were faced with a narrative that was too fractured, overwhelming, and incomprehensible to fit into a linear, progressive, or periodizing chronology. Instead of attempting to place their experience into these frames, people fell into mental habits that bear some comparison with contemporary reactions to a bewildering world. This not only questions whether they had made the shift to 'modern' conceptions of time, but may point to parallels between pre- and postmodernity that complicate the very notion of that shift. And in the search for known scripts in particular, the people of the revolution rejected 'modernizing' solutions to their psychological dilemma. Faced with astonishing change, they did not comfort themselves that transformation was the natural state of the universe, or with linear tales of progression, or that acceptance of turning points between eras could make sense of what they were experiencing. Instead, they insisted that had seen exactly this before. It is to the most vehement expression of such déjà vu that we now turn.

2

Time and the Constitutional Legitimacy
of the Revolution

2.1 Pre-Stuart Precedents

In a work of 1690, the politician and playwright Sir Robert Howard suggested he had remarkable political prescience. The book was a history of the reigns of Edward II and Richard II; and both the volume's title page, and its preface, said that Howard had written the bulk of it back in 1685. The author had done this, he claimed, because he had seen close parallels between the mistakes that had led to the deposition of the two medieval kings and government policy in the last years of Charles II and under his successor, James. Considering how 'exactly' the Stuart rulers had 'follow'd the steps' of their 'unfortunate' predecessors, Howard had 'then expected to see a Revolution resembling theirs'.[1] Given that a revolution, and yet another monarchical deposition, had indeed come in 1688–9, it would be easy to dismiss Howard's claim as a retrospective construction of his own political acumen—except that the author seems to have been warning of parallels between the late Stuart and the late medieval eras for some time. In 1681, at the height of the exclusion crisis, he had published a stand-alone volume biography of Richard II.[2] This had showcased the articles drawn up against the monarch by Parliament at his deposition: by printing the charges in full, this Whig author used them to criticise Charles II, and so furthered his party's case against their contemporary king. With such an interest in the fourteenth century clearly in place before 1685, it does, after all, seem likely that Howard had begun his post-revolutionary work under James II. Yet, if we can admire Howard's political prophecy, we can also wonder at his use of the past. Like Dolben in the revolutionary convention, he understood the recent cataclysm through close analogy with centuries-old events.

The most noticeable feature of Howard's writing was its total lack of any sense of anachronism. As the preface and introductory passages boldly stated, the very point of history was to learn the directly applicable lessons of even distant events. Howard went through his reasons for studying the past, rather than engaging in other academic disciplines. As a Whig, these explanations were largely an exercise in gratuitous Catholic-bashing, but Howard's endorsement of historical writing

---

[1] Robert Howard, *The history of the reigns of Edward and Richard II* (1690), preface.
[2] [Robert Howard], *The life and reign of King Richard the Second* (1681).

The Revolution in Time: Chronology, Modernity, and 1688–1689 in England. Tony Claydon, Oxford University Press (2020). © Tony Claydon.
DOI: 10.1093/oso/9780198817239.001.0001

nevertheless underlined the vivid and living example of bygone ages. He rejected theology because it had degenerated into debates about doctrines invented by papists who had lived long after Christ. He dismissed philosophy as dry speculations on the preposterous propositions of medieval monks.[3] History, however, had great value. It revealed 'the best measures of men'; it showed the means by which states were preserved; and if one wanted to protect societies against the disasters caused by ambitious people, 'there [were] no Prescriptions so useful against this sickness as the Precedents in History'.[4] Most remarkably, it did not matter how far back one went for such instruction. Howard praised Machiavelli's *Discoursi* as the highest expression of the historian's art. This was even though this treatise had drawn lessons for Renaissance Italy from the Roman Republic. For Howard, there were no concerns about the applicability of the classical world to a situation a millennium and a half later: the *Discoursi* were wonderful because they supported what would otherwise be abstract political notions 'with Fact'.[5] Howard then went on to say his main purpose in writing was to show how wise rule led to glory, but that political folly led to ruin; and he argued that the best way to do this was to choose the clearest example in English history. For him, the best proof of his contention came from a period that was three to four hundred years before—so he analysed the rule of the three Edwards and of Richard II, stretching from 1272 to 1399.[6] Howard's confidence that the distant past could provide an instructive pattern for the present was considerable. The book's dedication to William III told him that the 'Fatal Methods' and 'Arbitrary Designs' of Edward II and Richard II were 'exactly copied by our two last unhappy princes [Charles II and James II]'. These kings' actions could teach us, because in English politics nothing material had changed since their day. We should study these two monarchs because they had lived 'under the same Constitutions' as ourselves; they were 'Presidents to our present Times' because they 'past under the same Laws and Government that we now enjoy'.[7]

Of course, Howard's work was not a handbook of general historical lessons. It was a contribution to the controversy that by 1690s was debating the legitimacy of the revolution in a massive and spirited pamphlet exchange. Much of the preface of the Howard's history lambasted the doctrine of 'passive obedience' to rulers that supporters of James II were claiming was the fundamental principle of politics, and that they complained had been broken when the old king was chased from the country. In the main part of the work, Howard used the depositions of Edward and Richard to show English rulers could legitimately be removed for their misdeeds. In deploying history to defend 1688–9, however, Howard was just one of a vast cloud of commentators. His characteristic use of the past, and the

---

[3] Howard, *History of the reigns*, 4–23.   [4] Ibid., 25, 27.   [5] Ibid., 26.
[6] Ibid., 28–9.   [7] Ibid., 1, 27.

assumptions about time that went with it, were an extremely common feature of arguments for the change of regime.

The material relating history to the legitimacy of the revolution is extensive. As one would expect, an event as significant as the removal of a king was the subject of much public theorizing. This began in the 1689 convention. When England's political elite met to discuss the state of the nation, it was clear that James's power had been broken and that very few people wanted him back (at least not with full royal authority); but what the exact constitutional position was, and what should happen next, was highly debateable. As a result they were hotly debated. Although direct press reporting of convention discussions was illegal and no official record of exactly what was said was made, we do have the notes of several people who were present, and these, along with a variety of supporting evidence, reveal rich theatres of argument.[8] The convention talked about whether James was still king—in which case a regency might be the solution to the general distrust of him—or whether the throne was vacant and could be offered to someone else. It debated how exactly James had lost the crown, if he had done so; and it discussed if any new monarch must be the hereditary heir of the old one. On a slightly different tack, the convention also pondered whether, and how far, the crown's powers should be limited to avoid the constitutional tensions that had marred the whole seventeenth century. Finally, the convention worried about its own status. It had not been elected as a Parliament; but could it declare itself to be one—especially once it had chosen a monarch to complete the elements of a normal legislature?

This intense debate rapidly spilled beyond Westminster. Even as the members gathered, the temporarily uncensored press advised them what to do. This did not cease once a constitutional settlement was made. As Howard's preface reveals, people continued to write about the revolution, even after the convention had declared that James was no longer king and had offered the crown to William in a joint monarchy with his wife, Mary. Continued comment was guaranteed partly because James still had supporters. As we shall see, they were able to evade the controls on print that were reimposed once the new regime was in place, and this in turn meant a press campaign to counter this 'Jacbobitism'—particularly since key groups, the clergy in particular, were given time to decide whether they would swear oaths of loyalty to the new monarchs.[9] Debate was stoked further because William's supporters were not agreed on why he was king. For some he enjoyed the right as a conqueror of the kingdom, and—or perhaps or—as a *de facto* ruler who had fought his way to power. For others, he had been offered a vacant throne after its previous occupant had voluntarily renounced it by running away to

---

[8] Most notes were later published, and have been collected in Jones, *A Parliamentary History of the Glorious Revolution*.

[9] See below, ch. 4.

France. For still others, he had been advanced by God as the providential saviour of the Protestant cause, or had been selected by the people, once James's misrule had broken the old king's contract with them, and so left them free to choose a new sovereign. These competing interpretations fed the divisions between Tories and Whigs that had become a feature of English politics in the late 1670s (the arguments becoming broadly more 'Whiggish' in the order they have just been presented). The result was a vigorous press 'allegiance controversy', which generated so much material that its closest student, Mark Goldie, could list nearly two hundred pamphlet contributions between 1689 and 1694. And, as Goldie admitted, this number included only those publications 'substantially' concerned with the legitimacy of the revolution.[10] Hundreds of other works entered the dispute, but were also about something else. Howard's work, for instance, did not make the list because it was mainly medieval history.[11]

These piles of controversial pieces, along with the convention debates, provide a detailed snapshot of the understanding, or at the very least of the presentation, of time within constitutional thought in the revolutionary era. And the overwhelming impression it leaves is *stasis*. As has already been stated, very many commentators on the revolution assumed that they had to find a historical analogy for what they had just witnessed. They sought an earlier set of events, very often very much earlier, which they argued should guide people to solutions whilst the nation's affairs remained in flux, and which they then claimed legitimated the arrangements that were finally made. As they did this, they denied significant or relevant change had happened over the intervening centuries. In contrast to the very immediate reactions to William's arrival, which had wondered if things were moving through a turning point to a new era, by the time people began to debate what had happened, most denied any meaningful historical process. If such things as the source of sovereignty, the rights of subjects, or the fundamentals of law had developed through time, then people in the past would have had different aims and ideals, and they would have operated in a different legal and institutional context. Their history might therefore be informative in some ways in the late seventeenth century (illuminating the origins of problems, or suggesting things about broad human reactions to change, for example), but it could not be applied directly, and without acknowledgement of the differing context, to determine or justify current action. Yet people struggling to understand the revolution *did* apply past histories in this unmediated way. They assumed an absolutely unchanging situation and so collapsed the long ages between their exemplars and themselves. A working label for this attitude to the past could be 'static

---

[10] Mark Goldie, 'The Revolution of 1689 and the Structure of Political Argument', *Bulletin of Research in the Humanities*, 83 (1980), 473–564, quote at 477.

[11] The preface engaged closely with [Abednego Seller], *The history of passive obedience since the reformation* (1689), and cited Samuel Johnson, *Some reflections on the history of passive obedience* (1689) in support of its arguments.

chronology'. Its prominence both challenges any theory of a move towards to a progressive view of time by 1688–9, and severely compromised any attempt to describe the revolution as a step into a bold new future.

It is true that the past was not always used to make exactly the same points about the present. Circumstances in the winter of 1688–9 posed a complex series of problems; the final settlement had a number of different elements, and as we have mentioned, Whigs and Tories came to understand what had happened in rather different ways. There were, therefore, a great range of different political principles and arrangements to be defended. Fortunately, however, English history provided a rich menu of possible moments that might be compared in some aspect to the fall of James, so writers chose quite flexibly from the variety. This meant that static chronology—whilst insisting that 1689–9 exemplified ancient principles—was not necessarily politically conservative in late seventeenth century terms. It could support positions that overturned recent practice: perhaps most dramatically denying that heredity must run its course in the choice of king—an idea that had been promoted to defend the restored monarchy since the 1660s, and that had triumphed in both the exclusion crisis of 1679 and at James II's accession in 1685. Static chronology could thus produce rather different pasts. Where this variety of positions did not differ, however, was in their basic conception of history. The fact that people across such a wide political spectrum all adopted the same approach to understanding time argues for its very considerable hold; this also addresses the important objection that we only see polemic in political argument. It is true that the witnesses we will quote were trying to persuade others. We therefore see them selecting particular arguments for particular dialectic purposes, rather than necessarily divulging their real or whole worldview. It is also true that this book will show the people of the late seventeenth century able to construct other senses of time in circumstances where they were not involved in constitutional dispute. Nevertheless, it must be significant that so many writers and speakers in these crucial debates treated chronology in the same way. They thought presenting a static time would do most to persuade, or simply to comfort, their audiences when they invited them to think about the legality of 1688–9.

In large part, the pattern of precedents followed the footsteps of Gilbert Dolben and Robert Howard. The royal depositions of the fourteenth century were cited again and again in the convention as people sought tools for analysing the end of James's reign. In the debates, the falls of Edward II and of Richard II were used to make the basic point that a reign could end, even if the king had not died, but party dispute about exactly what had happened when James fled in 1688 deepened interest still further, since speakers came up with different versions of 1327 and 1399. For Whiggishly inclined members of the convention, the fate of the medieval kings showed that subjects (especially when they were represented in Parliament) could depose a monarch, and that this might create a vacancy on the throne which would allow some choice of the next ruler. Tories countered that Edward and Richard had renounced office voluntarily (cutting out the people's role in removing them), and that far from producing a vacancy, the abdications had simply led to hereditary successors gaining the crown.[12]

The print material also concentrated closely on 1327 and 1399. Perhaps the most playful (if not the most constitutionally insightful) parallels were drawn by Charles Ceasar. His *Numerous infaustus* contended that being the second king of a name guaranteed bad luck, and so told the sorry tales of Edward II, Richard II, and James II—throwing in William II (killed by an arrow), Henry II (betrayed by his children), and Charles II (reigning over a divided nation rapidly heading for revolution), for good measure.[13] More closely in tune with convention debates were pamphlets such as *A short historical narrative*, which put the fourteenth century at the heart of its coverage of deviations from strict hereditary principle, or *The present case stated*, which argued people should take the oaths to William by narrating the stories of Edward and Richard. According to this latter, and clearly Whig, author, the monarchs' fates demonstrated 'the legal formalities that were then accounted proper for the deposing an unjust, oppressive king'.[14] Other writers joined in. Within a few weeks of the revolution, the Whig author of *A brief vindication* of the proceedings against James used 1327 and 1399 to stress that Parliament had formally deprived rulers for their misdeeds.[15] Another early pamphlet, answering the argument that James II had been forcibly chased from the throne, made a different (and more Tory-inflected) point. Like James, the medieval monarchs may have had no choice but to abdicate—but this did not mean their demise was illegitimate, because every political decision is dictated by circumstance.[16] Over the next few years, direct application of the fourteenth-century depositions continued. In 1693, for example, the author of an attack on the Tories' interpretation of the revolution insisted they were wrong to think the Middle Ages demonstrated that only conquest or providence could transfer power. Instead, Edward III had claimed to have succeeded his father because Edward II had forfeited authority by misrule; Henry IV had then displaced Richard II on exactly the same principles.[17]

Whilst much of this coverage drew out the similarities between 1327, 1399, and 1689, some paradoxically stressed the closeness of the events by *not* comparing distant history to the contemporary world. Quite often, works appeared that

---

[12] See for example, Grey, *Debates*, x, 12, 19, 23, 55–61; *The debate at large between the Lords and Commons at the free conference* (2nd edn, corrected, 1710), 39–44.

[13] Charles Ceasar, *Numerus infaustus* (1689).

[14] *A short historical narrative touching the succession to the crown* (1689), 1; *The present case stated: or the oaths of allegiance and supremacy* (1689), 16.

[15] *A brief vindication of the parliamentary proceedings against James II* (1689), 56–7.

[16] 'An answer to the desertion discussed', in *A complete collection of papers in twelve parts, relating to the great revolution* (1689), x, 1–16 at 13.

[17] *A letter from Oxford concerning Mr Samuel Johnson's late book* (1693), 15–18.

provided medieval narrative, without gloss. They simply assumed that historical events were so obviously repeated in recent ones that audiences would apply them without any authorial guidance. For example, a tract produced by the Whig bookseller Richard Baldwin in the weeks after the revolution, and entitled *A true relation of the manner of the deposition of Edward II*, was just that. It launched into the story, feeling no need to explain why it had appeared at that moment. Its appendix, reproducing articles against Richard II, similarly mirrored the charges against James in the 1689 Declaration of Right (which accompanied the convention's offer of the crown to William) without comment.[18] Even more remarkable was another book that Baldwin put out a year later. This was, in fact, a version of a romanticized account of the reign of Edward II, written in the 1620s by the gentlewoman Elizabeth Cary. Unpublished at the time, it had appeared in print in 1681, mistakenly attributed to Elizabeth's husband, Henry. Early in William's reign, however, Baldwin reproduced it again. This time it did not claim to be the work of any named author, but it did have a snappy new title. Cary's prose had made its 1681 debut as *The history of the life, reign and death of Edward II*. Now, however, the front cover declared simply: *The parallel*. It only explained in a subtitle what it was about, and no explanation was provided for what this tale was supposed, in fact, to reflect. Baldwin was sure his audience would understand that the falls of Edward II and of James II were essentially the same, without him having to labour the point.[19]

Constitutional discussion of the revolution did extend outside the fourteenth century. Other periods were examined for precedents and analogies: but none was very recent. The latest to receive much detailed attention was the Tudor age and especially the reign of Henry VIII. This period interested commentators because Henry had used Parliament to alter the succession as his revolving choice of wives had changed his notions of inheritance. Whigs, in particular, and true to their principles, thought this proved that representatives of the people had a role in determining who should be king and could override strict heredity. They were particularly fond of pointing out that without Parliament, Mary Tudor and Elizabeth could not both have been valid heirs of Henry. Whatever view you took of the great king's marriages, one—if not both—of his daughters must have been illegitimate. This allowed some to stress that the great Queen Elizabeth had been an entirely parliamentary monarch. She relied on the earlier legislative act of succession for her right to the crown (never, for example, attempting to reverse her bastardization); and she herself had passed a statute declaring it treason to deny Parliament's sovereignty over who was monarch.[20]

---

[18] *A true relation of the manner of the deposition of Edward II* (1689).

[19] *The parallel: or the history of the life, reign, deposition and death of King Edward II* (1690).

[20] For example, *Letter from Oxford*, 18; James Parkinson, *An examination of Dr Sherlock's book* (1691), 9; Samuel Masters, *The case of allegiance in our present circumstances consider'd* (1689), 23; *The late King James's letter to his privy counsellors* (1692), 19.

Other periods analysed were further back in time. Again following Dolben's lead, the Wars of the Roses were picked over. Whilst it was principally Whigs who cited the fourteenth-century royal depositions as evidence that misgovernment could lead to forfeiture, and the Parliament-controlled succession of the Tudor age, Tory philosophy could be more comfortable with the lessons provided by changes of monarch in the chaos of the fifteenth century. This was because many Tories found a way to accept William III by thinking of him as '*de facto*' king. That is, they accepted one should obey a monarch who was actually exercising power (as the prince of Orange did, once his rule was established), even if that ruler's legal title was questionable. For Williamite Tories, opposition to such a person would mean endless disorder, or might quibble with the divine providence that had brought the ruler to power, or could lead ordinary subjects into dangerous speculations about where true right lay. Wanting to promote this view, some commentators turned to the conflicts between Lancastrians and Yorkists and showed that two rival dynasties had repeatedly displaced each other from the throne—but that each time they had done so, they had been recognized as legitimate authorities, at least until their power was, in its turn, displaced.

One 1689 pamphlet, for instance, cited a number of cases where people had accepted *de facto* rulers, but made the reactions of English subjects in the fifteenth century key to the case. In the time of 'the wars between York and Lancaster', the author pointed out, ordinary folk had tended to ignore competing claims to the throne, but instead had just obeyed whoever happened to be in power. When they had done this, they were not simply choosing an easy life. Rather they were taking the only rational course of action in a difficult situation. They were avoiding pointless allegiance to lost causes and trying to avoid further chaos by stirring up rebellion. 'He would', the pamphleteer noted, 'be very severe upon his own ancestors, who would make them all perjurers who then swore to the reigning king, while another at the same time claimed the crown.'[21] The author of another 1689 work analysed the '*de facto* statute' of Henry VII's reign. He suggested that the act had indemnified people who had merely obeyed kings in actual possession over the preceding decades (so they were not guilty of treason); and he boldly stated that Henry VII could only owe his title to *de facto* principles, since his other claims descended from usurping Lancastrian rulers.[22] Speakers in the convention also referred closely to the era, and its endless and irregular changes of regime. We have seen the Tory Dolben open discussion by citing 1470, and the Tory Earl of Nottingham engaged closely with the period in the 6 February debate in the convention to try to settle differences over a vacancy of the throne. In his contribution, Nottingham wanted to avoid declaring the regal office empty. He feared

---

[21] *A letter to a dissenting clergyman of the church of England concerning the oaths of allegiance* (1690), 14–15.

[22] *A friendly conference concerning the oaths of allegiance* (1689), 3–5.

this would annul hereditary rule and open the door to monarchical election. But he openly admitted that nonhereditary succession had been common, especially in the fifteenth century; and he hinted that the trick to accepting this had been to cover illegal usurpations with claims of hereditary title, however 'specious'. This was a recipe for normalizing *de facto* rule that he was hinting might be used in 1689.[23]

Whigs did make some use of Wars of Roses. They stressed that the kings of that era had not followed in hereditary order; or had had their titles confirmed by Parliament; or had fallen as a result of misrule—1485 was particularly ripe for this last point, given the poor reputation of Richard III.[24] Yet Whigs were rather more interested in another era, this time one even earlier than the deposition of Edward II. This was the epoch of the Baron's Wars in the reigns of King John and Henry III (1199–1272). These conflicts could be used to support Whig principles, since they seemed to involve subjects rising against tyrannical monarchs, and even imposing binding limitations upon them. Since these limitations had been repeatedly cited and respected in the succeeding centuries, this history seemed to prove subjects' right to resist. At the core of interest was the Magna Carta of 1215. This list of liberties had been extracted from King John after aristocratic revolt: so, for those of a Whiggish turn of mind, it was an invaluable rhetorical reference point—particularly given Magna Carta's reputation as a cornerstone of English government and its status as the first fully recorded statute.[25] For some, in fact, the concessions forced from King John more or less *were* the English constitution. Thus White Kennett asserted that the chief function of the 1215 document was to declare, beyond all doubt, that royal power had to be exercised under and within the law.[26] Similarly, the author of a pamphlet published in the summer of 1689 used Magna Carta to establish the illegality of James II's rule. The deposed monarch had breached terms in that first statute, and lawyers had long agreed that all such actions were void.[27] Others wove Magna Carta into a narrative of continuing English opposition to any king who overstepped the bounds of his authority, and so made heroic freedom fighters of the revolting barons of the thirteenth century. Samuel Johnson complained that any attempt to deny the legitimacy of popular resistance made traitors and rebels of those who had risen against John and Henry III.[28] Similarly, the veteran polemicist Daniel Whitby

---

[23] *Debate at large*, 51–7, esp. 55.

[24] See, for example *Brief vindication of the parliamentary proceedings*, 13–16; p. 40; [Daniel Whitby], *An historical account of some things relating to the nature of the English government* (1690), 34–9; *Late King James's letter*, p. 4; and some of the Whig contributions to the 6 February debate on the vacancy in *Debate at large*.

[25] On Magna Carta's status, see Corrine C. Weston, 'England: Ancient Constitution and Common Law', in J.H. Burns and Mark Goldie, eds, *The Cambridge History of Political Thought* (Cambridge: CUP, 1991), 374–411, at 379.

[26] [White Kennett], *Dialogue*, 15.   [27] *A brief account of the nullity of King James's title* (1689).

[28] Samuel Johnson, *Remarks upon Dr Sherlock's book, intituled, The case of allegiance* (1690), 11–12.

('Whigby' as he had been badged by enemies during the exclusion crisis) provided a long and lionizing account of the Barons Wars in the historical account of English government that he penned to answer critics of the revolution.[29]

2.2 Seventeenth-Century Silences

So, in the aftermath of 1688–9, the past was widely used, across the political spectrum, to justify current action. And it was the distant past. Everything we have just surveyed occurred before 1600. The Stuart age was neglected to an astonishing extent—at least as a source of directly applicable constitutional precedent (though, as we shall see later, an account of recent decades *did* emerge to understand the political and cultural processes that had led to the crisis of James's reign, and some of the scripts that had been used to make sense of the immediate events of William's invasion had been drawn from seventeenth century).[30] Part of the surprise here is simply that recent history seemed to count for less than ancient narrative. The further back in time the people of William's England went, the more energy they appeared to put into finding close analogies. The result was to sunder the revolution's constitutional settlement from the decades that had led up to it: something that enhanced the atemporal nature of the prevailing arguments. Yet perhaps even more remarkable was the fact that the seventeenth century was neglected even though it had witnessed a series of events that looked like very close parallels for 1688–9. For example, in 1628, Parliament had voted a 'Petition of Right' that could have been seen as a forerunner of the 1689 'Declaration of Rights'. In 1642, a rebellion had broken out against a king, Charles I, who was accused of exceeding his powers. In 1649, that same king had been judged and deposed. In 1660, a constitutional convention, composed in the same way as the one of 1689, had invited a new king to rule the country, and in the 'exclusion crisis' of 1679–82, the nation had debated whether the natural inheritance of the crown could be interrupted for the public good.

Of course, it is obvious why some of these events were not widely used in the discussions of 1688–9. The exclusion crisis, which had given rise to the Whig and Tory parties, simply provided the wrong lesson. It had resulted in victory for the Tories and their insistence that monarchy was unconditionally hereditary. Any Tory who now wished to endorse William was therefore embarrassed by the exclusion era. Whigs, meanwhile, could not use the crisis as a legitimating precedent for their position because they had lost. Though a few from the party, understandably, gloated that they had warned of the consequences of letting heredity bring James to the throne and some repeated arguments that had been

---

[29] [Whitby], *Historical account*, 6–30.   [30] See below ch. 5, and above ch. 1.4.

used between 1678 and 1683, the occurrences of those years never formed a major element of Whig argument after 1688.[31]

The impossibility of using 1649 as a precedent was clearer still, but is worth discussing at much greater length. The trial and execution of Charles I was the only deposition of a monarch in the preceding two hundred years (unless one accepted the removal of Lady Jane Grey in 1553 as the conclusion of a true, if short, reign). It might, therefore, have been possible to cite it, along with the events of 1327, 1399, 1470, and possibly 1485, as a moment proving that misbehaving kings could be removed—and one that had the added power of living memory. Yet the silence on the event from supporters of William was pretty deafening. There were a few attempts to deal with the legacy of the regicide, which we will deal with below. Overwhelmingly, however, 1649 was ignored. The reason, of course, was the absolute denigration of what had happened to Charles I in subsequent decades. As the royalist party had regrouped in the 1650s, and even more so after Charles' son was restored to the throne in 1660, the regicide had been painted as the deepest, perhaps the original, political sin of the English people.

The process of vilifying the regicide began almost as soon as it had occurred. Executing Charles was deeply resented by the majority of English people, and royalist propagandists moved to exploit this sentiment.[32] Their masterstroke was to publish the tract *Eikon basilike* within weeks of the king's death, a work that purported to be Charles' autobiography.[33] This presented the king's constant concern for his subjects and nation and paraded his willingness to be a martyr for English law and religion, his fidelity to friends, allies and family, and his unceasing attempts to find a compromise solution with those who opposed him. The work proved hugely popular, and it naturally cast the rebels in the darkest light.[34] These messages were reinforced by the restored monarchy in 1660. The illegality of the regicide was underlined by the treason trials of those who had signed the death warrant and the grisly infliction of hanging, drawing, and quartering, even on the bodies of those, such as Oliver Cromwell, who had already died.[35] The evil of the rebellion was driven home by the institution of the anniversary of Charles' death, 30 January, as an annual fast for the English to atone to God for their fault in resisting heaven's anointed king. Over the next years, vast quantities of legislation, sermons, poems, plays, tracts, pictures, and broadsides stressed these messages; by the early 1680s, Tories could swing the debates of the exclusion crisis in their

---

[31] For example: [Daniel Defoe], *The advantages of the present settlement* (1689), 6.

[32] For a recent summary of work on the regicide, see Philip Baker, 'The regicide', in Michael J. Braddick, ed, *The Oxford Handbook of the English Revolution* (Oxford: OUP, 2015), 154–69.

[33] Sharpe, *Image Wars*, 390–403.

[34] *Eikón basiliké: the povrtraicture of his sacred maiestie in his solitudes and svfferings* (1648 [ie 1649—the work was brought out immediately after Charles' execution at the end of January, so before the Lady Day, 25 March 1649, taken by many as the start of the new year until calendar reform in 1752]).

[35] Laura Knoppers, *Historicizing Milton: Spectacle, Power, and Poetry in Restoration England* (Athens, GA: University of Georgia Press, 1994), ch. 2.

favour by suggesting Whigs were the heirs of the thoroughly disgraced regicides.[36] After 1688–9, therefore, any suggestion that 1649 was a precedent for the revolution was inconceivable (unless one wished to denounce what was going on), and indeed, a highly positive image of Charles continued into the 1690s.[37] Given that any discussion of Charles I's reign was likely to raise uncomfortable questions about the wisdom or morality of opposing a Stuart king, silence might seem the best policy.

And that silence fell very early in the reactions to the revolution. It was the principal response to a major, and very early, embarrassment for those who were contemplating the removal of James II. Just two days after the convention began substantial debate, the calendar demanded observance of the 30 January fast to atone for Charles I's murder. The convention, however, sabotaged the solemnity. It declared the day after the fast to be a thanksgiving for William's providential deliverance of the country (in London and nearby counties, at least; the rest of the country was given another fortnight to prepare). This was almost certainly intended to neutralize the fast, at least for that year, without the controversy of cancelling it explicitly, and it seemed to have had that effect. Contemporaries reported that very few pulpits saw the sorts of denunciations of rebellion that usually occurred on the 30th. Only one sermon for the occasion was published (and this stressed that the rebels had murdered an astonishingly virtuous king— thereby reducing applicability to the current case); other clergy who used the event to stress the legitimacy of hereditary Stuart rule, or to oppose resistance to rulers in all circumstances, were subject to heavy criticism.[38] By contrast, the thanksgiving was widely celebrated. In the early weeks of 1689, therefore, Charles' fate was suppressed, drowned out, and forgotten.

This pattern largely persisted in the press commentary on the revolution over the next years. The regicide was not raised as a precedent for the revolution, except by those opposed to William's regime.[39] Supporters of the new government dealt with Charles I sparingly, and when they did, it was almost always to deny parallels between the two depositions. This line of argument began in the very early weeks after James's fall. In March 1689, Daniel Whitby popped up to admit that greeting William's arrival as providential might draw accusations that Cromwell's triumph

---

[36] For royalist propaganda, see the early chapters of Kevin Sharpe, *Rebranding Rule: The Restoration and Revolution Monarchy, 1660–1714* (New Haven: Yale UP, 2013). For the main strands of Tory propaganda in the exclusion crisis, see Harris, *London Crowds*, ch. 6; See also Andrew Lacey, *The Cult of King Charles the Martyr* (Woodbridge: Ashgate, 2003), ch. 5, for the continuing development of the cult of Charles I between 1660 and 1688.

[37] See the remarks on the king in numerous 30 January sermons, and in such works as *The life and death of Charles I* (1690).

[38] Tony Claydon, 'The Sermon Culture of the Glorious Revolution', in Peter McCullough, Hugh Adlington, and Emma Rhatigan, eds, *The Oxford Handbook of the Early Modern Sermon* (Oxford: OUP, 2011), 480–94, esp. 485–6. William Stainforth, *A sermon preached in the cathedral and metropolitical church of St Peter in York, January 30th, 1689* (1689).

[39] See below, ch. 4.2.

must be celebrated in the same way—but he then showed why the two instances were not at all similar. In 1649 the regicides had only pretended to uphold liberty, and the execution of the king had not had the broad popular support enjoyed by the elevation of the prince of Orange.[40] At around the same time, Daniel Defoe, in one of his earliest publications, stressed that the trial of Charles I had been illegitimate because the earlier king, unlike James II, had not broken the fundamental law of the kingdom.[41] Another writer drew a contrast between the valid resistance to the tyrant James and what had occurred in 1649—which he labelled 'the unjust deposing and murdering a pious king, who had not…designed to alter either the government or religion'.[42] Later pamphlet writings also took such lines, though the regicide could still enter into party dispute.[43] When the cleric William Sherlock decided he could support the revolution, after an initial hesitation, he was attacked from the Whig side for not making sufficiently clear how different Cromwell's regime had been from William III's. Samuel Johnson accused him of accepting 1689 on a Tory principle—namely that one should obey *de facto* power—which would have fully legitimated the wicked republic of the mid-century.[44] In fact, Johnson did have a point here. Tories had very occasionally suggested that people in the 1650s had been right to suffer Cromwell patiently: this to defend their *de facto* argument for supporting William.[45] But even then, they stressed the protectorate should have been deplored as well as suffered, and they never argued for any justice in the regicide that had created the republic. 1649 was no precedent for 1688–9, though the fact that most English people had lived peaceably under Cromwell might just be for elements of what came after.

Preachers followed pamphleteers. They remained pretty reluctant to publish any sermons marking 30 January for some time after William's arrival, but eventually a few accepted the challenge of discussing 1649 without having it disparage 1688–9. One strategy was to depoliticize the regicide. Clerics such as Richard Kidder could make 1649 stand for all sins generally, could then make vague calls for repentance, and then hope this would call down God's blessing on the people and their new governors.[46] Others, though, emphasized gulfs that separated Charles' execution

---

[40] [Daniel Whitby], *A letter from a city minister* (1689), 12–13.   [41] [Defoe], *Reflections*, 48–9.

[42] *The new oath of allegiance justified from the original constitution* (1689), 20–1.

[43] See for example, *Letter to a dissenting clergyman*; Timothy Wilson, *God, the king, and the country, united in the justification of this present revolution* (1691), 38–9; *A vindication of the present settlement* (1692), 15.

[44] Johnson, *Remarks*, 32–3; [Thomas Long], *Resolution of certain quearies concerning submission to the present government* (1689), 60–1.

[45] See, for example, [Edmund Bohun], *The doctrine of non-resistance and passive obedience* (1689), 12–13, 27; or references to Robert Sanderson's earlier argument that one should obey unjust usurpers such as Cromwell in such works as [Thomas Comber?], *A letter to a bishop concerning the present settlement* (1689), 26–7; [Francis Fulwood], *Obedience due to the present king* (1689), 6.

[46] Richard Kidder, *A sermon preached before the Lords Spiritual and Temporal in the Abey-Church at Westminster, the 30th of January, 1691/2* (1692); in a similar vein, Richard Bynns, *A sermon preached before the honourable House of Commons, January 30, 1692* (1693).

from James's fall. They did this by suggesting the regicide had been the result of national sins of division and ungodliness that had let in popery, and that only now—with the good Protestant regime installed—did the country have a chance to break free of the cycle.[47] Perhaps trying to clear himself from continuing Whig charges that he lacked enthusiasm for the revolution, William Sherlock produced a particularly vivid example of this sort of rhetoric for the House of Commons in January 1692. For him, the sin of 1649 was like the sin of the Jews in murmuring against Moses after the Exodus from Egypt. Israel had been punished with forty years in the wilderness before arriving in the promised land; England had suffered forty years of political instability before 1688–9 offered them the possibility of redemption.[48] In such writing, Williamite commentators did not challenge the obloquy under which the regicide had fallen. Rather they tried to exploit it by emphasizing how very different, and how infinitely better, the events of William's arrival had been. The result, though, was to sever any link between the present and the recent past; or in the case of preachers such as Sherlock, to link them only as opposites: 1689 was the cure for 1649.

As for the other possible seventeenth-century parallels with the Williamite revolution, 1642 was caught in the same web of denunciation as 1649 and was similarly unavailable as a precedent. Although some arguments for resistance to Charles I were recycled (for example tracts from the early 1640s were reprinted at the time of the revolution), writers knew the great mid-century rebellion had ultimately led to the regicide.[49] It was therefore part of the same felony and so could not be used as a template for those who had chased away James II without calling attention to the illegality, treachery, and ambition of their actions. When arguments were recycled, therefore, they rarely admitted when they had had their first outing. Also, and as with the regicide, some authors talked of the early 1640s to draw the deepest contrasts with William's arrival that they could think of. One explicitly stressed the greater valence of distant medieval events over seventeenth-century history by saying the barons who had opposed King John and Henry III were far closer to men of 1688–9 than the parliamentarians of the civil war era.[50] Again, there were a few attempts to look at the political demands made on Charles I in 1640–2 and to suggest these were legitimate, or at least understandable, expressions of grievance, rather than the wicked demagogy of ambitious men.[51] These, however, were isolated: standardly, writers presented the king as the true defender of English law, though they could insist he was defending a balanced

---

[47] See, for example, William Lloyd, *A sermon preached before the queen at Whitehall, January 30* (1691).

[48] William Sherlock, *A sermon preach'd before the honourable House of Commons at St Margaret's Westminster, January xxxth, 1691/2* (1692).

[49] For example, Philip Hunton's 1643 *Treatise of monarchie in two parts*, which argued England's constitution was a mixed and limited kingship, was reprinted as [Philip Hunton], *A treatise of monarchy* (1689).

[50] *Letter to a dissenting clergyman*, 22–6.

[51] See, for example, *The history of self-defence in requital to the history of passive obedience* (1689), 29.

constitution that granted his subjects rights—as, for example, when quoting his 1642 *Answer to the nineteen propositions*, which had been composed as a deliberately conciliatory appeal to moderate opinion.[52]

The events of 1628 and 1660 were more interesting. The Petition of Right of the first of these years was used in Whig discourse to outline some of the rights this party claimed people had against a monarch. But there was some nervousness about allowing it to do too much work. Parliamentary assertiveness in the late 1620s could look like the origins of the revolt that toppled the sainted king, so the Petition was usually deployed in lists of declarations of English liberty that stretched back into the Middle Ages, and so lost any radical bite.[53] There was consideration of the events of 1660, since commentators could draw attention to a very close parallel with the revolution without instantly offending the prevailing interpretation of Stuart history.[54] In 1660 there had been no king in England to call a Parliament that might discuss the lack of legitimate ruler. Consequently, the militarily dominant General Monck had arranged for a convention—constituted in the same way as a Parliament—to decide what to do, and this had resolved to invite King Charles II back to England to take up the duties of monarch. One could argue that this was exactly what happened in 1688–9 (with William playing both Monck and Charles' roles); and many might have hoped for a repetition of the Restoration's peaceful inauguration of popular and traditional rule. Despite these potentially attractive similarities, however, analysis of 1660 was not nearly as common as one might expect, once events moved passed the first gathering of the convention in January 1689. This scarcity of analysis could have stemmed from nervousness about the legitimacy of irregular gatherings of national representatives. Both the body that had met in 1660, and the one of 1689, reconstituted themselves as legal Parliaments as soon as they had chosen kings, and they retrospectively enacted some of their earlier actions as normal statutes. Few seemed to want to encourage frequent ad hoc gatherings of the people's delegates outside a parliamentary framework: it smacked too much of popular sovereignty. Also, of course, there was the embarrassment that 1688–9 undid the settlement of 1660 in crucial respects. It ejected the very hereditary dynasty that had been so carefully put back in place. By resorting again to a convention without a monarch to decide the nation's affairs, the revolutionaries defied the Restoration's careful statements that nothing valid could be done without Commons, Lords, and King acting together.[55]

So, with some partial exceptions, the Stuart era was not used as a source of constitutional precedent after 1688–9. Far from undermining static chronology, however, this effectively reinforced it. It created a caesura in history. With the seventeenth century largely missing in action, events could not flow from the

---

[52] For example, *The present conjuncture* (1689), 4–5.   [53] See below, ch 2.3.

[54] See for example, [Francis Fulwood], *Agreement betwixt the present and the former government* (1689), 49–50; *The late honourable convention proved a legal parliament* (1689); see also contributions to the convention debates: Grey, *Debates*, x, 93–103.

[55] For example in the 1661 Treason Act: 13 Car 2, st.1, c.1.

distant past, through recent decades, to a present that was the result of this continuous historical development. Instead, the present was severed from its immediate antecedents and connected only to happenings that were a century old or more. The only vision in which such a gap made sense was static chronology. In this, history was a random-access storehouse of exemplars. Some parts of the past, most notably the last two or three generations, might be thin on usable data, but this did not disrupt the coherence of history because history was not an evolving story. So long as justifying precedents could be gleaned from somewhere, whole swathes of human experience could be more or less ignored.

2.3 The Ancient and Unchanging Constitution

This general downplaying of Stuart precedents left commentators focused primarily on the Middle Ages, albeit with forays into the Tudor decades. In fact, many were drawn even further back in time. This was because they presented their medieval exemplars as expressions of an 'ancient constitution' that had been inherited from the very first centuries of English history. The notion has been quite extensively studied, but it is important to look at it in more detail. This is both because it played a very significant role in debates about the revolution, and because that role seems to contradict some of the scholarly conclusions about the discourse that have been reached over the last decades.

In broad outline, and as overwhelmingly presented in the post-revolution debates, the theory of the ancient constitution was simple. It was that the English had retained a system of government, which enshrined the rights of subjects, from the very foundation of their national community. From at least the days of the Anglo-Saxon kings of the Dark Age 'Heptarchy' (and probably before: the Anglo-Saxons had inherited their polity from their German forebears, or perhaps also from the Britons who had lived in England before the Romans arrived), the legitimate power of kings had been balanced by the freedoms of the people. Subjects had been represented in Parliament-like assemblies; they had been consulted in the exercise of government; their liberties and properties had been secure in law against their rulers; they had played an active role choosing—or at least approving—their monarchs; and they had been able to depose kings when it became absolutely necessary for the public good. This system had survived the Danish and Norman invasions because the conquerors had accepted English laws and customs. It had been confirmed by Magna Carta and coronation oaths through the Middle Ages, and it had lasted into the seventeenth century in the form of the common law, the role of Parliament, the acknowledgement that kings ruled within the constitution rather than above it, and in strong subjects' rights.[56]

---

[56] For fuller descriptions of the ancient constitution, often concentrating on the more subtle pre-1689 uses and debates, see J.G.A. Pocock, *The Ancient Constitution and the Feudal Law* (Cambridge: CUP,

As just presented, the ancient constitution encouraged static chronology. Because the system of government had survived through the centuries, the passage of those centuries could be ignored. Distant precedents were still relevant because they illustrated the exact same rules under which people still lived. However, we cannot simply chalk up any talk of the ancient constitution after 1688–9 as more evidence of the temporally frozen worldview of the revolutionaries, because scholarly analysis of the concept has raised important questions about its exact nature, and its vigour, in the later seventeenth century. John Pocock, the pioneering modern student of the ancient constitution, has argued it was starting to weaken by the time of the revolution. He saw the early Stuart decades as the golden age of belief in the idea, but thought it had got into trouble under Charles II as it became entangled in party dispute. As the Whigs claimed Parliament had the right to deliberate on the succession during the exclusion crisis, Tory scholars moved to undermine that body's authority by denying it was part of an ancient system of government. In particular, the historian Robert Brady assembled evidence that many of the key features of English law and government were relatively recent, and—even more damningly—had been granted by monarchs instead of being the birthright of the people. Parliament had first been called by kings, and only in the thirteenth century; common law had evolved from feudal grants made by rulers since the Norman conquest. According to Pocock, this expertly argued case had fatally damaged the ancient constitution as a serious intellectual position. He admitted it had been used to defend the revolution, but the overall tone of his work was that this had been a temporary throwback.[57] By 1688–9 the key trends in political philosophy were either to break free from history—as John Locke was to do with his abstract reasoning on natural rights—or to follow the very different and developmental analysis encoded into the language of civic humanism, which Pocock examined at length and that we shall come to later in this book.[58]

Other scholars have gone beyond suggesting that the reign of the ancient constitution was ending by 1688–9. They have questioned whether it had ever actually led people to believe that the fundamental government of England had remained unchanged through aeons. For example, examinations of the writings of early Stuart lawyers and historians—particularly John Selden—have revealed that although most of these thought the English constitution was ancient, they tended to mean this was because it had never been totally disrupted and replaced.

1957); Glenn Burgess, *The Politics of the Ancient Constitution* (Basingstoke: Longman, 1992); Janelle Renfrew Greenberg, *The Radical Face of the Ancient Constitution* (Cambridge: CUP, 2001); Paul Christianson, 'Royal and Parliamentary Voices on the Ancient Constitution, 1604–1621', in Linda Levy Peck, ed., *The Mental World of the Jacobean Court* (Cambridge: CUP, 1991), 71–98; Paul Christianson, 'Ancient Constitutions in the Age of Sir Edward Coke and John Selden', in Ellis Sandoz, ed., *The Roots of Liberty* (Columbia, MO: Liberty Fund 1993), 89–146.

[57]   Pocock, *Ancient Constitution*, 229.
[58]   Pocock, *Ancient Constitution*, esp. ch. 9; Pocock, *Machiavellian Moment*; see below ch. 4.

They did not think it was utterly unaltered since the Dark Ages. Selden and others stressed that invading Danes and Normans had adopted much existing English law, but they stressed that they had also adapted it, introducing some novelties that suited their purposes. In addition, these early seventeenth-century writers believed the most constant feature of English government had been its mechanism for evolution. Kings, for example, had consulted the people when it became clear that the law needed to be changed to cover issues that had not arisen before. This was why parliamentary statute was the highest form of authority, and why common law rested on axioms that had been established gradually through a series of legal judgements, responding to cases that had arisen in different ages. For these writers the resilience of the constitution lay in its flexibility and development: any talk of constancy was a rhetorical fiction, rather than a historical claim, or it was an attempt to describe how the essence of a thing could remain, even as its individual parts were renewed and replaced.[59]

These interpretations are important. They demonstrate that seventeenth-century people were capable of sophisticated thinking about English government that recognized progression through time. They may even have become more capable of this as the Stuart age wore on. However, progressive ways of thinking about government were not evident in constitutional responses to 1688–9. The reaction to the revolution may have been a last burst of celebration of an ancient and unchanged law, but it was a glorious one, and it must cast doubt on how far people were escaping the static chronology that it encapsulated.

For commentators on 1688–9 went beyond their extremely frequent reference to medieval precedent. As people discussed the revolution, they made explicit, and sometimes extended, reference to a timeless system of government that had been inherited, virtually unaltered, from folk living over a millennium before. A particular pertinent example is that of William Atwood. He had entered the lists on behalf of an ancient constitution before William's reign. In the years of the exclusion crisis, he had been one of the main opponents of Robert Brady, insisting—in the face of that Tory's proofs that Parliament was a relatively recent and royal invention—that national assemblies had in fact been part of a fundamental con-stitution of England.[60] J.G.A. Pocock's account of that debate assures us that Atwood lost it, at an intellectual, as well as a political, level. He was convincingly bested by superior evidence and logic.[61] Perhaps so; but if Tories triumphed over

---

[59] Burgess, *Politics of the Ancient Constitution*; Christianson, 'Royal and Parliamentary Voices', 83–5; Weston, 'England: Ancient Constitution', 388; G. J. Toomer, *John Selden: A Life in Scholarship,* vol. 1 (Oxford: OUP, 2009), ch. 6; Donald R. Kelley, 'History, English Law and the Renaissance', *Past and Present*, 65 (1974), 24–51; William Klien, 'The Ancient Constitution Revisited', in Nicholas Phillipson and Quentin Skinner, eds, *Political Discourse in Early Modern Britain* (Cambridge: CUP, 1993), 23–44.

[60] Debate had been sparked by Robert Brady, *A full and clear argument to a book lately written by Mr Petyt* (1681), denying the notion of an ancient parliamentary constitution. Atwood replied with such works as *Jus Angelorum ab antiquo* (1681); and *Argumentum anti-Normannicum* (1682).

[61] Pocock, *Ancient Constitution*, ch. 8.

exclusion, this was not the end of the matter. In 1688–9, the outcome of the 1679–83 crisis was reversed (James was finally barred from the throne), and so, to a large extent, was any Tory advance in constitutional thought. After William's installation, Brady adhered to the defeated cause of the ousted king, and as soon as he was politically down, Atwood re-emerged to give him a good kicking. In a pamphlet rushed out in the immediate aftermath of William's acceptance of the throne, in an extended version published in 1690, and in proposals for an even longer second part of the larger work, Atwood described a fundamental system of government that had been operating for many centuries and had permitted the removal of James II.[62]

The cornerstone of Atwood's case was the originally elective, or at least selective, nature of English government. England, he believed, was a union of a number of Saxon kingdoms, all of which had initially created kings through the free choice of the people—and which had then retained the principle that subjects must consent to new rulers before they took up authority. To prove this, Atwood quoted a fourteenth-century work, *The Mirror of Justices*, which he claimed established that popular consent was the origin of royal power in England, and he also cited as much ancient Northumbrian and West Saxon history as he could uncover.[63] At least as importantly for Atwood, selection meant English monarchy was always conditional and revocable. In the first centuries of national history, kings had been appointed by the people to protect them, to uphold justice and the law, and to rule them well. This had been explicitly acknowledged in promises and oaths rulers had made at their coronations, and there were clear consequences for breaking this contract. If a king ceased to perform the political functions to which he had acknowledged he owed his power, that power was forfeit. As Atwood put it graphically at one point, 'for the most part during the Saxon Government, a king was but a more splendid general: nor could he hope to maintain his dignity, but by hardy actions, and tender usage of his people'.[64]

From this basic point, Atwood asserted that all subsequent kings based their authority on the same principles. English monarchy owed its power to the consent of subjects. So, right through the Middle Ages to 1688–9, those people had had the right to select, depose, or discipline their rulers. Accordingly, much of Atwood's work was taken up with a historical trot through some of the standard instances of this occurring; and since he was writing within the post-revolutionary allegiance controversy, he placed particular emphasis on illustrating that a subject's duty to an English monarch did not survive that ruler's break with constitutional rule. Thus there was a survey of the frequent depositions and elections of Anglo-Saxon

---

[62] William Atwood, *Wonderful predictions of Nostredamus* (1689); William Atwood, *The fundamental constitution of English government* (1690); William Atwood, *Proposals for printing the fundamental constitution of the English government* (1690).
[63] Atwood, *Fundamental*, 28–30, 36–8.   [64] Ibid., 39.

monarchs.[65] Then there was an account of the Norman dynasty that rested heavily on popular consent. William II was not direct heir to William I, and so came to power by agreement of the people; Henry I was not secure until he had promised good rule; the people had chosen King Stephen over his rival the Empress Mathilda, and then Mathilda's heirs over Stephen's.[66] The rebellions of the Baron's Wars against the early Plantagenets were put to the same use. King John's Magna Carta and the great charter issued by Henry III were acknowledgements of the limitations of monarchical rule after the legitimate defence of ancient rights by subjects.[67] From here, Atwood went on to discuss the depositions of Edward II and Richard II, and the dynastic shifts in the Wars of the Roses.[68] He even said he would have continued forward in time beyond these cases, but would stop at the dawn of the Tudor age because more recent events were still controversial. He feared that the case he was making would get lost in political argument if he ventured far into the last two centuries. This was a strong hint that he might have argued the debateable accessions of Mary Tudor, Elizabeth, and James I had in fact been approved by the people, or even that Charles I had been lawfully deposed for misrule.[69] This was more than random citing of precedent. It was an account of the survival of a kind of monarchy that had operated, continuously, at all points in history.

As important for Atwood as the persistence of Anglo-Saxon kingship, was the strong reassertion of the ancient existence of Parliament. This was the point on which he had been most embarrassed by Brady in the exclusion era. Now Atwood simply repeated the myths he had tried to peddle a few years before. If kings had always run the risk of being deposed, his tacit argument ran, there must always have been a body that had the judicial power to depose them. This body would be a representative of the people, so Parliament must have been as long-standing as the kingly office itself. Atwood scrabbled evidence together to prove this, as he had done when first facing Brady—but the result was scarcely more convincing. For the most part, scattered references to different kinds of gatherings of subjects were woven together to create an institutional continuity for the legislature, even though many these looked like ad hoc cabals of rebelling nobles. His earliest reference was to the 'folcmot' mentioned in the Laws of Edward the Confessor—though the reader had only Atwood's word that this referred to Parliament, and of course these laws had no provenance before their compilation (or downright fabrication), in the early twelfth century.[70] At other points, the fact that a king lost power, or faced rebellion, was used to insinuate that a representative of the people must have convened to manage the challenge to royal power. Absolutely typical of

---

65 Ibid., 36–8.   66 Ibid., 39–40   67 Ibid., chs 5–6.
68 Ibid., 57–8   69 Ibid., 58.
70 Ibid., ch. 4. For Edward's laws, see Bruce R. O'Brien, *God's Peace and the King's Peace: The Laws of Edward the Confessor* (Philadelphia: University of Pennsylvania Press, 1999).

Atwood's argument was his use an 'ancient statute' made during Richard II's reign to warn the king what might happen if he did not end his abuses. This law, it had been claimed, said a 'great council' of the nation had always had the right to depose a monarch and had been used some years before to get rid of Edward II. Unfortunately there was no modern record of such a law, but this, suggested Atwood, was (probably) because Richard had destroyed many of the records in the Tower as part of his bid for absolute rule.[71] Atwood's case was therefore thin, but the point is the confidence with which he asserted it. For him, 1688–9 was simply the latest exercise of a set of subjects' rights that had been inherited, as part of a coherent constitution, from the earliest English decades.

And Atwood was not alone. Many other commentators spoke of a systematic ancient constitution, passed down from Anglo-Saxon days, though only a few found the space to lay the argument out at Atwood's length. When the Lords of the convention called in leading lawyers to ask if English government was really founded on an original contract as the Commons resolution on the throne maintained, William Petyt said it was, and a very old one at that. He claimed a polity based on popular consent to royal rule had come over the North Sea with the Saxons and had been repeatedly reasserted through the Middle Ages.[72] Pamphleteers who agreed with Petyt, and traced a constitutional heritage back northern Europe, included Samuel Masters. Rebutting the claims of James's supporters that English law gave the king unchallengeable power, Masters asserted that just a 'little skill' in English history disproved this. The Saxons had brought their ideas about rule from Germany, where, as the Roman author Tacitus had described, 'Kings had not an unlimited or absolute power', and the 'same kind of government hath been transmitted by succeeding kings to the present age'.[73] The author of another 1689 tract that justified the actions of the convention concurred. The holding of assemblies of the people, even without royal summons, had been regular practice among the German tribes before they crossed the sea—so what had happened when James fled had the most ancient precedent.[74] Again, the writer Richard Booker founded English government on 'Gothick' (that was, German) principles of consensual law making, and was backed by a Tacitus-quoting author who argued that deposing kings for misbehaviour was in line with the very old and continental foundations of English politics.[75] Other authors did not trace constitutional law back as far as Germany, but they were sure it had lasted from the earliest periods of English history. Thus Peter Allix asserted a basic contract between the king and subjects had been agreed as the seven states of the

---

[71] Atwood, *Fundamental*, 32–5.

[72] HMC, *The manuscripts of the House of Lords 1689–1690* (1889), 15. It should be noted that other witnesses had a less 'historic' interpretation—see below ch. 2.4.

[73] Masters, *Case of allegiance*, 9.   [74] *The present convention a parliament* (1689).

[75] R[ichard] B[ooker], *Satisfaction tendered to all that pretend conscience for nonsubmission* [1689]; *New oath of allegiance*, 6–7.

heptarchy had united into one kingdom, and the author of a pamphlet produced immediately after the revolution chose the same historical moment as the point when Parliament had been enshrined in the constitution.[76] Daniel Whitby emerged again to state that the right to be governed by law rather than arbitrary will had been asserted constantly since the time of the Saxons (though he suggested they might have got the idea from the pre-Roman Britons as much as their German forebears); other contributors to the allegiance controversy thought the common law was of clear Saxon origin, or at least was the result of construction by 'good and wise ancestors'.[77]

The idea of an ancient constitution was therefore in rude good health in the immediate discussion of the revolution. Even when it was not explicitly laid out, it lay behind much of the reaction. All the precedent hunting across the medieval centuries that we have been chronicling assumed that one system of government had remained intact over a long period of time, whilst expressions of relief at William's arrival almost always thanked him for preserving 'ancient' or long established liberties. Witness, for example, the gatherings of gentry at Nottingham and King's Lynn as they heard of William's landing, or the speech of Sir George Treby, welcoming the prince to London in early December.[78] Those who raised objections to the fiction of immemorial liberties were shouted down. William Atwood was not the only writer to denounce Brady in the years after James's fall. The prolific writer Samuel Johnson also engaged extensively with the unfortunate Tory in the post-revolutionary years and was joined by others who argued the case at less length.[79]

But the ancient constitution not only survived in the aftermath of 1688–9, the version deployed in this era was peculiarly static. This is important, because, as noted above, some earlier understandings of ancient English government had allowed, even depended on, change. The utter stasis in constitutional thought was particularly evident in two features of post-1688–9 writing. The first was implicit in everything we have said so far. It was simply the promiscuous way commentators cited events and authorities. As they established the features of English government, the folk of the revolutionary era swept across centuries, mixing voices and happenings that had been separated by hundreds of years and ignoring all

<hr>

[76] [Peter Allix], *An examination of the scruples of those who refuse the oaths of allegiance* (1689), 3; *Four grand questions proposed and briefly answered* (1689), 1.

[77] [Whitby], *Letter from a city minister*, 8; *A friendly debate between Dr Kingsman, a dis-satisfied clergy-man and Gratianus Trimmer* (1689), 28; *Four questions debated* (1689), 1; *Brief account of the nullity*, 3.

[78] *The declaration of the nobility, gentry and commonality at the rendez-vous at Nottingham, Nov. 22, 1688* (1688); *An address by the mayor and inhabitants of King's Lynn to the duke of Norfolk, Dec. 7, 1688* (1688); *The speech of Sir George Treby…to his highness the prince of Orange, Dec. 20, 1688* (1688).

[79] Samuel Johnson, *An argument proving that the abrogation of King James…was according to the constitution of the English government* (1692): for others, see, [Daniel Whitby], *Considerations humbly offered for taking the oath of allegiance* (1689), preface; [Fulwood], *Agreement*, 13; *Letter from Oxford*, 8; James Tyrell, *Bibliotheque politica* (1694), *passim*.

developments in the ages between. This was a feature of the many works that trotted through the history of England to demonstrate the constant reiteration of basic principles. Above, we clarified which periods of English history were given special attention in post-1689 writing by separating out the authors' treatment of each epoch (Anglo-Saxons, fourteenth century royal depositions, Wars of the Roses, and so on). In the original rhetoric, however, these all jostled together. Although some responses to the revolution, such as Atwood's, were extensive histories that laid stories out at length, most used a summary of the English past as part of short political argument. They therefore covered the whole story, or at least very substantial parts of it, in a few paragraphs, and, of course, this eliminated the chance to discuss alterations or evolution. Chronological jumbling became even more severe when writers advanced through the centuries several times, going back to an earlier period to initiate discussion of a different feature of their constitution. For example, Daniel Whitby's *Historical account of some things relating to English government* was in reality several historical accounts.[80] He started by running through the kings from William I to Richard II to show they all promised to govern according to law, but he then doubled back to King John to begin an account of legitimate resistance to tyranny which he ran through to Edward I. He then covered the history again, from the early Middle Ages to the first Tudor king, to show monarchs were approved by Parliament. Finally, he repeated his coverage once more, listing rulers from William II in 1087 to Richard III in 1483 who had not been hereditary heirs to the throne. In other cases, all sense of where instances stood in time broke down. Writers simply grabbed examples randomly, from any period, to prove their points, with absolutely no chronological contextualization. Thomas Long provided an acute example. As his somewhat disorganized prose wrestled to persuade people to support the revolution, he cited—in this order, which was no particular one—the Roman invasion of Britain, Edward the Confessor's election, William II's accession, the Norman Conquest, Magna Carta, Henry VIII's coronation oath, King John's resistance to the pope, Simon de Montford's rebellion against Henry III, Henry VII's invasion, Henry IV's status as a *de facto* king, Aethered the Unready's similar position, William II's accession again, and the anarchy in the time of King Stephen and the Empress Mathilda.

Such ahistorical use of history affected legal authorities as much as events. Expertise on the English constitution was cited from all periods of English history, with no attempt to either contextualize its content or trace any evolution within political thought. The sources that were employed ranged back as far as Tacitus and fragments of Anglo-Saxon legal codes, but then went a long way forwards through a list of writings and documents that were used so extensively that they constituted a kind of constitutional canon. These included those spurious

---

[80] [Whitby], *Historical account*, 2–43.

laws of Edward the Confessor, Magna Carta, the thirteenth-century writing of Henry de Bracton, the early fourteenth-century *Mirror of Magistrates*, coronation oaths of all periods, the writings of Sir John Fortescue in the fifteenth century, and Sir Thomas Smith's late-Tudor *De republica Anglorum*. In fact, the mixing was a little more eclectic with constitutional statements than historical events because it extended into the seventeenth century. Although the course of politics in the Stuart age was too controversial to be used to prove legal principle, statements of what people had thought the constitution said were more admissible—especially if they supported the idea of a long-standing balanced polity or had been made by those monarchs who had been so treacherously attacked by rebels. The thoughts of Sir Edward Coke (1655–34) and the 1628 Petition of Right were thus joined by James I's musing on law-bound monarchy, and even by Charles I's support for the role of Parliament in his declarations and in his 1642 *Answer to the nineteen propositions*.[81] Rarely, if ever, were the opinions of this vast range of sources contrasted. Rarely, if ever, was there was any sense that opinions had evolved over time. In the arguments of those supporting William of Orange, all experts, of whatever period, sang harmoniously from exactly the same legal hymn sheet. And as with events, the writings could be crushed so tightly together that all historical specificity was squeezed out. For example, Samuel Johnson joined Atwood in claiming that Parliament's warning to Richard II rested on a now-lost statute that had allowed the legislature to depose a king—but the writer then said that if this could not be absolutely proved, the principle was anyway stated in numerous other places. He then rattled off (again in no particular order) the *Mirror of Magistrates*, Bracton, the style King Alfred had used—'king by will of God and the people', the Confessor's laws, Fortescue, and repeated coronation oaths.[82]

The stasis implied by such jumbling of past moments was underlined far more explicitly in a second feature of pro-Williamite writing. This was the treatment of the greatest potential challenge to an unchanging system of government: the Norman Conquest of 1066. On the face of it, the conquest made a mockery of the ancient constitution. William I had invaded the country without the consent of the English people. He had taken over by force of arms rather than by popular approval, and he had rapidly replaced the English landowning elite with a new Norman aristocracy. It was, therefore, most unlikely that a free constitution would have survived. Indeed, earlier in the seventeenth century, an important strand of thought insisted it had not. Radicals of the civil war era had advanced the notion of a 'Norman yoke', asserting that a free system of government had been lost in 1066, that the new regime had imposed a burden of tyranny, and that it was the

---

[81] For example, *King James the first his opinion of a king and of a tyrant* (1689); [Thomas Long], *A full answer to all the popular objections that have yet appeared for not taking the oath of allegiance* (1689), 8, 9, 38.

[82] Johnson, *Argument proving*, 26–9.

task of people now to challenge existing rulers to regain their ancient birthrights.[83] Similarly, Robert Brady, in his exclusion-era writings, had claimed that the Conquest had been a new foundation of government that had placed all power in the triumphant king and his armed followers. Yet despite the difficulty of asserting continuity either side of William's invasion, those discussing the success of another William, six hundred years later, did what they could to make this case. The characteristic mode in historical interpretation of the eleventh century was conquest denial.

The argument was made across the political spectrum. The veteran writer Thomas Long, who spent much of 1689 trying to persuade his fellow Tories that they could accept William without abandoning their principles, discussed the first Norman king as part of his attempt to resolve queries about the legitimacy of the new Dutch ruler. He argued that the Tory principle of non-resistance to rulers held in most cases—but that there were exceptions at moments of necessity, and that the English constitution had always made provision for the people to choose their rulers at moments of uncertainty and crisis. 1066, he asserted, was an example. William I, he suggested, had never claimed right by a conquest. Rather, he had done all he could to preserve the existing system of rule. He invaded because Harold Godwinson had usurped a throne bequeathed to the Norman duke by Edward the Confessor, and at the invitation of many Anglo-Saxon nobles. After the battle of Hastings, William had taken care to have himself crowned by the Anglo-Saxon archbishop of Canterbury in Westminster Abbey (and so had come to his title by the usual means); and he had taken the usual coronation oath, promising to preserve English laws and customs.[84] Whigs agreed. Samuel Masters stated that 'The Duke of Normandy, who we call the conqueror, was such only with respect to Harold, who usurped the crown, but not with respect to the kingdom, which he claimed as successor to King Edward'.[85] Daniel Whitby insisted that William had made repeated promises that his new subjects could enjoy their ancient rights and customs, and that he would govern them according to the laws of the Confessor.[86] As we would expect, William Atwood made continuity at 1066 an absolute axiom of history and would have demonstrated this at length if the second part of his *Fundamental Constitution* had appeared; a young Daniel Defoe launched his publishing career with the suggestion that the Norman duke had decided to confirm the ancient rights of England.[87] Meanwhile other authors insisted William was only a so-called conqueror because he owed his right to nomination by a legitimate predecessor and securing the people's consent, or they stressed once again that the new king's coronation oath proved his determination

---

[83] Christopher Hill, 'The Norman Yoke', in his *The Intellectual Origins of the English Revolution Revisited* (Oxford: OUP, 1997), 361–5.

[84] [Long], *Resolution*, 3.   [85] Masters, *Case of allegiance*, 9.

[86] [Whitby], *Historical account*, 2–6.

[87] Atwood, *Proposals for printing*, 2; [Defoe], *Reflections*, 41.

to rule according to established laws.[88] White Kennet made the slightly different, but closely related, point that William's right to the throne could not come from mere invasion, even if he had wanted it to. The conquest itself was illegitimate because it was 'barbarous and ambitious'. This was why the Norman had sworn his coronation oath, and had had himself approved by the people at the four corners of the platform in Westminster Abbey, as Anglo-Saxon kings had done.[89]

In this, the post-revolutionary writers were maintaining the dominant mode of seventeenth-century understanding of 1066. Even those adherents of the ancient constitution who had seen its essence in gradual adaptation, rather than utter constancy, had stressed it had survived the Conquest to avoid the sort of radical discontinuity that might have allowed greater claims for royal power. Yet Conquest denial after 1688–9 is still remarkable (for all that it may be understandable, given the reluctance of many to see the latest William as a conqueror, or to open a space for radical change at the revolution). First, it defied those assertions of total conquest that had been gaining strength in seventeenth-century historiography. The arguments of men like Brady were simply ignored by those who accepted the revolution: indeed, as Mark Goldie has shown, some Tory-leaning thinkers abandoned a Brady-esque reading of 1066 to endorse 1688–9. Writers such as Edmund Bohun, who had once seen the Norman invasion as a creating a constitutional clean slate, now endorsed a new theory of conquest—Grotius' notion of victory in a just war—that meant they no longer had to discuss the eleventh century.[90] Second, the denial of conquest was total, even naive. It lacked the subtlety of many earlier positions, which had admitted that, although the ancient constitution had survived 1066, it had been a close-run thing. As Glenn Burgess and Paul Christianson have pointed out, John Selden was closer to believing continuity was a necessary legal fiction rather than a strict historical fact, and he recognized that the Normans made considerable concrete changes under a show of conformity to old forms. Other thinkers, such as Thomas Hedley, had claimed the conquest had caused a temporary interruption in government by the ancient constitution that then had to be restored through the struggles that led to Magna Carta.[91] In contrast to this, almost all post-1688–9 commentators had William as a good Saxon monarch, for all his Norman blood. He ruled according to the old constitution and had been nominated by the last English king. Perhaps most dramatically, a major

<hr>

[88] *Brief vindication of the parliamentary proceedings*, 39; [Kennet], *Dialogue*, 14.

[89] [Kennet], *Dialogue*, 14–19.

[90] Mark Goldie, 'Edmund Bohun and *Jus Gentium* in the Revolution Debate, 1689–93', *Historical Journal*, 20 (1977), 569–86.

[91] Burgess, *Politics of the Ancient Constitution*, 66–7; Paul Christianson, *Discourse on History, Law and Governance in the Public Career of John Selden, 1610–1635* (Toronto: University of Toronto Press, 1996), 24–7. See also, J.P. Sommerville, 'The Ancient Constitution Re-assessed: The Common Law, the Court, and the Languages of Politics in Early Modern England', in R. Malcolm Smuts, ed., *The Stuart Court and Europe* (Cambridge: CUP, 1996), 39–64, at 52–3; George Garnett, *John Selden and the Norman Conquest* (London: Selden Society, 2013).

history of English parliaments—published by Nathanial Bacon immediately after the revolution—stripped away almost all of Selden's acknowledgement of change in 1066, even though it claimed to be based on that writer's manuscript notes. In Bacon's version of Selden, government by consent had been described by Tacitus among the German tribes, it had survived the Saxons' move to England, and it had persisted after William arrived. It was true that Norman kings had stretched the old powers of monarchy, especially over tax and forest law. But this was excusable given the pressures they faced, and the essential nature of their rule was shown in other actions. William got himself crowned in a Saxon-style ceremony and made a solemn covenant to uphold the laws, all the Norman kings consulted a Parliament-like council before altering the legal system, and even when they did go beyond old understandings of royal power, the new rulers rapidly reversed course to confirm all ancient rights the moment their subjects protested against such novelties.[92]

An absolutely unchanging ancient constitution was therefore at the heart of commentary on the revolution in the period immediately after it had happened. As one 1690 pamphleteer put it, summarizing the output of authors who had justified the revolution up to the point he was writing: 'they have, with great industry, sifted the legal constitution of the English monarch, and the history of all its monarchs'.[93] In all this prose, time was effectively frozen as people struggling to understand William's arrival presented it as simply the latest instance of principles that had not altered since at least Saxon times, and as they used distant events and authorities (usually very distant) to legitimate what they had done.

2.4 Universal Principles

If much constitutional comment on 1688–9 looked back to an enduringly ancient system of government, the most enduringly influential did not. This of course, was the work of the Whig commentator, John Locke. Long after the writings of Robert Howard and William Atwood had passed into obscurity, people would be discussing Locke's *Two treatises of government*. Although largely written during the exclusion crisis, these tracts were not published until late 1689 and were probably revised in the months after the revolution in order to provide more closely relevant analysis of it.[94] And, famously, the *Treatises* eschewed all reference to the English past. As John Pocock and others have pointed out, Locke grounded

---

[92] Nathaniel Bacon, *An historical and political discourse of the laws & government of England from the first times… collected from some manuscript notes of John Selden* (1689), 2–103.

[93] *Allegiance vindicated, or the takers of the new oath of allegiance to K William and Q Mary justified* (1690), 1.

[94] This dating first clearly made by Peter Laslett, 'The English Revolution and Locke's Two Treaties of Government', *Cambridge Historical Journal*, 12:1 (1956), 40–55.

constitutional legitimacy in 'principles of nature and reason which lie outside history and do not change with its changes'.[95] Government had rightful authority if it was founded on the correct axioms of rule. For Locke, this meant recognizing that power was a trust, with the purpose of protecting the people's natural liberties and property, and that could be forfeited if the trust were betrayed. It did not matter how, or even whether, such legitimate authority had passed down from earlier generations. This ahistoricity meant Locke's ideas remained worth discussing long after scholarship had debunked all theories of surviving 'Gothick' government, and that they could be applied in societies very different from that of seventeenth-century England. The *Treatises* therefore prove that late-Stuart minds were not inevitably caught in ancient constitutionalism. They could produce stimulating lines of thought with very different conceptions of time's relevance and nature.

And others aside from Locke defended 1688–9 without worrying too much about the historical provenance of government. It is true that his work has become the most famous of this kind of argument and was, in many ways, the most far-reaching. His writing was peculiar in its almost total lack of reference to the English past, and he formulated theories that would delegitimate tyrannous government, even if a nation had long accepted a system of law that seemed to allow it. But he was not unique in focusing on the purpose or principle of political authority, rather than justifying it by precedent—so he was not quite as unusual in his treatment of history as has been suggested.[96] Although those commentators who looked to the past froze time in a static chronology, others supplemented the appeal to precedent with arguments that did not depend on retrospection.

There was a parade of such thought as early as the January debates of the convention. On the 29th of the month, the House of Lords asked the opinion of leading lawyers about a thorny problem presented by the Commons. The lower house had voted that James II had lost authority because he had broken an 'original contract' with his people. But the Lords wanted to know if there was any evidence that such a contract had been concluded. As we have seen, William Petyt answered with a standard rehearsal of the ancient constitution.[97] But Petyt was, in fact, in a minority of one. All the other experts admitted they could not find an original contract in English history. There was, they acknowledged, nowhere where a fundamental agreement between kings and subjects was laid out in the legal or documentary record. Of itself, this did not contradict the idea of an ancient constitution. The original contract might have been so far back in time that the precise moment it had been concluded had been forgotten, and all documentation of it might have been lost: indeed the idea that English government had lasted so long that it had this 'immemorial' quality was one of its chief claims to legitimacy. As one of the lawyers, John Levinz, said, the basic rules on which

---

[95] Pocock, *Ancient Constitution*, 236.
[96] See, in particular, Pocock, *Ancient Constitution*, 235–8.   [97] See above, ch. 2.3.

English monarchy rested might be called 'an original contract, though you know not when it began'. Other opinions, though, used less chronological logic. They simply stated that English monarchy was limited, rather than absolute, and that one could not understand how this was possible unless there was some sort of contract governing that limitation. Thus Robert Atkyns, Edward Montagu, John Holt, George Bradbury, and William Whitelocke all admitted they could not find the contract in the records of the law. But they said respectively: that a consensus of people had said government was always founded on some sort of contract; that reason revealed there had to be basic agreement on which authority rested; that Fortescue had said England was a mixed and political monarchy, so there must be an underlying consent to define its powers; that the common law as it existed had the form of an agreement; and that the contract must be there to explain why English kings were not absolute. In all these contributions it was technically the present nature—or possibly even just the existence—of government that proved the contract. Any transmission of that agreement through the generations played a minor, or non-existent, role because that transmission could not actually be demonstrated.[98]

Once the pamphlet controversy began, both Whigs and Tories could deploy ahistorical argument. The Whigs' efforts in this area have been well catalogued and analysed by Mark Goldie. As part of his work on the allegiance controversy, he compiled a list of types of case used to justify the revolution, and one of these was contract theory founded on natural law. Some commentators, he showed, insisted government could only be just if it was founded in consent, and if its purpose was to protect certain natural rights (most basically that of self-preservation, but others could be added). Goldie noted fourteen works in his corpus that used this style of argument: examining these shows how historical events and precedents could become irrelevant.[99] Take, for example, Samuel Johnson's attack on Abednego's Sellar's notorious 1689 tract, *The history of passive obedience*. Sellar had argued clerics who transferred their loyalty to William had defied their church's long insistence that subjects must never resist their rulers. In reply, Johnson insisted not only that this had never been the position of the English clerical establishment, but that it could not have been, since it so clearly misunderstood the whole nature of government. For Johnson, rulers who abused their position to torment or destroy their subjects were usurpers. Their actions exceeded their legitimate power because they were beyond law; indeed they were against the very intention of law, which always was to protect people and their natural rights. Once this was established as a universal principle, Johnson did not have to delve the depths of English history. He simply had to show that James II had behaved as a tyrant and so a usurper, and the tract therefore concentrated on

---

[98] HMC, *House of Lords 1689–1690*, 14–15.   [99] Goldie, 'Revolution of 1689'.

the events of the very last few years.[100] Similarly, James Tyrell, in his *Bibliotheca Politica* (which Goldie called a 'vast, rambling compendium' of contemporary political ideas), gave a central place to the notion that all kings and supreme magistrates were given their prerogatives as a trust. They had a revocable duty to uphold the peace, happiness, and safety of mankind—the reasons they had been set up in their position by the people in the first place. This again bypassed any ancient English constitution. Tyrrell's principles could be discussed without reference to specific moments in the past; and for long passages, the author (who also quoted Locke) took this opportunity.[101]

Tories rejected all such logic. Indeed, the denial that government was founded in a contract would be central to any definition of Tory political thought after 1688–9. This did not mean, however, that they were incapable of ahistorical argument. At least one of their characteristic explanations of why one should obey the post-revolutionary regime rested on the basic nature and purpose of any government, and so did not need any appeal to events in the past. This was *de facto* theory. Tories who argued that people should obey whatever power happened to be in charge certainly backed this with static chronology: people had never been blamed for behaving this way; monarchs who clambered to power had enjoyed authority. But they also based their arguments on a theory of the abstract purpose of government. Rulers were needed to protect subjects from anarchy and from the rapaciousness of foreign powers. Resisting someone who was actually performing these functions would risk the chaos of civil strife, or alien invasion, and so would remove the protection which was the very point of any system of rule.

In some hands, this line of thinking could be as cleanly ahistorical as Whig natural law theory. For example, the author of a *Vindication* of those who had transferred allegiance to William put the purpose of loyalty, rather than its heritage, at the centre of his case. He admitted that James II had been a 'rightful and lawful successor' whose prerogatives had passed down to him legitimately from his forebears. But once the old king was no longer on the throne, the situation was transformed. James has stopped giving his subjects protection, so no longer earned their obedience. In strange echoes of the Whig natural law position, the *Vindication* asserted that, 'The Reason of all Law is the public good': James's authority had ceased because he was now incapable of exercising the function of any government anywhere. Events before 1688–9 were not needed to sustain this position, and the author's only protracted use of them was to back the wholly separate argument that James had tried to interfere with William's interests in England, thus giving the prince of Orange the right to declare war on the English

---

[100] Johnson, *Some reflections*, particularly 7, 11.
[101] Tyrell, *Bibliotheca Politica*: the principle of government as a trust was most clearly laid out at the start of the third dialogue, pp. 145–7. The work had clearly been in preparation from the early months after the revolution—the first dialogue had appeared as a stand-alone piece in early 1692.

king and ultimately to displace him.[102] Similarly, the Tory pamphleteer Robert Wynne opened his defence of the revolution with the abstract statement that the point of government was the security of the people. From there he argued that loyalty could not extend beyond its purpose—which was to support powers that were protecting those who were loyal—and that any oaths attempting to tie people further than this were invalid because all sworn loyalty had an implied reciprocity (it fell if the non-swearing party broke its side of the bargain). Having said all this, Wynne did not need to use much history. His chief interest in looking back before the revolution was to demonstrate that Charles II's Parliaments could not bind people to maintain allegiance to Charles' hereditary successors if these ever lost *de facto* power.[103]

There were other ahistorical arguments used to discuss 1688–9 that were not as clearly tied to party positions as contract or *de facto* theories. One was Cicero's principle '*salus populi suprema lex esto*'. This was the idea that, particularly in moments of crisis, the safety or the welfare of the people should supersede any rules of government that seemed to contradict it, and should therefore become the supreme law. It was invoked by both Whigs and Tories at points during the debates on the revolution—usually when folk were arguing for a quick settlement over wasting too much time ensuring that what was done would perfectly match existing English law. Sometimes it was deployed explicitly to bypass any appeal to the past. There was a particularly powerful outburst of such sentiment on 19–20 February 1689. Then the convention was debating whether it could act as a Parliament, even though it had not been summoned by a king. On this question, some used historical examples such as the irregular assembly that elevated William II to the throne in 1087, or the convention that restored Charles II twenty nine years before (one of those rare uses of the Stuart age in constitutional debate)—but others thought there was no historical instance close enough to help the present dilemma.[104] Instead, members said the extraordinary situation justified their actions. Sir Giles Eyre stated that, in the circumstances they faced, 'Necessity abrogates all Laws. The Precedents of this, that are demanded, are not to be expected [since] 'tis not in every King's reign that he abdicates the Government'.[105] Similarly, Sir Edward Seymour asserted there were no good past models for what was happening, but thought 'you are as well qualified to make Precedents as to follow others'; whilst John Howe mocked the whole precedent-hunting industry with a medical image: 'Tis unreasonable in a sick man not to take any physic but what has been prescribed him formerly'.[106]

---

[102] *A vindication of those who have taken the new oath of allegiance to King William and Queen Mary* (1689), pp. 5, 8 for quotes.
[103] [Robert Wynne], *The case of the oaths stated* (1689).
[104] Grey, *Debates*, x, 84–9.   [105] Grey, *Debates*, x, 99.   [106] Grey, *Debates*, x, 95, 92.

Commentators also used international comparisons. Rather than taking distant English precedents as their only source of examples to prove the legitimacy of the revolution, speakers and writers also looked to fairly recent events in other European countries. This demonstrated that what they were claiming had happened over the winter of 1688–9 fitted patterns that were generally accepted as legal, and were therefore rooted in universal, rather than historical, principle. Examples that were used included the abdication of the Emperor Charles V in 1555. This showed, some thought, that a monarch could renounce a throne, as some claimed James II had done by leaving the kingdom. The depositions of King Sigismond of Sweden in 1592 and of King Alfonso VI of Portugal in 1668 were thought to prove that subjects could protect themselves against damaging rule by removing a monarch. Curiously, given that the defeat of Catholicism was used extensively outside legal argument to justify William III's rule, some in the constitutional debates even pointed to the fact that Henry IV of France had not been allowed to accede to the French crown until he had adopted the Catholic faith in 1589. This, it was claimed, established that it was impossible—despite what James has claimed—to have a king and a nation of different beliefs.[107]

At an initial glance, these styles of argument pose an important challenge to our picture of a chronologically static commentary on the legality of 1688–9. They all seemed to rest on universal principles which did not rely on appeals to precedents within an ancient English constitution. But any longer look does a lot to dispel the impression. First, these sorts of universal argument—though not exactly unusual—were still heavily outnumbered by appeals to an unchanging English government. Some commentators did lay out the logical steps that should lead people to obey, or refuse to obey, rulers, but many more found it easier to secure their case with concrete instances from England's past. Moreover, the outnumbering often occurred within the very works that advanced ahistorical positions. One of the most striking things about commentary on 1688–9 was its blunderbuss nature. Authors and speakers usually ran a whole battery of arguments to convince their audiences, and the sort of ahistorical material we have just surveyed was usually mixed with lines of attack that relied heavily on precedent. As a result, although it is not hard to find natural rights theory in commentary on the revolution, or *de facto* reasoning that saw loyalty as a reward for protection, it is much harder to find works that put such cases without also including generous appeals to the past. So, among Whig contract theorists, Locke was in a small minority in his lack of interest in constitutional history. Looking through Goldie's list of allegiance controversy works demonstrates that even the

---

¹⁰⁷ See, for example, Grey, *Debates*, x, 16, 47; *The Lords and Commons reasons and justifications for the deprivation and deposition of James II* (1689), 2; *A protestant precedent offered to the bishops* (1689); [Long], *Resolution*, 19–20; 'An answer to the desertion'.

authors who advanced a natural law case for contract tended to suggest that the agreement was also embodied in the historical system of government.[108] Indeed some, such as Peter Allix and William Atwood, advanced natural law in only some of their works: in other tracts and pamphlets they relied wholly on history.[109] Similarly, Tory *de facto* theorists almost always bolstered their musing on the abstract purpose of government with analysis of the past: this was why they were so attracted to the period of the Wars of the Roses. In some cases, the piling of historical precedents overwhelmed the abstract case in principle as well as number. Edward Stillingfleet's 1689 *Discourse* against clergy who refused oaths of loyalty to William started with the basic point that promises to obey rulers must fall if this contradicted the public good, and that this happened if rulers ceased to provide the protection that was their part of the bargain. But this Tory argument gradually sank beneath waves of more Whiggish examples from the past. As Stillingfleet reached for any line of rhetoric that might win over his audience, he referenced not only kings whose authority had been recognized even though their legal title was suspect, but kings through the ages who had been chosen for the public good by Parliament even though they were not hereditary successors, and of ones deposed for tyranny—as if rule were by some form of contract.[110]

Sometimes the itch to back universal principle with historical example led to a reinterpretation of the ancient constitution. This construct was reinterpreted so that old systems of government came to embody the abstract argument being advanced. This happened, for example, with *salus populi*. Commentators sometimes suggested that necessity should overrule law in 1688-9—not simply on theoretical grounds, but because Englishmen had accepted that it might do so in the past. *Salus populi* was thus incorporated as an axiom of the ancient constitution. So, in the 19–20 February debates, John Howe said he was imitating 'our Ancestors, who always followed the necessity of affairs', whilst Giles Eyre said the convention should look to the depositions of Edward II and Richard II, even though he denied these could be directly compared with 1688-9. For Eyre, the parallel was not in exact legal situation, but in the broader principle that necessity had given medieval forebears sanction to dethrone kings: 'Where there is the same Necessity, there is the same reason'.[111] The actions of the 1660 convention

---

[108] Goldie, 'Revolution of 1689'. A good example is [John Humfrey], *Advice before it be too late* (1688), which told the convention they had the power to remake government on contractual grounds, but thought they might invest it in a king and the two houses of Parliament to gel with the ancient constitution.

[109] [Peter Allix], *Reflections upon the opinions of some moderate divines* (1689); and Atwood, *Fundamental*, mixed natural and historical contract theory—but [Peter Allix], *The anatomy of a Jacobite tory* (1690), and [William Atwood], *Dr Sherlock's 'Two Kings of Brainford'* (1690), took largely historical positions.

[110] [Edward Stillingfleet], *A discourse of the unreasonableness of a new separation* (1689)—this sort of ambiguity makes it hard to categorize Stillingfleet as a Whig or a Tory at this point.

[111] Grey, *Debates*, x, 99.

were also discussed as instances of *salus populi*. John Maynard cited the Restoration assembly, before quoting Cicero; whilst John Birch said the 1689 assembly could act with parliamentary power, 'by the best of precedents', and then recalled his own service in the 1660 body.[112] At that time, he said, everyone had laughed at those who had slowed the handling of the political emergency by demanding precise precursors.[113]

International commentary also did what it could to integrate its foreign examples into an unchanging English polity that validated the revolution through prescription and precedent. Various techniques were used to suggest that all nations had adhered to sets of inherited principles that were also embodied in England's laws: all Europeans were thus heirs to some sort of primordial and unchanging constitution, of which the ancient English one was the local variant. Sometimes this argument for congruence between England and the Continent was made simply by including foreign examples in the list of historical incidents used to establish timeless political truths. One of the most curious pieces produced in the post-revolutionary debates took this to the extreme of citing only French examples. This short 1689 pamphlet claimed French lawyers could not object to what had just happened among the English, because France itself had long-surviving principles of government that would excuse William's accession. These included subjects' right to resist tyrannous monarchs and the fact that abandoning the realm constituted an abdication; and the illustrative examples were as old as the familiar English ones. They reached back to the War of the Common Good against Louis XI in the fifteenth century, or the (albeit temporary) deposition of King Childeric a thousand years before that.[114] Another pamphleteer delved just as far back in French history. Richard Booker's short 1689 piece complained that James had sought help from Louis XIV in regaining his throne. This, Booker thought, was outrageous because Louis himself owed his title to the fact that his ancestor Hugh Capet had been chosen by the French people to replace the ineffective Carolingians.[115] Other works happily mixed foreign precedents with the standard English ones to create the sense of a universal ancient constitution. So the Whig pamphleteer James Welwood tried to establish the possibility of monarchical abdication by citing the precedents of several Anglo-Saxon kings, but threw in the examples of the Emperor Charles V and Queen Christina of Sweden for good measure.[116] In another striking example, the author of *A brief vindication* of the revolution ran through changes in the royal succession from the Anglo-Saxons to the Wars of the Roses, which he said proved people

---

[112] Grey, *Debates*, x, 93.

[113] Grey, *Debates*, x, 101–3. See also pamphlet literature on 1660, such as *Late honourable convention*; W[illiam] P[ayne], *An answer to a printed letter to Dr W.P.* (1690), 9.

[114] *A letter from a French lawyer to an English gentleman* (1689).

[115] B[ooker], *Satisfaction tendered*, 5.   [116] Welwood, *Vindication*, 11.

had always altered who was king for the common good; but he only did this after recounting histories of France and Spain to the same purpose. He also quoted English coronation oaths through the ages, to show rulers always undertook to protect the liberties of their subjects, but did the same for German, Polish, French, and Spanish promises by rulers.[117]

More concretely, some commentators traced the common features of European constitutions to common origins. Admittedly, this was sometimes little more than a vague reference to a 'Gothick' government, which was presumably established in the very extensive areas the Goths had invaded and settled at the fall of the Roman Empire.[118] Some accounts, though, were more detailed. For example, for Peter Allix (who, as a refugee from French persecution, had an appropriately international outlook) many continental nations could be shown to be the direct heirs of the German tribes. When the Roman Empire had collapsed, the Teutonic nations had certainly come to south Britain, and the author would trace their lasting establishment of limited monarchy there. First, however, he wanted to stress that these tribesmen had also settled in many other places, taking their free government with them. To prove this, Allix gave potted constitutional histories of the Spaniards, Navarese, Burgundians, Swedes, Hungarians, Lombards, and Portugese (all showing them electing and deposing monarchs according to the rulers' behaviour). He then expanding on the government of Poland and the Holy Roman Empire (whose open election of monarchs underlined the point) and went on to speak at even greater length of his native France. It was true, Allix admitted, that Louis XIV's kingdom looked absolutist, rather than Teutonically free. But this was because the Bourbon monarchy had spent the past hundred years subverting the ancient constitution that the French had inherited from the Franks. Their true polity was best illustrated in the depositions of Childeric (late fifth century), Louis the Good (833), Charles the Fat (887), Charles the Simple (922), Charles of Lorriane (987), and—much later—Henri III in 1588. It was also evident in the regular gatherings of the Estates-General. Since the late twelfth century, these had institutionalized the earlier open-field meetings, and conclaves of nobles, that had been held to discuss the nation's affairs since the German tribes had invaded.[119]

Rhetorical promiscuousness thus diluted abstract argument, sometimes to the point of simply incorporating it into visions of the ancient constitution. But there was a second, and deeper, reason why the existence of ahistorical logic did not transform understandings of time. Precedent and abstract political theory had deep temporal affinities. Ancient constitutionalism had asserted that the principles of government had not changed. It was therefore possible to cite instances from

---

[117] *Brief vindication of the parliamentary proceedings*, 26–47. See also the highly international approach of [William Denton], *Jus regiminis, being a justification of defensive arms* (1689), esp. chs 4–5.
[118] B[ooker], *Satisfaction tendered*, 5; Nathaniel Bacon, *Historical and political discourse*, 60.
[119] [Allix], *Reflections upon the opinions*, 56–77.

long ago as directly relevant to current circumstances, and so to collapse intervening centuries. Abstract theories of politics went even further along this line. They effectively stated that the principles of government could not change, because they were based on a logic and reason that would be the same at all periods. If this were admitted, one might as well illustrate (if one did not need to prove) the principles by citing past instances of them operating, and these instances could be ancient, because there had only ever been one way of founding legitimate government. As John Pocock suggested, writers of abstract theory may have continued to use history because the strong pull of the past meant they dragged it back into arguments from which it had technically just been eliminated.[120] But they may also have seen the polemical value of showing that many people in all ages had agreed that politics must always operate in certain ways. For perceptions of chronology, therefore, abstract theory had a virtually identical effect to ancient constitutionalism. Time froze because, in their fundamentals, governments could never evolve without ceasing to be legitimate.

It would be tedious to create a long list of examples of abstract theories rapidly turning to ancient historical example to enhance their case. As has just been suggested, this happened the large majority of times ahistorical logic was deployed, if the historical example was admittedly sometimes fleeting. Even when writers were proceeding on the most abstract grounds and applied these primarily to very recent events, they rarely resisted at least passing reference to deeper history. So, for example, Daniel Defoe's 1689 *Advantages of the present settlement* was, in the main, a catalogue of James's crimes, which were used to the Whiggish purpose of demonstrating the king had perverted the purposes of government, and so been legitimately deposed. Nevertheless, it observed, 'he is a mighty stranger to English history that knows not that some persons have been removed from the administration of regal power by the authority of parliament'.[121] On the *de facto* Tory side, Francis Fulwood argued that James had abandoned his role as monarch, so that obedience was no longer due to him. But he also referred back well before recent events and rooted his theoretical point in a long-standing constitution. For him, the Jacobites' notion that people should stand by a ruler, even though they no longer fulfilled the functions of rule, was 'against the light of nature, the primary end of [royal authority] being the safety of the kingdom', but also contradicted 'the sense of ancient and learned lawyers, and also of the plain acknowledgement and profession of our ancient kings and parliaments'.[122] Beyond these specific examples from each end of the political spectrum, the widespread use of authorities on the English legal system scattered over time underlined the tendency of commentators to support abstract lines of thought with concrete, if ancient, history.

---

[120] Pocock, *Ancient Constitution*, 238–9.
[121] [Defoe], *Advantages of the present settlement*, 20.   [122] [Fulwood], *Obedience*, 3.

Even if writers had established a constitutional principle through timeless logic, they frequently reinforced their case with quotations from King Edward's Laws, William I's coronation oath, Magna Carta, Bracton, the Mirror of Magistrates, Fortescue— or to come just a little closer in time, from Thomas Smith, or Edward Coke.

2.5 Classical and Biblical History

So, abstract reasoning could retain the use of precedent from an unchanging English constitution. But it could push analysis even further back in time and freeze chronology even earlier than the arrival of the English in Britain. This was because the universal applicability of political logic meant that writers could use examples to compare to 1688–9 from well beyond—and sometime well before— the records of England's constitution. In particular they mined two familiar sets of texts that allowed their interests to expand well before the Anglo-Saxon kingdoms. These, of course, were the Bible and the heritage of classical literature. These were works that spoke of societies several millennia old, but which were well known to educated Englishmen, and were familiar well beyond elites through popular retellings in sermons, poetry, folklore, and proverb.

Use of classical examples to illustrate axioms of government that were supposedly embodied in the 1689 settlement was a recurring feature of the commentary, but in truth it was a pretty scattered one. No particular moments came to dominate discussion in the way that 1327 and 1399 emerged as central referents in the English material; and no particular periods of the classical past were thought specially rich times to study. Part of the reason, of course, was the immense political variety of Greek and Roman history. A huge range of points could, and were, made by referring to different items on a very long menu of incidents and situations strung out across many centuries. This was compounded by the intimate knowledge of the histories among Stuart-era authors: an expertise imbued by the close study of the ancient past that constituted a good deal of higher education in the early modern era. Thus many of the commentators on 1688–9 knew the storehouse of classical stories well, and could usually find something, somewhere, in that cupboard that suited their rhetorical recipe of the moment. An almost random dive into the publications of the allegiance controversy provides a good range of examples. Peter Allix answered those who asked why James II's son had been excluded from the throne, given that he was innocent of his father's crimes, by saying that the children of deposed tyrants were unlikely to make good rulers and that the Romans had understood this when they destroyed the whole family of the Tarquins (the action that established the Roman republic in 495 BCE).[123] Arguing against absolutism, the author of a pamphlet—the

---

[123] [Allix], *Examination of the scruples*, 13.

suitably classically entitled *Political conference between Aulicus…Demos…and Civis*—wanted to stress that no sensible constitution left absolute authority in one set of hands.[124] The author illustrated this by saying that even the ancient democracies had not let the people rule unrestrained: Athens had had proconsuls, Sparta ephori, and Rome senators, to provide checks and balances to unfettered power. Thomas Long, pressing his usual *de facto* argument for obeying William, pointed out that the title of virtually all Roman emperors had been technically suspect. To demonstrate this he gave a potted narrative of the shenanigans surrounding the imperial successions of Claudius, Nero, and Caligula.[125]

As with references to the long-gone English past, such appeal to history collapsed time. Writers rarely pondered differences in political, social, and cultural context that might render lessons inapplicable. Certainly, the author of *A brief vindication* of James's deposition said he would skip over classical examples because some might think them 'too old and far fetched [and]…not to be precedents to us in these ages', but this looked more like a way to avoid boring the reader with endless evidence at a particular point in the argument, since the work did use examples from Greece and Rome in other passages.[126] And where the pamphlet did this, it illustrated the prevailing, and so unperiodized, approach by mixing its reference to the pre-Anglo-Saxon past with far more recent examples, which were seen as embodying exactly the same principles. For example, the work's discussion of limits on monarchy ranged from classical constitutions to the contemporary states of Europe.[127] Others too compounded ancient and modern. For example, to respond to those Jacobites who objected to the idea that James had abdicated because his flight from England had been forced by circumstances, the author of *The answer to the desertion discussed*, pointed out that virtually all abdications—even those that had been accepted as legally binding—had been unavoidable given the conditions at the time. To show this he cited the resignation of Diocletian in 305, made inevitable by his illness, but then also referred to the abdication of the Emperor Charles V (1,250 years later), who was also sick and had been exhausted by his failure to suppress the Protestant heresy in Germany.[128] Similarly, Thomas Long came close to implying that the Ceasars, as they had endlessly usurped each other, had expected their subjects to be familiar with Henry VII's statute telling them to obey whoever got themselves settled in power.[129]

Classical history, then, served political argument after the revolution in a way that paralleled the ancient constitution. Of course nobody claimed an unbroken heritage of law and custom that had come down to the English from the Greeks or

---

[124] *A political conference between Aulicus, a courtier, Demos, a countryman, and Civis, a citizen* (1689), 11.

[125] [Long], *Resolution*, 32–4.   [126] *Brief vindication of the parliamentary proceedings*, 23–6.

[127] Ibid., 10–13.   [128] 'Answer to the desertion discussed', xi, 12.

[129] [Long], *Resolution*, 38.

Romans. Both objective history, and majority assumptions about the immemorial origins of English government in the forests of Germany, denied that. But English government was thought to embody universally just and rational principles of rule that had underlain classical events and practices, so these could be cited without any need to dwell any unique historical contexts that might limit their applicability. The resources for precedent hunting were thus extended, obviously geographically, but also chronologically—citing the Spartan constitution took commentators back to the eighth century BCE.

The use of scripture in constitutional arguments after 1688–9 also stretched the period under analysis. But before we can examine the role of the Bible in discussion, we again need to wrestle with the atypicality of John Locke. The problem this time was not neglect. Locke was unusual in not referring to English history in his analysis of the revolution, but he was very willing to apply the Jewish past to the topic. Indeed, his first treatise of government—all 213 pages of it—engaged in close scriptural commentary to clear the ground for the natural law arguments of the second part of the whole work. But this was scriptural commentary of a peculiarly ahistoric kind. Locke did not use biblical events to establish precedents. Instead he used reason, and close textual analysis, to debunk a theory that scripture established a certain set of rules for political power. Some of this has been highlighted in Locke scholarship. For some decades it has been stressed that Locke's prime target was Sir Robert Filmer's *Patriachia* (a 1630s work that had been revived in the Restoration era) and that Locke was writing to counter its scripturally based assertion that monarchical power was an absolute inheritance from Adam.[130] What has not been noted is the unusual effect this had on Locke's conception of time. Whilst the *Second Treatise* was exceptional in ignoring precedent, the first went well beyond this to destroy attempts to justify present structures by using examples from the past.

Filmer was, in fact, an easy target. Although, as Locke pointed out, he exploited rhetorical skill to hide the fundamental implausibility of his position, the author had used biblical commentary to suggest that political power derived from a father's power within a family and that it must therefore be monarchical and absolute, since it had been passed down hereditarily from God's grant of dominion over the world to Adam (the first father as well as the first man). Although the common early modern analogy between kingship and fatherhood had perhaps made the difficulties with such an argument harder to see for its initial audience, it was riddled with absurdities, and Locke set out to expose these. Among his most powerful points were that God's grant to Adam was made before there were any other people, so it could tell us nothing about political societies, and could

---

[130] Again Laslett, 'The English revolution', refocused scholarship.

only have been over non-human things; that absolute patriarchal authority would contradict itself as soon as there was a third generation, because the grandchildren could then have two different 'absolute' masters (their father and grandfather); and—perhaps most famously—that if power had descended through Adam's heirs it must either have been divided among all his descendants—thus sharing it among all the world's population—or one person in each generation must have been his heir, in which case we must urgently find out who that person was so that all the rulers of the earth could surrender their authority to this one legitimate sovereign.[131]

What is clear, even from such a short summary of Locke's arguments, is that they were grounded in reason, rather than appealing to history. Locke engaged with Filmer's biblical scholarship—overwhelming with his commentary on the early chapters of Genesis—but it did not use the ancient events related there to establish principles by which we should conduct affairs today. Instead it denied that the passages Filmer cited contained explicit instructions from God about how politics was to be organized, and then demonstrated that the lessons Filmer drew from the scriptural past could not be correct, simply because they made no logical sense. This was a rational, not historical, mode of arguing. Locke repeatedly claimed his position was proved by 'scripture and reason', but it was reason that did the hard work.[132] He recruited biblical events simply as illustrations of what had already been shown by logical reflection. For example, having shown there was no rational grounds to decide who should inherit a father's power if he had more than one child, and thus that it must be divided between descendants, Locke cited the amicable division of flocks and land between Lot and Abraham— something only possible if authority could be split between different people.[133]

It is true Locke made some use of historical counterexample. For instance, in the last few sections of the *First Treatise* he pointed out that the Jews had governed themselves without absolute rulers, or even any kind of monarch, for long periods of their history (under the Judges, or during the Babylonian captivity), and that the kings they had had (people such as Saul, David, and Solomon) had never claimed to be Adam's heirs.[134] Yet this use of the past was intended to weaken the notion of precedent rather than establish it. Locke was arguing the Jews had lived under a number of political forms whilst continuing to be the elect nation of God, so it was impossible to see which style of regime had divine approval, and which should determine how other folk should organize their affairs. Such passages also took up rather less space in the work than the purely logical debunking of Filmer, and they were joined by arguments that reversed the

---

[131]   [John Locke], *Two treatises of government* (1690), chs 3–10.
[132]   As at Locke, *Two treatises*, 37.   [133]   Ibid., 173.   [134]   Ibid., 197–202, 212.

temporal direction of precedent-based argument, again to undermine the binding power of the past. For example, Filmer had argued that biblical patriarchs such as Abraham had demonstrated their absolute power by taking actions such as waging war and pronouncing death sentences. Locke pointed out, though, that in his contemporary world, non-sovereign and non-monarchical authorities did the same sort of things. He cited republics, which raised armies, and Jamaican plantation owners, who exercised extensive power over their slaves and tenants.[135] Here recent examples trumped precedent: in one other case so dramatically that it might just have cast doubt on the authority of scripture itself (though it is highly unlikely that this was Locke's intention). As he mocked Filmer's notion of indivisible power by pointing to another partition of sovereignty—this time of the earth between Noah's sons after the flood—he observed dryly that that story told nobody who was supposed to have got America in the carve up. This might hint that the Bible (or at least its earliest chapters) needed to be understood in the context in which it was written—in this case by people who did not know about the New World.[136]

Even if Locke had not intended any sly aside about the authority of Genesis, his treatment of scripture would have marked him out as a peculiar kind of thinker in the late seventeenth century. The majority of those who cited the Bible in favour of their constitutional arguments after 1688–9 joined Locke in linking abstract argument with God's word, but they did so in a way that reinforced the power of past example, rather than dissolving it. Standardly, the pattern of argument was to establish a principle of government (either from reason, or from instances of English history, or both), and then use a biblical incident to show it had applied among a people blessed by heaven. By implication this demonstrated that it was a divine, and so eternal, rule, and therefore one that should govern the revolution by its precedent. Though these commentators were writing in the age of Locke, they were, in their chronological assumptions, very much heirs of Filmer.

A clear illustration was the *History of self-defence* published in 1689 as part of the reaction to that notorious pamphlet by the Jacobite Abednego Sellar, which had argued that non-resistance to rulers had been the constant doctrine of the Church of England since the Reformation.[137] The debate over Sellar's tract formed a vigorous subset of the allegiance controversy, and those answering him took a variety of approaches, but the *History* rested its early passages on scripture, once it had laid out its basic stall.[138] The author opened with the claim that absolute obedience to rulers, no matter how they treated subjects, was against human

---

[135] Ibid., 160–71.   [136] Ibid., 177.   [137] [Sellar], *History of passive obedience.*
[138] Goldie noted seven pamphlet refutations, and one defence, of Seller's piece: Goldie, 'Revolution of 1688', 556.

nature. Not having the right to resist tyranny would reduce men to the level of dumb beasts and would fly in the face of the whole history of human dealings. To demonstrate this last point, the pamphlet swept through the whole past to provide a catalogue of legitimate rebellions, and it started with biblical events. Most prominent among these were the actions of the biblical King David, who—before coming to the throne—had led a revolt against the misrule of King Saul. The pamphlet also narrated the story of the rebellion against King Reheboam (in which the ten northern tribes of Israel had formed a separate kingdom in protest at oppressive taxation); it noted the defiance that many prophets—especially Elisha—had shown royal authority; and ended with the rebellion of the Macabees, which had restored Jewish independence after the Greek conquests and was reported in the Apocrypha, if not in the canonical Testament itself.[139]

This, of course, was a Whiggish use of scripture, but the Bible would also support Tory arguments. Once appointed bishop of Salisbury in 1689, William's chaplain and propagandist, Gilbert Burnet, sought to find arguments for the revolution that would appeal to Tory-leaning clerics in his diocese. In his *Pastoral letter* he argued for the revolution on firm *de facto* grounds, and whilst some of his case rested on the English past (there had been numerous usurpations, but everyone had accepted rulers who had actually come to secure their positions), he also reminded the clergy of the political stance taken by scriptural figures. For all that Old Testament prophets had criticized kings, Burnet reminded his audience, they had accepted the authority of all Jewish rulers. They had done this even though the historical books of the Hebrew Bible had shown how many of these monarchs had gained their thrones in highly questionable ways. Similarly, St Paul had preached obedience to Roman emperors, even though the imperial office was founded on the illegal overthrow of the Roman republic, and even though the emperors had then made a habit of overthrowing each other. Most importantly, Christ himself had endorsed *de facto* theory. When he told his followers to submit to Imperial authority in worldly affairs (to render unto Ceasar, that which was Ceasar's: Matthew 22:15–22; Mark 12: 13–17; Luke 20:20–6), he was contradicting the contemporary laws of Israel, that had insisted rule by alien powers was null. Jesus, by contrast, had simply told people to acquiesce in the power of the conquering Roman state: Christians' true calling was not in the political world; they should accept whatever political structures the world threw at them.[140]

Such scriptural appeal was common in the constitutional discussions after 1688-9, and its effect, as with the citation of classical examples, was to expand

<hr>

[139] *History of self-defence*, 3–11.
[140] Gilbert Burnet, *A pastoral letter writ by the right reverend father in God, Gilbert, lord bishop of Sarum ... concerning the oaths* (1689), 8–12.

the store of precedents well beyond English history. For commentators on the revolution, the richest section of the bible was that describing Jewish history between elevation of Saul as king, and the final Babylonian deportation. This was the period of the Hebrew monarchy covered in the books of Samuel, Kings and Chronicles. Certainly, a few writers urged caution in making parallels between this period and modern England, because Israel had been a theocracy under the direct political supervision of God rather than enjoying the more ordinary constitution that governed English affairs: but this was a minority view.[141] Many more (and even those who raised caveats, in other parts of their output) were tempted by the similarities in structure of the two governments to make direct comparisons. They were also tempted by the rich parade of events in this part of the Old Testament (a veritable catalogue of rebellions, usurpations, invasions, depositions, and general political uncertainty) that allowed a number of different arguments to be made, according to party taste. So, some writers joined Burnet in suggesting biblical conquests had been accepted by the Jews because they had brought *de facto* rulers to power (or at least should not be resisted, as they were the results of providence).[142] Some joined the author of the *History of self-defence* in citing legitimate, and divinely blessed, rebellions against tyrants (David's resistance to Saul being particularly popular).[143] Others used the bible make different points, for example showing that non-hereditary succession had been common, or reminding readers that the Jewish monarchy had been set up by the people against God's advice, so there was nothing blasphemous in overthrowing a king.[144] Whatever point people were making, however, deploying precedents from the era of the Jewish monarchy had the same chronological effect. It represented a freezing of time over a far longer period than appeal to either English or Roman history. The exact dates of the Hebrew monarchy are unclear, because of the almost total absence of cross reference to biblical events in non-scriptural or datable sources, but according to modern scholarship, it probably stretched from the mid eleventh century to the early sixth century before the common era. At least in the constitutional essentials, nothing had changed sufficiently to render exemplars anachronistic over more than two and a half thousand years.

There were appeals to the New Testament as well as the Old, as Burnet's use of St Paul and Christ illustrated. In particular, Tories pointed to the apparently *de facto* political philosophy of Christ, his apostles, and the primitive Christians.

---

[141] [Richard Claridge], *A defence of the present government by King William and Queen Mary* (1689), 3. William Sherlock, *The case of allegiance due to sovereign powers* (1691).

[142] Sherlock, *Case of allegiance*, 11; William Lloyd, *A discourse of God's ways of disposing of kingdoms* (1691), 22, 26, 52, 55.

[143] *A friendly debate between Dr Kingsman*, 44–7; [Kennett], *Dialogue*, 28–9; [William Eyre], *A vindication of the letter out of the north* (1690), 17–19.

[144] *Brief vindication of the parliamentary proceedings*, 2; [Defoe], *Reflections*, 9; Howard, *History of the reigns*, xxxiii.

These, it was claimed were clearly described in the Gospels, the Acts of the Apostles, and the New Testament epistles, as well as in some non-biblical accounts of early Christian history that functioned as quasi-gospel for these purposes.[145] As Burnet had done, Tory commentators deployed these texts to point out that the earliest, purest, followers of Christ had never challenged the temporal authorities that happened to be set over them: they had even remained politically passive in the face of persecution, and when their rulers had fought their way, illegally, to power.[146] As the author of one pamphlet pointed out, St Paul had written his letter to the Romans—telling them that the 'Powers that are, are ordained of God' (a summary of Romans 13)—at a time when Nero ruled, and Nero was not only a notorious enemy of Christianity, but had murdered both his predecessor and his predecessor's heir. Similarly, Jesus had told people to pay their taxes to Rome when Tiberius was emperor, and Tiberius was 'a Usurper with a Vengeance'.[147] Another writer argued for the legitimacy of William and Mary by stating that the new regime was far less objectionable than the governors that Christ, St Paul, and St Peter in his first epistle, had told their followers to obey (1 Peter 2: 13–14). Israel's displaced rulers had resisted imperial conquest, and Roman occupation had been against the people's wishes; James, by contrast, had abandoned the realm, and the vast majority of English people had welcomed the prince of Orange.[148] In citing such exemplars, commentators were deploying precedents from periods more recent than the reigns of David or Saul, or the Mesopotamian conquests of Palestine—but they were reaching back before the most distant understandings of the origins of the English constitution, and merged their sense of biblical and ecclesiastical analysis with their deployments of classical history. When the author who considered the *Case of the People of England* asked—rhetorically, indeed sarcastically—if the usurpation of power by the first Christian Emperor Constantine meant he should have been resisted as illegitimate, and if his Christian subjects should have remained loyal to his legitimate—but pagan—predecessor, the pamphleteer combined the classical understanding that emperors were emperors simply because they could hold on to power, with a Christian trust in God's ways of disposing worldly government.[149]

The use of scripture in constitutional argument after 1688–9 therefore tended to reinforce a static view of history, frozen in anachronistic precedent which could

---

[145] The non-biblical texts (where these were cited, rather than commentators assuming a general knowledge of early Christian behaviour and political beliefs) lent heavily on the early third-century apologetics of Turtullian as the most sustained insight into the principles of the primitive church.

[146] *Vindication of those who have taken the new oath*, 4; [Thomas Bainbrigg], *Seasonable reflections on a late pamphlet* (1690); [Bohun], *Doctrine of non-resistance*, 3–5; *The case of the people of England in their present circumstances* (1689), 15–17; *A letter to the authors of and answers to the case of allegiance* (1691), 2; *Allegiance vindicated*, 7, 13, 25–7. Lloyd, *Discourse of God's ways*, 6–7.

[147] *A letter to Mr James Parkinson, MA, in answer to his examination of Dr Sherlock's book* (1691), 7–8.

[148] *The plain case as it now stands with reference to subjection to the present government* (1690), 10–14.

[149] *Case of the people of England*, 17.

reach back millennia. Yet there was one important and sustained exception, and it came in reactions to the New Testament passages just considered. To an extent unusual in consideration of past events, these came to be carefully contextualized by some commentators, and this was specifically to prevent them becoming standards of modern behaviour. This raised at least the potential for a somewhat different model of time: historical circumstances for the earliest followers of Christ were shown to be different in significant ways.

The reasons the passages received this treatment are clear. Principally it was because the actions and opinions of the first Christians appeared such strong endorsements of a *de facto* view of authority, and that political position became highly controversial. As Tories clung to a theory of legitimacy from possession as a way to accept the revolution without abandoning their anathema of popular resistance to rulers, Whigs accused them of having no deeper attachment to William than his bare exercise of power. The Whigs hoped thereby to brand their rivals crypto-Jacobites, who would happily serve James II if French force put him back on the throne, and to pose themselves as the king's most natural allies. The struggle manifested itself in the print tussle over William Sherlock's tract *The case of allegiance* (1690). This cleric had originally rejected the revolution, but found his way back to support William on the grounds that the prince of Orange had come to enjoy secure possession of the throne.[150] Sherlock's tract described the results of his intellectual journey, but it was roundly denounced by Whigs as an insincere and unreliable conversion.[151] All this left a pressing problem for his detractors. As Whigs determined to defeat any argument for authority on grounds of mere possession, they faced the acute embarrassment that the most authoritative Christian figures—St Peter, St Paul, and Jesus himself—seem to have endorsed exactly such principles. It thus became vital for Whigs to explain—in practice, to explain away—these passages.

The techniques used largely fell into two categories. For some, it was important to understand the audience for the biblical statements. Both Christ and his apostles, some Whig writers claimed, had been facing a rigid strand of Jewish theology which denounced any power not founded on God's express command and law. To counter this view, the New Testament texts had stressed that God had set up non-Jewish authorities through the ordinary course of politics (which was anyway guided by providence), and that these were perfectly legitimate. Yet the Whig authors claimed that Tories took the Bible's words much further than this

---

[150] Sherlock, *Case of allegiance.*

[151] Mark Goldie found three Whig tracts that responded to Sherlock's conversion before he had published a print explanation of it—and twenty-three that responded to the *Case* from a Whig position, in addition to seventeen Jacobite attacks for apostasy. He was defended by nine other works, and many others—not among the numbers just quoted—referred to the dispute in passing. Goldie, 'Revolution of 1689', 557.

simple intention. They made the wholly unwarranted claim that people must obey existing powers in all circumstances whatever: this was to misunderstand completely the purpose for which the scriptural injunctions had first been made.[152] For other Whig writers, it was the nature of the Roman Empire that was important. Within the imperium, the primitive Christians had had no political or civil rights. Roman government was absolute, and Christians had exercised a faith that was unprotected by its law. Christ's first followers were therefore in a very different situation to Englishmen in the seventeenth century, and so had a much narrower basis on which to resist authority. Stuart subjects lived under a constitution that granted them liberties that rulers were supposed to respect, and that protected their religion as the established faith. This allowed them to take action to defend the law, and the church, against a monarch acting outside the accepted prerogative: these were privileges that the primitive Christians had simply not had.[153] There were other lines of argument (such as suggesting that Jesus obeyed Rome for the theological purpose of allowing the atonement to proceed, and so was not making any political point), but all of them denied the applicability of a biblical precedent, and did so in a way that at least hinted at change over time.[154] What had been said, or what dictated action, in the past no longer bound people because that past was different. Theocratic Judaism, and pagan absolutism, had gone away. As the cleric White Kennett put it, 'St Paul has no Relation to our Present Discourse'; whilst another writer, who suggested Jesus was only talking about duties towards autocratic Roman emperors, said scripture could not bind us over civil rights, because of subsequent 'vicissitudes of government'.[155]

The heat of party battle over the Bible therefore defrosted time, at least a little. It thus joins other flashes of evidence of a more fluid conception of chronology and shows that in particular rhetorical circumstances people might adopt more progressive views of time's operation. However, it is important not to overstate this phenomenon, and particularly not for pro-revolution constitutional commentary. Whigs were responding to a very particular discursive challenge when they used detailed historical context to question the apparent meaning of New Testament texts and the history of the very early church. Denying that one or two precedents from the first century could be used in a particular way in the heat of a polemical battle was not the same as rejecting the authority of distant precedents generally, or abandoning the prevailing attitudes that governed discussion. As we might expect from the general approach to scripture and the past in the debates

---

[152] [Kennet], *Dialogue*, p. 23; [Gilbert Burnet], 'An enquiry in to the measures of submission', in *A complete collection of papers in twelve parts,* ii, 6; [Long], *Resolution*, 36–8.

[153] B[ooker], *Satisfaction tendered*; [Kennett], *Dialogue*, 25–7.

[154] *History of self-defence*, 12–13.

[155] [Kennett], *Dialogue*, 27; *The grand problem briefly discussed* (1690), preface.

around 1688–9, the very writers who contextualized the behaviour of early Christians used lessons from ancient centuries quite confidently in other parts of their work. Certainly Whig arguments over Jesus' words point to ambiguities in Christian, and especially Protestant, conceptions of time to which we are about to turn. But overwhelmingly, scripture was used as an uncomplicated storehouse of historical examples for direct application today, and so joined the English constitution and classical reference in a tightly woven fabric of a static chronology.

3

The Revolution in Reformation Time

3.1 A Protestant Revolution

On 16 July 1690, Gilbert Burnet, the bishop of Salisbury, mounted the pulpit in the Chapel Royal at Whitehall. King William was absent in Ireland, where, half a month before, he had defeated the forces of his exiled predecessor at the Battle of the Boyne. Queen Mary, however, was present, and heard Burnet preach at the service to mark one of the monthly fast days that she had instigated to call down God's blessing on the military effort against James.[1] What the bishop said came close to official propaganda. Not only was the sermon delivered on an occasion sponsored by the government, and with a view to advancing its great military cause, but it was given by a man at the centre of its efforts in public relations. Burnet had performed this role even before William came to the throne. He had translated and edited the prince of Orange's manifesto for his invasion; he had travelled with William as his personal chaplain for the expedition; and had been busy over the winter of 1688–9 preaching and pamphleteering in favour of an offer of the crown to his Dutch master.[2] Once that crown was secured, Burnet continued in this role, writing tracts and sermons to support the new regime and suggesting publicity campaigns, such as the monthly fasting, to persuade the English of the justice and benefit of William and Mary's rule.[3]

What was a little unusual about Burnet's sermon was its deep rooting in history. Although there were certainly moral and theological arguments within the rhetoric, these were illustrated and supplemented with a vision of the human past that stretched over centuries. The whole second half of the work was a survey of historical narratives which, Burnet thought, elucidated the dangers and opportunities facing his audience. In particular, he set the current war in Ireland, and the revolution that had made it necessary, within a sustained (and for the genre of a sermon, extraordinarily detailed) account of the unfolding of the Protestant

---

[1] Gilbert Burnet, *A sermon preach'd before the queen at White-hall, on the 16th day of July* (1690)—Burnet briefly referred to the news from the Boyne at 28–9.

[2] Tony Claydon, *William III and the Godly Revolution* (Cambridge: CUP, 1996), 29–30. For works over the winter of 1688–9, see [Gilbert Burnet], *An enquiry into the present state of affairs* (1689); [Gilbert Burnet], *A review of the reflections on the prince of Orange's declaration* (1688); [Burnet], 'Enquiry into the measures of submission'; G. Burnet, *A sermon preached in the chappel of St James*; Gilbert Burnet, *A sermon preached before the House of Commons, 31 January, 1688/9* (1689).

[3] Claydon, *William III and the Godly Revolution*, chs 1–2. Key pamphlets by Burnet were cited in ch. 1; his sermon contribution is evident in this chapter.

The Revolution in Time: Chronology, Modernity, and 1688–1689 in England. Tony Claydon, Oxford University Press (2020). © Tony Claydon.
DOI: 10.1093/oso/9780198817239.001.0001

Reformation. William's arrival was presented as the salvation of a long process of Christian renewal that had started in Germany in the early sixteenth century, that had soon been adopted in England, and had then come through a series of perils to reach a point where it might now find final triumph under its providentially appointed leader.[4] All this appears at great remove from the constitutional defences of 1688–9. If lawyers, politicians, and pamphleteers had overwhelmingly frozen time when they put arguments for the legality of the new regime, this cleric gave it a majestic and evolving sweep. For Burnet, the revolution was a transformative rescue of a faith, that itself had been a transformative religious reform when it had first occurred in the early sixteenth century.

It was not, perhaps, surprising that Burnet read 1688–9 in this way. His worldview, as reflected in his extensive public writings, had rested on clear interpretations of history since the start of his publishing career in the 1660s, and had tended to analyse contemporary events with reference to a Protestant narrative.[5] And even by 1690, this bishop of Salisbury was still probably less famous for that episcopal appointment (made in the earliest weeks of William's royal patronage as a recognition for services rendered), than as the author of his definitive and hugely popular history of the English Reformation, which he had produced in two large volumes in 1679 and 1681.[6] But of course, while Burnet's Protestant interpretation of William's arrival was particularly intense, it was not unusual. The revolution was presented as a (usually providential) escape for the true faith in a vast range and quantity of material.

At the forefront of this was the huge number of sermons reflecting on 1688–9. To a great extent this was because the Williamite regime, and supporters of the revolution, used preaching as one of their prime media of persuasion. This had started as early as the constitutional convention. One of the first acts of that body had been to command the 31 January day of thanksgiving which we saw was designed to distract from the anniversary of Charles I's execution on the 30th.[7] The result of this decision was a sermon celebrating the arrival of William in every Anglican parish in the land, and in quite a number of dissenting meetings also.[8] Once the new government was settled in, it continued to tune the pulpits to its advantage, going well beyond the standard exploitation of the sermon genre as commentary on contemporary affairs.[9] Queen Mary was at the heart of

---

[4] G. Burnet, *Sermon…16th day of July*, 24–30.

[5] Tony Claydon, 'Latitudinarianism and Apocalyptic History in the Worldview of Gilbert Burnet, 1643–1715', *Historical Journal*, 51 (2008), 577–97.

[6] Gilbert Burnet, *The history of the reformation…the first part* (1679); Gilbert Burnet, *The history of the reformation…the second part* (1681)

[7] See above, ch. 2.2.   [8] Claydon, 'Sermon Culture', especially 483–4.

[9] For the role of sermons in public discussion, see Tony Claydon, 'The Sermon, the Public Sphere and the Political Culture of Late Seventeenth-Century England', in Lori Anne Ferrell and Peter McCullough, eds, *The English Sermon Revised* (Manchester: MUP, 2000), 208–34; McCullough et al., *Oxford Handbook of the Early Modern Sermon*, part iv.

this effort. She arranged for the sermons preached at her court to be published in unprecedented numbers—thus burnishing the image of the royal household as a pious and Protestant engine of the gospel, as well as broadcasting specific political messages.[10] She also multiplied occasions on which the populace were required to hear the government's preached message. Every year from 1689 she ordered monthly fasts to be held from spring to autumn to call God's blessing on the troops fighting Louis, whilst thanksgivings were organized for major military victories and at the end of the campaigning season. Much of this material was printed, and much of it reflected on the revolution that had started the war. Supporting this effort, clerical allies of the new regime also adapted the message of the regular round of preaching that happened as part of the annual festivals celebrating moments in English history, and which had become a solid Protestant and monarchical calendar by the late seventeenth century.[11] As has been shown, the annual fasting on 30 January to atone for the execution of Charles I proved tricky for Williamites, but some preachers nevertheless found ways to celebrate the revolution upon it, and two other annual thanksgivings were less problematic.[12] The one on 29 May to show gratitude for the restoration of Charles II could be dressed as a parallel salvation of Anglican kingship, even if the constitutional message of 1660 was ambiguous, whilst the one on 5 November could be exploited quite straightforwardly.[13] Sermons to give thanks for the discovery of the Gunpowder Plot in 1605 were easy to convert to an endorsement of the revolution, given the apparently similar rescues from popish threat.[14] Taking this material together, one can argue that 1688–9 was one of the most preached-over events of the seventeenth century.[15] This naturally meant that its place within ecclesiastical history, and Protestant narrative, were extensively extolled.

The run of fasts and thanksgivings created and exploited by the government produced official prayers as well as sermons. Such liturgy has recently gained the attention of historians, and it, too, placed 1688–9 within a Reformation chronology.[16] But this temporal framing was not exclusive to clerics. For instance, the constitutional and legal debate on the revolution had a version of a relatively recent Protestant era that was in some tension with the medieval precedent hunting that dominated discussions in this area. For some contributors to the allegiance debates, William's rule could be justified because he had rescued England from

---

[10] Claydon, *William III and the Godly Revolution*, 96–7. For Mary's memoires, see R. Doebner, ed., Memoires of Mary, Queen of England, 1688–93 (1886).

[11] Natalie Mears, Alasdair Raffe, Stephen Taylor, and Philip Williamson, eds, *National Prayers: Special Worship Since the Reformation,* vol. III (Woodbridge: Boydell 2013), lxxxviii–xc. David Cressy, *Bonfires and Bells: National Memory and the Protestant Calendar in Elizabethan and Stuart England* (Berkeley: Weidenfeld and Nicolson, 1989).

[12] See above, ch. 2.2   [13] See below, ch. 3.2

[14] Claydon, *William III and the Godly Revolution*, 102–4.   [15] Claydon, 'Sermon Culture'.

[16] Sharpe, *Rebranding Rule*, 369–73; Mears et al., *National Prayers*; Claydon, *William III and the Godly Revolution*, 83–4, 107–8.

the jurisdictional encroachments of the papacy. As we shall see, they thus integrated their constitutional history with a story of the reformed religion that began with Henry VIII's 1530s break with Rome, rather than rooting it in an Anglo-Saxon constitution.[17] More widely, almost all commentary on the revolution saw it—at least in part—as a triumph of, or a miraculous deliverance for, Protestantism. The earliest expressions of thanks to William as he advanced through southern England, and then met the nation's elites in London, centred on his work for the true faith, and this was echoed in histories, narratives, and accounts of the winter of 1688–9—starting with the very first published report of the revolution. John Whittel's *Exact diary of the late expedition* began its close description of its author's marching with the prince of Orange by outlining William's motives: the prince had 'espy'd the Mystery of Popish Inquity' in the politics of his day and had resolved to become the 'zealous Defender' of the Protestant religion.[18] Similarly, private reflections on, and expressions of relief about, James's fall lent heavily towards providential deliverance of reformed Christianity, as did the popular broadsides, and verse and ballad lyrics, that celebrated the prince of Orange's arrival (including Tom Wharton's anti-papal marching song, *Lilli burlero*, which has become, perhaps, one of the most enduring cultural legacies of the 1688 campaign).[19] This interpretation continued in the wide variety of print material that dealt, directly or indirectly, with the revolution through William's reign. The corpus included the propaganda for England's war with Louis XIV—presented as a fight to make good the defeat of popery begun with the change of regime in London; it encompassed audits of the state of the nation in almanacs and other compendiums (a country now set free, again, to uphold the true faith); and it extended into a very wide range of other social, political, religious, and cultural commentary that described the revolution as a milestone in the struggle against popish superstition, ignorance, and cruelty.[20]

In some ways, of course, the prevalence of this Protestant-inflected reaction to 1688–9 challenges fashionable ideas about changes in temporal perception over the early modern period. This was certainly not a secularizing interpretation of William's arrival. Since Protestants believed that theirs was the true faith, their vision of the revolution seemed absolutely full of a predetermined divine purpose. We shall return to these features of Protestant understandings later; but first we

---

[17] See below, ch. 3.2

[18] [John Whittel], *An exact diary of the late expedition* (1689), 1, 8; and see the material gathered in *A complete collection of papers in twelve parts.*

[19] For a tiny selection of the broadside, verse, and ballad material, see *Father Petre's farewell sermon* (1688); *Popery routed, or Father Petre's farewell to London city* (1689); 'The hieroglyphick', 'The dispensing judges', and 'The Papists' exultation', all in *Muses farewell*, and the examples analysed below. For *Lilli bolero*, see Galbraith M. Crump, *Poems on Affairs of State: Augustan Satirical Verse, 1660–1714, Volume 4: 1685–1688* (New Haven: Yale UP, 1968), 309–11.

[20] For consideration of much of this material, from related angles, see Claydon, *William III and the Godly Revolution*, and Tony Claydon, *Europe and the Making of England* (Cambridge: CUP, 2007).

should take up the more dynamic dimensions suggested by Burnet's preaching that seem to offer more comfort to recent ideas about the construction of time. As the preacher hinted, Reformation readings of the revolution might centre on God, but they could nevertheless suggest a fluid and developmental view of history. They imagined a past structured by long narrative arcs; they saw important dramas playing out through time; and they argued that action in the current moment could alter the future. But the body of material that demonstrated this vision was vast, and its chronological emphases varied. So to present the evidence clearly, Burnet's 1690 sermon will be taken as a multiple starting point, and the material will be discussed under two broad heads. The first is the assumption that God's providence had moved human history through radically different periods. The second was the deployment of Christian solutions to the problem of the continuation of time after Christ's atonement. These solutions—necessary for the faithful to discuss any period after the first century AD, and therefore utilized in discussion of 1688–9—both created forward-driving narratives and generated a sense of uncertain expectation in the present.

3.2 Protestant Periodization

Perhaps the most striking feature of Protestant interpretations of William's arrival was their strong periodization. People who talked about 1688–9 as a salvation for the Reformation tended to have a palpable sense of historical turning points. These had marked the boundaries between different eras, each of which had had characteristics peculiar to itself. In the commentary, this periodization was particularly evident in three characteristics of the discourse. First there was a sense of profound discontinuity in the early sixteenth century. Something fundamental had happened in 1517 when Luther had started the protest against Rome, and this had established a new era characterized by world-shaping struggle between popery and godliness.[21] Second, there was a sense of evolving fortunes within this new Reformation era. The period since Luther had not only started with a turning point, but it has its own internal structure. This was usually conceived as an initial period of miraculous success for the new faith, followed by increasingly disturbing divisions and reversals. Finally, there was the strong sense that William's triumph might begin a new era. For many, the revolution was an opportunity to re-found the Reformation. If all responded appropriately to God's deliverance, then the Protestant faith in England, indeed in Europe as a whole, could achieve new security, and might return to the purity and excitement of its first days. This would initiate another new epoch: 1688–9 might be a new 1517.

---

[21] The idea that the Reformation periodized history is explored in Anthony Keys, *The Estrangement of the Past: A Study of the Origins of Modern Historical Consciousness* (Oxford: OUP, 1991), esp. 79–84.

The early sixteenth-century discontinuity was handled fairly briefly in Burnet's 1690 sermon. He made no mention of Luther as the hero of a new movement and gave very little detail of what had happened in Germany in 1517. He did, however, talk of a 'first opening of the Reformation', making clear that a historical page had turned in the early sixteenth century, and—more dramatically—he laid out a new pattern of human affairs since that opening.[22] For the last seventeen decades, the world had seen an epic battle between the forces of godly Protestants and the might of popery, and this was obviously not a battle that had marked the ages before Luther. With a sustained account of the struggle—one that took in Charles V's wars in the Holy Roman Empire, Mary Tudor's reign in England, the wars of religion in France, the Thirty Years War in Germany, and the struggle between the Netherlands and France for domination in Europe in recent decades—Burnet created a distinct epoch in world history.[23]

This sense of a major historical rupture at Luther's protest pervaded much of the commentary on 1688–9. Yet before exploring it further, there are two important points to make. First, interest in the early sixteenth century was fuelled by more than simple recognition that the faith just rescued by William had been founded at that point in the past. It also rested on resurgence in interest in the history of the Reformation in Restoration Britain, encouraged by the ecclesiastical politics of the time. Since 1660, the Church of England had been defending itself against perceived Roman threats (from abroad, and from infiltrating popery at the royal court), and it had also been in dispute with Protestant dissenters, who refused to join the official establishment on the grounds that it retained too many features of the corrupted medieval church. In these conditions, it was natural for participants in the disputes to look back to the decades when the nature of the English Protestant church had first been defined, and the result had been a renaissance in Tudor studies. Burnet, for example, had written his massive history of England's break with Rome to answer Catholic accusations that this had been an unjustified schism. But he had also written to counter Peter Heylin's histories, published in the 1660s, that had presented the birth of the Church of England as a relatively limited reform of the old medieval structures, and so had downplayed the continental Protestantism which inspired dissenters. Burnet was thus using Reformation history to carve out a middle position between popery and Anglican intolerance and did so at a time when the Tudor past was widely invoked as the lack of press censorship during the exclusion crisis (1678–83) allowed open religious debate.[24] With the early sixteenth century so prominent in contemporary religious politics, it was understandable that 1688–9 would be discussed with reference to the rupture of that period.

---

[22] G. Burnet, *Sermon…16th day of July*, 24.   [23] Ibid., 25–30.

[24] Andrew Starkie, 'Gilbert Burnet's *Reformation* and the Semantics of Popery', in Jason McElligott, ed., *Fear, Exclusion and Revolution: Roger Morrice and His Worlds* (Aldershot: Routledge, 2006), 138–53.

The second point about the Reformation discontinuity was that its dating was vague. The rapid skim over the actual start of Luther's protest in Burnet's sermon was an example of this, but so were frequent references to a movement started 'in the last age', or 'at the time of our forefathers', without specifying a particular date or exact point in history. Partly, this was the effect of the confusion caused by the domestication of the wider continental movement. Reform in Europe had begun pretty definitively in 1517. William, however, had rescued an English Protestant church whose foundations were somewhat later, and whose exact dating could be disputed. Candidates for the establishment included the first reception of Lutheran ideas in England in the 1520s, the break with Rome in the early 1530s, the first systematic implementation of Protestant doctrine in the late 1540s, and Elizabeth's settlement in the late 1550s. Within this uncertainty, Henry VIII's reign posed a particular difficulty. As Burnet had shown in his *History of the Reformation*, considerable advances had been made by Protestantism under the second Tudor, without that being the monarch's intention.[25] Probably more important than these multiple possible origins, however, was nervousness about stirring tension between the diverse breeds of English Protestant. As has just been shown, religious dispute after the Restoration had a strong historical element. As has also just been suggested, Tudor church reform had been through a number of stages, of varying radicalism, and so might inspire a diverse spectrum of ecclesiastical positions. By the late Stuart era, a range of denominations, and of factions within the established church, looked back to different points in this complex history as the true birth of English godliness: so, given the potential for religious and political instability after James's fall, it was prudent for commentators to deploy vague dating formulas.[26] Of course this diluted the precision of a Reformation turning point. But as we shall see, it did not deny that a transformation had occurred, or soften the sense that history after this had been profoundly different.[27]

With the ground cleared, we can now explore the sort of material that constructed a Reformation period. One rich set of sources came from that first official marking of William's arrival—the thanksgiving called by the constitutional convention. The liturgy composed for the services on the day set the revolution in the context of the birth and subsequent preservation of English Protestantism. It offered glory to God 'for the blessed Reformation of this Church, in the days of our forefathers', and thanked the deity that he had 'ever since vouchsafed' it through 'the many wonderful Preservations, by which thou has manifested thy Fatherly Care of us'. It then incorporated recent events into this pattern by

---

[25] Burnet, *History of the reformation…first part.*

[26] For the historical disputes, see Claydon, *Europe*, 67–101.

[27] For more on dating the Reformation in late Stuart England, see Tony Claydon, 'The Reformation of the Future: Dating the Reformation in the Late Stuart Era', *Etudes-Episteme*, 25 (2017),https://journals.openedition.org/episteme/1831

expressing special gratitude for 'our late great and happy Deliverance, whereby we trust thou hast established to us all thy former Mercies'.[28] The official prayers thus conceptualized 1688–9 as the culmination of a clear period of history that had begun under the Tudors—though the language was fuzzy about when exactly this had begun. Preachers also fitted the revolution into a Protestant timeframe, which had had a transformative start (though they too were wary of giving a precise date). Most who spoke on the occasion assumed that church reform in the sixteenth century marked the start of an epoch of divine blessing for England that had just been spectacularly confirmed. So, speaking to his rural parish in Kent, Thomas Watts thought no nation had had such a remarkable run of providential salvation 'since our glorious Reformation'. John Tillotson (who was soon to be promoted archbishop of Canterbury) told his audience at Lincoln's Inn that God had just united and brought together all that he had done for England 'from the beginning of our Reformation'. Samuel Peck, minister of Poplar, similarly listed Catholic attempts to rebuild their evil 'Jericho' in England 'since our first Reformation', whilst a sermon to a country parish—said to be published without its preacher's knowledge, and intended to prove the geographical extent of the thanksgiving (right down to rural communities)—warned that England had been involved in a bitter struggle with popery 'ever since the Reformation, which is the Glory of our Land, first dawn'd and shone upon us'.[29]

This last work went on to detail some of the battle against Rome, and so underlined the particular nature of history since early Tudor times. This era, for the preacher, had been an epoch marked by papist attempts to extinguish the new light of the gospel. To show this, he narrated the persecutions under Mary Tudor, the plots and invasion attempts against Elizabeth, and the Catholic machinations in the Stuart age that had led to their final attempt to destroy godly Christianity under James II.[30] Other sermons arranged the past in the same way, even if they made less rhetorical effort to eulogize its start. So George Halley, giving the thanksgiving address at York Minster, rehearsed a litany of popish contrivances against godliness, strung out over the last 150-odd years. These included (in chronological, rather than performative, order) the Marian persecutions of the early 1550s, the 1572 massacre of the Huguenots in France, the 1588 invasion attempt by the Spanish Armada, the 1605 Gunpowder Plot, the 1641 Irish massacres, and the persecutions in France and Savoy since 1685.[31] At Poplar, Peck's

---

[28] *A form of prayer and thanksgiving to almighty God for having made…the prince of Orange the glorious instrument of this great deliverance* (1689).

[29] Thomas Watts, *A sermon preached upon Febr. the 14th being the day of thanksgiving* (1689), 18; John Tillotson, *A sermon preach'd at Lincoln's Inn Chappel, on the 31st of January, 1688* (1689), 30; *A sermon preach'd in a country church*, 8; Samuel Peck, *Jericho's downfall: in a sermon preached upon January 31 1688/9* (1689), 15–19.

[30] *A sermon preached in a country church*, 8–9.

[31] George Halley, *A sermon preached in the cathedral and metropolitical church of St Peter of York…fourteenth of February, 1688/9* (1689), 12–13, 17–18.

litany of popish horrors included the major designs of the Armada, the Gunpowder Plot, and James II, but there had been a number of 'smaller essays' that had filled the years between these highlights.[32] Gilbert Burnet, who spoke to the House of Commons, referred to the Marian persecutions, plots against Elizabeth, the Gunpowder Plot, and French Catholic ambitions in recent decades; and a work structured like a thanksgiving sermon, though probably not originally delivered as one, bundled together the cruelties meted out by Mary Tudor, the Armada, the 1605 plot, and alleged Catholic responsibility for the Great Fire of London in 1666.[33] The thanksgiving sermons for William's arrival thus established that a new era had begun in the early sixteenth century, and they identified its key and peculiar character. In particular, they deployed a canon of events since the Reformation that illustrated popish hostility to the gospel, and God's providential interventions to deliver it. These events both fitted into and defined a particular epoch, and they recruited the revolution as the latest part of the canon. This highly periodized vision was then disseminated through a range of genres to a wide variety of cultural milieu.

The most elite, and most substantial, medium was historical scholarship. In truth, and perhaps surprisingly, the revolution did not spark the craze for overarching histories of the Reformation that might have been expected if 1688–9 were being seen as part of an era inaugurated by Luther. But there were exceptions to, and possible explanations for, the lacuna. The explanations include the considerable work required to produce extensive histories to justify the revolution (as opposed to shorter forms, such as pamphlets or sermons, which could draw on the past quite as effectively) and also that very burst of interest in the sixteenth century that had marked the Restoration decades. Potential historians may have been dissuaded from going over ground that had been handled so extensively in recent years or duplicating volumes that were still generating active discussion. In particular, Gilbert Burnet's history had gained a reputation as a definitive study among mainstream Anglicans, and was still being debated by those outside that consensus, so others may have shied away from redoing his work.[34] As William Pudsey put it when excusing himself for skipping over ecclesiastical events in his 1698 account of Henry VIII's reign, 'there are particular Histories of the Reformation enow, and fresh in every one's Memory'.[35] Of the

---

[32] Peck, *Jericho's downfall*, 15–19.

[33] Burnet, *Sermon preached before the House of Commons*; *Rome's downfall: wherein is showed that the beginnings thereof call for praise and thanksgiving* (1689).

[34] Much of Burnet's immediate pre-revolution output had been concerned with defending his interpretation of the Reformation from criticism by others: see, for example, Gilbert Burnet, *Reflections on the relations of the English reformation* (1688); Gilbert Burnet, *A vindication of the ordinations of the church of England* (1688); Gilbert Burnet, *Reflections on Mr Varillas's history of the revolutions* (1686).

[35] William Pudsey, *A political essay, or summary review of the kings and government of England* (1698), 85.

exceptions, the most substantial and significant was that produced by Edmund Bohun. Bohun had been one of the earliest to write a narrative of the prince of Orange's invasion, but very shortly after producing this he revealed he had been working on a very much larger historical enterprise, and for some years. This had been to translate John Sleidan's sixteenth-century Latin account of the religious history of the Holy Roman Empire from 1517 to 1556 and then to extend the volume himself to the end of the Council of Trent in 1563. The result was a major piece of Reformation scholarship, printed only months after the change of regime.[36]

It was not only timing that tied Bohun's work to the revolution. The volume was dedicated to Queen Mary and claimed to be a response to recent political events. The author said he had laboured thorough Sleidan's very long work to comfort himself at a time when James's rule had put his reformed church in the most alarming 'degree of danger'. He had wanted to remind himself of God's work in promoting and protecting the Reformation in its early decades, as the movement faced its severe contemporary challenge. Since then, however, the change of regime in England had ended the threat from Rome. The 'late Wonderful Revolution' had brought Mary to England to be 'the Defender of our Holy Faith, and the deliverer of our oppressed church'. She was now free to fulfil her role as the 'chief Patroness of the Reformation', whose early story Bohun would relate.[37]

In this way, 1688–9 was fitted into a narrative begun in 1517, and the translation stressed what an extraordinary date that earlier year had been. Although the history itself plunged quite quickly into the dense details of Luther's actions, and although its original author had claimed to tell as impartial and accurate a tale as he could, Bohun included English versions of Sleidan's various forewords that left no doubt of the epochal significance of Luther's protest. No one, the dedication said, could view the story the book would tell with anything less than 'astonishment', 'admiration', and 'wonder'. One man, with a simple message, had transformed religion in large parts of Europe. Moreover, those alive at the beginning of the process could have predicted that something of overwhelming importance was happening, if they had had any awareness of the overall pattern of human history. For just when Luther launched his controversial career, Charles V was coming to inherit an empire more impressive than any European dominion since Charlemagne's. This should have alerted people to the possibility of transformation, because providence always concentrated power in one set of hands to prepare for great historical shifts. As Sleidan explained in Bohun's translation, 'God always raises up a great prince when the ecclesiastical or civil state is to be changed: as Cyrus, Alexander, Julius Caesar, Constantine, Charlemagne … [and]

---

[36] John Sleidan, *The general history of the reformation of the church from the errors and corruptions of the church of Rome*, trans. Edmund Bohun (1689), Bohun's epistle dedicatory.
[37] Ibid., Bohun's epistle.

now in our times last, CHARLES the V.'[38] The Habsburg dominance of Europe thus created a context for a revolution whose effects were compared to such things as the end of the Jews' Babylonian captivity; the Christianization of the Roman Empire; the transfer of imperial power to the successor kings of western Europe; and even (if this was what Sleidan meant by his reference to Caesar) the ministry of Jesus himself on earth. And Sleidan's description of what followed was close to Burnet's (appropriate, since Bohun quoted the Bishop of Salisbury's approval of Sleidan's skills as a historian immediately after the title page of his English version). For both scholars, and indeed for Bohun, too, since his continuation of the work to 1563 was in exactly Sleidan's vein, 1517 had introduced a new age of spiritual warfare.[39] History was now marked by the struggle for the gospel faith to survive in the face of great hostility.

Other works of historical scholarship underlined this periodization. One slightly curious piece appeared in two editions in 1692, advertising itself as an *Epitomy of ecclesiastical history*. In fact it was five short histories in one. First there was a potted version of Christ's life; then came an account of the early missions of the apostles; and then three collections of short biographies—of the primitive fathers, of the 'modern divines who carried on the glorious work of reformation', and of English monarchs since Henry VIII. This celebrated the revolution through the claim in its preface that the forces of Babylon had now been defeated in England, and, as its last two collections of biographies suggested, set this deliverance in the context of Protestant history. The narrative itself was rather scrappy. The biographies were brief and frequently got distracted by irrelevant trivia. However, the very fact that William and Mary's reign was placed at the end of a story begun by Henry VIII, and after a catalogue of Protestant heroes (which included founders of the movement such as Luther, Calvin, Bucer, and Beza), created a strong impression of a Reformation period, even without a remarkable pictorial frontispiece. This—closely following a common trope in Protestant iconography—was an allegory of the Reformation. Luther sat at the head of a table, surrounded by continental reformers,and by early English Protestants such as Tyndal, Latimer, and Cranmer. At the foot was a motley crew of papist monks and priests, who, despite their exerted puffing, complained that they could not extinguish the candle of the gospel that Luther had lit and placed in the centre of the picture.[40]

A second 1692 work, again a little odd, underlined this periodization. Produced by William Wake, it provided what its title advertised as *A brief history of several plots contrived, and rebellions raised by the papists...since the reformation*. This

---

³⁸ Ibid., Sleidan's original dedication.

³⁹ For the continuation, see Edmund Bohun, *A continuation of the history of the reformation to the end of the Council of Trent in 1563* (1689).

⁴⁰ J. S., *An epitomy of ecclesiastical history* (1692), frontispiece.

was not a cutting-edge work. It was arranged year-by-year, in the chronicle style that scholars of historiography, such as Daniel Woolf, have shown was going out of fashion by the end of the seventeenth century.[41] Nevertheless, it did much to reinforce the sense of a Protestant timeframe. It began its catalogue of Catholic crime in 1520, noting that this was 'about three years after Luther began to preach'.[42] It suggested that, whilst papists had long been corrupt, they had become far more vicious and untrustworthy since they had been busy trying to suppress reformed Christians—the period Wake described as 'these last hundred and fifty years'.[43] The list of events covered included the standard ones that established the character of the current era—plots against Elizabeth, the Bartholemew's Day massacre, the Armada, the Irish rebellion, and so on—but Wake rounded these out to show the continuity of papist treachery. The author found some instance of Catholicism undermining legitimate rule, fermenting rebellion, or conspiring to pervert royal courts for almost every date from 1520 through to James II's reign. In this way, he made clear that the canons of popish turpitude used in other sources were but the highlights of the continuous conspiracy to crush God's truth. The period of his title, '*since the reformation*', had a novel and horrifying unity that had infected its every moment.

These historical works were large and would have been expensive. Yet a vast range of other media took their chronological vision to a society far beyond elites. There is only space to consider a very limited sample in any detail here, but a huge quantity, and a great diversity, of material suggests the English public had already developed a strong sense of a Protestant era by the time the revolution occurred, and that when it did, it was incorporated into this periodization. One popular genre to promote the chronological culture was the almanac. These annual publications served a number of functions, but they were always based around a calendar for the year ahead which provided information about that forthcoming period. This usually centred on astronomical events, but could be supplemented by the dates of legal terms or fairs, guides to agricultural timings and meteorological forecasts, astrological prophecy, and a wider range of other stuff. Formatted as pocket reference works (they were printed in octavo, only a few inches in dimension), they were designed for frequent consultation, and were often intended to double as notebooks or diaries, with blank pages interleaved with the calendric tables. Many almanacs were also partisanly Protestant. These celebrated anniversaries that charted the struggle of the true faith against its papist foes (martyrdoms and massacres were popular), whilst short essays—inserted as prefaces to the entire work, or as monthly reflections or commentaries—denounced

---

[41] Woolf, *Reading History*, ch. 1.   [42] William Wake, *A brief history of several plots* (1692), 1.
[43] Wake, *Brief history*, epistle to reader.

the superstition, idolatry, avarice, or cruelty of papists. When almanacs had this confessional bias, they naturally reinforced the sense of a Protestant era.[44]

After 1688–9, a further feature of the genre integrated William's arrival into this pattern of history. Many of the works opened with a chronology of the world's, or of the British, past. Indeed, it has been suggested that this was the principle way ordinary people encountered numerical dates right through to the end of the eighteenth century.[45] This chronology placed significant events in a timeline that might provide a year for the occurrence, or, more frequently, stated how long it had been since it had taken place. Such items as '86 [years since] Queen Elizabeth dieth at Richmond', or '[Since] The conquest of Engl. by Duke William 615 years', were typical.[46] The kind of happenings celebrated in the chronological tables varied widely (from biblical stories to military conquests, fires, plagues, technological advances, and political intrigues), and they might range over the whole human past, or just recent centuries. For many, though, the start of the Reformation featured prominently. It was described by noting how long it had been since the first preaching of Luther against Rome, Henry VIII's break with the papal church, or the Elizabethan ecclesiastical settlement. Many also drew on the standard repertoire of key events in Protestant history familiar from the sermon literature (the Armada, the Gunpowder Treason, the Irish and Paris massacres), and some even incorporated other occurrences into their religious vision: for example, several noted the Great Fire of London in 1666, but described it as a plot by Jesuits to destroy the English capital. These had been standard features of the almanacs before the revolution, but when William arrived, his accession was smoothly integrated into the timeframe. 1688–9 was simply added at the end of the chronologies as the latest example of God's care of his people. For instance, for one almanac, 1690 was the one-hundred-and-seventy-fourth year since 'Martin Luther wrote against the pope', the one-hundred-and-thirty-first since 'Our deliverance from popery by Queen Elizabeth', the eighty-fifth since the 'The horrid design of the Gun-Powder Plot', and the second since 'Our Miraculous Deliverance from Popery by K. William'.[47] A product designed to enter into the quotidian life of its purchasers therefore confirmed that the revolution sat within a current age that had begun with the religious changes of the sixteenth century.[48]

An even more popular means of integrating the revolution into a Protestant epoch was the celebration of 5 November. Of course, this was not new in William's reign. For decades English people had marked the discovery of the Gunpowder

---

[44] For the almanac generally, see Bernard Capp, *Astrology and the Popular Press: English Almanacs 1500–1800* (Oxford: OUP, 1979).

[45] McConnel, 'The 1688 Landing of William III'.

[46] *Dove speculum anni, or, an almanac for the year of our lord God 1688* (1688), chronological table; William Gallen, *Gallen 1689: a complete pocket almanack for the year of our lord, 1689* (1689), 10.

[47] *The protestant almanack* (1690), chronological table.

[48] On the general tendency of these almanac timelines to periodize history, see Hannah Eagleston, 'The Texture of Time', *Renaissance and Reformation*, 32 (2009), 73–103, at 82–3.

Plot on its anniversary, in what had become a mass festival of England's Protestant character. Regular activities included lighting bonfires to burn effigies of Fawkes and the pope, the ringing of bells, the performance of Protestant puppet shows and civic ceremonies, fireworks, and the drinking to the damnation to the forces of Roman Catholic evil.[49] This had created a clear sense of a Reformation epoch at the popular level. Through such annual rituals, folk had linked their present day to a past moment of Protestant deliverance, and through yearly repetition of the festival, they had both celebrated and embodied a persisting Protestant cause. Popular memory recalled regular reiterations of a reformed identity, which had been possible because the faith had endured in England through generations.[50]

Gunpowder Day had also become part of a larger round of Protestant festivals. This structured the year into a cycle of confessional identity formation and broadened the popular sense of a Reformation history beyond the discovery of Fawkes' plot in 1605. After the 1660 Restoration, two new days of commemoration had been instigated: 30 January had been set up as public solemnity to remember the regicide of Charles I, and 29 May had been established as a thanksgiving for the return of monarchy in 1660. These events were now to be read as signs that God would protect Protestant monarchy, in spite of the Catholic plots that were held to have caused the civil war, the royal execution, and the English republic.[51] Some also marked 17 November as the anniversary of the succession of the great Protestant monarch, Elizabeth I, in 1558, and on 23 October people of Irish background remembered the outbreak of what they viewed as a massacre of Protestants in Ulster in 1641 to remind them of the threats facing the true faith.[52] The yearly round thus cemented the canon of key events that defined a particular Reformation period. Moreover, by William's reign, 5 November itself had gained additional levels of meaning. The anniversaries initiated in 1660 had incorporated the day into the official celebration of the restoration of the Protestant Stuart dynasty, but it had then become a point of mobilization against a possible Catholic heir. During the exclusion crisis of the late 1670s and early 1680s, 5 November had been a day to stage London's 'pope burning' processions. These had demanded the removal of the Catholic Duke of York from the royal succession by street

---

[49] Cressy, *Bonfires and Bells*, esp. 141–56; Walsham, *Providence*, 245–8. For the range of cultural practices surviving into the eighteenth century, see Colin Haydon, 'I love my King and my Country but a Roman catholic I hate: Anti-catholicism, Xenophobia and National Identity in Eighteenth Century England', in Tony Claydon and Ian McBride, eds, *Protestantism and National Identity: Britain and Ireland, 1650–1850* (Cambridge: CUP, 1998), 33–52.

[50] James Sharpe, *Remember, Remember the Fifth of November: Guy Fawkes and the Gunpowder Plot* (Cambridge, MA: Harvard UP, 2005), ch. 3.

[51] Cressy, *Bonfires and Bells*, 171–4.

[52] Cressy, *Bonfires and Bells*, 177–8; *The solemn mock procession…through the city of London, November ye 17th* (1679); *The solemn mock procession: or the trial and execution of the pope and his ministers, on Nov. the 17th at Temple Bar* (1680); T.C. Barnard, 'The Uses of 23 October 1641 and Irish Protestant Celebrations', *English Historical Review*, 106 (1991), 889–920; John Gibney, *The Shadow of a Year: The 1641 Rebellion in Irish History and Memory* (Madison: University of Wisconsin Press, 2013).

enactment of the horrors of Romish rule.[53] Later, under James, the day had been recognized as a point of possible resistance to the king and had been used as an opportunity for Protestant propaganda.[54] Thus, by 1688 repeated commemoration, and the memory of an adapting commemoration, ensured that the Gunpowder anniversary would recall a wide range of dates, scattered across, and defining, a Reformation period.

And then, in 1688, it gained yet another resonance, rapidly exploited by the revolutionary regime. By accident, or quite possibly design (there is some evidence this had been planned on board the Dutch invasion fleet), 5 November was the date on which William landed in England.[55] The day thus became a moment of renewed deliverance for Protestant England: probably immediately in popular consciousness, and certainly by the time the official meaning of Gunpowder Day festivities was altered for the first anniversary of William's disembarkation. From 5 November 1689, the day was to mark the dual providences of James I's rescue from Catholic plotters and the whole nation's rescue from his popish grandson. This, of course, incorporated the revolution into the Protestant epoch already constructed by the annual celebrations: those charged with explaining the revolution on the day did so by stressing that incorporation.

As with the 1689 January thanksgiving, the liturgy led the way. As Thomas Comber was to stress in his 1696 reflections on 5 November form of prayers, these had been adapted after the revolution to stress that 'now God hath made this day such [a double festival] to this Reformed Church, by two eminent Deliverances from utter Ruin.'[56] The prayers first appointed in 1689 repeatedly linked the two salvations of Protestantism, and so situated them within a period of history marked by particular divine care towards England. God, they claimed, had given a 'fresh instance of…loving kindness', had shown 'repeated goodness', and had 'filled our hearts again with Joy and Gladness'.[57] Sermons on 5 November in William's reign followed this up. Though these, inevitably, highlighted the events of 1605 and 1688, they argued that these deliverances were just a subset of God's attention to his true church since the sixteenth century. Some were explicit about a Tudor turning point. Thomas Knaggs, speaking to the Corporation of London, said the plots defeated on the 5 November typified Catholic attempts to 'ruinate'

---

[53] Cressy, *Bonfires and Bells*, 179–84; *The manner of burning the pope in effigies in London on the 5th of November, 1678* (1678); Sheila Williams, 'The Pope-Burning Processions of 1679, 1680, and 1681', *Journal of the Warburg and Courtauld Institutes*, 21 (1958), 104–18.

[54] The more popular elements of celebration had been suppressed by the government in fear of sedition: *At the court at Whitehall, the sixth day of November, 1685* (1685); and some had used 5 November sermons to advance the case against Catholicism, despite royal pressure not to—Edward Pelling, or his publisher, reprinted a 1681 piece, Edward Pelling, *The true mark of the beast* (1685). See also, Cressy, *Bonfires and Bells*, 184–5; Hutton, *Rise and Fall*, 255–6.

[55] Gilbert Burnet, *Bishop Burnet's history of his own time: volume* 1 (1724), 787–8.

[56] Thomas Comber, *A discourse of the offices for the Vth of November, XXXth of January and XXIXth of May* (1696), 2.

[57] *A form of prayer and thanksgiving to be used yearly on the fifth of November* (1690).

the Reformation 'ever since the stretched-out Arms of Almighty God deliver'd our Church and State from the Egyptian Darkness, and Tyrannous Yoke of Popish Superstition'.[58] William Talbot, preaching to William himself, said the day celebrated the preservations of godly faith, but also the 'raising up our holy Reformers, who cast off that insupportable Yoke…the tyranny of the Bishop of Rome', and Simon Patrick, addressing the House of Lords, said the two dates were a divine deliverance of a 'Reformation [that] itself was at first Effected by the extraordinary Providence of God'.[59] Other preachers focused less on the start of the Protestant era, but continued to package events since the sixteenth century as a unity. In 1689, on the first occasion 5 November marked the revolution as well as the Gunpowder Plot, Gilbert Burnet ran through a standard list of Protestant highlights as he addressed the House of Lords. He demonstrated the hand of God in the blessings of Elizabeth's reign, the defeat of the Armada, the Irish rebellion of 1641, and the 1660 restoration of monarchy, as well as the occurrences of 1605 and 1688.[60] Many others followed this familiar cannon of Reformation history, and some extended the range of example to continental Protestants. The 1572 massacre of the Huguenots in Paris was particularly popular—probably because it allowed a lurid imagining of what would have happened in England, had either Guy Fawkes, or James II, won through—though others mentioned such events as the suppression of Bohemian reform in the early years of the Thirty Years War.[61]

There is room to debate how far this official presentation of the revolution's place with a Protestant era altered wider understandings of 5 November. On one hand, sermons were supposed to be preached every year in every church in the land, and the dating coincidence of the two deliverances was striking, being noted from the very first. By the time the first printed accounts of William's expedition were being produced in December 1688, an author could note that the prince landed on 'a Day never to be blotted out of the Englishman's heart', and even before the prince of Orange had been offered the crown, Burnet would tell the House of Commons that the Lord had 'enobled' and 'enriched' the fifth day of November with a 'Second Blessing'.[62] On the other hand, it seems commemoration

---

[58] Thomas Knaggs, *A sermon preached before the right honourable lord mayor and court of aldermen at Bow-Church on Sunday, November the fifth 1693* (1693), 1.

[59] William Talbot, *The spirit of popery tried…a sermon preached before the king at Whitehall upon the fifth of November* (1699), 14; Simon Patrick, *A sermon preached before the Lords spiritual and temporal…on the fifth of November* (1696), 29.

[60] Gilbert Burnet, *A sermon preached before the house of peers in the abbey of Westminster, on the 5th of November* (1689), 4.

[61] Benjamin Jenks, *A thanksgiving sermon preach'd upon the fifth of November* (1689), p. 1.; John Sharp, *A sermon preached before the Lords spiritual and temporal…on the fifth of November* (1691), 22–3; William Fleetwood, *A sermon preached before the honourable House of Commons at St Margaret's Westminster…the 5th of November* (1691), 17–19; Richard White, *The church's security in the midst of all difficulties and dangers* (1694), 9–11.

[62] *The expedition of his highness the prince of Orange for England* (1688), 5; Burnet, *Sermon preached before the House of Commons*, 34

of 1688–9 rapidly disappeared into the far more established rituals marking 1605. Beyond occasional pulpit mentions of William's service for the nation, it is hard to detect much new Orange flavour to Gunpowder Day shenanigans beyond the first couple of years after the revolution, and the festivities may not, in fact, have occurred in every community in the land.[63] Whatever the true state of popular consciousness, though, it is hard to imagine that the fall of James did not take its place in the range of historical associations elicited by this late-autumn holiday in the English mind. When, in 1709, Henry Sacheverell appeared to preach against the political and ecclesiastical principles many thought had been established at the revolution, it was particularly shocking that he did so in a 5 November sermon.[64] The error that led to a state trial was at least partly a sin against the proper meaning of Gunpowder Day, as it had been adapted since 1688–9.

The point that the last century and a half was packaged as a peculiar Protestant era in the aftermath of the William's invasion risks becoming laboured. It was contained in a wide range of literary genres and cultural forms, but it would be tedious to survey them all in any detail. The notion of a turning point in the sixteenth century, and of special period since that break, were notable, for example, in the widespread sense that William had defeated a specifically Jesuit conspiracy against England.[65] This focused on the role of James II's Jesuit advisors, especially Father Edward Petre, but the emphasis on the Society of Jesus presented its plot as the latest example of what an English tradition of anti-Jesuit works had constructed as sustained effort to destroy Protestantism by an evil group set up in the sixteenth century in direct and hostile response to Luther.[66] The chronology was also clear in poetic response to the revolution. Much of the verse and ballad material was of poor literary quality and contained little sophisticated ideology (in fact most of it simply gloated at the fall of stalwarts of the old regime).[67] Nevertheless, many of the stock images of evil (hoards of relic-touting and avaricious monks, for example), suggested that the displaced king had tried to reinstate a world before the sixteenth-century reforms (which saw a turning point

<hr>

[63] For partial celebration of 5 November, see McConnel, 'The 1688 Landing of William III'; and Hutton, *Rise and Fall*, 257. The submergence of the Williamite element in Gunpowder celebrations was part of a wider, rapid, forgetting of the king's role in the revolution: see the 'Death, Character and Reputation' section of Tony Claydon, 'William III and II (1650–1702)', *Oxford Dictionary of National Biography*, Oxford University Press, 2004; online edn, May 2008, https://doi.org/10.1093/ref:odnb/29450.

[64] See Geoffrey Holmes, *The trial of Dr Sacheverell* (London: Eyre Methuen, 1973), 64.

[65] As in such works as *The Jesuit's exaltation* (1688); *The Jesuit in the pound* (1688); *The Jesuit unmask'd* (1689); *Three letters: 1. A letter from a Jesuit* (1689); *Great news from Bristol, being a true account of the apprehending of old father Petre, the Jesuit* (1689); *The Jesuit's memorial for the intended reformation of England* (1690).

[66] Material from Charles II's reign that had a strong sense of a persistence of Jesuit plotting since the society's foundation included: *The cabal of several notorious priests and Jesuits discovered* (1679); *A true narrative of the inhumane positions and practices of the Jesuits* (1680); *Pyrotechnica Loyolana: Ignatian fire-works or the fiery Jesuits temper and behaviour* (1667).

[67] Such pieces dominate two large collections of the material published in the immediate aftermath of the revolution: *Muses farewell*, and *A supplement to the muses farewell to popery and slavery* (1690).

in Tudor era, if it was blind to more sophisticated thinking about how Catholicism might have changed with the Counter-Reformation and confessionalization), and some works were more explicit about dating.[68] A verse entitled 'A sale of old household stuff' presented James dispensing with a 'Reformation / brought in by *Henry the Eighth* / and *Besses* grave Convocation', as well as flogging memorabilia of the Protestant historical canon—the tapestries in the House of Lords celebrating the defeat of the Armada and the discovery of the Gunpowder Plot.[69] Similarly Thomas Shadwell, in a congratulatory poem to William, talked of the restoration of a golden age, first established when 'our wise reformers' swept away popish tyranny and superstition; whilst another anonymous verse had priests surveying England to reverse Henry VIII's sale of monastic lands.[70] A Protestant era also impinged on popular visual culture. In 1689, a new edition appeared of Samuel Ward's cheap print from the early seventeenth century that had depicted God's deliverance of England from a popish conspiracy manifested in the Armada and Fawkes treason. Those behind this initiative clearly hoped the revolution had created a market for past defeats of popery.[71] One could go on through multiple media without unveiling radical new dimensions of chronology.

One final genre is, however, worth considering in a little more depth. This was the material generated by the allegiance controversy. This was not only because the sense of a Protestant epoch in this stuff had a somewhat different emphasis, but also because constitutional writing could suggest that the Protestant era was even more profoundly unlike what had come before than was suggested in other sources. Although Williamite works insisting on the legality of 1688–9 were dominated by versions of an ancient constitution, some also had a strong sense of the Protestant epoch. They stressed Henry VIII's eradication of the pope's judicial authority in England, presenting this as the establishment of England's true independence (as a speaker in the convention put it, Henry was 'the first Prince that totally shook off the Pope's power'), and they presented the period as a continuous defence of this autonomy, which had now culminated in William's eradication of papal influence in government.[72] Such commentary produced a Protestant constitutional era to run in parallel with the ecclesiological one. Popery had not only struggled to extirpate true faith over the past sixteen decades, it had tried to destroy England's imperial monarchy, and the liberties of its subjects.

Significantly, this dimension of the defence of William's right to the throne generated a sense of historical context, even of anachronism, that had been missing from almost all the rest of the legal debate. In fact, it was clearer than in

---

[68] For example, 'A new song on the calling of a free parliament', and 'A new song to the tune of *Couragio*', in *Supplement to the muses farewell*, 126 (wrongly paginated 204), 131.

[69] 'A sale of household stuff', in *Supplement to the muses farewell*, 107–10.

[70] Thomas Shadwell, 'A congratulatory poem on his highness the prince of Orange, his coming to England', in *Supplement to the muses farewell*, 215; 'The explanation', in *Muses farewell*, 119.

[71] *The popish powder treason* (1689).   [72] Grey, *Debates*, xi, 29.

theological works. The times since the break with Rome not only had a new historical narrative for constitutional thinkers, but that narrative had created contexts so different that it had changed the meaning of events and of people's actions. For example, the new and particular circumstances of the Protestant era affected understanding of political duty. Very soon after William had been declared king, it became clear that the oaths of allegiance to him were going to be stumbling blocks, as people considered if they could transfer loyalty to the new ruler. Many, particularly the non-juring clergy, objected that they could not swear to obey the new monarch, given they had already promised their fealty to James. Pamphleteers, however, tried to counter such scruples by explaining that one must understand the oaths of allegiance in the context of their post-Reformation times. Oaths had been introduced by Elizabeth and James I, not to tie subjects to monarchs no matter how they behaved, but as part of the ongoing struggle against Rome's political ambition. Their purpose was to exclude the pope's authority from England by securing people's loyalty to their domestic ruler. It was, therefore, inappropriate to use the oaths to support a king who had wanted to reintroduce Rome's yoke.[73] In a similar way, constitutional pamphleteers who discussed the crimes of bad monarchs from history made a distinction between examples from before and after the Reformation. Kings of the Middle Ages—whatever their other faults—were not criticized for their Romish religion. Everyone recognized that figures such as Richard II or Edward II had had no Protestant alternative to their Catholic faith. Yet James II and Mary Tudor were both castigated for popery as part of the legal case against them.[74] Their religious adherence was incorporated into the analysis of their threat to an English constitution that—by the time they ruled—had become not only free, but also essentially Protestant. In both these cases, the discontinuity of the break with Rome had created two very distinct eras. They were in fact so different that the events within them must be interpreted within contexts that were acknowledged to have transformed the lessons that should be drawn: once again the continuing vigour of religious assumptions in political debate melted the frozen chronology of legal and constitutional discussion.

To conclude this section: setting 1688–9 in a Reformation context produced a periodized view of the past. The practice assumed that a new era had begun with a transformation in the sixteenth century (whatever the—perhaps deliberate—haziness in dating this turning point for England). It mapped a new pattern of history since that origin: the narrative now centred on the defence of godly reform and a Protestant nation from papist attack. It even began to suggest that

---

[73] See, for example, *The present case stated*; *Some considerations touching succession and allegiance* (1689); [Long], *Resolution*, 10.

[74] Attacks on James were, of course, ubiquitous; for attacks on Mary, see *Popish treaties not to be rely'd on* (1688).

circumstances had become so different after the Reformation that parallels could no longer be drawn directly over that discontinuity. The precise legal case for this put in some allegiance controversy pamphlets was a subset of the wider impression that living after Luther's protest was a wholly different experience from the lives of folk before. People of the Protestant era faced new threats, they had new duties and rights, and they had a new understanding of their relationship with God.

But the Reformation context for 1688–9 periodized the past at a second, somewhat finer level. It drew the revolution into an existing sense that the Protestant era had had an internal history, with sub-periods within the overall reformed epoch, and this, of course, enhanced the impression of time flowing from one set of circumstances to the next. Again, Burnet's 1690 sermon to the queen can start the illustration. His introduction to his account of Protestantism exemplified one of the commonest divisions perceived within the history of the Reformation—namely the distinction between an early period, when the faith had done well, and a more recent block of time in which it had got into severe trouble. As Burnet put it, 'Upon the first opening of the Reformation, all the World ran into it. The Corruptions and Ignorance of Popery were things of Which all Men were so weary, that they with Joy welcomed the Light and Purity of the Gospel'. After a while, however, the hypocrisy and greed of many of those who had joined the new movement began to tell. As a result, 'God punished them severely'. Protestant strength melted away, and a series of trials began, some of which came close to destroying the faith. 1688–9 was understood within this context. It was because things had been going so badly that William's providential rescue of the cause had been needed, and was why people must continue to support the struggle for the true faith that his war against Louis represented.[75]

It is worth making two points about Burnet's sense of a fundamental turning point within the Protestant past in his Chapel Royal sermon. First, of course, it was firmly based in reality. It was simply the case that Protestantism had spread extraordinarily rapidly in its early decades, but that it had later got into difficulty. Its Catholic opponents had begun to find strategies which slowed its advance from around the middle of the sixteenth century, and then the movement had begun to retreat in seventeenth.[76] Second, Burnet's dating of the end of the first era of the Reformation was earlier in his 1690 sermon than he usually placed it. Preaching to the queen, he suggested the times of trial had begun in the early 1550s when Charles V had been (at least temporarily) triumphant in Germany at the head of his Catholic forces. Yet in the substantial number of other works

<hr>

[75] G. Burnet, *Sermon…16th day of July*, 24.

[76] For the impact on English politics of this decline, see Jonathan Scott, *England's Troubles: Seventeenth-Century English Political Instability in European Context* (Cambridge: CUP, 2000), 27–33 and *passim*.

where Burnet discussed the unfolding fortunes of the true faith, he tended to place the turning point around 1600. This produced a neat pattern of sixteenth century advance, followed by seventeenth century failure, which was widely apparent in reactions to the revolution.

In fact, it was Burnet himself who did much to popularize the notion that the Reformation had been the proverbial game of two halves. Much of his writing before 1688–9 had suggested that something had gone wrong for the true church in the seventeenth century, but he was to state this explicitly in one of the earliest pieces of propaganda he produced for William in England.[77] Preaching to the prince a few days after Dutch forces had arrived in London, Burnet suggested this triumph might reverse the lamentable pattern of recent history. In the last 'age' (the contemporary term for century), God had set up the 'glorious work' of reformation. Now in this current age, the true faith had been brought 'low', and even risked final suppression.[78] The vision was even clearer in the work Burnet published in 1692 to propose a new agenda for the Church of England after 1688–9. His hugely influential *Discourse of the pastoral care* charted a new approach for clerics. It suggested that the revolution, and the associated Toleration Act, now called for moral example, for Christian instruction, and for parochial leadership— rather than legal coercion—to hold on to the population. Yet the problem the *Discourse* sought to address was a specifically seventeenth-century one. Protestants had come to depend on the law because they had lost their original purity and zeal. As a result, a Reformation that had enjoyed extraordinary success in its first century was 'in this present age…not only at a stand, but going back'.[79]

This 'contrasting-centuries' model of a Protestant past was most explicit in Burnet's work, but, as the famous historian of the Reformation, he was an important and respected interpreter of the last century and a half, and he was not alone. A good deal of commentary on the revolution saw it as a chance to reverse a religious decline that had started with the Stuart dynasty around the turn of the sixteenth century. In particular, such reaction glorified the reign of Elizabeth as an age of Protestant energy that had subsequently been lost to popish infiltration and corruption. Here is not the place to examine the discourse in detail. It combined with complaints about the court's political mistakes since 1603 to create a distinct 'Stuart age', which will be a subject of a later chapter.[80] To give just one flavour, though: the convention debates of early 1689 might have steered clear of using seventeenth-century precedents to discuss legal and constitutional matters, but in the realm of religion, speakers were prepared to denounce a popish influence in England that had been increasing over recent decades. In the debate in the lower House on 29 January that ended in the resolution that England could

<hr>

77 See Claydon, 'Latitudinarianism', esp. 586–7.
78 G. Burnet, *A sermon preached in the chappel of St James*, p. 5.
79 Gilbert Burnet, *A discourse of the pastoral care* (1692), 9.   80 See below, ch. 5.

not, in future, be governed by a popish prince, Colonel John Birch claimed the nation had had to struggle to save its faith for some time, and cited instances of the problem scattered across the Stuart age. James I had been so fond of the idea of marrying his son to a Catholic that English foreign policy had been neutered and the Palatine had been lost to the Protestant cause. Charles I had married a Catholic and 'all things, from that time forward…tended to Popery, and a Civil War'. When Charles II had allowed his brother James to marry a papist, many had predicted a new campaign to destroy the Protestant religion, and Birch asserted this would have happened if God not intervened by sending the Dutch. All of this created the impression of a great era of trouble for the true faith since 1600: a period when 'we have been scrambling for our Religion, and have saved but little of it'.[81]

More widely, the idea that Protestantism had done well for a season, but had then suffered a dramatic reverse, was implicit in the frequently expressed sense that the faith was facing an existential crisis by 1688–9. Much of the relief that was expressed that William had won the English throne centred on the fact that he had secured one of the last bulwarks of the Reformation, after so many others across the European continent had been swept away, and many saw the revolution as a chance, indeed a divine demand, for the cause to rally and correct the reversals of recent decades. To go back to the convention debates: many members urged a quick resolution of the constitutional crisis, and one that left William in charge, because they thought the very survival of the European Reformation was in the balance. As early as 22 January, Henry Capel stressed that the fate of all the Continent's reformed churches depended on English deliberations and that foreigners were waiting uneasily 'till they hear how we proceed'. In the main debate that ended with the lower House's resolution that the throne was vacant, members emphasized that—even as they talked—the last acts of European Protestantism might be being played out. Louis XIV had been striking down the Reformation in the territories he conquered; Ireland had again fallen into the hand of a Catholic rebellion; and there was 'no Popish prince in Europe, but would destroy all Protestants' as they had already done in France and the Habsburg lands.[82]

The same pessimism was evident beyond the Westminster debating chambers. As one would expect, fasts for the war against France treated both the revolution and the conflict that it had led to as signs that God was at last allowing some succour for a cause that had nearly been lost. The liturgies for these occasions included a revived prayer for foreign reformed churches that stressed their 'sad

---

[81] Grey, *Debates*, xi, 26 (note, Birch was actually reported saying the scrambling had lasted 'these forty years', but this was not consistent with the examples he then cited to illustrate the principle. He must have misspoken, or been misrecorded).

[82] Grey, *Debates*, xi, 6–25, quote at 12.

and mournful state' and their suffering under 'superstitious and merciless men', and then implored heaven to come to the aid of those who were now 'Sheep appointed to the Slaughter'.[83] Preachers piled on the agony. They described the 'Whips, and Gibbets, and Racks', the 'Blood, Fire, and Destruction', that currently faced Protestants abroad; they pointed out that England had only narrowly avoided the fate of true churches in Germany, France, the Netherlands, Ireland, and Savoy; and they explained that all reformed Christians looked to William's realm as the last great 'bulwark and support' for their cause.[84] They were also clear this was no merely recent problem. The accounts of suffering took in Louis' steady increase in pressure on his French Protestant subjects, and examples from his wars spread over decades, leading Gilbert Burnet to observe that the cruelties had gone on for 'twenty Years, with very little interruption'.[85] All this suggested an unfolding tragedy very different from the first epochs of Protestantism, and at least one preacher drew an explicit contrast between the sixteenth and seventeenth centuries. Speaking to the House of Commons on the first fast day for the war, Thomas Tenison painted Louis as the epitome of popish cruelty, against whom the English had been engaged by William in 'the Evangelical Cause'. Yet to win that fight, they needed to rediscover the zeal of their Elizabethan forebears. The challenge now was to bring 'again the Spirit of our Illustrious Ancestors, which appeared gloriously in former days, and particularly in the reign of that Excellent Princess, who settled our Reformation'.[86]

Secular propaganda joined this chorus. Although there was plenty of room for geopolitical explanations of the war that presented France as a potential 'universal monarch' and called on all other nations—of whatever faith—to unite against her to preserve a balance of power, pamphlets that urged support for William's cause mixed this with a strong sense of confessional crisis that had brought the Reformation to the point of ruin.[87] Part of this effort was contained in simple histories of the persecutions in Europe over the last years. There was a burst of these from 1689, both because they provided a context for the conflict England was now conducting, and because a Protestant government no longer used censorship to discourage such publications.[88] Pamphlets, tracts, broadsides, and

---

[83] 'A prayer for all the reformed churches', in *A form of prayer to be used the fifth day of June* (1689); 'A prayer for all the reformed churches', in *A form of prayer to be used on Wednesday the twelfth day of March* (1690).

[84] Simon Patrick, *A sermon preached before the king and queen at Whitehall, April 16, 1690* (1690), 28; William Talbot, *A sermon preached at the cathedral church of Worcester… September 16, 1691* (1691), 23; Gilbert Burnet, *Some sermons preached on several occasions* (1713), 39–40; John Tillotson, *A sermon preached at St Mary le Bow… Wed 18th June, 1689* (1689), 23.

[85] Gilbert Burnet, *A sermon preach'd at Whitehall before the king and queen on 29th April, 1691* (1691), 24.

[86] Thomas Tenison, *A sermon against self love… 5 June 1689* (1689), 22–3.

[87] For the mixture of these rhetorics, see Claydon, *Europe*, 152–92.

[88] For example, Jacques Pineton de Chambrun, *The history of the persecutions of the protestants by the French king* (1689); *The French king's decree against protestants* (1689); *The pastoral letters of the*

printed speeches also wove the decline of the Reformation into their rhetoric. An early piece, preparing the ground for war, created a sense of urgency as it printed a parliamentary address to William, promising to support his international alliances. It asserted that his expedition to England had been absolutely necessary to uphold the Protestant interest in Europe and that resistance to his enemies was now essential to prevent their unfolding 'extirpation' of the faith.[89] In the same vein, William Lloyd, outlining theories of just war in 1691, said conflicts to protect co-religionists elsewhere were legitimate, and he underlined this by suggesting Louis' attacks on Protestantism exceeded heathen cruelty and were expanding from his own subjects to those of neighbouring princes.[90] Adding to the gloom in 1689 and 1690, reports and histories arrived from Ireland, detailing such privations for Protestants as the sufferings of the besieged population of Derry and the exile of reformed Christians terrified of Tyrconnel's popish government, which was in rebellion against the London regime.[91] The horror came in pictures as well in words. The frontispiece to *The most Christian Turk*, a catalogue of Louis' crimes, showed him triumphant and attended by a Jesuit priest, as a town that had opposed him was burnt in the background and its inhabitants cruelly slaughtered (Fig. 3.1).[92] All this created a sense of pressing crisis very different from the miraculous expansion of Luther's movement, or the security of Elizabeth's Protestant polity. Whilst not all visions had the grand sweep and dating neatness of Burnet's work, there was a general sense that the Reformation had had a periodized internal history of progress and then retreat.

There was one final, and rather more hopeful, element of periodization within the Protestant framing of the revolution that was again exemplified in Burnet's 1690 sermon. This was the belief that William's arrival might represent such a significant triumph for the Reformation that it would mark a new turning point and so inaugurate a whole new era. Many dreamed that 1688–9 would secure the future of the faith, reverse the pattern of recent decline, and offer an opportunity for the reformed churches to attain spiritual perfection under their new patron, the prince of Orange. In Burnet's address, the excitement was palpable. William's achievements and destiny were described in such glowing terms that there could be little doubt he was an instrument of God, with a far more than ordinary role in the narrative of the true religion. It seemed clear to the preacher that 'Angels

incomparable *Jurieu* (1689): Richard Strutton, *A true relation of the cruelties and barbarities of the French king* (1690). There had been a similar burst of publications during the lapse of censorship in the exclusion crisis.

---

[89] *The address of the Lords spiritual and temporal, and Commons assembled in Parliament…5 March, 1688* (1688): for the original address see *Commons Journals* x: 40–1; *Lords Journals* xiv: 139.

[90] Lloyd, *Discourse of God's ways*, 38–9.

[91] For example, from a large selection of material, George Walker, *A true account of the siege of London-derry* (1689); George Walker, *The substance of a sermon, being an incouragement to protestants* (1689); William King, *A sermon preached at St Patrick's church, Dublin, on the 16th Novemb.1690* (1690).

[92] *The most Christian Turk, or a view of the life and bloody reign of Lewis XIV* (1690), frontispiece.

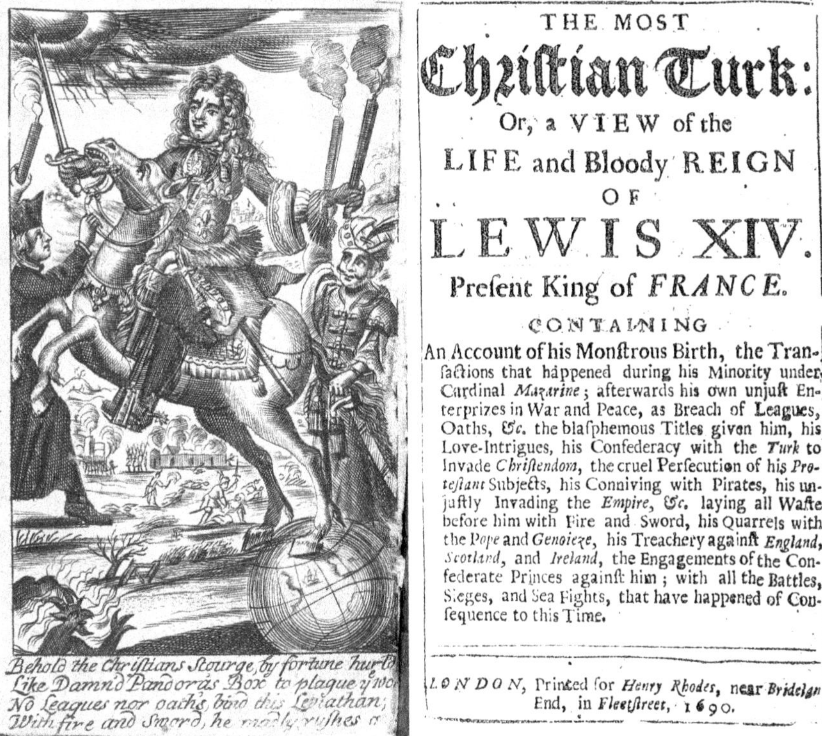

THE MOST

Chꝛiſtian Turk:

Or, a VIEW of the
LIFE and Bloody REIGN
OF
LEWIS XIV.
Preſent King of *FRANCE*.

CONTAINING

An Account of his Monſtrous Birth, the Tranſ-
factions that happened during his Minority under
Cardinal *Mazarine*; afterwards his own unjuſt En-
terprizes in War and Peace, as Breach of Leagues,
Oaths, *&c.* the blaſphemous Titles given him, his
Love-Intrigues, his Confederacy with the *Turk* to
Invade *Chriſtendom*, the cruel Perſecution of his *Pro-
teſtant* Subjects, his Conniving with Pirates, his un-
juſtly Invading the *Empire*, *&c.* laying all Waſte
before him with Fire and Sword, his Quarrels with
the *Pope* and *Genoieze*, his Treachery againſt *England*,
Scotland, and *Ireland*, the Engagements of the Con-
federate Princes againſt him; with all the Battles,
Sieges, and Sea Fights, that have happened of Con-
ſequence to this Time.

LONDON, Printed for *Henry Rhodes*, near Bridelan
End, in *Fleetſtreet*, 1690.

Fig. 3.1 Frontispiece to *The most Christian Turk, or a view of the life and bloody reign of Lewis XIV* (1690). By kind permission of The Bodleian Libraries, The University of Oxford: Douce BB 538.

watch over' William, that his 'Scene of Success' was not complete, and that soon not only England, but all Europe would 'by his Means' be delivered.[93] Protestants might be more than safe under the new king of England, however. They had also been provided with an opportunity to reinvigorate their movement. As the closing passages of the sermon made clear, Burnet's audience must respond to their deliverance with efforts to live a godly and Protestant life: if they did so, a whole new chapter in history might begin—a chapter in which, he hinted, the final defeat of the evils of popery might be achieved.[94]

Many other preachers echoed Burnet's sentiments in the years after 1688–9, and we shall examine some of their addresses when analysing apocalyptic below. Yet excitement about the future spilled beyond the pulpit into an eclectic range of material. It was perhaps poetic convention that drove versifiers such as John Dennis to predict a new 'Golden Age' after William's salvation of the country

---

[93] G. Burnet, *Sermon … 16th day of July*, 29.   [94] Ibid.

from the 'Tyranny of Hell and Rome', but similar predictions also marked prose panegyrics of the new ruler.[95] Two biographies, published in 1689 to introduce the new monarch to his English subjects, related his work defending the European Reformation before he invaded England, and suggested strongly that his destiny lay in his finally destroying the scourges of popery.[96] As the preface of one of them stated: 'it cannot be thought that the progress of so great a Prince's fame can ever make a halt', and that heaven still had much in reserve to immortalize his story.[97] Similarly, the most enthusiastic supporters of the new monarch in the allegiance controversy could spill over into highly optimistic language. Announcing his lifelong devotion to William in a pamphlet published three months after the revolution, Daniel Defoe saw the prince of Orange's arrival as—at least potentially—an invitation to a promised land for the English.[98] Musical material also thought 1689 was a new beginning. Excitement was clear in two odes by the poet Thomas Shadwell that he had penned to celebrate the royal couple's birthdays in their first years in England, and which he intended to become the lyrics of musical performance (the one for Mary did actually achieve a fine setting by Henry Purcell). Shadwell's gift to William suggested a future European paradise, brought about by his efforts to deliver the continent from Louis XIV's popish tyranny.[99] His verse for the queen suggested she would soon come to outshine the existing star of the English Reformation: 'No more shall we the great Eliza boast / For her great name in greater Mary's will be lost'.[100] Summing the mood of so much of this material, Guy Miege prefaced his otherwise prosaic description of the geography and political structures of England (intended as a reference work) with an introduction that suggested the whole nation had been transformed by William's defeat of popery. He explained the title of the work in its opening sentence: 'tis the late *Revolution* that has given birth to this Piece of Work; a New Face of Things required a *New State of England*'.[101]

One more-focused set of material that presented the revolution as the dawn of a new Protestant age was the stuff produced by the movement for the reformation of manners. This has been extensively covered by scholars—starting with Dudley Bahlmann's suggestively entitled *Moral Revolution of 1688*—and it consisted of coordinated efforts through William's reign to improve the behaviour of Englishmen.[102] Clergy discouraged vice through pulpit exhortation, pastoral care,

---

[95] John Dennis, *An ode upon the glorious and successful expedition of his highness the prince of Orange* (1689), 5, 7.

[96] *An historical account of the memorable actions of the most glorious monarch, William III* (1689); *The history of the most illustrious William, prince of Orange* (1688).

[97] *History of the most illustrious William*, epistle dedicatory.   [98] [Defoe], *Reflections*, 1–2.

[99] Thomas Shadwell, *Ode on the anniversary of the king's birth* (1690), 2–3.

[100] Thomas Shadwell, 'Now does the glorious day appear', in *Supplement to the muses farewell*, 223.

[101] G[uy] M[iege], *The new state of England under their majesties K.William and Q.Mary* (1691), epistle to the reader.

[102] Dudley W.R. Bahlmann, *The Moral Revolution of 1688* (New Haven: Yale UP, 1957).

and diocesan visitation; the monarchy joined in with proclamations against common sins and self-consciously virtuous example at court; and laymen founded Societies for the Reformation of Manners—voluntary bodies dedicated to bringing adulterers, Sunday traders, profane swearers, drunks, and sex workers before the magistrate. The political, cultural, and social meaning of the movement was varied, and has been debated, but very much of it claimed to be a response to 1688–9.[103] For the reformers, the revolution had given England a second chance. Such a providential deliverance allowed, indeed demanded, action by good Protestants to remove the blemishes that had encouraged the spread of popery, or had provoked God to punish the nation by Catholicism's advance.

Manifestations of the reformation of manners movement, and its sense of the revolution as a moment charged with the possibilities of renewal, ranged through a variety of media. Sermons, as so often, led the way. The societies commissioned a series for annual meetings from the late 1690s, but moral reform had been the concluding theme of almost every fast or thanksgiving performance from the start of William's reign—rhetoric that presented the king's accession as the starting gun for a dual campaign against popish persecutors abroad and popish vice at home.[104] Other genres concurred. Two early broadsides encouraging religious and moral renewal suggested that 1688–9 had been the crucial date. One described the first lay initiative for reformation of manners (a push against bawdy houses in Tower Hamlets) as having been inspired by William's letter to Bishop Compton of London on the first anniversary of his acceptance of the throne, telling him to lead the church in a crusade for godly behaviour.[105] The other encouraged all people, and clerics especially, to get behind 'this glorious day of a reformation, begun by their present majesties, William and Mary' (and presented its text below a picture of the royal couple, crowned and enthroned).[106] Longer tracts too carried the message. Burnet's *Pastoral Care* put the encouragement of godly behaviour in parishes at the heart of its instructions to clergy and made clear, in its preface, that the revolution had created the space for this initiative.[107] When Josiah Woodward came to write a history of the Societies for Reformation of Manners in 1699, he portrayed them as a response to a general promotion of the vice that had prevailed until the revolution, and that could only be resisted once William had banished popery and Mary had lent her active support to efforts for moral reform.[108]

---

[103] The debates were at their hottest in the last decades of the twentieth century: see Claydon, *William III and the Godly Revolution*, 110–21; Craig Rose, *England in the 1690s* (Oxford: Blackwell, 1999), chs 5–6.

[104] Claydon, *William III and the Godly Revolution*, 100–10.

[105] *Antimoixeia, or the honest and joint design of the Tower Hamlets* (1691).

[106] *A caution to Christians, or serious maxims of a desired reformation* (1690).

[107] G. Burnet, *Discourse of the pastoral care*, preface.

[108] [Josiah Woodward], *An account of the societies for the reformation of manners* (1699), 2–6.

Such excitement about 1688–9 sometimes became so intense that it toppled over into the full-scale apocalyptic. In some formulations, expectation of a radical break with the past led to predictions that Protestant history might finally be moving to its culmination, with the final victory of God's church at the end of the world. One early example, a verse panegyric to William, began in shock at the suddenness of God's salvation, proceeded through promises that the new king would settle England and Scotland and then rescue the oppressed Protestants of Ireland and France, and ended with the suggestion that he would overthrow 'Babylonish' Rome itself and so prove the 'Morning Star; to usher in the glorious promis'd Reign of Christ.'[109] Rather than analyse this sort of sentiment here, however, consideration of apocalyptic should wait because it fitted within the wider Christian understandings of time that are about to be described. For now, it should be clear that, in the aftermath of the revolution, many English Protestants believed they had just lived through a crucial moment in the history of their faith. More than a page had been turned. This was (or at the very least had the potential to be) a completely different chapter, or even a new volume, with a new plot.

Such a sense, of course, reinforced the highly periodized, perhaps even progressive, view of the past created by the other characteristics of Reformation thinking about 1688–9. Not only had the world changed in the early sixteenth century (and perhaps so profoundly that old truths were no longer valid), and not only had the time since that transformation been divided into clear sub-epochs of heroic advance and then terrifying retreat, now the world was going to be, or at least had a very good chance of being, wholly different again. When people thought about the revolution as a Protestant event, they saw their nation, and humanity as a whole, moving forward through successive states of being, and so, perhaps, took a step towards 'modern' chronology.

3.3 The Evolution of Christian Time

Protestantism, then, offered a far more fluid picture of history than the frozen chronology of so much constitutional thought. In fact, though, this is not surprising. It is, to an extent, simply what one might expect from people who professed the Christian faith. Christian thought had exhibited a developing sense of time across the centuries before 1688–9, and this had been particularly marked within those movements—such as Protestantism—that saw themselves as expressing, or reasserting, pure doctrine in a corrupted world.[110]

---

[109] Robert Fleming, *Britain's jubilee* (1689).

[110] For Protestantism's general promotion of a progressive view of the past, see Ernest Lee Tuveson, *Millennium and Utopia: A Study in the Background of the Idea of Progress* (New York: Harpur and Row, 1949); and Nisbet, *History and the Idea of Progress*, 124–39.

Christians had always had some sense of chronological development. Their beliefs emerged from a Jewish religion that had divided history into four great eras. Judaism had posited a time before the creation of mankind; a period in which humanity had existed in paradise before its first disobedience to God's commands; an epoch between that 'Fall' (as Christians later called it) and the arrival of a messiah; and an age after the messiah, in which time would continue, albeit with society now existing in a perfected state. The Jewish faith had set the turning points between these periods in real time. The creation, the expulsion from paradise, and the messianic coming were understood as temporal events, for all that they might also be sacred mysteries or symbolic images, and they divided eras in which relations between the deity and his people would be of different kinds.

But the Jewish faith had done more than create great spiritual periods. It had also had a strong sense of providentially directed history within each of these. In particular, it had explained the spiritual nature of current age—that after the 'Fall'—by telling forward-driving narratives. As the Hebrew Bible/Old Testament made clear, God's dealing with mankind after he had thrown them out of Paradise had been marked by an emerging self-revelation. He had shown the pattern of his judgements through events such as the scattering of mankind from Babel, and Noah's flood. He had then selected the Jews as a chosen people, concluded covenants with them, and dealt with his elect nation—according to their faithfulness or backslidings—both in order to maintain the covenant and (as became increasing clear in those parts of the Testament written later in the development of scripture) as an example to other nations who might eventually, themselves, receive blessing. These divine interactions with mankind had occurred at potentially dateable points (even if texts did not, in fact, date them), and this allowed a scripture that, for long passages, related spiritual truth through a developing historical narration.[111]

Early Christians had retained much of this chronological sense as they had worked out their faith. Most importantly, they had accepted the Hebrew Bible as the true word of God. This meant agreeing that divine interventions in the world would mark out different spiritual epochs and that divine nature was revealed through chronological narration. The early Christians then elaborated the vision in key ways. First, they inserted two new turning points in divine chronology. They claimed that the deity had taken human flesh to become the messiah foretold by the Jews (and at a very recent point in real history), and they insisted that he would then return to rule on earth before a final remodelling of the universe at a last judgement of all souls. The Hebrew Bible's pattern of creation, expulsion, and messianic coming thus developed into the even more periodized Christian schema of creation, fall, incarnation, millennium, and last judgement. Second, Christians wrote new and updated narratives—a New Testament—to explain and

---

[111] For the Jewish God's intervention in history, see Patrides, *Grand Design of God*, ch. 1.

illustrate divine truth. The gospels were life histories leading to Jesus' crucifixion: the point of Christ's incarnation became manifest in his biography as he moved towards his atonement for mankind on the cross. Similarly, the Acts of the Apostles illustrated God's purposes for Christians by relating the early events of ecclesiastical history, and the book of Revelation (and hints within the gospels and epistles of St Paul) appeared to lay out a sequence of future events—albeit in highly mystical and allegorical language—that would lead to Christ's second coming and the last judgement.[112]

Christians thus had a dynamic view of chronology—divine truth unfolded in periodized and narrative-filled time—and this arguably became more important to them the longer their religion survived. In fact, they had to elaborate further visions of history to cope with a surprise. The most obvious reading of Christ's promises to his people suggested that the millennium (or, in his own formulation, the 'kingdom of heaven') would follow shortly after his incarnation. But as decades passed and Christ failed to return, his followers were challenged to explain and find meaning in the delay. One response was to develop visions of time that continued to evolve even after Jesus had returned to heaven, and to do this, Christians looked to particular parts of scripture. Some drew analogies between their own experience and that of the Jews as it had been related in the Old Testament. Just as an old chosen people had been enlightened through God's action over time in preparation for the messiah's first coming, the new chosen people would be prepared by a series of trials and blessing for his second sojourn on earth. Others looked to Revelation, interpreting it as a guide to a considerable earthly history that would precede the millennium, and making attempts to locate their present moment in its allegorical story. Both approaches produced a strong sense of a providential, evolving, and narrative pattern of post-incarnation history. This was evident, for example, in Eusebius' third-century *Ecclesiastical History*. This portrayed the expansion of the faith within the Roman Empire, and its ultimate conversion of the imperium, as the means to Christ's final triumph, and its rhetorical tone and devices, especially in its closing books, echoed those of Revelation.[113] It was also clear in the Venerable Bede's seventh-century *History of*

---

[112] For a good, brief, summary of all this—and comment on how far Judaism and Christianity differed in their essential historicity from the other religions of the ancient world—see J.L. Russell, 'Time in Christian Thought', in J.T. Fraser, ed., *The Voices of Time* (Amhurst, University of Massachusetts Press, 1981), 59–77, esp. 59–65. See also, Taylor, *Secular Age*, 56; Turetzky, *Time*, 56–8; Karl Löwith, *Meaning in History* (Chicago: Chicago UP, 1949), ch. 11; Hampton, *Writing from History*. Manuel, *Shapes of Philosophical History*, ch. 1, asserts there were cyclical as well as linear elements in early Christian thought and stresses a multiplicity of spiritual periodizations—but nonetheless emphasizes the generally 'progressive' vision of Christian time.

[113] Eusebius, *The History of the Church*, trans. G. A. Williamson (Harmondsworth: Penguin, 1989), esp. books 9–10.

the English. This effectively depicted this people as a new Israel, coming to secure possession of its land through fidelity to the truth faith.[114]

Centuries later, the Old Testament, and Revelation, proved relevant for Protestants, and so for English Protestant readings of 1688–9. To start, these parts of the Bible encouraged the highly periodized view of history that we have been exploring. A God who had offered the Hebrews covenants at particular points in time, and who would come at an exact moment in the future to judge mankind, was capable of creating a new era with the sixteenth century Reformation, or of doing so again by saving the true faith at the revolution. But these sections of scripture also encouraged English Protestants to think in terms of providentially driven narrative within the periods heaven had carved out through its major interventions in history. Revelation, and the historical parts of the Hebrew Bible, seemed to show that God was constantly involved in human affairs, revealing his nature, plan, and expectations in the everyday weft of political and social life. Consequently, the revolution, like all other events, had to be interpreted within an unfolding divine story. This meant the English, as Protestants, were brought closer to a 'modern' chronological sense as they contemplated William's arrival, than the same people had been when deploying constitutional worldviews. As we are about to see, their prevailing modes of thought meant time flowed forward, and also that the present was destabilized. God required action on the part of believers in response to his providence; whether they obeyed his call would shape their fate.[115]

The Old Testament dominated English Protestant culture. From the early sixteenth century, England was compared to Israel in a wide range of spiritual literature, with close analogies being drawn between stories from the Hebrew Bible and the unfolding experience of the English Reformation. Thus monarchs from Henry VIII onwards claimed to be new incarnations of Kings David, Solomon, or Josiah, or (in Elizabeth's case) the Judge Deborah, and so to be leading their people to the true faith.[116] More widely, national triumphs and disasters were interpreted as divine blessings or chastisements with close reference to Old Testament examples, and sermon audiences were encouraged to reflect on the fate of ancient Jews as they faced temptations. Scriptural history confirmed that virtue would have its reward, but did so by telling forward-moving narratives that were supposed to match the unfolding of contemporary events. Preachers

---

[114] The biblical parallel is particularly clear in Bede, *The History of the English Church and People* trans. Leo-Shirley Price, revised R. E. Lantham (Harmondsworth: Penguin, 1968), book 2, ch. 2, which treats St Augustine, the apostle of the English, as an Elijah-like figure, triumphing over (Celtic) enemies who had fallen into error. See also Schiffman, *Birth of the Past*, 126–34.

[115] It has been argued that Protestantism placed unique emphasis on interpreting divine meaning in the successive unspooling of events, rather than stressing typological harmonies between periods: see for example, Alison A. Chapman, 'Now and Then: Sequencing the Sacred in Two Protestant Calendars', *Journal of Medieval and Early Modern Studies*, 33 (2003), 91–123.

[116] For a full survey of royal presentation, see Kevin Sharpe, *Selling the Tudor Monarchy: Authority and Image in Sixteenth Century England* (New Haven: Yale UP, 2009); Sharpe, *Image Wars*.

also described an overarching story mapped by the Hebrew Bible, and then applied this directly to the history and fate of English Protestants. The Jews, it was claimed, had been blessed by God, but then had failed to live up to his standards. They had been warned to repent by a series of chastisements, but despite some partial and temporary improvements that had earned providential deliverances, they had ultimately tested God too far. He had accordingly rejected and scattered them soon after their refusal to accept the gospel of Christ. The English, clerics had been sure, were on the same historic journey. Blessed by the Reformation, they had been tested and chastised (for example by Mary Tudor's reign or the civil wars), as well as cherished and rescued (for example from the Gunpowder Plot). Their ultimate fate would depend on their behaviour, but that of the Jews was held up as a constant and dire warning.[117]

This vision, first adumbrated from pulpits, penetrated deep into popular culture in media including song, theatrical performance, cheap tract, and verse.[118] This meant that when the revolution occurred, it could be easily poured into an Old Testament mould. Although some scholars have argued that it was difficult to portray the post-revolution regime in biblical terms, because this seemed to deny a divine right of monarchy supposedly endorsed in Hebrew scripture, or was most suitable for Jacobites because of the Old Testament's frequent stress on exile and return, this narrows down a high-polyvalent textual source to a few, and internally contested, elements.[119] There were, in fact, many different lessons that could be drawn from pre-Christian scripture, and commentators on 1688–9 were happy to exploit the possibilities. So, the fall of James was widely seen as demonstrating God's love for a favoured nation that had shown resilience in the face of a Catholic ruler, with James's reign often being presented as punishment for their former sins. The deliverer, William, was celebrated as a successor to some of the more admirable Israelite kings: he had a chance to lead England, as they had led Israel, back to obedience to heaven. The English were warned that they must respond to this extraordinary providence with renewed efforts to uphold godliness, just as the prophets had repeatedly exhorted the Jewish people. Burnet's 1690

---

[117] Michael McGifford, 'God's Controversy with Jacobean England', *American Historical Review*, 88 (1983), 1151–74; Patrick Collinson, 'Biblical Rhetoric: The English Nation and National Sentiment in the Prophetic Mode', in Claore McEachern and Debora Shugar, eds, *Religion and Culture in Renaissance England* (Cambridge: CUP, 1997), 15–45; Walsham, *Providence*; John Spurr, 'Virtue, Religion and the Government: The Anglican Uses of Providence', in Tim Harris, Paul Seaward, and Mark Goldie, eds, *The Politics of Religion in Restoration England* (Oxford: Wiley Blackwell, 1990), 29–47.

[118] The standard work on the transmission of Protestant culture to the popular level is Tessa Watt, *Cheap Print and Popular Piety, 1550–1640* (Cambridge: CUP, 1991); but see also Walsham, *Providence*.

[119] Murray Pittock, *Poetry and Jacobite Politics in Eighteenth-Century Britain and Ireland* (Cambridge: CUP, 1994), 9–10; Andrew McKendry, '"No parallels from Hebrew times": Troubled Typologies and the Glorious Revolution in Daniel Defoe's Williamite Poetry', *Eighteenth Century Studies*, 50 (2016), 81–99. A work to stress the continuing purchase of typology in a post revolution literature is Manuel Schonhorn, *Defoe's Politics: Parliament, Power, Kingship and* Robinson Crusoe (Cambridge,: CUP, 1991).

sermon demonstrated such thinking with its opening reflections on God's dealing with Jews in the Davidic period, and his closing exhortation to further reform and repentance, but it was a feature of most Protestant thinking about 1688–9.[120]

Illustration can come from a wide range of sources: the pulpit certainly, but also from other genres, and from the very early weeks after the Dutch invasion. For example, the liturgy for the day of thanksgiving on 30 January 1689 was disproportionately steeped in the Hebrew Bible. It included, not only the standard Old Testament reading (Jeremiah's thanks for ending the Babylonian exile), but also a specially composed hymn stitched together from psalm verses (most of these supposedly written by King David to express his gratitude to God for blessings on himself and his nation). It even turned one of the New Testament readings needed for a properly constructed church service back towards the years before Christ. The passages used as the epistle did not come—as was usual—from an apostolic letter, but rather from a section of Revelation that referred to one of Moses' songs of thanks to Jehovah for leading his people out of Egypt.[121] Similarly, a very early account of the Dutch expedition over the winter of 1688–9 presented a key moment in quite extraordinary biblical terms. When the prince of Orange was met by deserters to his cause at Sherborne (including Prince George of Denmark) they were described greeting him with words from I Chronicles 12: 'Thine are we, David, and on thy side, thou son of Jesse.'[122] Around the same time, a pamphlet compared William to Josiah, the Old Testament king who had rediscovered divine law and imposed it on his erring people; and Burnet would publically tell William, as he arrived in London, that he was achieving the same national unity that David had created when displacing Saul on the Jewish throne.[123] This sort of material provides a context for understanding the presentation of a Bible to William and Mary at their coronation in April 1689. Among other messages this was clearly meant to remind them to consider their biblical forebears when they set their style of rule.[124]

If Old Testament reference was widespread in readings of 1688–9, it was most concentrated in that burst of sermons released by the regime's attempt to preach its way to legitimacy. Pulpits echoed a familiar set of tropes that had structured Protestant thought since the sixteenth century: the revolution was the latest in a series of deliverances for Protestantism in England that closely mirrored the blessings God had sent to the Jews, but the English must respond in a way that contrasted with the first chosen people. They must show deep and genuine

---

[120] G. Burnet, *Sermon…16th day of July.*

[121] *Form of prayer and thanksgiving to almighty God.*

[122] 'The expedition of the prince of Orange for England', in *A complete collection of papers in twelve parts*, iii, 7–8;

[123] *The fall of Babylon; or, good King Josiah revived by the happy arrival of his highness the prince of Orange* (1688); G. Burnet, *A sermon preached in the chappel of St James'*, 7–9.

[124] *An account of the ceremonial at the coronation of their excellent majesties* (1689); Claydon, *William III and the Godly Revolution*, 61–2.

repentance, not a rapidly fading burst of joy. This was the message—repeated to the point of absolute predictability, if not *ad nauseam*—in the bulk of the thanksgiving sermons in 1689, in the 5 November sermons, in many of the sermons published out of Queen Mary's court, in the sermons on the fast and thanksgiving days for the war, and in sermons to mark particular later blessings, such as William's escape from assassination in 1696.

Particular illustration is almost pointless, given that anything chosen would stand for literally hundreds of other examples, but two classes of performance can be picked, virtually at random. The surviving printed fast sermons for William's war from the summer of 1691 are a rich seam. In fact, all of these provided an exegesis of an Old Testament text to explain the pattern of English history. Two preachers, William Sherlock and Gilbert Burnet, cited the psalms to show God's dealings with England followed the same script as his dealings with the Jews over time: the recent revolution was a blessing to which the nation must respond with faithfulness.[125] Two more, William Talbot and Lilly Butler, quoted prophets who warned of the impending destruction of the Jewish monarchy by the Persians to illustrate the fate of nations that did not learn the lessons of God's cycles of chastisement and deliverance.[126] Two further clerics, John Tillotson, and Thomas Cary, used the state of the Jews after the Babylonian captivity. The return to Jerusalem was a parallel to the salvation of 1688–9, but this could not be—as the prophets Ezra and Zechariah warned—a time to relax efforts for godliness.[127] Finally, Richard Meggot used the dilemma faced by King David after sinning against God in numbering his people, to draw lessons about the importance of putting the nation's fate in divine hands in the conflict with France inaugurated by the revolution.[128]

If works produced for a particular category of occasion illustrate the pattern, so do the sermons of one particular cleric. William Wake was a close ally of Gilbert Burnet, and a chief cheerleader for the post-revolutionary regime. He preached on a number of official occasions through the 1690s, and when doing so, he frequently turned to the standard stock of providential interpretation of the Old Testament. On the first fast day for the war in 1689 he used the words of the prophet Joel to insist that England's sins, especially after the recent deliverance from James II, demanded repentance.[129] Addressing the Corporation of London

---

[125] G. Burnet, *A sermon preached at White-Hall…29th of April*; William Sherlock, *A sermon preached at White-Hall, before the Queen, on the 17th of June, 1691* (1691).

[126] Talbot, *Sermon preached at the cathedral church of Worcester*; Lilly Butler, *A sermon preached at St. Mary-le-Bow, before the Lord Mayor, Court of Aldermen and citizens of London* (1691).

[127] Thomas Cary, *A sermon preached in the parish-church of St. Philip and Jacob, in the city of Bristol* (1691); John Tillotson, *A sermon preached at White-hall before the Queen on the monthly fast-day, September 16th 1691* (1691).

[128] Richard Meggott, *A sermon preached before the queen at Whitehall on the fast, July 15* (1691).

[129] William Wake, *A sermon preach'd before the honourable House of Commons, at St. Margaret's Westminster June 5th. 1689* (1689).

at a thanksgiving in 1691, he used David's encouragement to his people to rejoice to suggest that a proper response to the blessing of William's arrival would ensure this was 'only the Beginnings of that Great Felicity we shall henceforth enjoy'.[130] Speaking to the lawyers of Gray's Inn to mark Queen Mary's funeral in 1695 (in a performance that exhausted several editions in its print version), he deployed Old Testament salvations, such as that from the wrath of Haman as related in the book of Esther, to comfort the nation that continued faith would retain God's blessing, even after the loss of such a great ruler.[131] Giving thanks for the discovery of the assassination plot against William in 1696, Wake told a Westminster congregation that David's career showed the protection God would give a righteous monarch.[132]

In all this, Protestant interpretations of 1688–9 encapsulated important elements of a forward-flowing chronology. By mapping English experience onto an Old Testament narrative, commentators confirmed a historical unfolding of providence. God acted over time in the world. He punished and rewarded nations after, and in response to, their sins and repentances. In turn, people were supposed to respond in time. Warned by prior chastisements or encouraged by earlier blessings, they were to turn to God: they were to reform from a former lax state to a later improved one. And taken together, these providential challenges created an overarching story for the English experience. Just as for the Jews, the nation was moving towards an ultimate decree. In the end, it would either be destroyed or set up as God's great example to other peoples. Thus the Hebrew Bible scripted a forward-driving narrative: the deity was revealing his nature, and the English were determining their destiny, as history unfolded.

But the challenge to react to God's temporally structured judgement also had an effect at a more personal level, and one that destabilized the present moment. For the deity had dealt not only with nations in the Hebrew Bible, but with particular people. At key points he had given individuals choices of huge magnitude at exact points in time. Their presents were thus invested with a terrible fluidity and uncertainty, because their fates—and often those of many others—would be determined by how they responded to God's calls at that instant. Cases included the divine order to Jonah to preach repentance to Nineveh (a challenge he flunked, until his sojourn inside a great fish changed his mind) and the demand that Abraham sacrifice his son Isaac (a challenge he nearly accepted until excused at the last moment). These illustrations were particularly dramatic, but there were numerous other illustrations scattered through scripture, and the Old Testament made it clear these were but vivid examples of a choice that faced every person at every point in their lives. The nation God judged had been, clearly, a collection of

---

[130] William Wake, *A sermon preach'd before the Lord-Mayor and court of Aldermen in the church of St. Mary le Bow, on Thursday the 26th of November* (1691), 35.

[131] William Wake, *Of our obligation to put our trust in God, rather than in men* (1695).

[132] William Wake, *A sermon preached in the parish church of St. James, Westminster, April xvith, 1696* (1696).

individuals. Every Jew had therefore faced a constant choice. Would they help avoid chastisement by living according to God's law or endanger themselves and their neighbours by sin? Through the prevailing analogy between the Israelites and the English, God confronted every Protestant with the same challenge.

And two points of theology deepened the sense of personal crisis in each lived moment for the faithful at and after the revolution. First, there had been a recent shift in theories of salvation. By the time of William's arrival, large sections of the Anglican communion, and elements within Nonconformity, had abandoned the strict predestinarian Calvinism of the earlier seventeenth century. As a result, many now believed that individuals's moral choices affected, not just how they would fare on earth, but the fate of their soul after death.[133] This eased the pastoral problem of explaining the apparent arbitrariness of God's dealing with mankind within the Calvinist worldview (neatly summarized by Alexandra Walsham)—but it also removed the one great comfort within that creed: that however disorientating the present, one's ultimate future was guaranteed.[134] This shift placed great stress on immediate amendment of life. For instance, the reformation of manners movement tended towards anti-Calvinist soteriology, and it emphasized that a person's reformation could not be delayed for a moment in case sudden death left one with an unfavourable balance of righteousness and sin.[135] The second theological factor was the considerable emphasis in early modern English Protestantism on the ability of individual repentance to save much larger groups of people. God had made it clear he did not simply count numbers of virtuous and reprobate when deciding whether to punish a community. A few sincere conversions might excuse multitudes: Jehovah had, for example, promised to spare the city of Sodom if ten good men could be found there. Such instances were used to encourage moral reform even among those demoralized at the vice all around them, but it put even greater pressure on those who heard the message to act in their critical moment. As William Lloyd said in a 1690 fast sermon to William and Mary themselves, 'Oh! if we could all attain to this [purity of life]! if any number of us could do it! I will not say the whole nation, but a considerable part of it! What favours might we not hope, the whole nation would have for their sakes?'[136] Such a divine moral calculus not only heaped vast responsibility on those who might be prepared to repent; it ramped up uncertainty since one could never really tell if one's efforts towards godliness would work. Perhaps God would

---

[133] C.F. Allison, *The rise of moralism* (London, 1966) gives the broad outline.

[134] Walsham, *Providence*, 8–32.

[135] This was a major theme of Burnet's, *Discourse of the pastoral care*—a good pastor must stress this urgent renewal—whilst those Nonconformists most involved with the reformation societies, such as Daniel Williams, were the moralist party within a Presbyterian soteriological dispute in the 1690s: Williams attacked predestination in his *A sermon preached at Salter's Hall to the societies for the reformation of manners* (1698).

[136] William Lloyd, *A sermon preached before the king and queen at Whitehall, March the twelfth, 1689/90* (1690), 31.

be satisfied by the efforts of a few righteous. Perhaps, however, they would fall short. Heaven had provided no clear mathematical formula to decide.

Such factors destabilized the present by filling it with a terrible uncertainty, and it also emphasized its fluidity by demanding immediate action to change the future. The current moment was filled with an *urgent* duty to amend ways of life. That great tidal wave of preaching demanding repentance in the wake of the revolution did not present this as a cool fact about God's dealing with nations. It cajoled; it begged; it insisted. The time for change had to be *now* because the Hebrew Bible showed that no one could tell how much longer God would be patient. To prevent the sample size simply exploding, the 1691 fast sermons can again provide examples. Preachers (who often referred to the case of Sodom to prove what effects even one sincere response might have) focused on the moment in which they spoke as they stressed the urgency of what they were demanding.[137] So Talbot urged that everybody '*this day* resolve and enter upon a course of penitence and newness of life'; Tillotson said his congregation should start efforts as soon as they went 'away from this solemnity [the church service]'; Cary told sinners they could not 'put far from us an evil Day' by imagining punishment might be delayed—'God by his providence speaks *now* to us'; Butler fired the starting pistol for a moral race asking his audience to strive to see who would be first in amending their lives.[138] Italics have been added to the original sources above to bring attention to the immediacy of the rhetoric, but they almost certainly represented the tone of the preaching in its original oral delivery. As historians of the early modern sermons have begun to explain, these could be passionate performances, with audiences swept into greatly heightened psychological conditions through verbal emphasis, emotive performance, and emphatic gesture.[139] As the stress on immediate action tended to come towards the end of sermons, when preachers built to their polemic climax, there is little doubt that those attending the original delivery would have been impressed by the urgency and present-centredness of their duties.

The Old Testament framing of 1688–9 thus created a progressive view of time in several ways. It patterned understanding of the revolution on narratives of God's dealings with nations that ran forward through time and suggested a possible grand arc of divine action, in which the English were moving towards an ultimate judgement in the future. But comparing England and Israel also turned the present into a forward-facing moment. The future was being created in the 'now' by the responses of sinners to God's deliverance or forbearance. It thus flowed out of the

---

[137] Talbot, *Sermon preached at the cathedral church of Worcester*, 29; Butler, *Sermon preached at St. Mary-le-Bow*, 23; Sherlock, *Sermon preached at White-Hall, before the Queen*, 26–7.

[138] Talbot, *Sermon preached at the cathedral church of Worcester*, 28; Tillotson, *Sermon preached at White-hall*, 3; Cary, *Sermon preached in the parish-church of St. Philip and Jacob*, 20–1; Butler, *Sermon preached at St. Mary-le-Bow*, 23.

[139] Walsham, *Providence*, 315–25.

present as a consequence of actions made in the moment, and it was fluid because it might be altered by changing those actions. It was true that at a technical, theological level, and even within non-Calvinist soteriologies, God's foreknowledge of whether people would repent might fix and fill time—but at the common level of sermon rhetoric, this sounded much like the present in 'modern' views of empty chronology. People were shaping their forward narrative by what they did.

The sorts of impact made on temporal understanding by thinking in Old Testament terms were just as relevant to the second dimension of traditional Protestant approaches to time. This was the tendency to understand the post-atonement past, including the story of the Reformation, in terms of the book of Revelation. As Luther's protest against the papacy had matured, he and his followers had tried to place themselves in history with reference to the mystical account of the future of mankind contained in the last section of scripture. In particular, Protestants had identified the growing power of the Roman church with the vicious figures of Babylon and the Antichrist described therein, and had seen themselves as the book's remnant of the faithful who had stood against this corruption. This remnant, Revelation's mystical allegory seemed to suggest, would be persecuted to near extinction as the Antichrist engrossed worldly authority. But the tiny band of truly faithful would then triumph with Christ's second coming and ultimately be rewarded with a life of eternal bliss in a New Jerusalem.[140] English Protestants had taken these ideas up energetically. It provided a convenient way to denigrate the Catholic powers that threatened them, and offered comfort as they were subjected to a series of defeats, threats, and setbacks. Although discouraging, the persistent power of Catholicism was explicable: Satan would dominate the world until Christ's sudden, but certain, victory.

This tendency in English Protestant thought led to broad use of apocalyptic language. The pope was often denounced as the Antichrist, and his church as Babylon, and influential Tudor authors such as John Bale and John Foxe developed a 'two church' view of history in which a false *ecclesia* constantly oppressed its suffering, but faithful, counterpart. More specifically, some writers attempted precise eschatology. They tried to calculate where exactly in the mystical narrative the Protestant movement had reached, and so to predict when its final triumph might come.[141] The most influential attempts had been by Thomas Brightman, who had provided a detailed historicist reading of the book of Revelation, finding predictions of the religious changes of the sixteenth century in scripture, and by Joseph Mede, who had concluded that the thousand-year reign of Christ lay in

---

[140] The progress of the movement to this position had been gradual—Luther himself had started doubting Revelation's status as scripture, and had initially read apocalyptic passages in the Bible allegorically—see Katherine R. Firth, *The Apocalyptic Tradition in Reformation Britain* (Oxford: OUP, 1979), ch. 1.

[141] Richard Bauckham, *Tudor Apocalypse* (Oxford: OUP, 1978); Paul Christianson, *The Reformers and Babylon* (Toronto: University of Toronto Press, 1978).

the future and was not merely a mystical description of the existing church.[142] Such ideas had become particularly important in the crisis of Charles I's reign. Some found justification for rebelling against the monarchy in the idea that they were God's true people, participating in the final overthrow of Antichristian tyranny.[143]

As will be seen, exactly how far this tradition shaped reactions to William III's triumph can be debated. But there is no doubt about the general use of apocalyptic rhetoric once James had fled. 'Antichrist' and 'Babylon' were bandied around to describe the enemy just defeated. To take examples from 1689: one balladeer (who appeared to have no real command of either rhyme or scansion) hoped God would complete the revolution by deposing the Pope: 'We also hope that God will put from his throne / That Antichrist, that Whore of Babylon'.[144] In that same year, a pamphlet appeal to stand by the new government used its preface to celebrate God's deliverance from its 'Antichristian Adversaries'. Meanwhile a broadside mocking James's withdrawal from England claimed he had tried to 'advance the Kingdom of Antichrist'; the Whig writer Richard Claridge argued any continuation of James's rule would have indeed have installed that Satanic kingdom; and a welcome poem for William said religion was now rescued 'from the toyls of Babel's whore'.[145] A couple of years later, the cleric Lewis Atterbury provided one of the most prominent uses of this sort of language. Publishing a sermon preached before the Corporation of London that had reflecting on the blessings of the revolution, he entitled it *Babylon's downfall*.[146]

Words and images from Revelation were thus widely used in reactions to 1688–9. Quite a number of people took the further step of interpreting the revolution as directly prophesied, and of asserting that the final victory of Christ was at hand. Those from communities suffering persecution were particularly confident in their assertions: it is probable that such folk hoped a returning messiah might end their trials, and so were drawn to bold scriptural readings. Nonconformists such as Thomas Beverley, Benjamin Keach, and Israel Morland, and the French Huguenot, Pierre Jurieu, fitted this pattern.[147] Some of these even took the risk of

---

[142] Thomas Brightman, *Apocalypsis apocalypseos* (Frankfurt, 1609; English translation, 1611); Joseph Mede, *Clavis apocalyptica* (1627; English translation, 1643).

[143] Claydon, *William III and the Godly Revolution*, 32–44, provides a basic primer for the extensive literature on all this, but see especially Paul Christianson, 'From Expectation to Militance: Reformers and Babylon in the First Two Years of the Long Parliament', *Journal of Ecclesiastical History*, 24 (1973), 225–44.

[144] *England's great deliverance, or Britain's fears and tears in joy completed* (1689).

[145] *The absolute necessity of standing by the present government* (1689), preface; *The king's reasons (with some reflections upon them) for withdrawing himself from Rochester* (1689); Richard Claridge, *The second defence of the present government* (1689), 12; *To the most illustrious and serene prince, his royal highness* (1689).

[146] Lewis Atterbury, *Babylon's downfall…the substance of a sermon preached before the Lord Mayor…June 28 1691* (1691).

[147] See, for example, Benjamin Keach, *Antichrist stormed* (1689); Pierre Jurieu, *The reflections of the reverend and learned monsieur Jurieu* (1689); Israel Morland, *A short description of Sion's inhabitants* (1690)

being dateably precise about where the revolution sat within apocalyptic narrative. Beverley, for example, was sure the world would end in 1697.[148] Beyond these particular writers and communities, evidence for eschatological sentiment is patchier, but it nonetheless suggestive. The historian Warren Johnston has argued for a vigorous apocalyptic tradition in late Stuart England and has usefully catalogued a wide variety of instances of people reading the revolution in Revelation.[149] In particular, he stressed this was a vigorous discourse within the established church. He cited people who would be central to William's bench of bishops, including commentators such as John Tillotson, Simon Patrick, and Gilbert Burnet.

There are grounds for caution, which will be covered later, but it is certain that excitement about 1688–9 as a turning point in history took many Anglicans to at least the borderlands of apocalyptic assertion. In his 1690 sermon in the Chapel Royal, Burnet spoke in rapturous terms about what would happen if the English built on their recent deliverance. God would 'perfect' their lives, and righteousness would cover the whole land.[150] As will be seen later, Burnet had been similarly excited in the first months of William's time in England, and some of his allies such as Tillotson and Patrick had been moved to comparable passion. As Johnston and Margaret Jacob have argued, this group of pro-Williamite clergy could present the war against popish France—inaugurated by the revolution—as an accomplishment of scriptural prophecies about the final fall of Babylon.[151] In those same post-revolution years, the Anglican cleric Thomas Burnet produced his account of the geological and astronomical processes that would remodel the physical world at the end of days, and, as Lionel Laborie had pointed out, earlier Anglican prophecy made a vigorous reappearance.[152] The civil-war-era predictions of the archbishop of Armagh, James Ussher, were reprinted, and applied to the current struggle with Louis XIV.[153]

Such eschatologically exact language may not have been typical of the official church's thought, but the general willingness to think in apocalyptic terms reinforced the temporal effects of Old Testament thinking. Even if people were just

---

[148] See for example, Thomas Beverley, *The late great revolution, argued according to Revelation 17* (1689); Jurieu, *Reflections of the reverend*.

[149] Warren Johnston, *Revelation Restored: The Apocalypse in Later Seventeenth-Century England* (Woodbridge: Ashgate, 2011); Warren Johnston, 'Revelation and the Revolution of 1688–9', *Historical Journal*, 48:2 (2005), 351–89. See also, Jeongku Park, 'The Rational Apocalypse of the Latitudinarians in Restoration England', PhD Thesis, University of Swansea, 2018.

[150] G. Burnet, *Sermon…16th day of July*, 33–4.

[151] Margaret C. Jacob, 'Millenarianism and Science in the Late Seventeenth Century', *Journal of the History of Ideas*, 37 (1976), 335–41; Johnston, 'Revelation and the Revolution', 352.

[152] Thomas Burnet, *The theory of the earth…the last two books* (1690); Lionel Laborie, 'Millenarian Portraits of Louis XIV', in Tony Claydon and Charles-Edouard Levillain, eds, *Louis XIV Outside In: Images of the Sun King Beyond France, 1661–1715* (Aldershot: Ashgate, 2016), 209–28, at 219.

[153] James Ussher, *A French prophecy, or an admonition to the English* (1690); James Ussher, *An admonition to the English…to which is added, Archbishop Usher's prophecy* (1691); George Walker, *The protestant's crumbs of comfort containing…the bishop Usher's prophecy concerning Ireland* (1697).

using terms such as Antichrist and Babylon without specifying where in the Revelation story affairs had reached, they were deploying a discourse with a strong assumption of developing narrative.[154] Current struggles with popery were part of a grand providential design that would lead to the fulfilling of God's purposes in the final fall of his enemies. Each new event was a stage on that path, just as each new event could be interpreted as part of a grand story that paralleled that of the Jews. Furthermore, for those who thought there was any chance that the revolution was a herald of the last stages of the design, the present became crucial in ways that echoed the anxiety generated when people engaged with the Old Testament. For, in apocalyptic the current moment was invested with supernatural excitement. If not exactly fluid (God was controlling events within all under-standings of Revelation providence), it was at least destabilized because of the enormity of what might happen next. The consequences of an apocalyptic present might break all rules of normal history, natural science, or human behaviour. Gilbert Burnet promised his audience at St James's chapel in December 1688 a 'New Heavens and New Earth', and Thomas Burnet believed the apocalypse would start with a 'fiery chaos' breaking out near the seat of the Antichrist at Rome and would then spread, via eruptions of volcanoes and other cataclysms, to destroy the planet.[155]

And the apocalyptic present might demand urgent action, as much as it antici-pated wholesale transformation. Audiences were told they must prepare for coming transformations, and that they had an immediate duty to help God effect them. Those preachers who saw William's arrival and war as stages in the defeat of the Antichrist, did so in sermons that demanded energetic support for the ruler. People must arm militarily, bring down divine blessing by rapid moral reform, or both. The more systematically apocalyptic writers had even more pressing and specific agendas—Thomas Beverley's voluminous works in the aftermath of 1688–9 spent many pages analysing Revelation to prove his theory that the millennium would start before the turn of the century—but they also had detailed instructions for everyone in society. Rulers must strike mercilessly against the Beast (a call for a united assault on the papacy and its supporters); bishops must remove all vainglory from the church; clergy must search scripture to confirm Beverley's predictions, and teach them to their parishioners; and ordinary people must repent, bowing down before God—wearing sackcloth in the author's oft-repeated phrase—to prepare themselves to meet Christ.[156] With just a little more self-interest, Beverley

---

[154] For the general tendency of Protestant apocalyptic to generate forward narrative, see Kemp, *Estrangement of the past*, ch. 3.

[155] G. Burnet, *A sermon preached in the chappel of St James*, 21; T. Burnet, *Theory*.

[156] See, for example, Beverley, *Late great revolution*, epistle; Thomas Beverley, *The prophetical history of the reformation* (1689), preface; Thomas Beverley, *An humble remonstrance concerning some add-itional confirmations of the kingdom of Christ* (1690), 4; Thomas Beverley, *The catechism of the kingdom of our lord Jesus Christ in the thousand years* (1690), epistle to the bishops; Thomas Beverley, *An appeal most humble* (1691), 1; Thomas Beverley, *The blessing of Moses on the tribe of Asher* (1693), preface.

also urged Parliament to grant him financial support to go on churning out his warnings.[157] Benjamin Keach was as insistent that signs of the last days demanded response. His huge published argument that William's triumph was the first act in the overthrow of the Antichristian papacy was prefaced by hopes that his writing would stir up its audience to complete the 'work still to be done, both here and abroad, before that glorious state of the church comes in.'[158] The Baptist minister Drue Cressener's equally enormous proof that Rome was Babylon, and would soon fall, was dedicated to Queen Mary. It thanked her for her role in reviving the Reformation, and expressed the hope she would unite all Protestants in a final push against popery.[159]

Such expectation of wholesale change, and such urgent calls for action, focused attention on the present and transformed it into the pivotal point of world history. In apocalyptic, a supercharged 'now' was revealing itself as the supremely significant moment when the course of the cosmos was turning its most decisive corner. It was the point at which one's spiritual response would matter more than at any other. This produced a highly destabilized, anxiety-inducing present and created the sort of hunger for news that has been posited as a mark of modern temporal sensibility. People were put on high alert for signs that this was indeed the start of the end of the world, so a nervous demand for information was palpable in the apocalyptic sources. To take just one example: Cressener's preface to the queen was certain, in general terms, that the Antichrist would soon be defeated. It was also fairly confident that the revocation of the Edict of Nantes, which had ended the toleration of French Protestants in 1685, had started the countdown to victory, as it had been the brutal—but final—act of Babylonish persecution. But precisely how far the narrative had run depended on correct reading of the very latest news. Perhaps the very recent return of the Protestant Vaudois to their Alpine valleys was the start of a general godly revival. Perhaps, however, everyone needed to wait just a little longer, until the tide turned in France itself. Only more news, eagerly awaited, would tell.[160]

Apocalyptic, then, completed the forward-driving dynamic of Protestant interpretations of 1688–9.[161] Indeed, it contained something of all the dimensions that have been covered. Suggesting the world was about to enter a new era, it confirmed the highly periodized character of Reformation time. Seeing the revolution as the first harbinger of these new times, it magnified the sense of anticipation and excitement that was the capstone of that periodization. Stressing a developing

---

[157] Thomas Beverley, *To the high court of parliament* (1691).

[158] Keach, *Antichrist stormed*, preface.

[159] Drue Cressener, *A demonstration of the first principles of the protestant applications of the apocalypse* (1690).

[160] Ibid.

[161] For the tendency for apocalyptic to generate 'progressive' views of history, see Tuveson, *Millennium*, ch. 3, for coverage of the seventeenth century.

narrative, made comprehensible by the Bible, it complemented the Old Testament's tendency to see an evolving providential script in world affairs. And reinforcing the uncertain, response-demanding, present of immediate moral choice already created by reflections on Israel, it destabilized the current moment and orientated it towards the future. In fact, and perhaps paradoxically, it may have created a present more 'modern' (if by this is meant one fixated on a thirst for information and an acute anxiety about how to respond to what was known) than secular news culture ever could. Protestantism, it seems, was the supreme solvent of static chronology.

3.4 Static Christian Time

But there was a problem. Whilst the people of 1688–9 periodized the event within Reformation eras, and drew on dynamic elements of Christian chronology, they were also, as both Protestants and Christians, heirs to wholly contradictory features of their faith. Just as believers had encouraged time to flow, they also insisted it was frozen.

These contradictory features of religious chronology were as old as its progressive faces, and they arose because there were varied responses to the unexpected delay in Christ's second coming. Whilst some of the faithful had used a continuing narrative of God's dealing with chosen peoples, or apocalyptic, to fill the temporal space between the incarnation and the final completion of God's plan, others focused on a doctrinal difficulty with claiming any evolution in history after Christ's death. The problem was that Jesus' ministry, or at least its culmination in the atonement, was supposed to have fulfilled God's purposes on earth. Sinners had been provided with the means for reconciliation with heaven, so it was unclear what could meaningfully happen before that reconciliation was effected at the Last Judgement. This was no great difficulty in the very first years of the new faith. Then, Christ's second coming was expected imminently, so there was very little history to explain, or explain away. But the problem became increasingly embarrassing. The longer the last days were delayed, the deeper the question of what the new period of time might mean; and whilst some Christians coped by adopting the providential and progressive narratives just described, others denied anything of importance was really going on, or asserted that it was hopeless to try to fathom the significance of the events they were living through.[162] In fact, narrative-stilling options became more attractive when the Roman Empire in the west collapsed in the fifth century. This represented a shocking setback for a Christian faith which had grown to dominate that empire and now faced invasion

---

[162] Denial that humans could understand their history was a common Christian trope: Manuel, *Shapes of Philosophical History*, ch. 2.

by pagan nations. Denying any profound meaning to recent events was a comfort in the face of that catastrophe: what might have been an existential crisis could be reduced to a trivial epiphenomenon.

There were several ways to empty post-incarnation history of importance. The first was that exemplified by St Augustine. This philosopher–bishop, whose writing straddled the disaster of the first sack of Rome in 410 AD, treated time largely as an illusion, stressing that it only existed in the world God had created. The deity himself inhabited a timeless eternity outside that creation, and in so far as God contemplated his handiwork, he saw all its moments simultaneously. For him, history was a static pattern. This truth was still being expressed by early modern English Protestants over a millennium later, as Alexandra Walsham has shown.[163] Augustine also insisted the past and future were really mental constructions in the present. The past was simply current recollection and had no meaning outside that immediate ratiocination; the future was simply current expectation; and—at the spiritual level, accessible through prayer—all of God's purposes were gathered in the present moment.[164] This gave sustained and coherent exegesis to a strong time-freezing tendency in Christianity, which would be bolstered by the influence of strands of Greek thought that stressed the unchanging nature of the cosmos.[165]

A second means to deny significance to post-incarnation events sprang from that early Christian connection to the Jewish faith that was explored above. Christians claimed Jesus was the messiah predicted in the Hebrew Bible. But they did not do this simply by saying he fitted the descriptions of the saviour in the Old Testament. They also drew strong analogies between Jesus' life and role, and incidents in the earlier scripture, to show he carried the same divine message. Christ was not only predicted by the Hebrew Bible, but prefigured by it. Thus, for example, Christ's rule of the Kingdom of Heaven had been foreshadowed by King David's rule in Israel, and Christ's sacrifice—as God's only son—had been pre-enacted by Abraham's near sacrifice of his sole male child, Isaac, at God's command. In technical terms, the Old Testament character or incident was the 'type' of its New Testament fulfilment or 'antitype'. This typological approach tied the two parts of the Christian Bible together, but also became a central plank of the new faith's apologetic, and consequently soon came to be extended to post-incarnation history. Events in the Christian centuries came to be seen as antitypes of incidents in the Bible.[166]

---

[163] St Augustine, *Concerning the City of God Against the Pagans*, trans. Henry Bettesen (Harmondsworth: Penguin, 1984), book 9, chs 4–6; St Augustine, *Confessions*, trans. Henry Chadwick (Oxford: OUP, 1991), book 11, chs 7–13, 31. Walsham, *Providence*, 9–10.

[164] St Augustine, *Confessions*, book 11, chs 16–21; Taylor, *Secular Age*, 57; Turetzky, *Time*, 58–66.

[165] Russell, 'Time in Christian Thought', 66–71. For a survey of arguments for the atemporality of God in Christian thought, see William Lane Craig, 'Divine Eternity', in Thomas Flint and Michael Rea, eds, *The Oxford Handbook of Philosophical Theology* (Oxford: OUP, 2009), 145–66.

[166] Northrop Frye, *The Great Code: The Bible and Literature* (New York: Houghton, 1981), 78–83.

This understanding of the current age had ambiguous effects. It could invest meaning to post-incarnation history, as it did for Eusebius and Bede. It could provide a way to understand an advancing narrative as illustrations of God's plan, as it did for those who looked back at Old Testament stories to think about 1688–9. But it could not give history any significant *new* meaning. This was because the incarnation had to stand as the supreme fulfilment of earlier types. Although later events might be understood by connecting them to biblical precursors, they must not be thought of as adding anything substantial to the revelations of the gospel. That would risk dethroning scripture as the source of authority (a particularly sensitive issue for Protestants who accused their Roman rivals of inventing non-biblical doctrine) and would endanger Christ's status as the pivotal figure in world history. Current events were thus reduced to a playing out of spiritual truths that had already been mapped by their biblical types. Nothing essentially novel could happen: indeed, drawing analogies with the Bible ensured the meaning and significance of events was already fixed by moments in the past. This approach was manifest in Gregory of Tours' sixth-century *History of the Franks*. As Zachary Schiffman has pointed out, this was so systematically structured by analogy with Old Testament occurrences that it destroyed any distinctiveness or autonomous meaning in recent goings-on.[167] Such a lack of true novelty was probably a comfort in the darkening times of late antiquity. But it froze time profoundly when the same mental habit persisted into the early modern era. As Christians, the English Protestants who commented upon the revolution were conditioned to understand it as another manifestation of unchanging truths.[168]

This tendency affected and infected all the elements of Protestant dynamic that we noted in reaction to 1688–9. Even the first and perhaps most impressive—the peroiodization created by the profound discontinuity perceived in the early sixteenth century—offered less sense of progress through different stages of history when seen in the context of Christianity's insistence that truth, and the spiritual state of mankind, could not change. At a most basic level, Protestants' division of the past into eras before and after Luther was weakened by their need to insist their beliefs were not new. God's truth must be the same at all times, so Protestants denied innovation. Instead, as mountains of apologetic insisted, Luther had merely restored the pure doctrine and practices of the 'primitive' Christians (those who had lived in the first decades after the incarnation), and, Robert Ingram has argued, this became the characteristic mode of Protestant engagement with the

---

[167] Schiffman, *Birth of the Past*, 119–26; Martin Heinzelmann, *Gregory of Tours: History and Society in the Sixth Century* (Cambridge: CUP, 2001).

[168] For the general chronological *statis* created by typology, see Frye, *Great Code*, 78–83; for the degradation of history as a meaningful narrative created by its conception as manifestations of unchanging spiritual patterns, see Löwith, *Meaning in History*, ch. 11.

past.[169] According to the reformed, they were endorsing the faith as it had been before it was corrupted—from about the third century onwards—by the greed, ambition, and lies of the papacy. This had one of two consequences for the notion of a new Protestant era. Sometimes it suggested it was a continuation of the primitive epoch after a long submersion of true faith. This was not quite the same thing as a new era, and it tended to collapse the intervening medieval centuries in a way not entirely consistent with the view that history moved forward through periods. The long epoch of papal dominance became, effectively, an irrelevance: the depraved Middle Ages were reduced to an empty time waiting for the re-emergence of truth. Sometimes, though, Protestants shied away from the idea that their movement was a sudden resurrection of faith. When asked by Romanists where their church had been before Luther—a question designed to force them to admit that their creed was, after all, novel—Protestants often pointed to minority groups who, they claimed, had kept alive the flame of genuine godliness through the bitter ages of popish dominance. For example, the great English martyrologist, John Foxe, had made much of medieval movements that had protested against Roman doctrine. His catalogue of suffering included folk such as Lollards and Hussites, who—it might be argued—prefigured much of Luther's teaching, but had also reached out to earlier heretics such as the Waldensian and Albigensians, whose proto-Protestantism was a very considerable stretch.[170] This approach again compromised Reformation periodization. A true Christian community had survived from the primitive church right through to Luther's protest, so although the Protestant era was marked by a new success for this community (there was now a much more favourable balance between numbers of people espousing the true faith and those who did not), it was *not* fundamentally different from what had come before.

Such deep historical continuities were not often expressed explicitly in commentary on 1688–9.[171] As noted above, the revolution as a religious event was overwhelmingly understood as a salvation of English Protestantism—so rhetorical horizons tended to be limited to the years since England's Reformation. But everyone understood Protestant belief was not new, and the argument had been strongly reinforced in the reign of James II. Then, the Anglican church had reacted to the king's attempt to promote Roman Catholicism with a print and pulpit

---

[169] Robert Ingram, *Reformation Without End: Religion Politics and the Past in Post-Revolutionary England* (Manchester: MUP, 2018). Though, interestingly, this may not have been Luther's own view: he thought the church had degenerated from primitive ages, but he insisted that God's word, rather than any particular point in the past, was normative: see John M. Headley, *Luther's View of Church History* (New Haven: Yale UP, 1963), ch. 2.

[170] Stephen Reed Cattley, ed., *The acts and monuments of John Foxe* (1837), vols 2–3.

[171] For Protestants' denial of change generally in the late seventeenth century, see John Spurr, 'A Special Fondness for Dead Bishops: The Church, History, and Testimony in Seventeenth Century Protestantism', in Paulina Kewes, ed., *The Uses of History in Early Modern England* (San Marino, CA: Huntington Library Press, 2006), 307–28.

campaign upholding its doctrinal positions.[172] This effort—which involved those who would become William's chief clerical polemicists—insisted that popish deceptions were also innovations. According to the rhetoric, error had come in after an initial period of Christian perfection, and had been promoted expressly to subvert it. Fortunately, however, truth had been preserved in scripture, and perhaps among surviving communities of the godly, so the Reformation was a resurgence, not an invention.[173] After this education, audiences knew that—as a contributor to the campaign under James II had put it—'Our religion is the same with that of the early Christians, martyrs and professors'.[174] Occasionally this comprehension rose above the implicit in reactions to the revolution. When Sir George Treby welcomed William to the City in December 1688, he asserted that the prince's had saved English Protestantism, which he explained was a revival of the faith of the first, 'primitive', Christians.[175] A 1689 pamphleteer, celebrating God's deliverance from popish thraldom and ignorance, entitled his piece the *Innovations of popery* and outlined the stages by which truth had been corrupted, before Protestants rediscovered it.[176]

If the novelty implied by a sixteenth-century discontinuity was illusory, this had a knock-on effect for the Protestant age that came after it. Its character as a new period was compromised. As has been outlined, the sense of a Protestant era had been created among commentators on 1688–9 by citing a standard series of events, which stretched from Luther's day to the late seventeenth century, and which mapped this as an epoch of existential struggle for truth against the massed ranks of popery. But if Protestantism was not new, the struggle could not be new either. The travails of the godly after 1517 were simply a continuation of the battle that the truth had always had with evil.

Perhaps the most striking illustration of this type of continuous struggle in post-1688–9 commentary was contained within the widespread insistence that God's deliverance from James II brought a duty to help persecuted Protestants across Europe. The revolution, as a string of fast sermons and other material insisted, had been part of God's salvation for the whole Reformation, so England

---

[172] The print part of this became so voluminous as to stimulate two annotated catalogues of the titles: [William Clagett], *The present state of the controversy between the church of England and the church of Rome* (1687); and [William Wake], *The continuation of the present state of the controversy* (1688).

[173] These arguments ran as a leitmotif through the works Clagett and Wake cited: see, for example, [John Patrick], *Transubstantiation no doctrine of the primitive fathers* (1687); [Edward Pelling], *The antiquity of the protestant religion* (1687); [Thomas Comber], *A discourse concerning the second council of Nice, which first introduced...image worship* (1688); [Edward Gee], *The primitive fathers no papists* (1688); [John Patrick], *A full view of the doctrine and practices of the ancient church relating to the eucharist wholly different from the practices of the present Roman church* (1688).

[174] [Gregory Hascard], *A discourse about the charge of novelty upon the church of England* (1685), 5–6.

[175] George Treby, *The speech of Sir George Treby...to his highness the prince of Orange, Dec. 20, 1688* (1688).

[176] W[illiam] T[omlinson], *The innovations of popery in the church of Rome* (1689).

must move to relieved the foreign oppressed.[177] This certainly meant helping to defend the Netherlands against Louis XIV, and giving succour to Protestants fleeing persecution, but significantly, the duty also encompassed aid to the Vaudois of the Alpine valleys. These folk had been attacked by the popish forces of the Duke of Savoy (as a burst of pamphlets appearing in the first years after William arrived in England underlined), but crucially, they were also widely believed to have retained true Christian belief, virtually uncorrupted, through the years of papal dominance.[178] As historians explained (in frankly fantastic accounts), relative isolation in remote mountains, as well as accidents of ecclesiastical history, had meant that Rome's efforts to stamp out the truth of the gospel had failed in this one corner of Europe and that the Vaudois had been able to give succour to both medieval heretics who defied the papacy and to the first Protestants.[179] This survival was linked to the revolution because William was presented fighting the same cause as the Alpine faithful. The king was told in a dedication of Vaudois history by Abel Boyer that, 'You maintain, as they, Sir, the cause of God'.[180] 1688–9 was thus placed in the context of a very long struggle, and one in which the decades since Luther had not been particularly significant. The Vaudois' recent misfortunes were just the latest in a long saga of survival; helping them was only partly an act within a Protestant-era drama. As Burnet told William, the king had saved a Vaudois community that was 'the first begotten of the Reformation, or rather the last Remnant of True and Primitive Christianity'.[181]

Such assumptions about a much longer standing struggle between the papacy and truth soaked many other post-revolution accounts. This was guaranteed by the model of popery that had it starting to corrupt Christianity even within its earliest centuries. The catalogues of popish crimes against the Reformation in revolution commentary frequently reflected back to medieval antecedents, and the lists of godly heroics stretched way before Luther. One of the clearest examples came in John Seller's *History of England*, published in 1696 and dedicated to William (whom the author lauded as having saved the country from popery and slavery at the revolution, and had thus, perhaps, brought it to its greatest glory in the whole tale Seller told from Saxon times).[182] For the most part, this work was a chronicle-like trot through history, arranged reign by reign. Yet, after relating the

---

[177] Claydon, *Europe*, 241–53.

[178] *A journal of all that happen'd in the march of the Vaudois* (1689); *The declaration and manifesto of the protestants of the vallies of Piedmont, called the Vaudois* (1690); *A full and true account of the late revolution in Savoy* (1690); Henri Arnaud, *The present state of the Vaudois* (1691); Peter Boyer, *The negotiations of the embassadors sent to the duke of Savoy by the protestant Swiss-cantons* (1691).

[179] Perhaps the clearest account of this came with William Wake, *The case of the exiled Vaudois and French Protestants stated* (1699), but see also Samuel D'Assigny, *A short relation of the brave exploits of the Vaudois* (1699).

[180] Peter Boyer, *The history of the Vaudois* (1692), epistle dedicatory.

[181] Gilbert Burnet, *Sermon preached before the king and queen at Whitehall, the 1st day of October, 1689* (1690).

[182] John Seller, *The history of England* (1696), epistle dedicatory.

events of Mary Tudor's rule, the writer paused to provide a martyrology of those 'that have suffered the tortures and persecutions under Popery in England'. Crucially, whilst this was deliberately placed at an iconic point in Protestant history—'after a Reign, wherein the Blood of those of the Reformed Church, was shed like Water'—and whilst it illustrated the adversarial pattern of history since 1517, it also ruptured any simple Protestant period by providing stories 'before' as well as 'since' the happy Reformation'.[183] Seller named a large number of folk who had suffered for resisting the tyranny of Rome in the decades after Wycliff's protests in the late fourteenth century, and he suggested there had always been true Christians who had tried to keep the light of the gospel alive through the Middle Ages, when 'the Purity of the Primitive Churches was Clouded and *almost* [italics added] Obscured by the Roman Traditions, Errors, and Superstitions'.[184] He did accept that things had changed in the early Tudor era. 'The appearance of Martin Luther in Germany', and 'The Noble Mystery of Printing', had encouraged people to join the 'Gospel Professors in England and other Nations'. However, this was clearly only a magnification of a pre-existing movement; and as if to underline the point, Seller followed his observation about print and Luther with a list of martrydoms from 1511 and 1514—times before a new German movement could have inspired anyone in the Tudor realm.[185]

Such continuity was manifest in other histories, including the ones surveyed above to establish a Protestant periodization within interpretations of 1688–9. William Wake's long narrative of popish plots and rebellions certainly concentrated on the 'last hundred and fifty years... since the reformation', but his introductory paragraphs made it clear such treachery had a long pedigree. 'Diabolical machinations', and 'hellish Conspiracies of Priests', had marred 'the whole Course of History'; papal ambition had been the main theme of the last 'five or six hundred years'; and monks and friars had plagued society 'for several ages'.[186] The *Epitomy of ecclesiastical history* meanwhile failed to make clear in the main text where its section on Reformation divines took over from its one on admirable figures of earlier ages (with the result that several medieval figures might be read as precursors, or early instances, of the Protestant reformers), and the pictorial frontispiece also smudged the time frame (Fig. 3.2). Certainly Luther and other Protestant heroes filled two sides of the table around the candle of the gospel, facing down priests who tried to extinguish it who were ranged along a third. But, somewhat alone, on the last side, sat John Wycliff: a medieval critic of the papacy who had clearly played a key role in the preservation and promotion of Christian truth.

This assumption that the Reformation—at least as a resistance to the pope's spiritual tyranny—had had a continuous history through the Middle Ages broke the surface elsewhere in material linked to the revolution. For example, a prose

---

[183] Ibid., 532.   [184] Ibid., 533.
[185] Ibid., 535.   [186] Wake, *Brief history*, epistle to reader.

Fig. 3.2 Frontispiece to J. S., *An epitomy of ecclesiastical history* (1692). By kind permission of the Huntington Library.

preface to an early verse celebration of William's arrival presented 1688–9 as a providential continuation of the mercies God that had shown to England since the Tudor restoration of true faith. But it also suggested the nation had been blessed by an early conversion to Christianity in the first century and then by 'many great and venerable worthies' who had resisted Rome's corruption, 'which laudable endeavours of our renowned ancestors were preparatory steps to the reformation.'[187] A very early pamphlet justifying William's war with France, and warning that papists were not to be trusted (indeed it presented the emerging conflict as something of a crusade against Catholic dishonesty), collected instances of betrayal of Protestants since the sixteenth century, including St Bartholomew's Day and the plots against Elizabeth and James II. But it was careful to include the cases of John Hus and Jerome of Prague. These 'Good Men' had protested against Romish errors from the late fourteenth century and had been executed at the Council of Constance, despite promises of safe conduct.[188] When Edward Stillingfleet (appointed bishop of Worcester by William, and a cheerleader for the king) promoted moral renewal in his diocese in 1690, he encouraged godly preaching by claiming that Wycliff had stirred folks' thirst to hear the gospel; Thomas Beverley's apocalyptic reading of 1688–9 as an immediate presage of the end of time identified the Reformation as an earlier blow against the Antichrist, but gave the same status to the emergence of medieval heretical movements such as the Waldensians, Lollards, and Utraquists.[189]

A strong sense of pre-Protestantism even shaped the constitutional version of a Reformation era. Whilst writers within the allegiance controversy celebrated 1688–9 as a preservation of the freedom from Roman jurisdiction won in the 1530s, they also stressed that these freedoms had not been new. They reminded their readers that Henry VIII had regained a liberty lost to the papacy in the high Middle Ages, they set him within a tradition of earlier English kings who had battled to recover national autonomy, and they suggested that England had retained some of its independence through the medieval period.[190] Of particular interest had been the resistance of King John and of Henry II to papal bullying—a line of commentary that easily spilled over into narrative histories of England, such as Seller's.[191] Constitutional history thus mirrored theological: options for understanding the sixteenth-century Reformation ranged over revival, continuity, and sudden success—but all within an essentially unchanged struggle.

If such stasis smoothed over any discontinuity in the early sixteenth century, it obviously did the same for any sense of periodization within the Protestant epoch: that sense that history had moved forward through an early phase of Protestant expansion, and then on to more difficult time of retreat, division, and corruption. Looking back at the detailed rhetorical structure of Burnet's 1690 sermon to the

---

[187] *Lvx occidentalis, or, providence display'd in the coronation of King William and Queen Mary* (1689), preface.

[188] *Popish treaties*, 78.

[189] Edward Stillingfleet, *The bishop of Worcester's charge to the clergy of his diocese, in his primary visitation begun at Worcester, Sept. 11, 1690* (1691), 9. For Beverley, see Thomas Beverley, *The testimony of T. Beverley according to Scripture prophecy* [1691?].

[190] See, for example, [Long], *Resolution*, 10–12; Grey, *Debates*, x, 28–9.

[191] Seller's account of John and Henry's reign centred on resistance to 'proud' and usurping popes—Seller, *History of England*, 256–9, 282–5.

queen, it becomes clear that his account of advance and then contraction of true religion was intended less to sketch out a particular and characteristic history of the Reformation than to illustrate a moral truth that had held through all ages. Burnet's account of Luther's movement was preceded in his sermon by what he called 'a series of history'. This was a set of narratives that proved that 'the Nature and Promises of God are still the same', and which boiled down to the simple lesson that God rewarded people when they followed his injunctions, but punished them for backsliding.[192] To show this the preacher ran through a series of historical cycles. The Old Testament Jews had prospered under the patriarchs, but had then been delivered into captivity in Egypt for their sins. They had been great under David, but had then transgressed and been 'given up as prey to the King of Babylon'. They had been delivered from Babylon and reformed by prophets such as Nehemiah, but on corrupting themselves again, had fallen into the hands of the Kings of Syria. Nor had the pattern stopped with the Jews. Burnet told the history of the early church according to exactly the same script.[193] Early Christians had shown a purity and zeal, so that their faith 'had spread itself over the whole Roman Empire'.[194] Then, however, their fortune had bred luxury and complacency so the 'Church did soon degenerate'.[195] What followed was a series of plagues, the incursions of the gothic tribes, and the rise of Islam, which had put an end to the Christian civilization of antiquity.

In this context, the sense of advance through periods implied by Burnet's account of the Reformation's internal history largely evaporated. The two ages of Protestantism were not so much significant historical stages as opposed moral states, between which mankind was always alternating and had to choose. Protestant history was not an evolving continuation of a grand narrative, but at best a repetition of earlier patterns, and at worst simply a static microcosm of the human condition. Interestingly, Burnet introduced the section of the sermon on events since the Reformation by suggesting his audience take a 'narrower' view of his subject. He was not claiming to take a 'later' or a more up-to-date view. Burnet therefore denied any linear progress through periods of history. Indeed it made it hard to discern much movement of any kind. Although the preacher outwardly endorsed a cyclical view of the past, this was not his point. Rather, he stressed the standing moral decision that always faced humanity.

This was underlined in the preacher's more detailed description of the 'second' period of Reformation history. The decay that marked this era had not advanced in a steady narrative, but had rather been evidenced in repeated crises. These had included the 1550s with Charles V's near triumph in Germany and Mary Tudor's persecutions in England; the 1580s, when the Catholic League had formed with the aim of crushing the French Huguenots, and Phillip II had planned to invade

---

[192] Burnet, *Sermon…16th day of July*, 19.   [193] Ibid., 19–20.
[194] Ibid., 21.   [195] Ibid., 22.

Elizabeth's realm with his Armada; the 1620s, as the Reformation collapsed in the Habsburg lands and France's Protestants lost their last military strongholds; and the recent disasters of the 1680s, including the revocation of the Edict of Nantes and James II's accession. God had reiterated his warnings to his people of the consequences of their sins through these periodic crises; as a result Burnet's pattern of history began to look what geometrists call a fractal. A fractal is an apparently complex mathematical figure, which is in fact simpler in than it appears, because it demonstrates the same pattern in whatever part and at whatever scale it is examined. For example, a tree has fractal qualities: the pattern made by the trunk and large branches resembles the pattern of each of its large branches and the smaller ones that come off them, and this in turn is much like the tracery of the small branches and their twigs, or of the veins within leaves. Burnet's address was fractal in that, having demonstrated the unchanging 'nature and promises' of the deity in the first part, he examined these historically: first in long-term narratives and then in shorter-scale cycles that nested within these. He made clear that all his stories had the same structure and meaning—however long they had taken to play out, or wherever they were placed in the past. They were essentially identical manifestations of divine will.

Of course, the events that constituted Burnet's Protestant crises were also those that established the defining characteristics of the Reformation epoch. They were those—like the Marian persecutions, Armada, and James II's reign—that were widely used to suggest history had been a struggle between popery and faith since 1517. But Burnet was using them, not to create a periodization, but effectively to abolish such divisions of the past. And this was at least part of their effect when used by others. Listing of a canon of events to describe a Protestant era effectively froze the flow of time within that era. As has been shown, Protestant commentary on 1688–9 ran together events such as the St Bartholomew's Day massacre, Phillip II's aggressions against the Dutch and English, the Gunpowder Plot, the Irish revolt, the Great Fire of London, and the revocation of the Edict of Nantes, presenting them as mutually reinforcing examples of the popish threat.[196] But as the discourse did this, it robbed each moment of its historic individuality, and of any sense of a place in unfolding historical processes. The events were, spiritually, equivalent: there had been no real evolution between them. Their sole message was the fractal tale that papists kept plotting, that Protestants were in unending danger, but that a constant God would always be ready to deliver a faithful people.

This point was particularly striking in the use of chronological coincidences to prove the role of providence in James's fall. As has been shown, the annual 5 November thanksgiving was adapted to celebrate William's triumph as well as the deliverance from Guy Fawkes. But this was joined by an additional resonance.

---

[196] See above ch. 3.2.

Polemicists soon noted that it had been exactly one hundred years since another great salvation of England from Catholicism. The revolution was paired with the defeat of the Armada in 1588.[197] A doggerel verse set to the tune of *Lilli Bulero* and relating the events of December, had 'One Thousand, Six Hundred, Eighty and Eight' as its refrain (a clear attempt to establish a resonance with the Armada), and preachers at the official thanksgivings for the Dutch expedition underlined the link.[198] John Flavell, the Presbyterian minister, told his Devon congregation that God often marked the hundredth anniversary of a work of providence with another, and George Halley told those assembled in York Minster that the year eighty-eight had now seen two deliverances from papal tyranny.[199] At its most eloquent, these coincidences could be used to present the revolution as a sort of glorious summary of all God had done for English Protestants. But this again collapsed change over time. In his 1689 thanksgiving sermon, the future archbishop of Canterbury, John Tillotson, noted that William's arrival had happened 'just a hundred years after' the Armada and 'the same day' as the revelation of the gunpowder conspiracy. But this was far more than a tidy coincidence. 'God seems in this last deliverance, in some sort to have united and brought together all the other great deliverances which he hath been pleas'd to work for this nation against all the remarkable attempts of popery'.[200] Here Tillotson was cementing 1688–9 into the canon of Protestant history—but he was also tacitly insisting that the revolution was nothing new. At most it might be some sort of fulfilment, the most perfect instance, of something that had happened repeatedly since the Reformation.

The third and final element of Reformation periodization in revolutionary discourse was also undermined by the stasis of Christian chronology. Unless one understood 1688–9 as part of a closing apocalyptic unfolding of human affairs (of which, more below), any sense that the revolution itself might usher in a new era was compromised by the difficulty of describing the novelty of that new era, given that the spiritual state of mankind had been fixed over one and a half millennia before. At best, 1688–9 might be a return to a purity of belief, worship, and manners that had been lost in intervening times. But since the Protestant worldview already made this claim for the sixteenth-century Reformation, the revolution could not be the start of a very novel period, and anyway, reform of belief, worship, and manners could only ever be a change in human response to God's fundamental and unchanging offer of salvation to sinners. Any new era was not,

---

[197] Halley, *Sermon preached in the cathedral*, 12; Tilloston, *A sermon preached at Lincolns-Inn-Chappel*, p. 30; Peck, *Jericho's downfall*, 15.

[198] Galbraith M. Crump, ed., *Poems of Affairs of State*, vol. 4: *1685–9* (New Haven: Yale UP, 1968), 317–19.

[199] John Flavell, *Mount Pisgah: a sermon preached at the publick thanksgiving, February xiiii, 1688/9* (1689), 2; Halley, *Sermon preached in the cathedral*, 12–13.

[200] Tillotson, *A sermon preached at Lincoln's Inn Chappel*, 30.

therefore, any more than a fresh opportunity, or a moment of reinvigorated resolution, to live according to God's ancient law.

These points were implied in the presentation of the revolution as an exceptional opportunity to revive the original Reformation of the sixteenth century. This was perhaps inevitable given that William's triumph was seen as a salvation of Protestantism, but it had the temporal effect of blunting the existential newness of that victory since it took the audience back to the first moment of reform. Instances could be drawn from a wide variety of material, but Burnet's words will be used here because of the richness of his commentary on 1688–9, and because he was, arguably, the person in later seventeenth-century England who knew most about the original break with Rome. Repeatedly, he presented the revolution as an extraordinary point in time—but only because it set the clock back to the Tudor era. It provided the same opportunities as had been offered to the first reformers: the English could now repeat their work in restoring true Christianity, or—in an only slightly more progressive formulation—they might complete it after the struggle had been interrupted. So, in his first published sermon back on English soil, Burnet told the prince of Orange that a new 'Reformation' was needed in response to God's miraculous salvation of the true faith in England.[201] At the January 1689 thanksgiving, he told the House of Commons they had a rare and precious chance to 'give the last finishings to our Reformation'.[202] In November of the same year, he told an audience at Bow Church that the revolution was posing the same pressing challenge to unite for godliness that had occurred at 'the first beginnings of the Reformation'.[203] By Christmas Day, he was telling the king and queen that 'so great a Revolution' demanded 'visible Reformation'.[204] In October of the next year, he explained the purpose of William's new regime as giving the Reformation 'a recovery and a new lustre'.[205] Essentially, Burnet was confirming the argument of several scholars who have suggested that, right into the high eighteenth century, English Protestants felt themselves confronted with the same call to action as the original reformers. Their assumptions about their duties created a very 'long' Reformation—one that began in the sixteenth century, but demanded the same duties, and set the same patterns of thought, for several hundred years.[206]

---

[201] G. Burnet, *Sermon preached in the chappel of St James*, 25–6.

[202] G. Burnet, *Sermon preached before the House of Commons*, 33.

[203] Gilbert Burnet, *An exhortation to peace and union in a sermon…26th Novemb. 1689* (1689), 23.

[204] Gilbert Burnet, *A sermon preach'd before the king and queen at Whitehall on Christmas day, 1689* (1690), p. 34.

[205] Gilbert Burnet, *A sermon preach'd before the king and queen at Whitehall, the 19th day of October, 1690* (1690), p. 26.

[206] Ingram, *Reformation Without End*; Jeremy Gregory, 'The Making of a Protestant Nation: Success and Failure in England's Long Reformation', in Nicholas Tyacke, ed., *England's Long Reformation, 1500–1800* (London: UCL Press 1998), 307–34.

Such qualification of the novelty of any fresh start was also clear in calls for a transformation of moral behaviour after 1688–9. The self-chosen name for these initiatives—appeals for a *'reformation'* of manners—again connected the movement to the early sixteenth century, and the material promoting the campaign made it clear that people's duty to behave in a godly manner had been long-standing (for all that gratitude for the revolution should provide an additional motivation). William's arrival was not the first encouragement that God had given to moral renewal: it was the succession of earlier missed chances that gave such urgency to the movement. In fact it could be argued that that whole initiative had been launched among fears about the repeated failure to respond to providence. The earliest call for a systematic renewal of morality in the face of the revolution was Burnet's address to William on 23 December 1688. This explained that the English must react to God's mercy if they were to secure the promise of this 'most glorious beginning of a noble change in the whole face of affairs', but it also stressed that efforts were particularly important because the nation had blown a similar chance to perfect its relationship with God only three decades before. The 1660 Restoration had been a divine deliverance comparable to William's intervention, but people had greeted it with an immediate spate of drunkenness and then with the fashionable contempt for virtue which had marked Charles II's reign. The result had been the divine wrath that had brought a Catholic regime to power, 'so in order to the preventing the return of the like Evils, we must avoid relapsing into the like Sins'.[207] This line of argument also emerged as 29 May thanksgiving sermons were deployed to stress that the revolution demanded greater efforts for godliness. When William Lloyd preached on the day in 1692, the Restoration was presented as an earlier chance to restore national righteousness—but one that had proved abortive, and one whose promise could be completed only now that the corruptions of the restored regime had been swept away.[208] Of course, as this writer has argued elsewhere, much of this material was anti-Jacobite propaganda which accused the exiled regime of squandering chances for godliness.[209] Nevertheless, its very prevalence in post-revolution discourse blunted any sense that William's arrival had presented a wholly new kind of opportunity for spiritual renewal.

So far, we have considered the stilling of time within a Protestant interpretation of 1688–9 that undermined its potential for periodization. But the static quality of Christian chronology also weakened the sense of temporal progress that had been created by use of the Old Testament and the book of Revelation. The effect of engagement with the Hebrew Bible was fairly obvious, given everything that has been said so far, and can be dealt with reasonably concisely. Its main

---

[207] G. Burnet, *A sermon preached in the chappel of St James*, 20–1.
[208] William Lloyd, *A sermon preached before her Majesty on 29 May* (1692).
[209] Claydon, *William III and the Godly Revolution*.

consequence was to suggest that the basic pattern of history had remained unchanged for a period longer even than that of the Christian era.

To explore this, it is worth remembering why English Protestants adhered so closely to the Old Testament. Apart from their insistence on the Bible as the sole source of religious truth, this was almost certainly because of the vulnerable state of England's Reformation through most of its history. Surrounded by hostile Catholic neighbours, and wrestling with a domestic population prone to popish infiltration and spiritual indifference, Protestants recognized helpful analogies in the history of the Jews. The Hebrew Bible offered endless tales of God protecting his chosen people when they were threatened by idolatrous, cruel, and ambitious heathens, and, gratifyingly for those disappointed in fellow countrymen, of his smiting those backsliding Jews who failed to meet his standards. But whilst this was all very comforting, and whilst it did provide some sense of narrative as biblical stories were applied to the modern world, it was also a quintessentially typological approach to the distant past. Protestants were using biblical instances, from thousands of years before, as prefigurings of current circumstances. They therefore assumed a cosmos in which divine dealing never changed: indeed, it was one in which even the incarnation had not altered the basic relationship between heaven and humanity.

This mental habit was clear in reactions to 1688–9. As we have explored, the sermons that established a canon of Protestant events, and that incorporated the revolution among these, frequently used Old Testament stories as types of events in the Reformation age. To take another set of examples: all the texts for the surviving thanksgiving sermons for William's arrival in the early months of 1689 came from the Hebrew Bible (the New Testament was excluded entirely). Preachers spoke of the Protestant deliverance as echoing God's salvation of the Jews from Egyptian servitude in the book of Exodus; or incidents of God's mercy during the Judaic monarchy—as covered in the books of Samuel, Kings, Chronicles, and Psalms; or the state of Israel at the end of the Babylonian captivity—when the Jews were allowed to return to their homeland and rebuild their temple, as narrated in Jeremiah and other prophetic literature. This was remarkable, not least because it tied recent events to a very, very distant past. The return from Babylonian captivity had occurred in the late sixth century BCE; as we noted when discussing constitutional thought, the Judaic monarchy stretched back from the early sixth to the eleventh century; and the Exodus, though hard to date because of its debateable historicity, could not have happened much later than the end of the thirteenth century BCE.[210]

At its most extreme, this tendency to think typologically created multiple frameworks of related instances that trapped time hopelessly in a rigid grid. Take, for

---

[210] For particularly good examples, see Halley, *Sermon preached in the cathedral*, 12–18, and *Sermon preach'd in a country church*, 8–9.

example, the sermon by Tillotson on the 1689 thanksgiving. This took a passage from the book of Ezra, expressing thanks to God for the deliverance from Babylonian exile, and applied it to William's rescue of England from popery. This made Ezra's circumstances the type of Tillotson's, and so stressed that in all ages God could reward a people more richly than their sins deserved. But as we have seen, this same sermon also presented 1688–9 as a culmination and repeat of the mercies of 1588 and 1605. William's arrival thus became the anti-type, not just of a biblical type—the deliverance of Ezra's day—but of the non-biblical types that Tillotson minted from the dating coincidences—the mercies under Elizabeth and James I. Moreover, these new types must also, logically, be anti-types of Old Testament precursors. They had certainly been described in exactly that way in celebrations of them since they occurred, and—as we have seen in the case of November 5—continued to be so in William's reign. This was a temporal universe of endless, mutually reinforcing, self-reference. Unlike the physicists' 'arrow of time' (which can only operate asymmetrically, in one, forward, direction), Tillotson's events could speak to each other both forwards and backwards because God's nature and dealing never changed. In the rhetorical performance, the return from the Babylonian exile gave meaning to 1688–9. This then gave meaning back to 1588 and 1605, so that both modern and biblical events ended up in a rich web of reciprocal conversation, deepening—but not altering—the significance of each other. This time was not only fractal, but symmetrical. It defied the assumptions of the emerging natural sciences, and of 'modern' chronology more generally.

The one element of Christian thinking that might have broken the temporal tyranny of types was apocalyptic. Revelation suggested that, towards the end of time, Christ would once again intervene in worldly affairs in significant ways that would change the spiritual economy of the universe. He would finally defeat the forces of Satan and remake heaven and earth. As a result, the faithful would never again face the moral choices and temptations that typological examples were evoked to elucidate. If apocalyptic responses to 1688–9 had been widespread and profound, therefore, there would have been a mode of Protestant thinking that could have had a truly progressive view of time. Yet, while some people clearly did react to William's arrival in these terms, and while some scholars have argued for a strong survival of the apocalyptic tradition into the late seventeenth century, there is a need for real caution. As a number of historians have argued, confidence that one could interpret the apocalypse and apply it to current events may have been badly dented in the civil wars of the mid seventeenth century. Many who had believed the victory of parliamentary forces would initiate some sort of millennium of godly rule had been disappointed: hopes had been blasted by the division and violence such views unleashed, by the use of Revelation to promote a disturbing cornucopia of political and religious ideals, and simply by the fact that the victory had been so spectacularly reversed in 1660. After that bitter experience, some scholars have suggested there was reluctance, fear, and embarrassment in making strong claims of eschatological certainty. It is perhaps possible to trace—as Christopher Hill most prominently claimed he had—a waning of apocalyptic in the Restoration decades, or at least its modification into other kinds of thought.[211]

Examining closely how prophetic language was used in the revolution's aftermath suggests a position between the competing scholarly interpretations of the prominence of Revelation in the late Stuart era. As we have seen, there were plenty of statements that seemed to express apocalyptic optimism after 1688–9. Yet frequently, phrases or tone made caveats. When this happened, rhetoric collapsed back into a typological world of unchanging moral truths. This was especially true for members of the established church: the group whose enthusiasm needs to be proved before eschatology is accepted as common outside the minority groups who definitely did espouse it. For example, Tillotson's sermon at the January thanksgiving in 1689 (which is emerging as a remarkably rich source of temporal conceptions) was sufficiently excited by recent events to hint at apocalyptic expectation. The preacher urged his audience to reform their lives, taking as a warning the Jews, whom God had finally abandoned for their immorality, and said these unfortunate folk served as examples to his audience, 'upon whom the ends of the World are come'. To drive this home, Tillotson told the English not to 'tempt Christ, who is beginning the Glorious Deliverance of his Church from the Tyranny of Antichrist'. Yet the notion that the Lord was just 'beginning' his final defeat of evil said rather little about how long this would take (so left the apocalyptic timescale vague), and even more significantly, the fact that the eschatological utterance came within a comparison between England and Israel (and in a sermon which had spent a long time in its early sections establishing the parallels) meant it could be read as simply a particularly vivid typological statement. England's position was the same as that of the ancient nation. It was not being (or at least had not yet been) transformed by processes leading to the end of the world. To underline this, Tillotson used explicitly typological language. Quoting St Paul, he said of the punishments the Jews had suffered, 'Now all these things happened unto them for Examples, or Types, and they are written for our admonition'.[212]

Other Anglicans also used caution, often bottling apocalyptic within a less radical language that simply illustrated static moral truths. Simon Patrick, preaching on the same day as Tillotson in 1689, suggested that God would soon heap further blessings on his people, and that this meant that he, or at least 'his name', was near. After using that phrase, however, Patrick spent some paragraphs explaining what it meant. It turned out mainly to indicate that the deity brought a variety of blessings

---

[211] William M. Lamont, *Godly Rule: Politics and Religion 1603–1659* (London: Macmillan, 1967), ch. 7; Christopher Hill, *Some Intellectual Consequences of the English Revolution* (Madison: University of Wisconsin Press, 1976); Christopher Hill, *The English Bible in the Seventeenth-Century Revolution* (London: Penguin, 1993), ch. 19; James R. Jacob and Margaret C. Jacob, 'Anglican Origins of Modern Science: The Metaphysical Foundations of the Whig Constitution', *Isis*, 71 (1980), 251–67, esp. at 259.

[212] Tillotson, *A sermon preached at Lincoln's Inn Chappel*, 22–3.

to the peoples he favoured and who lived according to his word, and that these blessings could reinforce each other (for example, political peace stemmed both naturally and providentially from social harmony).[213] He then proved this with a range of historical examples: examples which were deployed as types. Similarly, Gilbert Burnet's apocalyptic statements tend to dissolve on closer analysis. He had indeed become excited on two pulpit occasions shortly after William's arrival in England. In the address to the prince at St James in late December 1688, and at his coronation service a few months later, Burnet had seemed to promise 'a New Jerusalem'; an imminent start to Christ's thousand year reign on earth; and the new heavens and new earth. But examined more carefully, these predictions were very cautious. The new heavens and earth in the St James performance were, in fact, just a way of speaking. They were a state of blessing and virtue that 'may' be 'termed' this new cosmos 'according to the Prophetick Style'. The talk of the New Jerusalem and of the millennium in the coronation address was merely a metaphor for what the world would look like if all kings were as virtuous as William, and this admirable state was illustrated from a range of past exemplars. Again, apparent apocalyptic turned out to be little but a colourful expression of long-standing moral lessons.[214] Finally, another clergyman, this time Thomas Burnet, described the ultimate divine remodelling of the world in his *Theory of the earth*. Yet, although he dedicated the last two sections of this work to Queen Mary when he published them in 1690, and although he said that the example of the post-revolutionary regime made the millennial rule of the saints more conceivable, he also carefully distanced himself from any precise dating or expectation of the events he proposed, explaining that the Bible was hard to interpret on this point.[215] The overall impression, therefore, is of excitement following the revolution that might spill over into quasi-apocalyptic language, but that most people were being careful not to be too exact, and that most remained firmly rooted in a universe structured around moral precedents.

Typology and notions of spiritual constancy within Christianity thus blunted the sense of periodized and forward progress through time within Protestant readings of 1688–9. Their effects on perceptions of the present were more equivocal, but still qualified any vision of a 'modern' temporal awareness in the commentary. Certainly, biblical types did not remove the urgency of action in the current moment. Presenting the horrors of God's judgements upon nations who did not respond to his warnings or protection (the fates of Sodom and of Jerusalem took

---

[213] Patrick, *A sermon preached at St Paul's*, 30–6. Patrick had told the prince of Orange a week before, that his arrival 'may' herald the millennium: Simon Patrick, *A sermon preach'd in the chappel of St James…20 January* (1689), p. 32.

[214] G. Burnet, *A sermon preached in the chappel of St James*, 21; Gilbert Burnet, *A sermon preached at the coronation of William III and Mary II* (1689), p. 20.

[215] T. Burnet, *Theory*, epistle dedicatory, 31. For another qualified hope that final deliverance might be coming, see Edward Pelling, *A sermon preached before the king and queen at Whitehall, Decemb. 8 1689* (1690), 26–8.

centre stage), could only underline the pressing need to reform, and would stress the range of possible futures arising from the current moment. If godliness were sincere and complete enough, England would be rewarded as God's favoured nation. If not, the horrors being inflicted on Protestant churches abroad were held up as warnings of what would come—and that was only if God chose to punish the kingdom by the ordinary, human, means of French invasion.[216] Destruction by (super)natural catastrophe was also an option. For example, the earthquake felt in London in 1692 was deployed to show a Sodom-style fate was a real possibility.[217] And yet, while God's unchanging relationship with mortals invested the post-revolution present with a particular intensity of anxiety, an expectation, and a sense of action within the moment, it also provided a limiting script that made the future less uncertain. It thus, perhaps, helped to stabilize the present. The range of what God might do was extraordinary, but the rules by which he would decide what to do were clear and fixed and had been illustrated repeatedly in the past. In that sense, the future was predictable from the typology, and it was even controllable if folks drew the right lessons. Repentance would bring salvation. By this same token, although God's unchanging law made action urgent in the present, it also made duty clear. One might not know if what one was doing would prove sufficient to assuage divine anger, but there could be no doubt about what one was supposed to do. The predictable litany of recommended responses to God's mercy in 1689—temperance, mutual charity, sincere worship, and so on—was so standard as to become the most tedious feature of Protestant discourse under William.

At a deeper level, the providential element in the present's shaping of the future removed even more of its fluidity. It was God who determined consequences of current actions. And God stood outside time. He had foreknowledge of what would happen, and what would happen fitted a preordained divine plan leading to the apocalypse—even if that apocalypse were not starting to arrive just yet. In all these senses, the English Protestants in the years after 1688–9 knew that the future was fixed. It was already 'full' of God's design for it. There was uncertainty was in human knowledge about how the present would lead to the future, but there was absolutely no uncertainty about how it would actually do so. It is, admittedly, difficult to find concrete evidence of these philosophical considerations breaking the surface of Protestant commentary on the revolution—but that commentary's fundamental nature, as Christian discourse, ensured those considerations were there. And perhaps there was an echo in the comforting tone of some responses to 1688–9. Sermons stressing the urgency of response, for example, would

---

[216] For such warnings, see Burnet, *Some sermons*, 39—this from a sermon preached on the first fast day for William's war, unpublished at the time; Simon Patrick, *A letter of the bishop of Chichester to his clergy* (1692), preface, x.

[217] Thomas Doolittle, *A sermon preached upon the late earthquake* (1692).

reassure with insistence on its efficacy. If this was the time that a Christian people finally turned to their God, their God would welcome them as his own. There was, on reflection, little anxiety or unpredictability in such a present.

The impact of Protestantism on the psychology of the current moment was therefore a microcosm of its whole impact on time. On one hand, it encouraged a dynamic sense of forward movement through stages of being that allowed lives to unfold as narrative and suggested transformations between great periods. On the other, and probably stronger, hand, it insisted that nothing fundamental could ever change. In images already used, Protestant time was fractal (its patterns were the same at every period and over whatever timescale one examined it) and it was symmetrical (it could be read as easily backwards, from later events to earlier ones, as it could forwards). Such a chronological awareness could invest the revolution with excitement and the possibility of great historical significance. But it was not the framework to understand 1688–9 as radically new.

4

Time and History in Opposition Rhetoric

4.1 The Origins of Opposition

Perhaps the most striking thing about the campaign against William's intervention in England was how long it took to start. Although the Dutch were assembling their invasion force through the summer of 1688, and although news of the mobilization meant James knew something was afoot, his keen sense of family loyalty, and his wager that political forces in the Netherlands would restrain the prince of Orange, meant he refused to believe that his son-in-law would attack his realm until the fleet was very nearly ready to sail.[1] As a result, little propaganda was directed at William by the Stuart court until the early autumn. Then, however, an energetic series of pamphlets, public prayers, and royal declarations suddenly began to warn the English of the horror of what might unfold.[2] One of the very earliest pieces, a short tract entitled *The Dutch design anatomised*, ended with a striking historical analogy. Presenting an interpretation of the 1588 Armada that was markedly different from that which would soon appear in Williamite propaganda, the author urged his audience to support the government in rendering 'the Invasion as ineffectual, and as fatal to the most unjust Aggressors, as that was a hundred years since'.[3]

Such a use of the past was, of course, essentially typological. It ignored political and religious context as it used a point in history to apply direct political lessons to the present. The century between the Habsburg and Orange invasions, and the considerable ideological difference between them, collapsed as the English were asked to fight alongside their forefathers in defence of the kingdom. The lesson drawn may have opposed the stance of the material this book has examined so far: but it created the same static chronology. Other parts of the pamphlet fitted this pattern. For instance, the author used the examples of the Saxon invasion of Britain, and the Norman Conquest of England, to suggest that rulers who came to power by force always imposed a tyranny on their new subjects.[4] Again,

---

[1] John Miller, *James II: A Study in Kingship* (rev. edn, London: Methuen, 1989,), 193–4.
[2] Tony Claydon, 'William III's *Declaration*', esp. 91–7.
[3] *The Dutch design anatomized* (1689), 40.   [4] Ibid., 11–18.

The Revolution in Time: Chronology, Modernity, and 1688–1689 in England. Tony Claydon, Oxford University Press (2020). © Tony Claydon.
DOI: 10.1093/oso/9780198817239.001.0001

this was the very opposite of the reading of historical events that would be offered by William's apologists, but, again, the past was treated as an unproblematic source of immediately relevant lessons. From these examples, it may seem the only difference between the supporters of the revolution and its detractors would be in the political points made, not in their deployment of history. Jacobites and Williamites cherry-picked the past for morals, even if they reached for different cherries.

Yet Jacobite, and other oppositional, material is a bit more interesting than this. It included alternative approaches to chronology: indeed there were hints of this even in that first anti-Williamite tract. The *Dutch design* used the past typologically, but it was also issuing warnings, so it presented history, not as something to be celebrated and repeated, but as something to avoid. As it said of earlier invasions of England, James's subjects were in danger of suffering 'the like miseries the Britons did under the Saxons, the Saxons under the Normans', if they did not rally to repulse the Dutch.[5] In a subtle, but significant, shift in the lesson drawn from the precedent, history did not bind, but must rather be transcended by avoiding the mistakes of the past. The tract's warnings also began, at least imaginatively, to map out a post-revolution narrative, and the story it told would remodel the nation. If William triumphed, the pamphlet implied, monarchy would be abolished by his king-hating allies, and the people would (in another use of precedent as horror story) receive the same treatment the Dutch had meted out to English merchants in the notorious 'massacre' at Amboyna in the East Indies in 1619.[6] Political revolution would thus accelerate history. The consequences of Dutch occupation would sweep away all old certainties: security, welfare, liberty, the old English government itself, would become mere memories.

This first anti-Williamite work thus contained, in embryo, themes that would develop in oppositional thought over the following months and years. There was a contrasting reading of precedent that—among other things—would reinterpret England's participation in the Reformation, repackage the ancient constitution, and open the seventeenth century as a source of historical analogy. There was also an emotional and intellectual distancing from precedent, when the past was read primarily as warning or lament rather than as inspiring guide. And there was the construction of a post-revolution narrative that would engender a sense of rapid change, and ultimately of underlying transformative processes. Opposition understanding shared much with the chronological world of the Williamites, but it also pointed to a more fluid, dynamic, and evolving sense of time.

---

[5] Ibid., 15.   [6] Ibid., 16, 19.

4.2 The Re-engineering of Precedent in Jacobite Argument

In the face of the catastrophe of 1688–9, the most urgent task facing Stuart loyalists was to counter the interpretations of William's arrival put out by the regime. At the core of the Jacobite argument was the illegality of what the prince of Orange had done in taking the throne. He was a foreign usurper; no honest Englishman could therefore give him their allegiance, and the whole legal framework of government had been compromized. Appealing to law in an English context meant appealing to history, so the Jacobites—no less than their Williamite rivals—dived back through the centuries of the English past. As one early pamphleteer put it, the revolutionaries had sinned in making the crown elective 'which for above 600 years has been successive'; and as another argued, they wished to reverse the long-standing judgement of King John's reign, that deposition was anathema to the English constitution.[7] But, of course, Jacobite reading of the precedents had to contest that of their enemies, and their choice of past examples would diverge as well. The result was a vision of the national story very different from that left by either Whig or Tory narratives.

The central point Jacobites wished to make was that hereditary monarchy was the essence of the English constitution. As Paul Monod has stressed, this principle lay at the heart of much of the popular material they produced. Doggerel verse, and visual imagery, emphasized the family succession of James II; it also insisted on the king's true fatherhood of his son, James Francis Edward—whom some Williamites slurred as a fraud, smuggled into his mother's birthing chamber to cover her inability to provide an heir, but whom loyal artists depicted as the very image of his parents.[8] In more sophisticated political polemic, some authors stressed heredity to the exclusion of other considerations—whilst many others argued that it was the keystone of the constitution, without which all other laws, rights, customs, and privileges would fall. Precise ideology thus varied, but all of those who rejected the revolution agreed that the indefeasible legitimacy of the hereditary heir was the first and founding axiom of English politics. This allowed them to paint the accession of William as a breach of fundamental law, but it also meant they had to deal with a barrage of Williamite precedent. As we saw in chapter two, supporters of the revolution plundered history for examples of nonlineal succession that had been accepted as legitimate, so to make their argument, Jacobites needed a cogent rebuttal.

The most instructive battle was fought over the Wars of the Roses. As we have seen, Whigs and Tories clashed over this ground, but Jacobites departed radically

---

[7] *A remonstrance and protestation of all the good protestants of this kingdom* (1689), 5; [George Hickes], *A letter to the author of a late paper* (1689), 6.

[8] Paul Monod, *Jacobitism and the English People, 1688–1788* (Cambridge: CUP, 1989), 70–80.

from either party's use of the era. For James's supporters, the key events were not the termination of reigns by the people's representatives, or the *de facto* acceptance of rulers after they had chased each other off the throne, but rather a statute of 1461 and a marriage in 1486. The statute had been that passed by Edward IV to confirm his title. This might appear to uphold the principle that Parliament had the right to decide who was the monarch, but Jacobites ignored this implication to concentrate on the clauses of the act that had declared Henry IV, Henry V, and Henry VI to have been usurpers.[9] Using these as confirmation, opponents of William argued that what had happened in 1399 could not have been the legitimate removal of a king by the legislature, since Parliament had had no right to do such a thing. Rather, it had been an illegal seizure of the crown by a man, Henry Bolingbroke, who was not the royal heir. Henry had then passed this illegality—and the inevitable political instability it came to breed—down to his own heirs, until Edward's capture of the throne had returned the true hereditary line.[10] The lesson of the Wars of the Roses was not, therefore, the mutability of succession, but rather the very opposite. Violence and uncertainly had stemmed from the exclusion of true monarchs. Certainly, Edward had accepted the validity of legal acts under the Henrys, and so had seemed to acknowledge the authority of *de facto* kings. But this had been to avoid the chaos of unpicking great swathes of previously settled law, and to protect subjects who (not being versed in the complexities of dynastic succession) had innocently obeyed the ruler who seemed to be in charge.[11]

The marriage was that between Henry VII and Elizabeth of York. When Henry had won the battle of Bosworth Field, Jacobites insisted he had not legitimately gained the throne because he had not been the hereditary heir of the last rightful monarch, Edward V (Richard III's kingship was another of the usurpations so common in the era). His rule was therefore illegal, and the '*de facto*' statute that he passed, which seemed to uphold the principle of legitimate rule by whoever had secured the throne, was in fact a worthless piece of partisan posturing. It was exactly the position one would expect the latest usurper to adopt as he tried to distract people from investigating his thin hereditary claim. However, by marrying Elizabeth of York, who was the sole surviving representative of the legitimate line by this point, Henry began to repair the situation, and Jacobites insisted that

---

[9] [Jeremy Collier], *The desertion discuss'd in a letter to a country gentleman* (1689), 5; [Robert Brady], *An enquiry into the remarkable instances of history and parliamentary records* [1690?], 40; [Henry Dodwell], *Concerning the case of taking the new oaths of fealty and allegiance* [1689], 8. *A review of Dr Sherlock's case* (1691), 39.

[10] [Collier], *Desertion discuss'd*, 4; [Dodwell], *Concerning the case*, 8; [Jeremy Collier], *Animadversions upon the modern explanation of II Henry 7 cap.1* (1689), 2; [Jeremy Collier], *Vindiciae juris regii* (1689), 7; *The character of Thomas Merkes, bishop of Carlise* (1689); [Charlwood Lawton], *The Jacobite principles vindicated* (1693), 3.

[11] [Collier], *Animadversions upon the modern explanation*, 2; Thomas Browne, *The case of allegiance due to the king in possession* (1690), 14.

the marriage proved Henry knew he had to do this. The first Tudor could now suggest he had united his false claim to the throne with his wife's true one, and his son, Henry VIII, could be recognized as a fully legitimate monarch, though as the successor to his mother, not his father.[12] In such writing, the Jacobites were constructing a different sort of 'Ancient Government'.[13] Theirs was not rooted in the rights subjects enjoyed against their monarchs, but rather in a continuous hereditary succession. This might not always operate in practice, but the precedents focused upon proved it would eventually be re-established as people came to acknowledge their errors.

This vision shaped the Jacobites' use of earlier medieval events. For example, the deposition of Edward II in 1329 could no more be an illustration of Parliament's rights than the events seventy years later. Instead, it was interpreted either as a moment when heredity had asserted itself despite political turmoil (Edward II had been succeeded by his eldest son upon his resignation), or as another case when a departure from true heredity had been reversed. If Edward III had not been the legitimate king whilst his father was still alive, he was unquestionably so once the old ruler had died.[14] The reign of King Stephen was also reinterpreted away from Williamite norms. It did not illustrate the power of subjects to choose a non-hereditary ruler. Rather it again demonstrated the horrific effects of usurpation, and the tendency of the English crown to return to the correct line. The bloody civil war between Stephen and the Empress Mathilda (who should, in Jacobite thought, have been the unchallenged queen regnant) ended when Mathilda's son, Henry II, came to the throne by general agreement on Stephen's death. This agreement was reached because internecine turmoil had convinced everyone of the need to put the monarchy back in its proper course.[15]

Jacobites thus used medieval precedent to establish that the claims of true heredity were never extinguished, and that displacing it had lamentable consequences. Yet drawing this lesson produced a far more dramatic contrast to Williamite uses of the past than simply reinterpreting the Middle Ages. It opened a wholly new and raw era—the seventeenth century itself—as a storehouse of historical example. Unsurprisingly, James's supporters did not share their enemies' reticence in discussing the rebellion of 1642, the regicide of 1649, or the English republic. The generally accepted understanding of the Stuart age made the points they wanted, so they were more than happy to rehearse the narratives that the Williamites had

---

[12] James Montgomery, *Great Britain's just complaint* (1692), 23; [Collier], *Animadversions upon the modern explanation*, 6–7; Browne, *Case of allegiance*, 27–45; [Samuel Grascome], *Two letters written to the author of a pamphlet entituled Solomon and Abiathar* (1692), 21–2.

[13] The phrase was used early in Jacobite material, from James's first propaganda against William's invasion—see *Prayers to be used in all cathedral, collegiate and parochial churches…during this time of public apprehensions from the danger of invasion* (1688).

[14] [Collier], *Desertion discuss'd*, 4; Montgomery, *Great Britain's just complaint*, 23; [Collier], *Animadversions upon the modern explanation*, 4; [Brady], *Enquiry into the remarkable instances*, 39.

[15] *Character of Thomas Merkes*, 7; [Brady], *Enquiry into the remarkable instances*, 23–31.

so carefully suppressed. Indeed Paul Monod has claimed that a 1688 ballad, which presented the prince of Orange's advance from Devon as a re-enactment of Cromwell's Good Old Cause, was the earliest piece of Jacobite propaganda.[16] Opponents of the revolution thought the seventeenth century demonstrated in spades (and even better, did so within living memory) that rebellion brought murder and misery, that judging or removing a ruler did not suppress his hereditary right, and that, in time, God's providence was likely to return monarchy to its true succession.

Surprisingly, although Jacobites made frequent reference to the heinous sin of regicide, this was rarely the meat of their case. In most instances, citing Charles' execution was a brief rhetorical gambit that attempted to make links between the moral character of people who would put a king on trial, and those who would chase one out of the country.[17] It could even be used to suggest the latest revolutionaries were worse than those who had risen against Charles I because, for instance, they had not bothered to assemble hard evidence against the deposed ruler, or because the English had lazily allowed a king to be removed without the great struggle that had characterized the 1640s.[18] However, the regicide itself tended to receive passing comment, rather than extended analysis; occasionally it was used in unexpected ways. For example, James Montgomery claimed abuses by government under William were worse than those that he admitted had started the discontent against Charles—so he opened the possibility of criticizing the martyred monarch that was rarely taken by the Jacobites' opponents.[19]

This lack of coherent focus on the regicide is a bit puzzling. It was perhaps because the parallels between 1649 and 1689 did not, in truth, go far beyond the basic deposition of a ruler. James II had lost power, but he had not been put on trial and executed. It may also have been because Williamites had succeeded in putting distance between the two sets of events. As we have seen, supporters of the revolution insisted Charles I had not broken the law as his son had done and that he had been removed by an ambitious faction, rather than with the general consent of the political nation. Theories of conquest, abdication, and providential deposition in 1688–9 had also been designed to negate any suggestion of a repeat of 1649.[20] Presented with these obstacles to using the regicide to condemn the revolution, Jacobites instead concentrated on the regimes of the 1650s.

---

[16] Monod, Jacobitism, 49–50.

[17] See, for example, Animadversions upon the declaration of his highness the prince of Orange (1688), 21; [Sir Thomas Prendergrass], A short history of the convention (1689), 1; Observations upon the late revolution, 7; A letter from a loyal member of the church of England to a relenting abdicator (1689), 32; [Charlwood Lawton], The Englishman's complaint (1689), 2; [Collier], Vindiciae, 45–6; [Grascome], Two letters, 16; [Charlwood Lawton], Some paradoxes presented as a new-years-gift (1693).

[18] Remonstrance and protestation, p. 5; The loyal martyr vindicated (1691), p. 36.

[19] Montgomery, Great Britain's just complaint, 71.   [20] See above, ch. 2.3

There were, perhaps, two further reasons for this. First, the relevant parallels were far closer than with Charles I's execution. The Commonwealth, and Cromwell's Protectorate, had established effective power in England, just as William had done; but they were challenged, exactly as he was, by a legitimate Stuart exiled abroad. The choice of who to accept in these circumstances could thus be made to look almost identical in the two instances. Probably more importantly, however, Jacobites focused on the 1650s because so much of their fire was directed at *de facto* theories for William's authority. This was partly because they thought Tories (who relied on this sort of argument) might be easier to persuade than Whigs (whose party had been created in opposition to the idea of James's rule), but also because they were enraged into paroxysms of pamphleteering by the conversion of William Sherlock. As we have said, this tract-writing cleric had originally come out against the revolution, but in his 1691 *Case of allegiance,* he had announced that he was now willing to accept William on the thoroughly *de facto* grounds that the Dutchman had achieved a settled control of the country.[21] The sense of betrayal, and the consequent itch to attack Sherlock's new position, drew the Jacobites to the 1650s because they thought this was the easiest way to expose the monstrosity and absurdity of their bogeyman's arguments.

The first stage in the Jacobite case was simply to establish that their targets' rhetoric, and especially that of Sherlock, would justify the regimes of the 1650s as effectively as that of the 1690s. This was easier than one might expect. Sherlock's position did in fact come very close to the simple argument that one must obey those in power, whoever they were, because they were granting people protection from the dangers of anarchy and foreign invasion. One of the most sustained treatments of this theme came in John Kettlewell's lengthy and sophisticated refutation. Suggesting that Sherlock's argument 'would leave no such thing as a usurper in the world', Kettlewell pointed out that the Rump Parliament of the Commonwealth had been in longer, and more confident, command of the British Isles, than William had been, up to his opponent's point of writing. So, if the prince of Orange was justly ruler of England because he had now secured control, then the regicides had enjoyed exactly the same legitimacy.[22] Another extensive answer to Sherlock, this time by Robert Jenkin, gloried in the fact that Oliver Cromwell had been settled in power with full *de facto* control over the country for five years, so must, on his opponent's logic, have been legitimate, and a great cloud of other writers took the same line.[23] George Hickes stressed that any political action whatever could be justified as providential if it worked, and he challenged his opponents to say why their principles did not excuse the Lord

---

[21] For Sherlock's switch, see Kenneth Padley, 'Rendering unto Caesar in the age of revolution: William Sherlock and William of Orange', *Journal of Ecclesiastical History*, 59 (2008), 680–96.

[22] [John Kettlewell], *The duty of allegiance settled on its true grounds* (1691), pp. 48, 61, 62.

[23] [Robert Jenkin], *The title of a usurper after a thorough settlement examined* (1690), p. 71.

Protector or the Rump.[24] Thomas Browne pointed out that if Cromwell had made himself king, the idea that possession brought authority would have allowed him to execute all Charles II's followers as traitors.[25] An anonymous *Review* of Sherlock's *Case of allegience* kept coming back to the point that *de facto* power excused the regicides' rule, and a jaunty poem of 1690 made more or less the same case: 'Some idly fancy, that protection / doth nat'rally infer subjection [the basic reciprocity at the heart of de facto theory] / To which I say, if this were true / Subjection were even Cromwell's due'.[26]

Such rhetoric exposed the logical consequences of Williamite *de facto* theory for understandings of the mid seventeenth century, but of course it also packed an emotional punch. Given the near-universal, and relentlessly sustained, denigration of the republican regimes since 1660, Jacobites could paint supporters of the revolution as apologists for evil. They suggested that appealing for loyalty to William because he was in settled possession was to use arguments that would excuse the sins of the regicides because those sins had led to their political dominance. It would also overturn the widely accepted verdict on the mid-century revolution, and—perhaps worse—it put Williamite opponents in the company of Thomas Hobbes. In his famous *Leviathan*, Hobbes had argued for loyalty to the Commonwealth in the 1650s on the grounds that obeying whoever was exercising actual power was the logical choice for anyone who wished to avoid the chaos and constant bloodshed of ungoverned anarchy. But his reputation had been destroyed in the republic-denouncing decades after 1660, and he had become something of an icon of unprincipled, and probably atheistic, cynicism—so supporters of the exiled Stuarts therefore delighted in asserting that Williamites were spouting plain Hobbism.[27] In a related line of attack, Jacobites simply pointed out that *de facto* theory overturned the accepted view of the republican regime as an illegal usurpation and those who had opposed it as heroes. As an anonymous 1691 pamphleteer put it, when Charles had 'retired for his safety' and 'continued many years out of England', 'no man living ever thought…that he had abdicated the crown'; and, as George Hickes pointed out, the Restoration authorities had given short shrift to those who had tried to defend actions under Cromwell because his success suggested he had been a providentially appointed ruler.[28] Combining the standard view of the English republic as illegal with moral horror, John Lowthorp quoted statutes and declarations from the early years of Charles II's reign (though of course he insisted this had begun in 1649, not 1660). These had made it clear

---

[24] [George Hickes], *An apology for the new separation* (1691), p. 4.

[25] Browne, *Case of allegiance*, 46–7.

[26] *Review of Dr Sherlock's case; The new oath examined and found guilty* (1690).

[27] For the denigration of Hobbes, see the last section of Noel Malcolm, 'Hobbes, Thomas', in the *Oxford Dictionary of National Biography* www.oxforddnb.com.unicat.bangor.ac.uk/view/article/13400?docPos=1, accessed 08.06.16. For accusations of Hobbism, see [John Richardson], *Providence and precept* (1691), p. 15–17; [Hickes], *Apology*, p. 4.

[28] *Loyal martyr vindicated*, p. 20; [Hickes], *Letter to the author*, 13.

that the regicides were 'usurping tyrants' and 'exercrable, perfidious traytors', whilst the decision to make Cromwell protector had been 'wicked, traytorous and abominable'.[29] Meanwhile Thomas Wagstaff contrasted those clerics who had betrayed principle by defecting to William III with those Anglicans who had suffered at least career martyrdom under the republic in defence of political truth.[30] In 1692, Samuel Grascome observed that the Orangeists had tried to draw distinctions between the 1650s and 1690s, but 'there is scarce any arguments of them, that is not equally valid against the one as the other; nay I am sure some are more valid against the P of O. then O.C.' Emphasizing how large a part this logic had played in Jacobite writings, Grascome excused himself from detailed demonstration of his point: 'this hath clearly been done by so many hands already, that I am ashamed to repeat them.'[31]

Whilst weaponizing the 1650s was the most notable way that William's opponents forced the recent past into the political debates from which his supporters had so carefully excluded it, there was another route by which Jacobites introduced the seventeenth century to discussions. This was through their peculiar conception of the post-Reformation era—at least in England. Here we are not talking about Catholic Jacobites (who obviously rejected Williamite views of the last 170 years as an endlessly reiterated struggle against popery), but rather those who wrote from within the Protestant movement, but who disagreed about the basic meaning of history since the Tudor age. The key figure here was Abednego Sellar. In a 1689 response to the revolution—which generated a sub-controversy within the general print discussion of allegiance—this nonjuring clergyman re-read the time since Henry VIII's rejection of the Roman church.[32] For Sellar, this period—including the Stuart decades—had certainly been marked by a characterizing struggle against popish principles, but the key battle had not been against a corrupted theology, but against the doctrine that kings could be deposed for misbehaviour. This false doctrine, the author argued, had been the foundation of Rome's claims to worldly dominion in the Middle Ages; so, since 1517, good Protestants had insisted that monarchs were appointed by God, and could thus only be held to account by him. To prove this, Sellar quoted a great cloud of Protestant witnesses 'since the reformation' as the title of his pamphlet defined his topic. He began with English authorities, including Tyndal, the Henrician bishops, and Latimer and Cranmer, but then continued through a whole series of Elizabethan and early Stuart-era divines, and culminated in statements since the Restoration.

---

29   [John Lowthorp], *A letter to the bishop of Sarum* (1690), pp. 18–19.

30   [Thomas Wagstaff], *A letter to the author of a late letter* (1689); [Thomas Wagstaff], *A letter out of Suffolk* (1694).

31   [Grascome], *Two letters*, 30. For other passages drawing parallels with the 1650s, see *Letter from a loyal member*, 32; [Kettlewell], *Duty of allegiance*, p. 63; [Jenkin], *Title of a usurper*, p. 70–1. [Collier], *Desertion discuss'd*, 7; [Dodwell], *Concerning the case*, 2; [Richardson], *Providence and precept*, pp. 15–17.

32   [Sellar], *History of passive obedience.*

These included the era's bestseller, *The whole duty of man*, and (chosen for maximum embarrassment) the early views of clergy who had welcomed Charles II but went on to support William—men such as Simon Patrick and John Tillotson. Sellar then took his argument abroad. He quoted the founders of continental Protestantism (Erasmus, Luther, Beza, Calvin), but also a list of later European thinkers stretching through the seventeenth century, in order 'to shew...the Harmony of the Confessions, as in other things, between us and them, against the Papists'.[33] Sellar's effort sparked a series of replies that accused him of reading Protestant writings selectively—and that were especially fond of pointing out good Protestant monarchs such as Elizabeth and James I had helped rebels against royal authority in Scotland, France, and the Netherlands.[34] But he also had defenders, and the charge that Williamites had betrayed the doctrinal heritage of the Church of England became standard in Jacobite rhetoric.[35] This polemic placed particular stress on the outpourings of Anglican denunciation of rebellion since the civil war.

In the areas covered so far, James's supporters were both reinterpreting, and reselecting, precedent. Compared to their Williamite rivals, they drew different lessons from past events and picked a different set of events to cite. But they did not question the basic structure of historical argument. Endorsing a static chronology of their own, they reached back through time to draw immediately relevant morals, or to quote immediately applicable authorities, for current politics. Indeed, in opening up the seventeenth century for political analogy, they extended the realm of precedent. Bulldozing Williamite distinctions between the 1650s and the 1690s, they insisted the two decades were exactly the same.

Yet, whilst challenging supporters of the revolution on their own grounds was a large part of the Jacobite case, it was not the whole. In ways that were surprising for such a conservative political movement, James's supporters broke with the stifling typology of precedent, and began to construct more fluid and developmental models of time. A hint of this came with that very concentration on the Stuart age that their opponents had avoided. In Jacobite rhetoric, the seventeenth century was treated as a source of uncomplicated political truth, but at least this was drawn from very recent years (even from the life history of those still around)—and this reduced any sense of anachronism. A good number of the Jacobites' supposed lessons from the past did not have to ignore changes of context over centuries, as almost all Williamite constitutional argument did. More

---

[33] Ibid., p. 125.

[34] See, for example, *History of self-defence*; [Edward Fowler], *A vindication of the divines of the church of England* (1689); [Thomas Long], *The historian unmask'd* (1689); Johnson, *Some reflections*; Thomas Bambridge, *Seasonable reflections on a late paper* (1690).

[35] See [Hickes], *Letter to the author*; Thomas Ken, *Lacrymae ecclesisa Anglicanea* (1689 edition), epistle; *The sad estate of the kingdom* (1689); John Lake, *The declaration of the right reverend father in God, John, late bishop of Chichester* (1689).

concretely, among James's supporters, the Stuart age was treated more as a warning than as a precedent. Its lessons were more about what to avoid than what to emulate—and as we are about to see, this involved a substantially different attitude to time.

4.3 Warnings from History

To see the effects of Jacobite complaint about the past, is it useful to resume the backwards march through medieval history that we interrupted to discuss the Stuart age and the Reformation. Not long before the reign of King Stephen there had been the Norman Conquest. Jacobites had a particular set of attitudes to 1066 that meant that, for them, it could not be a precedent. As we saw, Williamite responses to the arrival of the Normans ranged from denying the discontinuity of a conquest (and so discussing it as another iteration of the ancient constitution), to trying to distract attention from the battle of Hastings by discussing Grotian theories of just war.[36] For Jacobites, by contrast, the Norman invasion might simply be a conquest, because they—or at least some of them—were happy to retain theories of absolute royal power. Some commentators argued that the Normans had established the unchallengeable rights of their monarchy over the territory and people they had conquered. These rights had been passed down by heredity to James II, and were the reason his subjects had sinned in removing him. As M.A. Thompson pointed out, the most vociferous advocate of this position was Jeremy Collier's early 1689 work, *Vindiciae juris regii*.[37] This tract asserted that the origin of English government had been in the conquest of 1066, which was interpreted as an unconditional triumph for William I that had bestowed an absolute and hereditary authority on his successor monarchs. To those who argued the Norman ruler had accepted Edward the Confessor's laws, Collier quoted a string of early medieval writers who described the Conqueror treating his new subjects arbitrarily, and he suggested any law that had been confirmed was criminal rather the constitutional. There was no real dispute about how thieves and murderers should be treated, so William upheld existing codes out of convenience, not because he was in any way bound by them.[38]

At first glance, this looks like just another debate within a precedent-based chronology. Both Jacobites and Williamites were drawing directly applicable lessons from the past, even if these were different lessons. But a number of considerations in fact meant the Jacobites did not, and could not, use 1066

---

[36] See above, ch. 2.3.
[37] M. A. Thomspon, 'The idea of conquest in controversies over the 1688 revolution', *Journal of the History of Ideas*, 38 (1977), 33–46.
[38] [Collier], *Vindiciae*, 8–12.

typologically. First, to argue that the Norman invasion founded an absolute hereditary monarchy was not, in fact, to appeal to a precedent. Rather, it was to construct an origin story for English government. The point of a precedent was to justify doing the same thing again, but an origin story could not, by definition, be repeated, at least not within the same legal and political framework. 1066 had been moment of constitutional foundation, so it could not be re-enacted without establishing a wholly novel political system, and in this new system, all precedents would fall. Belonging to a now-superseded political universe, former actions could no longer legitimate anything: as one Jacobite writer in fact put it, 'conquest cuts off the laws of the old constitution'.[39] Second, Jacobites avoided treating 1066 simply as precedent because this created an obvious problem. If a conquest by William I were a historical exemplar, its lesson was that anyone fighting their way to the throne would become the legitimate ruler, and this could be used to justify William III's rule.[40] Collier may have been partly blinded to this difficulty when he wrote, because in early 1689 it was not clear that William had yet conquered the Stuart realms (there were still substantial lands left in James's hands in Scotland and Ireland, and the loyalty of the English to their new-minted regime was not absolutely certain), but he and other Jacobites soon saw the peril. As Mark Goldie pointed out, *Vindiciae juris regii* was unusual in stressing the absoluteness of the Norman Conquest.[41] Though some Jacobite pamphlets did root duties to monarchs in the feudal law the Normans had introduced, many put the stress somewhere very different.[42]

The predominant emphasis in anti-regime writing on 1066 was the suffering of the people. The conquest had brought misery and slavery, and this was asserted from the start of the propaganda campaign. As we saw, the very early pamphlet *The Dutch design anatomised* drew a parallel between the brutality of William the Conqueror and the likely brutality of William of Orange, and this work was joined by other pieces written in the autumn of 1688 to counter the Dutch intervention. Some stressed the immediate bloodshed and martial rule that resulted from foreign invasions generally, but at least one used 1066 to mock the later William's claim that he had come to secure a free Parliament. The Norman army, like all invading forces 'from the beginning of the World', intended 'nothing but to

---

[39] *Review of Dr Sherlock's case*, 29.

[40] Most famously, though controversially, in Charles Blount, *King William and Queen Mary conquerors* (1693), but it formed at least part of the case of a number of pamphlets: Goldie, 'Revolution of 1689'.

[41] Mark Goldie, 'Edmund Bohun and *Jus Gentium* in the Revolution Debate, 1689–1693', *Historical Journal*, 20 (1997), 569–86.

[42] See, for example, [Dodwell], *Concerning the case*, 4; [Theophilus Downes], *A discourse concerning the significance of allegiance* [1689], pp. 4–5.

master where it comes', so English rights and liberties would be lost now.[43] Later Jacobite works also stressed the horrors of conquest, though they were sometimes wary of making explicit reference to 1066. Perhaps a sense that the English hereditary monarchy they were defending had begun with William I prevented them from being too direct in criticizing his rule. Nonetheless, their picture of a nation losing its rights when conquered would have evoked images of the Normans in an audience which had—earlier in the century—heard both Tory and radical arguments that this was exactly what had happened to the people in the eleventh century.[44] So when James Montgomery dismissed the case from conquest in the allegiance controversy by stating the principle meant 'Adieu to Rights and Privileges, Liberty and Property', and said that all of history's annals chronicled the slavery of conquered peoples, readers' minds would have slid to the Battle of Hastings.[45] Similarly, when Charlwood Lawton denied Jacobites were planning an invasion from France, because they realized how much the English would suffer in such an enterprise—and anyway charged that it was William who was behaving as the absolute conqueror—audiences would have read 1066 between his lines. A more open reference to the arrival of the Normans, this time by Robert Brady, illustrates how treatment of the conquest was changing among supporters of absolute, hereditary, monarchy. Before the revolution Brady had been the scholar who had done most to prove that English government was a Norman imposition that had established the indefeasible rights of kings. By 1690, however, his emphasis had shifted to the plight of those who had been overrun. Denying that the people had played any role in the election of the monarch in 1066, or for some time after, he asked how they could possibly have done so, since the people were Saxons enslaved by Norman masters, and so quite incapable of expressing their interests or influencing events.[46]

Of course, none of this was far from typological thinking. The past taught a lesson that was directly applicable: conquests led to widespread privation. But there were subtle differences between this sort of argument and justifying precedent. First, although emphasis had moved from the origins of royal power within the Tory thought of the exclusion era, to the sufferings of the Anglo-Saxons, both interpretations saw the possibility of radical discontinuity. An entire society and legal system had been replaced in 1066 and a new era had been inaugurated. This considerably weakened the hold of distant eras over current practice. Events were

---

[43] *Animadversions upon the declaration*, p. 28. For other works warning of bloodshed, see *Some reflections upon his highness the prince of Orange's declaration* (1688), 11–12; *Prayers to be used; By the king, a declaration, given 6 November 1688* (1688).

[44] For the classic studies of Norman domination after the conquest, see Hill, 'Norman Yoke'; Pocock, *Ancient Constitution*, 361–6; for exclusion-era Tories' insistence on absolute conquest, see above, ch. 4.2

[45] Montgomery, *Great Britain's just complaint*, 24.

[46] [Brady], *Enquiry into the remarkable instances*, 28–9.

only relevant to understanding current politics if they had occurred after the Conquest, and—more importantly—the foundation of authority was not an immemorial ancient constitution that demonstrated its principles through endless reiteration, but rather the imposition of new rules at a specific point in time. Second, and perhaps more significantly, the past here was not an exemplar, but a warning. It should not be repeated, if this could possibly be avoided. The lesson of history became the need to behave differently from people in the past; in fact the pattern of history must be transcended to create (or for Jacobites, recreate) a more just world. All this put multiple kinds of distance between the past and the present.

The treatment of 1066 by William's opponents was a specific case of divergence in historical interpretation, and in the relationship of the past to the present. But it illustrated dimensions of an alternative, Jacobite, sense of chronology that was evident in consideration of large swathes of history, and that differed markedly from the largely static vision of pro-revolution writers. After a few moments reflection, the reasons for the difference are fairly obvious. Williamites wanted to affirm the post-1688–9 order, and so, naturally, had a tendency to weave it into familiar patterns. This encouraged a vision that played down discontinuities, and that wanted to incorporate all points of history into an endless chorus of approval for what had just happened. But Jacobites were not celebrating the present. They were rejecting it. This encouraged a contrasting chronological sense, and one that, in particular, loosened the hold of the past over the current situation. For example, protesting against the present state of affairs (particularly if arguing for the return to an earlier one) implied that societies could deviate from their ideal condition—and thus that profound change was possible. It also opened the possibility that some periods of the past might be compromised as sources of exemplars. If the current moment were a perversion of truth, other points in history might be too. Both these consequences of protesting against the here and now undermined typological thinking. The first hinted that the world might change too much for old lessons to be applicable; the second raised the possibility that sometimes the real lesson of the past was the illegitimacy of former events. Within this worldview, deployment of precedent would always be questionable: commentators would have to pay very much more attention to context, and to potential differences between past and present, before historical comparison could be thought valid. Added to all this, was the simple rhetorical and political pressure to challenge easy typology. So heavily reliant was pro-revolutionary argument on past examples that it may sometimes have seemed easier merely to deny history's power to bind. The only alternative to this kind of blanket scepticism about history would have been to slog through a cloud of dead Williamite witnesses, refuting or amending the supposed principle that each was supposed to have established, one by one.

A particular, but illustrative, example of such distance from the past came as James's supporters tackled the issue of treason. This was obviously a hot topic, given that Jacobites were tried and executed for opposing William's regime, and opposition commentators took aim at the legality of such prosecutions.[47] There were a number of ways of doing this (including condemning trial irregularities and the use of informants and *agent provocateurs*), but at least some writers tried to present the law itself as outdated. It was, they claimed, invalid because it had not altered to reflect changing social or legal circumstances. An instance was Samuel Grascome's exculpation of the execution of William Anderton for publishing anti-government tracts in 1693. In this notorious case, whose conduct became a vivid point of contention, the regime claimed to have acted within the law governing treason. As it did so, it took refuge within the ancient constitution: the legal framework governing treason rested on Edward III's act of 1351—but this was held to have codified, without modifying or extending, the immemorial common-law traditions in the area. Faced with this position, Grascome might have engaged in legal minutiae and debated the exact meaning of statutes and legal cases. There was plenty of this sort of dense writing within the allegiance controversy. Instead, however, the pamphleteer cited technological and cultural changes to dismiss a thicket of earlier rulings. Nothing in the statutes or trials of the Middle Ages could relate to Anderton, Grascome claimed, since his supposed crime had been to *print* opposition propaganda. Printing had not been invented when the medieval cases had occurred, so they told us nothing about whether publishing a tract in this way could be treason. Citing one supposed precedent for Anderton's execution, Grascome exclaimed 'What is my Lord Chobham's case to printing? That famous Wicklivite lived in the reign of Richard the Second, some scores of years before printing was thought on'.[48] Similarly, Bartholomew Shower, arguing for tighter regulation of treason trials to prevent William's opponents being summarily dispatched, suggested that new and updated law was needed. Hitherto, he complained, exaggerated reverence for the age of the medieval statute had meant it had never been altered. This was despite numerous cases over the centuries that demonstrated that its wording was dangerously unclear, and that its operation could be manifestly unjust. In a pointed mockery of such rigid ancient constitutionalism, Shower asked why any new statute on any subject had been needed after Magna Carta. If that great contract had contained all that was needed to define an Englishman's rights (as some seemed to imply), all subsequent legislative activity had been superfluous.[49] In these examples, Jacobites were not so much challenging precedent, as dissolving it. They were pointing to

---

[47] For the most recent study of the government campaign, see Rachel Weil, *A Plague of Informers: Conspiracy and Political Trust in William III's England* (New Haven: Yale UP, 2013). For attacks on legality, see, for example, William Anderton, *True copy of the paper delivered to the sheriffs* (1693); [Robert Ferguson], *A letter to the right honourable Sir John Holt* (1694); [Thomas Wagstaff], *A letter out of Lancashire to a friend in the country* (1694).

[48] Samuel Grascome, *An appeal of murther from certain unjust judges* (1693).

[49] [Bartholomew Shower], *Reasons for a new bill of rights* (1692).

changes in social context, or evidence of imperfections that had accumulated over time, to rule what had happened in the distant past out of current discussion.

At a more systematic level, the fact that Jacobites were protesting against their current situation opened the possibility of illegitimating whole, and long, periods of history. In virtually all versions of Williamite thought, there was an understandable tendency to read the post-revolution regime as the latest instance of unchanging truths, and so to see all earlier periods as equally valid proofs of those verities. For Whigs, some version of the ancient constitution had always governed the power of kings; for Tories, all ages provided illustrations of *de facto* and providential principles. Jacobites, by contrast, believed William's government was invalid—so they looked for other illegitimate regimes with which to compare it. As they did this, they created ages from which no justifying precedents could be drawn (the very best these periods could offer would be horror stories to avoid)— and there were a surprisingly large number of them.

For English history, the most discussed was the republic of 1649–60, and we have already explored some of the use that was made of this. But the years of Cromwell's dominance were joined by other, sometimes prolonged, periods of illegitimate rule. In 1553, there had been the nine-day reign of Lady Jane Grey. Jacobite commentators had used this to mock Sherlock as effectively as they had used Cromwell: Grey's partisans had gained effective control of London and government, leaving the legitimate ruler, Queen Mary, to wrest power back in what must, for *de facto* thinkers, have been a rebellion.[50] Far more extensive had been the period from 1483 to 1507. These had been years of successive usurpation: first Richard III had stolen the throne of his nephew Edward V, and then Henry VII had ruled by virtue of naked conquest. Even longer had been the epoch from 1399 to 1461. For all these decades, Lancastrian kings had excluded the true Yorkist branch of the Plantagenet dynasty, following the illegal deposition of Richard II.[51] Equally invalid had been the first days of Edward III (a usurper until his father died); the rule of King Stephen (1135–54); and technically that of William II as well. When William the Conqueror had been killed in a fall from his horse in 1087, his eldest son Robert should have inherited the kingdom, if proper primogeniture had been followed. According to some Jacobite commentators, this made the second Norman king a usurper; indeed, it also raised questions over the bulk of Henry I's reign, given that Robert's line did not die out until 1128.[52] If one also included the pre-Norman period (invalid, not because of usurpation, but because it occurred before the modern monarchy had been instituted), nearly half of the time the English had been established in Britain had been lived outside current

<hr>

[50] See, for example [Collier], *Animadversion upon the modern explanation*, 7; Browne, *Case of allegiance*, 13.

[51] For Jacobite discussion of these periods, see above, ch. 4.2.

[52] See above, ch. 4.2, and the list of those rulers who had 'docked the intail' on the crown in *The price of the abdication* (1693), 17.

constitutional norms. Over a century and a half had fallen into this category, even restricting attention to the time since 1066.

The Jacobite creation of legal and illegal periods of constitutional history had a number of consequences. It meant, most crucially, that one had to be careful from which period of the past one drew one's precedents. If an invalid era was chosen, the lessons might be null, or even misleading and dangerous. This, in essence, was what the Jacobites were saying as they attacked Sherlock. His arguments established a connection between the post-revolution era and the 1650s (albeit tacitly, and against his own insistence), and so ended up justifying a murderous and illegal regime. This weakened the direct hold of the past over the present, both because it enjoyed demonstrating that it might be counterproductive to use historical events in current political argument, and because a sense of context was now needed to distinguish between history that could be deployed as a justifying precedent and history that could not. At a very basic level, one had to know if a king was legitimate before citing public acts, or political circumstances, under his rule. For example, and as we saw, Jacobites could dismiss Henry VII's *de facto* statute because it was the self-serving measure of a usurper, from a period when right rule had been suspended; and the support Henry IV got from the English could not make him a legitimate king—the practical precedent did not overrule the hereditary principles.

The most sustained working out of these considerations came with Robert Brady's main contribution to the allegiance controversy. We have cited his 1690 *Enquiry into the remarkable instances of history and parliament records* at points above, but it is time to consider the overall rhetorical strategy of the piece. This was to dismiss claims that precedents affirmed popular control over monarchical succession by retelling English history as a pretty constant battle between legitimate hereditary kings and ambitious and conspiratorial subjects. The wicked plotters had been successful on many occasions—but this could never justify using their mendacious slogans about the people's rights to change their rulers as evidence for the true axioms of the English constitution. In Brady's vision, two periods of history—both dear to Whig writers—could be dismissed pretty much outright as sources of political truth, because central monarchical authority had been too overwhelmed by ambitious subjects to assert its legitimate authority. Early Anglo-Saxon history, far from illustrating an ancient 'Gothick' constitution, could not provide 'authentick and well-grounded precedents' since it had been a period of chaos when robber barons were engaged in 'invading, plundering and burning one another's countries, frequently killing and murthering their kings'.[53] Similarly, the centuries after the Norman invasion, which had produced Magna Carta, were lawless, having featured 'so many Tyrants as there were Lords of

---

[53] [Brady], *Enquiry into the remarkable instances*, 1.

Castles'.[54] Other canonical illustrations of the ancient constitution were dismissed as systematically. Edward III had succeeded only because rebelling nobles had assembled a stronger army against his father, whilst Richard II had been deposed by the machinations of party, and by naked military power.[55] Claims for the public good in all these events were mere window dressing. One could see this in a telling comparison with the mid-seventeenth-century usurpation. The rebels of 1640 to 1660 had produced declarations and remonstrances 'all filled with the Consent, Rights, and Authority of the People…holding forth Common Good and Publick Interest', but these had been fig leaves for their armed domination of the country. The overriding lesson of England's story was thus, not the persistence of true constitutional principles, but their vulnerability and lapses. As Brady put it, 'the best laws in the World cannot keep Men from being wicked, nor secure the Government from the attempts of intruders and usurpers, when they think they have the opportunity and means to set themselves up'.[56]

Such long periods of illegitimate rule meant history could only be used with great care. But they also opened up the possibility of undermining the Williamites' entire precedent-based project. In some of the boldest attacks on the historical justification of the revolution, Jacobites adopted a tone of scepticism about the past—particularly the distant past—as a whole. If, commentators implied, so much history was so badly compromised that it had no relevance to the modern world, then it might be a mistake to seek any guidance from bygone centuries. To take an example, Thomas Browne followed Brady and a number of other Jacobites in examining the irregularities of the Wars of the Roses. Like them, he did so to cast doubt on *de facto* theories of legitimacy. But his point was not so much that some of the rulers of the fifteenth century had been usurpers, but that the two sides in the conflict had behaved in ways that cast doubt on everyone's rule. In that era, the notion that might brought right had allowed anyone seizing the throne to act as a lawful king. Because there had been no higher principle in deciding between dynasties, the Yorkists and Lancasterians had continually sought 'all opportunities to dethrone each other'[57] Moreover, the rival factions had denounced each other in such a mess of reciprocal condemnation that it left the reader struggling to remember if anyone had a right to the crown. Edward IV had attainted those who had helped Henry VI before the former had displaced the latter. But Henry reversed the charges when he fought his way back to power; and then Edward threw the whole legal machine into the opposite direction again when he regained his regal position. Kings themselves had been declared traitors and usurpers by their successors. Henry IV and Henry VI had been condemned by Edward IV; Edward IV had suffered the same fate at the hands of Henry VI, and

---

54 Ibid., 29.   55 Ibid., 30–9.
56 Ibid., 17.   57 Browne, *Case of allegiance*, 46.

Richard III and been declared an illegal ruler by Henry VII.[58] When combined with Browne's general lament that 'there is hardly any Monarchy wherein there have been more Usurpations than there have been in ours', the impression left was of an English past so besoiled by impropriety that it could hold no useful lessons for the late seventeenth century.[59] Indeed, the prevailing tone of Browne's piece was that what had happened must never be a guide to what should happen, because so much of what had happened had been wrong.

A similar scepticism towards political typology can be found in Robert Jenkin's 1690 pamphlet, *An answer to a vindication of the letter from a person of quality*. As its title suggested, this was part of one of the intense pamphlet exchanges within the allegiance controversy, and it upheld Abenego Sellar's argument that non-resistance to rulers was a key principle of English Protestantism. At one point, however, it discussed the clause in Magna Carta that seemed to allow subjects to take up arms against an unjust king. This stimulated a burst of Jacobite historical contextualization that ballooned into a general attack on the precedent industry and the ancient constitution that underpinned it. Jenkin first pointed out that this clause did not appear in later charters that laid out subjects' rights. It therefore looked to him, not like a fundamental axiom of English government, but merely a temporary victory for aristocratic rebels, which had been extorted when the monarchy had been very weak, and had been reversed when it recovered.[60] Yet Williamites had used it to justify illegal revolution, and Jenkin charged that this was typical of their whole approach to the past. He insisted there was unambiguous law barring resistance to monarchs. It included the legislation surrounding James I's act of recognition and his oath of allegiance, and the statutes passed after the 1660 to condemn the 1640s civil war. But instead of following these recent, and unequivocally unrepealed, acts, Williamites blathered about ancient and doubtful precedents. 'Some', Jenkin complained, 'have sent us to Tacitus, and as far as [ancient] Germany to learn our English constitution'.[61] Others had sought examples of resistance from the 'monkish' chroniclers of the Middle Ages, but (as the monkish adjective implied) such examples were inevitable in this kind of source because the authors belonged to a corrupted church that had always tried to undermine the English monarchy. Other Williamites again had looked to the Tudor succession legislation to show the people could determine who was monarch, but these acts, Jenkin pointed out, were plain 'contradictory'. All in all, Jenkin wondered why it was necessisary to look back any further than the legislation of the last few decades, and as he did so he illustrated the characteristic Jacobite distance from the past.[62] For him, as for other commentators on his side,

---

[58] Ibid., 9–10.   [59] Ibid., 6.
[60] [Robert Jenkin], *An answer to a vindication of the letter from a person of quality in the north* (1690), 21.
[61] Ibid., 22.   [62] Ibid., 22–3.

precedent always had to be contextualized—and could often be contextualized away. What mattered was legal and moral principle, and recent law, since neither could be rendered irrelevant by circumstances that could change radically over time.

4.4 Discontinuity at 1689: The Corruption of New Times

So, Jacobite discontent at current circumstances damaged close links with the past. Today was a lie; much of the past had been as well. But criticism of the post-revolutionary regime disrupted static chronology in another way. As Jacobites underlined the illegitimacy of William's rule, they were naturally tempted to chart its lamentable effects, as well as its basic illegality. For them, the misstep of 1688–9 had led to a series of dire consequences, and this had soon created a new narrative of degeneration, begun at the revolution but spiralling downward the longer the usurping ruler remained in power. This produced an evolving, and process-driven, view of recent history, which presented it as a corrupted new era and foresaw a continual worsening of conditions. Adopted and adapted by Tory and radical Whig critics of the regime from the late 1690s, this gave rise to a novel chronology, with a new periodization, and strong sense of forward—indeed perhaps accelerating—development.

The idea of degeneration occurred in much Jacobite writing, but the heavy lifting in developing the notion was done by the group of 'Whig' Jacobites.[63] This was a relatively small, and itself diverse, category of people, consisting of those who adhered to James's cause, despite their deep commitment to the liberties of English subjects. Some had been won over by the exiled king's commitment to religious toleration. Some had been disappointed that the revolution had not gone further in securing freedom (or this had become a rationalization of their disappointment that they had personally failed to profit from it). Some had been alienated from William by the inevitable authoritarianism of a regime conducting a war for its survival, and had come to think a chastened James might be more willing to agree to substantial limitations on monarchical power. Whatever route these figures took to Jacobitism, they became the polemical powerhouse of the movement. By the early 1690s they were pouring out a stream of invective against the post-revolutionary government that frequently set the terms for public debate. Charges that these writers made against the regime became the focus of parliamentary investigation, print controversy, and popular scandal.[64]

---

[63] For this group, see Mark Goldie and Clare Jackson, 'Williamite Tyranny and the Whig Jacobites', in Esther Mijers and David Onnekink, eds, *Redefining William III: The Impact of the King-Stadholder in International Context* (Aldershot: Ashgate, 2007), 177–200.

[64] Most notably, when Charlwood Lawton's *A short state of our condition* (1693)—otherwise known as the 'Hush Money Paper'—sparked a parliamentary investigation into its claims that MPs were being bribed.

The broad areas of Whig Jacobite complaint are well known, and can be summarized rapidly. For them, 1688–9 had been a wasted opportunity to defeat royal absolutism. Instead of using the collapse of James's government to reach a clear constitutional settlement, forever limiting the crown's power, the nation had been distracted by the supposed urgency of getting a Protestant on the throne, and so had offered William the crown with only minimal restrictions. As a result, the post-revolutionary regime had proved certainly equally, and probably more, tyrannous than its predecessors. It misused its authority to inflict torture and trumped up treason allegations against supposed enemies; it ignored basic freedoms in its suspension of *habeus corpus*; and it resisted attempts to complete the revolution settlement with further restrictions on royal prerogative. Jacobite writers joined 'country' campaigners in calling for measures to prevent the court-corrupting Parliament. These included 'place bills' to exclude those who held posts in the administration from serving as MPs, and 'triennial bills' to force the king to call fresh elections every three years and so prevent him perpetuating a tame legislature.[65]

Outside legal and constitutional affairs, Whig Jacobites stressed the punishing costs of William's war. This conflict, which James's supporters rightly insisted was the inevitable effect of 1688–9, had had, they clamed, catastrophic consequences for English economy and society. Trade with France had been suspended, denying the country a lucrative source of prosperity. Naval confrontations had disrupted commerce more widely, depressing a major source of the nation's wealth. War had been expensive, leading to crippling taxes on the population. In fact, the conflict had been so costly that even heavy fiscal exaction had been insufficient, leading to an escalation of public debt that mortgaged the future of the national community. Meanwhile, the machinery of the state had expanded to manage the war, and this had both enlarged opportunities for the embezzlement of public funds (financial scandals in the civil service was meat and drink to Jacobite rhetoric), and had distorted the balance of society. Landed gentlemen and enterprising merchants had suffered from the advance of new classes of people (revenue officials, army officers, contractors, public creditors, and so on) who had been created by an expanding state, and were subservient to it. Social and constitutional analysis thus converged in concern for liberty in Whig Jacobite thought. A government that had been left with too much legal power, and that was seizing more, was also re-engineering the whole nation to neuter centres of resistance to its rule.[66]

---

[65] See Paul Monod, 'Jacobitism and Country Principles in the Reign of William III', *Historical Journal*, 30 (1987), 289–310.

[66] These dimensions of Whig Jacobite thought receive some analysis in Goldie and Jackson, 'Williamite Tyranny', and in the pamphlets laying out historical process since 1689 analyzed below.

As we will see, this critique fed into non-Jacobite criticisms of government in the later parts of William's reign, and became standard opposition rhetoric in the eighteenth century. What is important here, though, is not so much the details of the arguments as the fact that William's corruption was presented as progressive. Corruption was more than a standing fact about the post-revolutionary government: it was a process creating an unfolding narrative. Of course, this was largely the result of the Jacobite desire to denigrate the new regime. To prove the error of 1688–9, it was natural for writers to insist that conditions after the prince of Orange's arrival were worse than they had been before (which inevitably created a periodization, a sense of new times that were different from the past), and it was natural for them to ascribe the change to the evil of the new ruler and his supporters (something that provided them with a cause, and an explanation, of further changes even after the revolution). Yet, if the basic reasons for claims of degeneration were simple, the chronological effects were profound. Very rapidly, they constructed a far more dynamic sense of history than any of the political or constitutional discourses that have been examined so far in this book. Unlike Williamite precedent, Jacobite time flowed forward.

This feature was evident in the very first Jacobite statements. Even before James had fallen from power, those who tried to rally support for his cause lamented the consequences if the Dutch invasion succeeded. They painted a dark picture of England under Orange domination—and so created a future that would be very different from the legitimate Stuart present. The earliest warnings—such as that in the king's own declaration of 28 September 1688—concentrated simply on the threat of coming violence, but the rhetoric moved remarkably quickly to suggest that a new, and perverted, world order would arise if William triumphed.[67] Official prayers to be used during the invasion called for God's help to preserve the nation from the 'Effusion of Christian bloud', but they also appealed for divine protection of the nation's holy religion, and its 'Laws and Ancient Government'. This hinted all these would soon be gone.[68] Responses to the prince's manifesto made similar insinuations. Some printed *Animadversions* on the prince's document charged him with planning tyranny, since he was already dictating what the 'free' Parliament he called for would decide, and argued that William would establish Psresbyterianism in England to match his own religious preferences.[69] *Some reflections* upon the same manifesto pointed to its author's suppression of Dutch freedom on his coming to power in 1672, and his supposed brutality in disciplining Dutch armies, again to suggest that England's liberties would be extinguished after an Orange conquest.[70] *The Dutch design anatomised*, and some *Modest remarks* upon William's arguments, treated the people of the Netherlands

---

[67] *By the king, a proclamation…28th day of September* (1688).   [68] *Prayers to be used.*
[69] [Collier], *Animadversions on the declaration*, 28–9.
[70] *Some reflections upon his highness the prince of Orange's declaration*, 11–12.

as perpetrators, rather than as victims, in the coming catastrophe, but the temporal pattern was similar to the other pamphlets.[71] If James were defeated, England's laws and autonomy would be sacrificed; she would be governed solely by the will of her new masters; and her religion and society would be remodelled in the Dutch image.

Such warnings about a depraved new epoch shaped Jacobite polemic after the revolution. Having asserted that the future would be radically different if William came to power, James's supporters started documenting this transformation as soon as the regime changed. In fact, narratives of degeneration could be said to be the characteristic mode of Jacobite writing in the 1690s. Most anti-regime rhetoric was structured around rapidly evolving stories of corruption and decline, as the terrible effects of the revolution were shown playing themselves out. One 1689 pamphlet marked the transition from the dire predictions of the 1688 material, to the jeremiadical reporting of later works, by using early trends in William's rule to forecast a dark future. The author of some *Obsevations* on the revolution feared for the future of the English church, given the destruction of episcopacy on William's accession in Scotland; he feared for English liberties, given occupation by a Dutch army; and he feared for property, given the heavy tax demands already made and the decay of trade in the newly declared war.[72] As time went by, Jacobite authors had more concrete material to illustrate their theory of decline. Many of their works became little more than catalogues of tyrannies, impoverishments, bereavements, and plunderings by government and its foreign allies.[73] All of this created a developing story which could be projected into the future to predict an incipient final destruction. Samuel Grascome, condemning Williamite tyranny in 1693, warned that 'We must expect our Dear Native Country, will e're long be overwhelmed, and be buried in its own ruins.'[74]

Of course, this sense of chronological flow—of process operating through history—was a natural result of denouncing the post-revolutionary regime. If 1688–9 had been a disastrous mistake, and had introduced a regime bent on corrupting all that was good in England, then the revolution would inevitably be presented as a turning point that divided eras. Yet other features of the discourse used by James's Whiggish supporters reinforced this dynamism, and are worth exploring. They made Jacobitism more interesting than mere pessimistic mourning for a lost utopia and clarify its important contribution to later opposition worldviews.

---

[71] *The prince of Orange his declaration … with a short preface and some modest remarks upon it* (1688), 16; *Dutch design*, 7–11.

[72] *Observations upon the late revolution*, 4.

[73] See, for example, [Nathaniel Johnston] *The dear bargain* (1689); [Lawton], *Englishman's complaint*; [Montgomery], *Great Britain's just complaint*; *Sad estate of the kingdom*; [William Anderton], *Remarks upon the present confederacy* (1693); *Price of the abdication*; [Robert Ferguson], *A brief account of some of the latest incroachments* (1695).

[74] [Samuel Grascome], *New court-contrivances* (1693), 8.

The first significant feature has been recognized in existing studies. As Mark Goldie and Clare Jackson have pointed out, some writers attacked the post-revolutionary regime from the 'civic humanist' perspective that had emerged as an anti-court rhetoric in the earlier seventeenth century, and that rested on a theory of long-term economic and social change.[75] There is no need to cover the subtleties of this discourse at this point, other than to note that it assumed (following the writings of the mid-century republican James Harrington) that political influence was determined by patterns of wealth, especially landed wealth, in a society, and that this was prone to shift over time, creating crises when power got out of step with underlying economic patterns. Among the Jacobites, this sort of understanding was manifest in such writers as Charlwood Lawton and Nathaniel Johnston, who analysed their world by pointing to new classes of property holders who had arisen since the Middle Ages. Lawton, for example, argued that the constitutional tensions of the Stuart decades had been the result of kings failing to accommodate advancing groups who were represented in the House of Commons. Over the past centuries, he explained, the collapse of feudalism had allowed gentry and merchants to gain at the expense of the military aristocracy, but monarchs had not recognized this. Lawton argued that order could be restored if a chastened James agreed to a new Magna Carta that would strengthen parliamentary power, and so would refashion the constitution to fit the transformed social structure.[76] Meanwhile Johnston and others fretted that new types of people—especially the army officers and government employees of an expanding state—had started to upset the political balance of the nation. This process, they implied, had been accelerated by William to create and to reward a set of cronies who would support his rule.[77] Such writing injected a real sense of long-term historical change into strands of Jacobitism, but we should recognize it was a partial phenomenon. Only a small minority of the movement, on what might be called its extreme 'liberal' wing, stressed changes in property holding over the basic illegality of William's rule, or less-theorized lament about its consequences.

Rather more widespread, and so perhaps significant, historical dynamism arose from three other features of Whig Jacobite argument. The first was its anti-Dutch xenophobia. As one might expect, this was prominent in attacks on William. His enemies drew on a rich stream of panegyric that had been deployed in the three Anglo-Dutch wars of the 1650s, '60s and '70s, and used it to suggest that the old enemy was now exploiting (indeed may have engineered) the revolution to complete its destruction of England. And as the Jacobites did this, they revived a set of discourses from the earlier conflicts with the Netherlands that had developed a strong sense of sociological process to prove the intractable malice of the

---

⁷⁵ See Goldie and Jackson, 'Williamite Tyranny', 186–90.
⁷⁶ [Charlwood Lawton], *Honesty is the best policy* (1692).
⁷⁷ [Johnston], *Dear bargain*, 6; *Price of the abdication*, 6–7.

nation's assailants. Anti-Dutch xenophobia had exhibited this sense of historical development for two main reasons. First, the Netherlands were a new world power. Unlike other national enemies, such as the Spaniards and French, the Lowlanders' hostility to England could not be explained by long-standing rivalries and clashes of interest, because the Dutch had not existed as major geopolitical player until well into the Stuart age. Those who denounced the Dutch were thus forced to explain why they had become such a danger so quickly and recently, and so talked in terms of particular features of the Netherlanders' society that had transformed the nation since its first rise in the later sixteenth century. Second, the Dutch were Protestants. In another contrast with France and Spain, there was no off-the-peg explanation for their *animus* against godly England, based on a timeless Black Legend of evil popery. Netherlanders could not simply be the latest incarnation of the false church's eternal conspiracy against holy religion. Instead there had to be an explanation of how fellow followers of the Reformation had gone bad.

In the polemic of the earlier wars, Dutch society had been poisoned by flaws in the people's moral makeup. The origins of the process lay in 1560s, when Netherlanders had rebelled against the Spanish king and had endorsed an anti-episcopal Calvinism. These actions had turned the Dutch against all forms of hierarchy, and had thus rendered them fundamentally insubordinate. They had come to believe ordinary people could, and should, strive to greatness, and this creed had resulted in a vaunting ambition that was unrestricted by codes of natural deference, order, or honour. A dimension of this ambition was a gnawing avarice. For lowly folk, greatness was most easily achieved by gathering wealth—and this dimension of the national character was reinforced by the relative poverty of the Netherlands as territory. Lacking natural resources, the Dutch had had to graft for economic survival, but this had given them an unhealthy attachment to material accumulation. Taken together, ambition and avarice had created a people who wished to dominate the world and monopolize its trade, but these aims had then further corrupted Dutch morals. Worldly objectives had been promoted at the expense of Christian values, and Netherlanders had accordingly come to see ends justifying almost any means. In particular, the Dutch had become perfidious and cruel. To advance their own interests, they would betray those who trusted them, and used brutality against those who resisted. The story of the 1619 Amboyna massacre, during which—it was claimed—Dutch traders in the East Indies had deceived and then slaughtered honest English merchants, was endlessly recycled in the English press as a synecdoche of this whole national pathology.[78]

This set of ideas was incorporated into Whig Jacobite rhetoric after 1688–9. It was easy to present William's usurpation as the latest stage in the Dutch conspiracy

---

[78] For this earlier polemic, see Claydon, *Europe*, 132–52.

for hegemony—especially as it came with a host of supposed advantages for the new king's countrymen. These stretched from prominence at court, and opportunities to steal trade in wartime, to the chance to make profits lending to an indebted English government, and the use of English troops to defend Holland. As this interpretation was deployed, it organized Jacobite complaint as a temporally evolving narrative. Dutch depravities had emerged from the political, economic, and cultural conditions in which Netherlanders had found themselves and had then driven an emerging campaign for global domination that was now playing itself out in England. Effectively, Jacobites claimed, the Stuart realm was being remodelled—either in the Dutch image, or to serve Dutch interests—according to a long-term plan. Thus, one of the most vehemently xenophobic pamphlets of the Jacobite campaign, *The people of England's grievances*, listed the familiar series of disasters since 1688–9 (spiralling taxes, mounting debt, costs of war, and export of coin) and then ascribed this to a 'general cause'. This cause was 'Dutch Counsels and Dutch Measures of action', resulting from the prominent position of Netherlanders in the ministry and at court.[79] William Anderton, in the pamphlet that had him executed for treason, dated the source of the trouble before 1688–9. For him, the revolution had been managed by the Dutch to capture English resources for their own purposes, and its consequences had been the loss of English life on the battlefields of Flanders, the collapse of England's trade, and the sacrifice of English liberties.[80] Other pamphlets rooted their criticisms of Dutch behaviour in the old tropes of the Anglo-Dutch wars, and supported their analysis with the pre-revolution actions of the Netherlands in order to demonstrate the continuities of process. Nathaniel Johnston related Dutch commercial expansionism through the seventeenth century to explain their rapaciousness since 1688–9; Robert Ferguson told Dutch national history as a record of treachery against the English who had first helped them against their Spanish masters in the Elizabethan era; and an anonymous pamphleteer, counting the price of James's abdication, deployed traditional animal imagery to describe the United Provinces, calling them leeches and cormorants whose avarice consumed the wealth of other nations.[81] Of course, much of this was the sort of xenophobic name-calling that often emerges when societies come under economic or cultural pressure. But late-seventeenth-century anti-Dutch prejudice had a stronger sense of historical development than some other kinds of bigotry. The enemy was not just evil: one could see how it had become evil, and one could note how its perfidy had deepened and spread.

A third feature of Whig Jacobite rhetoric to inject a chronological dynamism into the cause was that precedent-weakening view of time that we noted in the

---

[79] *The people of England's grievances offered to be enquired into* (1693), 3.
[80] [Anderton], *Remarks*.
[81] [Johnston], *Dear bargain*, 4–6; [Ferguson], *Brief account*; *Price of the abdication*, 5, 8.

more mainstream parts of the anti-Williamite movement. Although the exiled king's Whig proponents placed more emphasis on people's rights than was common in much Jacobite ideology, they shared the sense that the breach in hereditary succession was a profound discontinuity that broke the hold of the past, and so had allowed their process of degenerative change. Whilst the Whig heritage of some writers drove them to static ancient constitutionalism (William had destroyed timeless fundamental law, so it was no surprise things had gone to pot), other commentators found that their strongly narrative understanding of post-revolution history was given conceptual space by the Jacobite legal argument.[82] In contrast to the Williamite constitutional case that forbade radical change, the opposition doubted that right government was guaranteed. For them, there was no immemorial constitution, nor timeless principles of good behaviour, that had ensured English history stayed within acceptable norms. The past had seen profound ruptures and departures from legitimate rule that had done considerable damage. Jacobites believed in seismic shifts (such as the Norman Conquest) and made no attempt to hide long periods of illegal governance—periods they claimed had caused ever-increasing anarchy and perversion (note their lurid descriptions of conditions during the Barons Wars, the Wars of the Roses, and Cromwell's rule).[83] Within this mindset, it was easy to think that a government could corrupt a society, and so to create a prolonged narrative of decline.

One very concrete example of mainstream Jacobite constitutionalism opening the door for an evolving process of post-revolution corruption was a 1695 pamphlet by Robert Ferguson.[84] This argued that Parliament ought to have been dissolved on the death of Queen Mary in December 1694; and its technical case was that Mary, as the sole even remotely plausible element of true government after the revolution (she was, at least, James's daughter), had been the only thing that had bestowed legitimacy on the legislature. Yet the work ranged well beyond this. Its emotional heart was the charge that William used posturing about liberty to hide a wicked scheme to his own selfish ends. The king was implementing a plan to enrich his cronies, to 'bring the Kingdom into an expensive and ruinous War' to defend his homeland, to reduce England to 'Poverty and Slavery', and to promote his tyranny.[85] And, crucially, Ferguson insisted that history had seen this sort of thing before. Suggesting that 'the Vices of the Age' sprang naturally from 'the Effects of Unjust Government', and picking up on the mainstream Jacobite insistence that there had been long eras of usurpation in the English past, the

---

[82] For Whig Jacobite ancient constitutionalism, see [Charlwood Lawton and William Penn?], *An honest commoner's speech* [1694]; [John Wildman], *An enquiry, or a discourse between a yeoman of Kent, and a knight of the shire* [1693]; [Lawton], *Jacobite principles*, 17; [Charlwood Lawton], *Some reasons for annual parliaments* [1693], though the last of these, having quoted practice under Alfred, Edward III, and Richard II, also stated that it didn't so much wish to 'dote on antiquity' as to revive a practice that was reasonable and advantageous (p. 2)—revealing Jacobite scepticism about a binding past.

[83] See above, ch. 4.3

[84] [Robert Ferguson], *Whether the parliament be not in law dissolved* (1695).   [85] Ibid., 4.

pamphleteer suggested that there had been earlier illustrations of illegal rule leading to social and political perversion.[86] For him, the Parliament that continued to sit at Westminster—and that was driving the nation to 'impoverishment, enslavement and ruin'—was in the same position as the illegal assembly that had fawned on the usurper Richard III. It was in the same position as the Rump, which had continued to sit after the regicide of 1649, and had needed to defend itself with mobs and force. It was in the same position as the so-called Parliaments of Cromwell's protectorate, which had been called to saddle the country with taxes, or even to discredit the idea of representative assemblies with their inevitable excesses.[87] Ferguson thus used Jacobite interest in discontinuities in right rule to illustrate and enliven his claims about a current, and ongoing, process of decline.

A final dimension of Jacobite writing to provide a chronological dynamism was the most basic. This was the simple idea that decline was driven by conspiracy. For enemies of William, things had been getting worse since the revolution because a group of plotters had got to the heart of government and were managing affairs for their own self-interest. This notion drew on the other features of the movement that we have been examining, and in some ways provided an abridged summary of them. The conspiracy was rooted in the new social groups posited by civic humanism; it aped and allied with Dutch disruption of old structures; and it exploited a usurping king's need to build a party to back his illegal power. Fired by the avarice and ambition of such motives, plotters were transforming England as they constructed a huge war state whose resources they could plunder, and whose expense would cripple the honest landowners and merchants of England.

One of the earliest and clearest expositions of this idea was Nathanial Johnston's late 1689 tract, *The dear bargain*. As its title suggested, this pointed to the losses England had suffered as a result of its change of ruler, but it was clear these were not just misfortunes or accidents. In a term used in its first paragraph, there was a 'Cabal' operating—and Johnston soon outlined what its plan was. Asking why so much money had been voted to the king, and why attempts to investigate misappropriation of these funds had been frustrated, the pamphlet explained that conspirators wanted to maximize the funds available for embezzlement of the public. 'Their design was to get Money to support the present government, that it might support them'.[88] The rest of the pamphlet detailed the baleful effects of having such men in positions of influence, and painted moral portraits of these figures (driven by a ravening personal ambition). This set a pattern that shaped almost all Jacobite writing. Although anatomizing the plot was not always the prime purpose of commentary, and if its precise anatomy could be unclear, the assumption that there was such a conspiracy lay behind the vast bulk of the movement's output. It emerged when people assumed particular miscarriages

---

[86] Ibid., 5.   [87] Ibid., 52–3.   [88] [Johnston], *Dear bargain*, 1.

were part of a wider pattern, as when Thomas Wagstaff noted that the informers at treason trials were too stupid to have come up with their own stories.[89] It emerged in the language in which those in charge of post-revolution England were described. They were 'robbers' and 'montebanks', 'ill' and 'voluptuous' men, people who 'preferred their own private Gain and Advancement before the public good', or 'parasites' with a 'separate interest' to that of the nation.[90] It emerged in comparisons to earlier plot-ridden eras: particularly to the 1670s, when, all assumed, the court had set out to corrupt Parliament in order to engross all power to itself.[91]

The notion of a deep-laid plot provided a dynamic to post-revolution politics in the thought of James's Whig supporters, but initially this was tempered by the most common identification of who the plotters actually were. In the first few years after the revolution, there was a tendency to suggest that the malefactors were those who had been behind corruption in Charles II and James II's reign. This suggested an essentially old problem—people had crept back to the centres of power and were now up to their old games.[92] As time when on, however, the identification of the evil cabal at the heart of public affairs shifted. Especially as a group of 'court' or 'junto' Whigs took prominent positions in the ministries of the mid 1690s, Whig Jacobites came to see that clique as a novel species of villain. In this emerging story, a whole section of the party had turned coats to work with the corrupting power of a usurping government. Betraying all the ideals on which Whiggery had been founded, they now used tyranny to still criticism, they imposed heavy taxation to destroy their rivals, and they benefitted from an expanded military machine to embezzled money and gain places of profit. Robert Ferguson put the point pithily. The Whigs, he charged, had spouted a language of liberty as they had overthrown James, but their behaviour since had been wholly selfish (and perhaps this was unsurprising given that the Whigs had emerged from the ambitious supporters of Cromwell's republic).[93] 'By enriching themselves', Ferguson said, 'they…bring the Kingdom into Indigency, Dishonour, and Bondage'.[94]

The Whig Jacobites thus promoted strong elements of historical evolution beyond their basic claim that the nation was on a slide to ruin. Civic humanism saw long-term economic change behind political crisis; anti-Dutch xenophobia introduced a sociological pathology that had been developed in earlier war propaganda; assumptions about the consequences of illegal rule had vice spreading from

---

[89] [Wagstaff], *Letter out of Lancashire.*
[90] [Grascome], *New court contrivances,* 1; *An honest Commoner's speech* (1694), 3; *The people of England's grievances* (1692), 6; [Lawton], *Short state* (1693) 1.
[91] *Some reasons for annual parliaments in a letter to a friend* [1693?], 5.
[92] *Honest Commoner's speech,* 4; [Lawton], *Some paradoxes;* see also Goldie and Jackson 'Williamite Tyranny', 184.
[93] [Robert Ferguson], *A letter to Mr Secretary Trenchard* (1694), 43.
[94] [Ferguson], *Whether the parliament,* 5.

an original sin of usurpation; and conspirators drove a process of decline as they pursued their selfish ends. The latter two of these elements also produced a strong sense of periodization. They insisted the revolution was a turning point that had initiated the new era of degeneration. The chronological sense of Jacobitism thus came to belie its conservative ideology. A movement that protested against the constitutional innovations of the revolution ended up embracing views of history that were far more open to process-driven transformations than the mental worlds of those who had accepted the new settlement. As we are about to see, this paradox spread outside the Jacobite movement in the later 1690s. The years after the ending of William's war with France in 1697 saw a refiguring of the political landscape that brought some of the ideas and images used by James's supporters into more general political debate. This ended the chronological *stasis* of Williamite discourse, but again, it did so most powerfully among those with deep criticisms of the post-revolutionary regime.

4.5 Periodization and the Urgent Present in Opposition Rhetoric after 1697

In brief, the story of the political remodelling of the 1690s runs as follows. Although William received the overwhelming backing of the English in the early parts of his reign, discontent with features of his rule soon emerged, even among his supporters. Debates in Parliament, and criticism of the court in print, revealed growing concern about the cost of the war, about an erosion of civil liberties, and about the advantages the Dutch seemed to be gaining under the new king. These were, of course, the grievances Jacobites had tried to tap—but before 1697, it had been difficult for them to coalesce into a coherent language of opposition among Williamites. There were two principle barriers. First, agreement with the court on the legitimacy of the revolution, and the necessity of the war to preserve it, limited how deep any criticism of government could go. There could certainly be questions about the details of royal policy and how the war was being conducted, but these were contained in support for the regime's objectives as a whole.[95] The second impediment to a full oppositional language was that the court had stolen the traditional discourse of criticism. In the bulk of the seventeenth century, concern about government had generally been expressed in a 'country' rhetoric. This feared popish influence around the king, and demanded greater parliamentary scrutiny to contain this. The attacks upon Charles I's court in the 1620s, those on Charles II in the 1670s, and those on James II had all followed this script. But after 1688–9, the new regime itself appropriated this language of parliamentary

---

[95] See, Robert McJimsey, 'A Country Divided? English Politics and the Nine Years War', *Albion*, 23 (1991), 61–74; Claydon, *William III and the Godly Revolution*, 208–13.

anti-popery. This happened at a practical level, since William exhibited none of the classic symptoms of popish infection, and had accepted its traditional remedy. There were no Catholics among his family or immediate household; his foreign policy was unimpeachably Protestant (he launched a crusade against the persecuting popish French); and he met his legislature every year for a substantive session. But it happened at the level of polemic as well. William adopted large swathes of traditional country argument, putting himself at the head of a campaign against court popery, and coming out in favour of parliamentary scrutiny. This started with his manifesto for his invasion, which blamed the ills of the nation on Catholic counsellors of the king and called for a freely elected Parliament as the universal remedy.[96] Once king, William presented himself as a godly Protestant ruler, and his court as the powerhouse of moral and spiritual renewal.[97] He also, particularly in his speeches to the Lords and Commons, treated his legislature as a partner in a drive against corruption: for example, offering the royal accounts for parliamentary audit.[98]

In the war years, therefore, it was difficult to construct a coherent critique of William's government, since the court was already using the standard arguments of seventeenth-century opposition. But this changed in the late 1690s. The obvious reason was the 1697 Treaty of Ryswick. This peace of exhaustion ended the conflict with France that had provided a basic consensus on policy between the king and any potential opposition. Under the terms of the treaty, Louis was no longer trying to reverse the 1688–9 revolution (so a common enemy disappeared), and, as a result, a bitter dispute opened about the level of military preparedness that England should retain. Peace also removed an important plank of the king's self-presentation as a Protestant champion. He was no longer confronting the forces of popery on the battlefield. Perhaps more importantly, however, the passage of time exposed those with concerns about the government to alternative rhetorics of criticism. With traditional country language compromised, people needed new explanations for what they felt was going wrong, and the ideas promoted by the Jacobites began to step into the breach. This happened quite rapidly with anti-Dutch xenophobia. Those who accepted the revolution could, nevertheless, complain that it had benefitted the Netherlands disproportionately—this was standard in parliamentary and pamphlet concern about the court from the early 1690s.[99] By the late decade, however, such suspicion of foreigners was joined by a sense that emerging classes of people within England were driving dangerous processes of social, cultural, and political change. As this happened, a coherent opposition polemic finally coalesced: and it contained a new temporal dynamism.

---

[96] *The declaration of his highness, William Henry, prince of Orange.*
[97] Claydon, *William III and the Godly Revolution, passim,* but esp. ch. 3.
[98] See, *Journals of the House of Commons,* x, 200, 271, 425.
[99] See, for example, the speeches recorded in Henry Horwitz, ed, *The Parliamentary Diary of Narcissus Luttrell, 1691–93* (Oxford: OUP, 1972), 216, 267, 288–90, 304.

The old country discourse of the earlier seventeenth century had been dominated by static chronology. Its anti-popery was rooted in a timeless battle between the false and true church, its parliamentarianism in the doctrine of the ancient constitution. By contrast, the new opposition discourse shared and borrowed some of the Jacobites' accounts of evolution through time.

The *locus classicus* of the new worldview—identified in existing work on 'Commonwealth' thought—was the standing army controversy of 1697–9. When the war ended, William wished to retain a large professional military to counter any new threat from France, but a majority of the House of Commons—and, crucially, a small group of energetic pamphleteers—rejected this idea as a financially wasteful threat to English liberty. The writers, labelled 'commonwealthsmen' by later scholars, were radical Whigs who had been alienated by the pro-court stance of their party's grandees in the mid-decade.[100] Believing themselves to be 'true' Whigs, they claimed to be heir to the movement's traditional suspicions of the executive, and, as John Pocock suggested, they deployed a 'civic humanist' discourse that had emerged, along with the Whig party itself, in Charles II's reign.[101]

The work that kick-started the print exchanges of the controversy was John Trenchard and Walter Moyle's 1697 *Argument shewing that a standing army in time of peace is inconsistent with a free government*. This used a battery of debating points, but several hung on the idea that a paid military had arisen with the erosion of the traditional 'Gothick' balance of society. In the Middle Ages, this analysis suggested, governments had remained free because a natural tension between kings and ordinary people had been mediated by a militarily powerful class of aristocratic landowners, who had intervened if either monarchy or democracy grew too strong. Over recent centuries, however, these aristocrats had lost their economic, and so their political, independence; and the way had come clear for court influence to advance.[102] Somewhat more socio-economic flesh was put on this by the pamphleteer Andrew Fletcher in a separate work that argued for a citizen militia as an alternative to a standing army. The balance of society had been destroyed, Fletcher suggested, around 1500. At that point, a taste for classical and exotic luxury (facilitated by the growth of Renaissance learning, the invention of printing to spread new tastes, and the intercontinental trade permitted by the invention of the compass needle) had impoverished nobles, just as the introduction of gunpowder had made warfare too expensive for the individual knight to be effective.[103]

---

[100] The classic study is Caroline Robbins, *The Eighteenth Century Commonwealthman* (Cambridge, MA: Harvard UP, 1959)

[101] J.G.A. Pocock, 'Civic Humanism and Its Role in Anglo-American Thought', in *Politics, Language and Time* (Chicago: Chicago UP, 1989), 80–103.

[102] [John Trenchard and Walter Moyle], *An argument shewing that a standing army in time of peace is inconsistent with a free government* (1697), 2–3, 7–8, 13.

[103] [Andrew Fletcher], *A discourse concerning militias and standing armies* (1697), 5–12.

Thus, as Pocock has claimed, anti-army rhetoric gained some sense of forward process through its deployment of civic humanist analysis. But there are a number of points to be made about this. First, there needs to be acknowledgement of the role of Jacobitism in transmitting this style of long-term sociological argument to the army controversy. Supporters of James had been the most recent exponents of these ideas: they had been part of the intellectual relay that led to the classic statements of civic humanism in the 1690s, and this underlines the paradox of a conservative movement promoting a dynamic view of history. Second, however, we need to be cautious about the role and significance of this set of arguments. Civic humanism did not constitute the whole of the case against the army, and was not the most radical in producing a forward-flowing view of time.

At the core of civic humanist philosophy was the view that free government depended on the autonomy of citizens. This was guaranteed by their control of land (which gave them economic independence from their governors) and their bearing arms (which ensured coercive force was in the hands of people, not rulers). Historical change became central to this analysis, but it was not always forward-facing because the commentators who deployed it were most concerned about how freedom was lost. As Pocock pointed out, civic humanists described evolving processes, but did so principally because they wanted to show that liberty evaporated when citizens surrendered their estates and swords.[104] Their prevailing model of change was therefore one of corruption: in their standard narratives, societies collapsed from free, landed, and armed citizenries, to masses of mere subjects, who were militarily, economically, and politically subservient to rulers. Whilst this certainly produced chronological dynamism, it was also profoundly backward-looking. To start, it induced deep nostalgia. It located ideal liberty in a lost past. Thus writers lauded the medieval centuries of Europe, when land and arms were supposedly dispersed through society by the feudal system (a set of assumptions that allowed many to talk in terms of an ancient constitution underpinned by this social pattern).[105] Additionally, the 'humanist' element of the ideology (its interest in the examples of republican Rome and the Greek city states, which Pocock believed had been transmitted by the writings of Florentine theorists in the renaissance) also looked wistfully to distant centuries.[106] Perhaps even more importantly, this nostalgia could lead to static chronology. Even though the anti-army writers recognized game-changing transformations through history, their commitment to ideal states in the past led them to lionize long-vanished polities, and to tell tales of ancient corruption as directly relevant warnings to their contemporaries. So Trenchard and Moyle's *Argument* established the

---

[104] Pocock, 'Civic Humanism', 87–90, 95.

[105] For ancient constitutionalism in the pamphlets, see [John Trenchard], *A short history of standing armies* (1698), preface, vi; [Samuel Johnson], *A confutation of a late pamphlet* (1698), 33–5.

[106] Pocock, *Machiavellian Moment*.

incompatibility of mercenary forces and free republics by citing examples from early Athenian, Corinthian, and Syracusian history. It proved the inevitability that such forces would stage political coups by remembering the sixteen Roman emperors deposed and murdered by their own armies. It showed that a citizen militia could perform the roles of a professional force by citing the ancient Thebans and Achians, and so on.[107] Other works followed suit, particularly arguing that Rome had flourished as a republic with citizen forces, but had declined when Caesar had used his army to end the city's freedom and as the empire had started to rely on mercenaries.[108] John Toland, meanwhile, came up with a whole scheme for an English military based on the structures of the Roman republic; and an anonymous pamphleteer urged the House of Commons to show 'a true Roman resolution' when fighting William's demands for standing forces.[109]

Such immediate use of the past was so anachronistic that it drew rebukes from the king's supporters, as we shall see, and it was even criticized from within the anti-army camp. Thomas Orme questioned the need for professional forces, but on reading Toland's scheme for a republican-style militia, noted dryly that its author seemed to have 'read more of the Roman History, and their Method, than he has seen of the Practical Discipline of this Age'.[110] Yet the response of most anti-army pamphleteers to such challenges was to insist ever more vehemently on their ancient examples. They even denied that the profound changes that they, themselves, had charted had touched the essentials of military practice. So Trenchard and Moyle's *Argument* lamented the decline of feudal Europe, but did not accept that associated developments in warfare, such as the introduction of modern artillery, weakened their argument by requiring more professional forces.[111] Andrew Fletcher, in the very pamphlet that laid out the profound socio-cultural alteration that he thought had revolutionized the world since 1500, used the 1645 battle of Naseby to show that these shifts had not, in fact, altered military realities. When Cromwell's recently trained recruits triumphed over professional royalist forces, he had shown that the 'modern' arts of war could be learned by ordinary citizens, and so proved that 'Ancient histories', and 'those excellent rules…that the Ancients have left us', were still valid.[112] Similarly, Walter Moyle used recent success by militias to counter his opponents' claim that 'the world is strangely altered'; and John Trenchard opened his *Short history of standing armies* with a defiantly change-denying statement: 'we have not only our Experience, but

<hr>

[107] [Trenchard and Moyle], *Argument shewing*, 8, 22, 27, and *passim*.

[108] [John Trenchard], *A letter from the author of the argument against a standing army* (1698), 8; [John Toland], *The militia reformed* (1698), 67–9; [Trenchard], *Short history*, 38; [Walter Moyle], *A second part of an argument shewing that a standing army is inconsistent with a free government* (1697), 13.

[109] [Toland], *Militia reformed*, 70–8; *A letter to a member of parliament concerning guards and garrisons* (1699), 4.

[110] [Thomas Orme], *The late prints for the standing army* (1698), 21.

[111] [Trenchard and Moyle], *Argument shewing*, 24.   [112] [Fletcher], *Discourse*, 4, 23–4.

the Example of all Times, to prove that men in the same circumstances will do the same things.'[113] Finally John Toland, in perhaps the most sustained insistence that classical history held direct lessons for the contemporary world, rounded off his contribution to the anti-army controversy with a call for educational reform. He admitted the men of his era might not be ready to participate in a citizen militia because changing ways of life meant they had lost martial spirit. But the answer was for everyone to be taught the inspiring tales of victory and heroism achieved by citizen-soldiers in early Rome.[114]

Civic humanism, then, did less to endow anti-army rhetoric with an evolving vision of time than might at first appear. The campaign certainly had a strong sense of historical evolution, but this was less ambiguously supplied by alternative elements of discourse borrowed from Jacobitism. There were swipes at the Dutch, as a novel political force that was facilitating the rise of professional forces in England.[115] Reference to Cromwell's oppressive army also hinted at a close link between usurping authority and the need for a professional force to subdue the people, so the anti-army writers shared the sense among James's supporters that periods of illegal rule bred multiple perversions of politics.[116] Most importantly, however, there was a very strong sense that the revolution had allowed a conspiracy to subvert English liberty. The principle anti-army authors insisted that the king himself was virtuous (and so rejected the Jacobites' complaint that James's deposition itself had poisoned politics—the problem, they claimed, was what a future bad prince might do with a mercenary force), but they nevertheless agreed that a deliberate and planned corruption that had begun—or at least had been greatly accelerated—in 1688–9.[117] The revolution had been a turning point that had ushered in a new era: one in which wicked men had advanced a grand scheme to destroy England.

The sense of plot ran through anti-army writings as a leitmotif. It was introduced in the very first sentences of the campaign, the bitterly ironic dedication of Trenchard and Moyle's *Argument*. This sarcastically praised William's Whig ministers as a set of men who relied on a standing army to protect them, since the public had realized they had destroyed the wealth of the kingdom. The tone of angry mockery could have been lifted from any number of Jacobite efforts—and was maintained through the corpus of anti-army polemic. Those who worked to retain a paid force were 'projectors', 'court-flatterers', and 'placeholders'; they were men steeped in the deepest of personal vices ('ambition, avarice and luxury'); and

---

[113] [Moyle], *Second part*, 19–21; [Trenchard], *Short history*, iii.
[114] [Toland], *Militia reformed*, 70–8.
[115] For anti-Dutch sentiment, see, for example, [Johnson], *Confutation*, 30–1.
[116] For example, [Trenchard and Moyle], *Argument shewing*, 14; [Trenchard], *Short history*, iv, 1, 8–10; [Moyle], *Second part*, 13, 15–17.
[117] For defences of William, see [Trenchard and Moyle], *Argument shewing*, 6; [Trenchard], *Short history*, 38; [Moyle], *Second part*, 6–8, 22–4.

they were promoting an army to provide an expanded state machine on which they could feed.[118]

This, of course, looks like standard complaints of corruption at court—but the rhetoric was given greater chronological depth by the suggestion that England was seeing a wholly new species of threat. The conspirators were different in kind from the sort of parasites that had been drawn to courts from the dawn of time. The novelty of the plot had several dimensions. The most obvious, and perhaps most roundly denounced, was the political allegiance of the plotters. Taking up the Jacobite observation that Whigs had abandoned old principles to advance court power after the revolution, the anti-army pamphleteers railed against a group that had championed liberty whilst it was excluded from power, but had then forgotten all this as soon as it was enjoying its spoils. Casting these apostates as villains, rather than the old advocates of absolutism (such as papists, and perhaps Tories), the rhetoric added hypocrisy and opportunism to its portraits of the evil cabal.[119] More significantly, however, the anti-army campaign argued that the post-revolutionary conspiracy was different in scale and nature from anything that had been seen before.

It was different in scale because rulers had been trying to build a standing force in England for some decades, but had had only very limited success until recently. Several of the pamphlets set what was happening in the 1690s in the context of the seventeenth century as a whole, but claimed that a latent threat had become real only in the last decade. Trenchard and other writers assumed the decline of feudalism had cleared the ground for standing armies—but they explained that this had not initially happened in England because she had not been closely involved in the wars of Renaissance Europe, and, as an island, had been able to rely on the navy for defence. The rule of Elizabeth—a prince who wished to rule with the love of her people—had also delayed any project of military tyranny. In 1603 the queen had died—'and with her, the Virtue of the Plantagenets and Tudors'—but although the incoming Stuarts had tried to smother liberty with a professional army, their incompetence had meant they had not got far.[120] James I had been too luxurious to put much energy into any project; Charles I had been so politically inept that he had raised overwhelming opposition to his plans; and Charles II's progress towards military absolutism had been derailed by the papist bigotry of his brother, who had turned the country against the crown before it had the power to crush protest.[121] However, the situation was very different after the revolution.

---

[118] [Fletcher], *Discourse*, 3; [Trenchard], *Short history*, 23; [Moyle], *Second part*, 14–15; *Letter to a member of parliament…garrisons*, 4.

[119] [Trenchard], *Letter from the author*, 14; [Trenchard], *Short history*, 39; *A letter to a member of parliament concerning the four regiments* (1699), 7.

[120] [Trenchard], *Short history*, 3. See also, [Trenchard], *Letter from the author*, 10; [Fletcher], *Discourse*, 12.

[121] [Trenchard], *Short history*, 3–19. For an abridged version of this history, see [Fletcher], *Discourse* 12–14.

Parliament had been overly generous to a national deliverer, and the prolonged war with Louis had provided an excuse for vast forces. William now had at his command an army that was many orders of magnitude larger than the ones that had caused disquiet under Charles II, or that had imposed military dictatorship under Cromwell.[122] Trenchard's *Short history* identified the few months after the revolution as the crucial moment when English liberty had been lost. Rebellion in Ireland had not been suppressed with the speed that might have allowed it to be done with a small force—'through chance, inadvertency, or necessity for our affairs (for I am unwilling to think it was Design)'—and as a result a much larger army had had to be assembled.[123]

If the plot's effects had been different in scale from anything achieved before by evil men at court, it was also different in kind, because it aimed at far more than creating a coercive tool for the corrupted government. It was attempting a wholesale remodelling of English society, which would leave a supine country that could no longer question the fiat of the conspirators in power. Picking up on hints in the Jacobite literature that the plotters' ambition and avarice were upending established social hierarchies, anti-army commentators sensed a plan to destroy independent landowners and wealth-generators and to replace them with servile creatures of the court. Thus Thomas Orme talked of a new class of person 'who have leapt up great wealth in their stations'. They had done this by defrauding funds that taxpayers had intended for ordinary sailors and soldiers, and they must now be 'strip'd back to what they had in 1688'.[124] Walter Moyle spoke of conspirators who now had 'the keys to our Money and the Titles to our Land in their Power' and were now planning the ruin of all but themselves.[125] Trenchard cast one of his pamphlets as a complaint from traditional elites to the upstarts who were advocating the army. Opening his letter to John Somers (a leading Whig minister who had gone into print to defend a professional military), he drew a deep social contrast between them. Somers was an 'Adventurer', whose economic stake was now 'Considerable', but—as a consequence of its recent origin in political gambling—this had not brought proper responsibility. Trenchard, by contrast, 'was not of a desperate Fortune', but he was properly concerned about the fate of his property because it had been a trust from a long-established family.[126]

In truth, much of the talk of socially transforming conspiracy in the anti-army literature was fleeting, and without comprehensive analysis. The writing concentrated on the dangers of a mercenary military, and spent time outlining that, rather than detailing the developments that it hinted lay behind the new force. Yet these fleeting suggestions contained the most radical chronology in the corpus. Society was being transformed so that old verities would no longer apply, and the

---

[122] [Trenchard and Moyle], *Argument shewing*, 14–15; *Letter to a member of parliament…garrisons*, 5.
[123] [Trenchard], *Short history*, 22.   [124] [Orme], *Late prints*, 4
[125] [Moyle], *Second part*, 14   [126] [Trenchard], *Letter from the author*, 3–4.

processes that were ensuring this had been released very recently. It was only since the revolution that a new kind of conspirator had had unprecedented success in debauching and reconfiguring the nation. Such narrative-driven, and periodized, analysis looked both back and forwards. It looked back to the ideas in Jacobite writing, sharing that movement's sense that 1688–9 had been a turning point when new kinds of evil had entered into the English polity. But anti-army literature also looked forward to the opposition rhetoric of the very last years of William's reign.

For all its passion, the army dispute was over quickly. Outvoted in the Commons, William had to give up dreams of a large standing force, and settled for a few thousand men, with the vast bulk of the military disbanded. This, however, did not end political tension. As the controversy over the number of soldiers waned, it was replaced by argument over the geopolitical balance of Europe. When the king of Spain, Carlos II, died in 1700 and left his realm to a grandson of Louis XIV in a cadet line, there was a danger that the French crown would become hegemonic in Europe, adding the western Hapsburg lands to its empire, including such strategically vital regions as southern Italy and Flanders. Although all saw the potential threat of this, the English political nation divided over the appropriate response. As the king and his Whig allies pressed for direct military intervention on the Continent, the Tory–country alliance that had come together to disband the army was far more cautious. It wondered how far England's national interests as a maritime power were really threatened by French forces on the European landmass; it thought the navy and continental allies might well be able to contain the danger without the need for massive English mobilization; and it wondered if Spain and France would, in fact, work so well together, given that their crowns would remain separate and that the new French ruler in Madrid might go native.

The topic of debate thus moved on in the last years of William's reign, but it was closely related to what had gone before. The sides in the contest were much the same as in the army controversy, and the issues were congruent, since the row was again about England's military activism. This meant that the scheme of degeneration developed in the earlier tussle could be easily transferred. The Tory side not only challenged the geopolitics of the Whigs, but asked why they really wanted war. Given the weaknesses of their rivals' strategic case, Tories reasoned, there must surely be some ulterior motive for their policy—and this, of course, was the agenda of the post-revolutionary conspiracy. Defeated in their attempts to maintain an army and its attendant evils in peacetime, Whig plotters were agitating for a new conflict. The arguments of 1700–2 were thus very close to those of 1697–9, and could have been mentioned quite briefly here, had they not produced the richest and most complete account of post-revolutionary corruption in a work whose striking images and chronological assumptions shaped opposition material for decades to come. It is time to introduce the arch-villain, Tom Double.

Mr (soon to be Sir) Thomas Double was the fictional character central to two anti-Whig pamphlets written by the economist, essayist, and pamphleteer Charles Davenant.[127] These were publishing phenomena. The first, *The true picture of a modern whig* (1701), went through six editions in its first year alone. This probably meant it sold around 10,000 copies, and it would have reached a much larger audience than this, given likely reading practices. Pamphlets of this kind (it was a slim, unbound octavo of sixty-four pages) were left in inns and coffeehouses for the perusal of patrons, and were probably read aloud to groups seeking entertainment and information: indeed the dialogic form of this work may even have encouraged amateur performances. The success of the *True picture* explains Davenant's willingness to produce the sequel, *Tom Double returned out of the country*, in 1702. The second pamphlet sold well itself—and made a wry comment on the impact of its predecessor. As part of the fictive account of recent politics which formed the meat of both works, Tom Double complained that an election victory he had hoped to secure in a northern town had been thwarted when *The true picture* was declaimed to a public gathering in the constituency.[128]

In form, the pamphlets were conversations between Double and his sidekick, Mr Whiglove, which reviewed recent Whig plotting and made plans for further political mischief. As the names of these figures suggest, the approach was satirical: the works provided a witty and exaggerated caricature of the Tories' enemies and of their supposed methods and motives. Yet while the tone was light-hearted, the purpose was serious. Davenant used his satire to point to the profound and long-term damage he believed the Whigs were doing to England. As he did this, he provided a biting critique of a process of corruption that had been unleashed by the revolution, and was driving the nation into ever deeper peril. The basic ideological framework of the two pamphlets was familiar from Jacobitism and the standing army controversies. In his frank revelations, Double admitted he had spent the bulk of the 1690s in various contrivances to enrich himself, and destroy his political rivals, and that his latest aim was a war, 'begun and carried on against all right and reason', which would distract the nation from discovering his crimes and would provide new opportunities to pocket money raised for mobilization.[129] Where Davenant's work went beyond other opposition tracts of the late 1690s, however, was in its detail. It outlined a vast and coherent conspiracy, exposing the arts of political lying and electoral bribery at its heart, and particularly stressing the role of finance in its operation. Claiming that he had invented most of the fiscal expedients that the court had claimed were necessary to pay for the war, Double showed how they had all worked together to impoverish honest Englishmen

---

[127] Double had gained the knighthood by the time Davenant reprised his characters in the 1710 *Sir Thomas Double at court and in high preferments*.

[128] [Charles Davenant], *Tom Double returned out of the country* (1702), 73.

[129] [Charles Davenant], *The true picture of a modern whig* (1701), 11.

and advance men of his own ilk. Heavy taxation bore down upon gentry and merchants, but created a steady stream of funds for those close to government to embezzle. Deficit finance perpetuated the need for high taxes, but opened investment opportunities for those with ready cash (just stolen from the public) to lend. As war disrupted trade, it impoverished the landed and commercial ranks of Englishmen, but provided a bonanza for those who had mastered the new economics of public credit and contracting. The overall result had been vast riches for the Whigs (who could now afford luxuries such as the dinner party with lobster, birdnests, and Tockay wine described at the opening of *Tom Double returned*), but a humbled 'Ancient Gentry', who were now too weak to act on their knowledge that Double and his friends were 'Upstarts and Leeches' upon the kingdom.[130]

Such detail sharpened the chronological framing of the post-revolutionary plot that had been present in earlier writings. Davenant's pamphlets not only described degeneration under William, but used a precise narrative to emphasize its novelty, and its origin in 1688–9. This very title of the first work announced new times. Double was the very picture a *modern* Whig. Although the term 'modern' was only just developing its associations with innovation in the later Stuart period, Davenant was using it to indicate at least a distinction from earlier types of people. Double, the author made clear, had betrayed the honourable patriotism and suspicion of power that had marked the original Whigs of the late 1670s: the label 'modern' pointed to this apostasy. Also, the word seems to have begun to have taken on a sense of active and deliberate breaking with the past at almost exactly this point in history (the Oxford English Dictionary's first example is from 1701 itself).[131] Davenant may therefore have carefully chosen the label to paint court Whigs as a novel species of men making wholesale departures from existing norms; and it is even possible that his choice of the word, in the title of such a popular work, helped launch the more progressive interpretation of it. Double's biography, which occupied the first half of the *True Picture*, and good sections of its sequel, reinforced this sense of a radical new era. It put innovation at the heart of Double's career; showing that it had simultaneously fuelled his rise and refashioned the nation. Since 1688–9, the biography made clear, Double had spent much of his time involved in unprecedented experiments with public finance. The war could have been paid for with the old branches of revenue, had not the Whigs mismanaged it; but as the party's extravagance ensured demands for money rose, new initiatives that benefitted the group could be made attractive. 'We got a Bank [the Bank of England] erected', Double boasted; 'We devis'd Exchequer Bills'.[132]

---

[130] [Davenant], *Tom Double return'd*, 3–4, 32.

[131] www.oed.com.unicat.bangor.ac.uk/view/Entry/120618?redirectedFrom=modern#eid   accessed 15.07.2016

[132] [Davenant], *Tom Double returned*, 39.

The malt duty, window tax, and impositions on births marriages and deaths were the 'Off-springs' of Double's brain; no one would have thought of lotteries without him, and the *New* East India Company (my italics), erected to lend to the government, was another one of his designs.[133] Obviously the language here was satiric (no one person could have come up with all these schemes), but it also emphasized novelty. These were financial fantasies, dreamt up where there had been none before, and they were so unheard of that it had taken an arch-plotter and projector such as Double to imagine them.

Tom Double's world was thus an innovation—but it was also one with a precise, and very recent, starting point. Again the biography made this clear. Double had been born of lowly origin, the son of a shoemaker, but he had never rested satisfied with that trade, and had resolved to gain his fortune through embezzlement and parasitism on the public service. He had accordingly wangled himself a place in the customs office under Charles II, but, sadly, his career had not taken root. By the start of James's reign, he had been turned out of his job as a notorious fraud, and he sunk into poverty. Before 1688–9, then, Double's character had been the same as it would be through his whole life, but the times had not allowed him to prosper. Yet this was transformed by the revolution. 'At last', noted Double, 'fortune vouchsafed me a favourable smile, and it was the week after the king landed at Torbay'.[134] From the moment William arrived, the rogue found his skills paid off. Pretending to have been a spy for the prince before the invasion, he convinced the Orange regime to take him into its inner circle; bribery and perquisites began to fill his purse; and he started a promotion through the ranks of government placeholders that eventually bestowed the influence over financial policy that he could now parade.[135] The revolution had therefore been the turning point in Double's life, but it also, Davenant made clear, marked a new era in English social history. By the time Double and Whiglove were having their conversation, the elite had been entirely altered. Allies of the court Whigs had risen from obscurity to positions of great wealth and power; traditional landowners were trudging along in the dirt, as men like Double swept past them in coaches. And this change was very precisely dated. When Double talked of the rise of himself and his friends, he repeatedly stressed it had only been possible in 'these times', these 'brave times', and that the period of his good fortune had begun in 1688–9.[136] So, Whigs had got 'much better fortunes since the Revolution'.[137] 'Ten years ago', Double reminded Whiglove, they had not been 'worth a groat'.[138] 'What was such a Lord not long before the Revolution?', asked Double of a generic modern Whig: 'a little Jackanapes that people shunned because he could not pay his Club'.[139]

---

[133] [Davenant], *True picture*, 25,   [134] Ibid., 15–17.   [135] Ibid., 17–26.
[136] Ibid., 4–5.   [137] Ibid., 15.   [138] Ibid., p. 4.
[139] [Davenant], *Tom Double returned*, 22.

The decade since William's arrival was thus explicitly defined as a novel period of change, with that arrival identified as the divide between eras. And the effect of this detailed description of the last decade was to create further features that introduced a progressive chronology. Change had not only started at a point in the past, and so mapped out a new period, it had been bewildering rapid—and it was set to continue into the future. The speed was underlined by explicit comment (it had all happened 'in a very few years') and by noting the scale of what had occurred.[140] The new masters of England had been raised 'from nothing'; as recently as James II's reign, Double had had 'no shoes to his feet'.[141] Future transformation was indicated by the Whigs' plans for the next few years. William's nine-year war against Louis had effected the social revolution of which they boasted, but now they were stirring an even bigger and more endless conflict that would produce even greater consequences. The national debt would double, taxes to pay for it would destroy the entire landed class, and the vast expansion of public credit would yield ever fatter profits for 'Friends in Town, who have been the Chief Getters since the Revolution'.[142]

Such writing produced an impression of accelerated change that had a further effect presaging a 'modern' sense of time. It destabilized the present. Double's plot was moving so fast that Davenant's readers must have felt it was unfolding in the very moment they read. Double's words told of his ceaseless action to create the future as he promoted his conspiracy, and Davenant's prose created a novel-like specificity of narrative circumstance that rooted that action in a constantly updating now that could astonish witnesses with its potential flexibility. In the recent days before his conversations with Whiglove, Double had dreamt up ever more vicious financial schemes; he had travelled to constituencies for mendacious vote buying; he had planned the menus for dinners at which he would debauch and recruit others. Telling Whiglove what they needed to do to help the party, he moulded times to come by his behaviour in this current instant. And this demanded compensating action in the reader. Relating how he had sometimes been thwarted by honest opponents (for example, complaining about the witnesses who had blasted a local election campaign by revealing him to be the fraud he was), Double challenged his audience to respond in their turn. If his plot could be defeated by resolute opposition, such opposition became a pressing duty. The chronology of Davenant's pamphlets was therefore precisely periodized, but it was also startlingly progressive and fluid. Since the revolution, history had been marked by bewildering novelty, lightning transformation, and a battle for the future, whose nature would be decided by the political struggle in which the author tried to engage his audience. No other works of the print exchanges in the last years of William's reign had quite this chronological dynamism.

---

[140] Ibid., 19.   [141] [Davenant], *True picture*, 4, 15.
[142] [Davenant], *Tom Double returned*, 40–2.

And it is important to stress that Davenant produced dynamism without the tropes that have been identified for civic humanism. Tom Double's was a very modern and recent kind of degeneration. The pamphlets made few classical references and were more or less uninterested in theories of long-term economic change—though neither was incompatible with the vision: at one point Double admitted his plot was a repeat of Cataline's against the free Roman republic.[143] The key driver of the new era of change was neither inevitable cycles of decline from free civilizations, nor the end of medieval landholding, but rather the vicious action of a recently emerged breed of men. This allowed Davenant to suggest a new and unique species of evil was evolving, as he did when insisting Double had stooped well below the standard arts of court flattery that were familiar to those who had viewed Stuart politics, and more generally as he presented corruption feeding on levels of taxation, and new forms of public credit, that had only existed since 1688–9.[144] This was, in fact, the true chronological radicalism of Davenant's writing. The revolution had ushered in, not simply a different era, but an unprecedented one. These were utterly new times with challenges that were unlike anything that had been seen before.

A profound sense of novelty featured in another campaign that had run alongside protests about the effects of war in the late 1690s. This came from the Tory wing of opposition to William—and was about religious, rather than civil affairs. It was sparked by Francis Atterbury's *Letter to a convocation man* (1696). Atterbury was a London minister and preacher, who—like a number of his Tory colleagues among the clergy—had become concerned about religious developments since 1688–9. Few of those who shared Atterbury's fears called openly for a reversal of the revolution's religious settlement (which had allowed Protestant dissenters to worship outside the Church of England, if they met stringent doctrinal tests), but many began to complain that heterodox groups had taken advantage of legal change to push liberty far further than Parliament had intended in its 1689 'Toleration Act'. 'High Church' clerics, as they came to be called, worried that some dissenters took Anglican communion occasionally, and so qualified for public office, even though this was still supposed to be restricted to members of the established church; that dissenters were flaunting their freedoms and openly proselytizing; and that the 'latitudinarian' bishops William had appointed to the church were far too relaxed about these assaults on the establishment. Most specifically, Tory clerics worried that too little was being done to stem heresy. Alarmed by a number of post-revolutionary writings which debunked the Trinity or other core doctrines, many clerics called for something to be done. They found their rallying cry in Atterbury's pamphlet. It demanded that the church's own legislative body, convocation, be summoned by the king, and that it enact new

---

[143] Ibid., 95.   [144] Ibid., 20.

canons against the spread of unchristian opinions and to end the latitudinarian torpor of the establishment.[145]

Atterbury's piece was read, correctly, as an attack on William's ecclesiastical policies and appointments. It also generated a fierce printed exchange, known to scholars as the 'convocation controversy'. The bishops whom Atterbury had targeted argued against any legislative meeting of the clergy, fearing it would result in a witch-hunt against them.[146] In truth, the dispute rapidly descended into tedious legal argument. High Church writers insisted monarchs must call convocations every time they convened parliaments; their opponents argued there was no such requirement. As one would expect, this produced a great deal of time-freezing scholarship as the two sides trawled back through the centuries for examples that they imagined proved their case. Atterbury's main demand—a church that governed itself without interference from the secular state—was also based on deep precedent. He argued that this must have been the original state of the Christian community before the magistrate (in the form of the Roman emperor) converted to their faith, so he appealed back to the decades of primitive Christianity.[147] But, for all this, the opening shot in the debate had contained elements that were far more dynamic. The *Letter to a convocation man* had suggested something quite remarkable for doctrinal disputes: the rise of a new conspiracy, peddling novel doctrine. In the ecclesiastical sphere, it sensed a plot quite as unprecedented, and quite as recent, as Tom Double's great project to subvert the state.

This was remarkable because, as the last chapter demonstrated, English Protestants were reluctant to suggest there was much new under the sun in religious controversies. Whilst they accused popery of innovating as they themselves remained true to unchanging truth, they tended to date the main popish errors to the early centuries of the Christian era (the processes of corruption were well in train by the fall of the western Roman Empire), and they saw their struggle with Romanism as a continuation of the great battle against the false churches that had started with the Jews' defiance of heathens.[148] In more technical areas— such as the exact nature of a Trinitarian and incarnate God—commentators had rich veins of patristic dispute to mine. The considerable range of positions advanced by early Christians usually meant that any modern error could be mapped back to some ancient heresy, and so each tended to be discussed as its survival or resurgence, rather than as any truly original subversion of doctrine.

By contrast, Atterbury suggested he was facing something unprecedented. Partly this was simply the scale and intensity of the challenge to traditional beliefs. By pointing to a slew of writings that had come out 'of late', or were 'not long since'

---

[145] Classic studies include George Every, *The High Church Party, 1688–1715* (London: Church Historical Society 1956); G.V. Bennett, 'Conflict in the Church', in Geoffrey Holmes, ed., *Britain after the Glorious Revolution* (London: Macmillan, 1969), 135–154.

[146] The first major riposte was William Wake, *The authority of Christian princes* (1697).

[147] [Francis Atterbury], *Letter to a convocation man* (1696), 18.   [148] See above, ch. 3.4.

published, the writer created an impression of a sudden and coordinated burst of heresy: one that was undermining Christian faith to an extraordinary degree.[149] According to Atterbury, such ideas, now openly circulating, had had such 'mischievous effects' amongst the laity that there was a real danger that 'the next age' would cease to believe in Christian revelation altogether.[150] Since 'age' might, given contemporary usage, mean century—and since Atterbury's work had appeared only a few years before a century was due to begin—he came close to predicting an imminent collapse of a faith that had survived over a millennium and a half. But it was more than the scale and urgency of the challenge that was so unusual. The author implied the ideas that were eroding Christianity were new too. Naming the sort of people he saw behind the danger, Atterbury identified 'Deists, Socinians, Latitudinarians, Deniers of Mysteries'.[151] This was an unusual list because it included no classical heresies. 'Deist' (a word invented to identify those who rejected revealed religion, even if they accepted that reason justified belief in a supreme being) was a sixteenth century French neologism that arrived in England in the early seventeenth century. 'Socinian' (labelling certain species of anti-Trinitarians) was derived from the supposed founder of the ideology, Fausto Sozzini (Fautus Socinius), who had died in 1604. 'Latitudinarian' had emerged as a term in Restoration England, badging those who had tried to cool religious tensions by limiting the number of core and indisputable doctrines. 'Deniers of mysteries' was probably Atterbury's own coinage, riffing on the title of one of the works he was attacking—John Toland's *Christianty not mysterious*—which had appeared only a few months earlier. Using this string of recent terms, the author dated error to the last few decades, and he was even more explicit when calling for a check to 'bold innovators of the faith' and 'new-fangled opinions'; and praising the few steps that had already been taken to prevent people using 'any new terms' in outlining the content of Christian belief.[152]

This sense of a new kind of threat brought the Tory side of the convocation controversy to the same sort of chronological vision as Davenant. The parallels became even closer as Atterbury's dated the threat he identified, as he stressed that it was driven by conspiracy, and as he made energetic calls for immediate action. The pamphleteer was not absolutely precise about when he felt heterodoxy had burst the bounds, but there was a clear implication that this had been a post-revolution phenomenon. The works he specifically listed as spreading doctrinal poison were all from the 1690s. As well as Toland's book, he cited William Sherlock's *Vindication of the doctrine of the holy and ever blessed trinity* (1690); Gilbert Burnet's *Four discourses delivered to the clergy of the diocese of Sarum* (1694); and John Locke's *Reasonableness of Christianity* (1695). Moreover, Atterbury stated several times that the problems that the Church of England was facing stemmed

---

[149] [Atterbury], *Letter*, 4,7.   [150] Ibid., 6–7.   [151] Ibid., 6.   [152] Ibid., 8, 13, 14.

from a misinterpretation of 'toleration'. Against the clear sense of Parliament in 1689, which had intended a very limited measure, too many people had assumed they had been granted a 'universal, unlimited' religious liberty in the revolution's ecclesiastical settlement.[153] If corruption had started with William's reign, it—like Tom Double's treachery in the secular sphere—had been forwarded by plotting. The faith had been undermined and overthrown by a widespread 'conspiracy' among men intent on subverting Christian truth.[154] These people had recently wormed their way into high positions in the church, and were now in 'secret correspondence' with more open heretics abroad.[155] Echoing the tactics of junto Whigs when criticized by honest men, this pack denigrated anyone who challenged them. They misrepresented their motives and questioned their character, hoping to demoralize the forces that might bring them to account.[156] Given the depths of this plot, Atterbury demanded action against it as urgently as the anti-army and anti-war pamphleteers. There was need for a convocation 'now', the author insisted in his introduction: the rest of the work underlined this with pressingly immediate portraits of the threat, of the need to free the church to find a remedy, and of the enormities that would result from inaction.[157]

Atterbury's pamphlet, and the campaign to defend the church that it encouraged, thus rounded out the opposition to William in the late 1690s. It gave it an important ecclesiastical dimension, and animated the Tory wing of the alliance that was critical of the king's mid-decade policies and ministers. This alliance was extremely broad, encompassing people from a radical commonwealthsmen to rock solid Anglicans. Such variety bred tensions. Sharp-eyed readers will have spotted that John Toland, the leading anti-army pamphleteer, was also a heterodox bogeyman in Atterbury's work. As political historians have noted, it took considerable skill on the part of men like Robert Harley to keep such a diverse opposition together as an effective political force.[158] Yet a shared chronological framework may have helped to consolidate the movement. Both radical Whigs and adamant Tories had a very particular sense of time. Abandoning the *stasis* of most Williamite commentators in the early years after the revolution, the opposition of the late 1690s saw 1688–9 as a turning point which had ushered in a dizzyingly accelerating period of truly innovative change. Forces released at William's arrival had subverted politics, corrupted society, and undermined the church. This was rarely sophisticated sociological analysis. Transformation was being driven by evil men rather than deeper cultural shifts—but this added to the sense of an unstable, and rapidly evolving, present. Plots could, and must, be countered. Action in the current moment to expose conspirators, and to reverse the effects of

---

[153] Ibid., 3.   [154] Ibid., 6   [155] Ibid., 4   [156] Ibid., 9–12.   [157] Ibid., 2.
[158] For an appreciation of the balance in Harley's career, see W.A. Speck, 'Robert Harley', in H.C.G. Matthews and Brian Harrison, eds, *Oxford Dictionary of National Biography* Vol. 25 (Oxford: OUP, 2004), 317–26.

their machinations, became an urgent duty that should shape a different future. This agreement that the world had recently begun to change, and that this change must be challenged, probably provided enough common ground for the opposition alliance to function. The people involved had taken very different stances before 1688–9, but all now saw the time *since* that date as the truly significant era. Imagining those most recent years as a period of corruption united all in hostility to those who had been in power as it unfolded. What had originally been a Jacobite chronology therefore had an impact well beyond those who wished to bring the old king back to the throne. Suggesting a radical break in time at the revolution, it consolidated a pattern of politics that was to last for decades.

4.6 Opposition Time in the Eighteenth Century

This book has no space to cover the eighteenth century, even its first years, in extensive detail, but it is important to recognize that the criticisms of government developed after 1697 remained current for a considerable period and maintained the fiction of a conspiracy-driven degeneration since the revolution. The discourse was temporarily muted in Anne's first years. The new monarch (as a legitimate Stuart) was popular among the Tories who had been attracted to Davenant and Atterbury's formulations, and there was a reluctance to criticize her support for the new war against France which had been launched when Louis appeared to attempt to seize the whole of the Spanish empire. The war was also surprisingly successful. Spectacular military triumphs on the Continent, under the command of the Duke of Marlborough, restored England's military pride and honour, and made it hard to argue that the conflict was merely a plot to enrich domestic parasites of the state. Ecclesiastical politics also calmed for a while. Convocation was permitted to meet annually from 1700 (part of a deal to construct a Tory-led ministry, which seemed to William to be the only way to secure political stability at that moment); and High Churchmen were also reassured by the belief that Queen Anne was more sympathetic to the establishment than her brother-in-law had been.

However, the mood soon shifted again. On the military front, costs climbed. Attempts to remove the French candidate for the Spanish throne failed; and the conflict—in its main theatre of Flanders—became bogged down. At this point, Tories broke with the Whigs by calling for a compromise peace, satisfied that France had been so weakened that she was no longer a geopolitical threat. Religious disputes also reignited. As Whigs continued to support dissenters, Tories complained that non-Anglicans had gained too much political power through their occasional conformity and were being allowed to replicate themselves by running educational academies. As rancour mounted, the pattern of opposition polemic, with its characteristic chronological frame, re-emerged. There was, Tories insisted, still a plot, which had been hatched at the revolution, to use war and Nonconformity to remodel England and enrich wicked men.

The most graphic example of this rhetorical recycling was Davenant's release of a new instalment of the Double narrative. In his 1710 *Sir Thomas Double at court and in high preferments*, the author updated audiences on his creation's career—though in truth little had changed. Our hero had allied with the Whig ministry which had come to lead the war effort, and had continued his tricks to advance himself by feeding off the ever expanding wartime state.[159] More widely, this pessimistic portrait of the age was propagated in the increasingly bitter press campaign against Marlborough. Although the duke continued to win on the battlefield, the shine came off his image as he fell into an increasingly close alliance with the Whigs, and as the scale of personal rewards for his service became ever more questionable. By the end of the first decade of the eighteenth century, the Tories were mounting a full-scale campaign of print vilification. This reduced the duke to a cartoon villain: but a villain clearly modelled on Double. He was a man who had exploited wartime conditions, and influence in government, to disrupt traditional society. In the end, the detractors claimed, Marlborough was lording it over the monarch herself.[160]

Much of this material was satire, low scandal, and gutter-level slander, but it nonetheless inhabited the same temporal universe as the opposition works at the end of William's reign. There was a strong sense of process as Marlborough and his cronies corrupted the body politic, and there was stress on action in a fluid present to alter—effectively to redeem—the future. When Anne dismissed the Whig ministry from power in 1710, and Marlborough from his military posts the next year, the Tory press praised her decisive political strokes, which had redirected the course of the nation. A precise chronology of the plot the queen had thwarted was available from the essayist and Tory propagandist Jonathan Swift, as he joined the polemical efforts to end the war. In his contributions to the periodical *Examiner*, which became one of Marlborough's chief persecutors after the Whigs' fall—and in his seminal tract *The conduct of the allies*, which cheerled Tory calls for peace—Swift identified a conspiracy that had been running for 'these twenty years past'.[161] This, of course, placed its start immediately after the revolution.

The high-water mark of Tory ecclesiastical politics under Queen Anne came with Henry Sacheverell's 1709 *Perils of false brethren*. This infamous sermon by an Oxford cleric created a political tempest with its accusation that Whig leadership of the church and state since 1688–9 had incubated the republicanism, and the

---

[159] [Charles Davenant], *Sir Thomas Double at court and in high preferments* (1710).

[160] Tony Claydon, 'A European General in the English Press: The Print Image of Marlborough in the Stuart Realm', in John B. Hattendorf, Augustus J. Vennendall Jr, and Rolof van Hövell tot Westerflied, eds, *Marlborough: Soldier and Diplomat* (Rotterdam: Karwansaway, 2012), 300–19.

[161] Quote at *The Examiner*, 14 (9 November 1710).

heretical principles of faith, that now threatened England's constitution and religious establishment.[162] In truth, Sacheverell's timeframe was eclectic, borrowing from many of the discourses already covered in this book, and some elements of his diatribe were chronologically static. He claimed to be defending an ancient set of theological and political doctrines that had been handed down from the primitive Christians; and he believed that his enemies were ultimately energized by the ceaseless popish campaign against true faith.[163] Some sections were more dynamic, though they suggested varying points in history for the arrival of pernicious ideas in England. Sacheverell shared the Jacobites' sense that the republic of the mid seventeenth century had been a point of extraordinary evil that had tainted all that came after it, and he expounded the theory of the earlier Laudian cleric, Peter Heylyn, that a Puritan poison had entered the Church of England from Geneva in the mid Tudor period.[164] Despite all this, the sermon most closely fitted Davenant and Atterbury's notion of a new kind of conspiracy that had operated since 1688–9. Men bent on undermining monarchy, and allowing any kind of theological opinion, had hoped to destroy divine kingship, and the Church of England, when William arrived—but having been thwarted under that king, they were now using more subtle means. Crying up religious moderation, exploiting the toleration that had been permitted at the revolution, and insisting that James's fall had proved the theory of popular sovereignty, these 'false brethren' had infiltrated the church and state, and now sought to do by 'secret treachery' what they had failed to achieve by 'open violence' two decades before.[165] The preacher also emphasized that the plotters' ideas were new. These men were 'upstart novelists'; 'new preachers' of a 'new, and unheard of gospel'; they deployed 'new fangled terms of modern philosophy'; and Sacheverell accused them of being 'modish' and 'fashionable' to boot.[166]

For a few years after Sacheverell's performance, and to an extent as a result of it, the 'opposition' rhetorics we have been examining came to support the government, rather than criticize it. The Tories triumphed in the general election of 1710, propelled by a war-weariness encapsulated in Swift's prose, and by anger at Whig attempts to prosecute Sacheverell for his words. An administration under Harley accelerated peace talks, moved to restrict the freedoms of dissenters, and launched wholesale investigations of the displaced ministers—especially the Duke of Marlborough. The reversal did not last long however. Tories split over whether to invite James II's heirs back to the throne once Anne died; and the fact

---

[162] The best account is still Holmes, *The Trial of Dr Sacheverell*; though for a collection of more recent scholarship, see Mark Knights, ed., *Faction Displayed: Reconsidering the Impeachment of Dr Henry Sacheverell* (Oxford: OUP, 2012).

[163] Henry Sacheverell, *The perils of false brethren, both in church and state, set forth in a sermon preached before the right honourable, the lord mayor* (1709), 9. 17–18.

[164] Sacheverell, *Perils of false brethren*, 13, 19. For Heylyn's theories about church history, see Peter Heylyn, *Aerius redivus* (1670).

[165] Sacheverell, *Perils of false brethren*, 17.   [166] Ibid., 9, 10, 12.

that some of the party advocated this tainted it with a Jacobitism with which the chronological framing of its ideology, at least, had considerable affinity. As a result, when the post-revolution Stuart line failed in 1714, the Whigs rode to power on the back of the arriving Hanoverian dynasty. Tory advocates of the exiled Stuarts had proved too weak to prevent George I coming to the throne and earned the debilitating suspicion both of the new ruler, and many of the electorate (which might complain about conditions since 1688–9, but did not go so far as to wish to reverse it). The worldview we have been tracing thus passed back into opposition, where it continued bitter denunciation of a series of Whig ministries through to the mid eighteenth century.

There is absolutely no space to trace development of the rhetoric after 1714. But enough has been said to note a considerable irony. Modern historiography has portrayed the revolution of 1688–9 as initiating a modernizing transformation of England's culture, economy, and society. It expanded the state, created modern systems of public credit, encouraged particular patterns of capitalist enterprise, and it created new classes of people who benefitted from these changes. In some accounts of these processes, these were quite deliberate changes, orchestrated by groups allied, politically, with the Whigs, who had a new and different vision of the nation. Yet these were not the people who described all this most clearly, or who elucidated its dizzying chronological dynamism. Rather, it was (perhaps, on reflection, understandably) those who opposed change who focused upon it. It was Jacobites, and their intellectual heirs in the Tory-country opposition, who first insisted that 1688–9 was a point of temporal rupture which had introduced the processes that twentieth- and twenty-first-century scholars have outlined. These were the people who claimed that the revolution was a dramatic break with the past; that it initiated a novel era; and that this 'modern' epoch was marked by accelerating change. They were the ones who insisted that new times posed pressing moral and political challenges; that the future was at stake in a highly charged and unstable present; and that everyone had an urgent duty to act in the current moment to shape it. They were also the people who suggested what was happening was unprecedented, so that history could be no real guide, and who feared that if the threat they saw were not defeated, events would head with a linear determination to a strange new world. All of this stood in contrast to the protagonists of change who—deliberately or subconsciously—covered what they were doing in languages of defending an ancient and unaltered constitution, or continuing the ceaseless struggles of God's true church. If we are looking for people in the late seventeenth century who understood time as we do now, we will find them among the most conservative groups of late Stuart society.

5

Progressive Williamite Time

5.1 1688–9 as 'Year Zero'

A century after William's arrival in London, the English people faced a new revolution. From the summer of 1789, events in France unfolded in ways that suggested parallels with the ejection of James II and generated similar debate in Britain about the fundamental principles of politics. The most famous exchange was that between Richard Price and Edmund Burke. Price, preaching on 4 November 1789 (the anniversary of William's birthday, which radical circles had adopted as the annual occasion to mark his triumph), praised the initial stages of the recent rebellion in France as an emulation of English action to secure their liberty a hundred years before. Burke condemned Price's words as a complete misunderstanding of William's triumph and as a dangerous encouragement to violence and disruption. Yet despite this disagreement, both men posed as defenders of 1688–9 and presented it as some sort of new start in English history. This was clearest for Price, who celebrated a series of new freedoms (including religious toleration) won in the late seventeenth century, and saw the fall of James as a moment when 'an era of light and liberty was introduced among us'.[1] But Burke too accepted there had been a turning point. Certainly the men of 1688–9 had been very cautious in making changes. They had been aware that the constitution had evolved slowly through generations, that it therefore embodied much accumulated wisdom, and that any alteration should innovate in order to preserve. But even as Burke stressed the conservatism of England's revolution, he celebrated it as some sort of founding of English government. The men who had greeted the prince of Orange had done their job so well that they had made a definitive settlement: something that had perfected, if it had not invented, the best principles of England's law. Thus the men of 1688–9 became the kind of political seers lauded in origin myths. They were 'great lawyers and great statesmen' whose power to reframe government had been unlimited, but whose moderation in exercising that power had been their gift to future generations.[2] The Declaration of Rights that they had penned was, said Burke, 'the cornerstone of our constitution, as reinforced, explained, improved, and its fundamental principles forever settled.'[3] Thus, despite being

---

[1] Richard Price, *A discourse on the love of our country* (1789), 32.
[2] Edmund Burke, *Reflections on the revolution in France* (1790), 21, 27.   [3] Ibid., 21.

The Revolution in Time: Chronology, Modernity, and 1688–1689 in England. Tony Claydon, Oxford University Press (2020). © Tony Claydon.
DOI: 10.1093/oso/9780198817239.001.0001

bitterly divided on France, both Burke and Price operated within the common late-eighteenth-century assumption that liberty was newborn with William's arrival. They saw 1688–9 as 'Year Zero' of English government.[4]

This view of the revolution was obviously very different from the 'static chronology' of its first defenders. So when had this new way of conceiving 1688–9 emerged among its supporters? In his classic survey of debate on the revolution in the eighteenth century, H.T. Dickinson suggested it had been a tool of Robert Walpole's propaganda in the 1720s and 1730s. Walpole's enemy, Lord Bolingbroke, had tried to build an alliance of opposition Tories and discontented Whigs against Walpole by suggesting both parties shared credit for continuing the ancient constitution in 1688–9. For Bolingbroke, liberty had survived since Anglo-Saxon times because all Englishmen had united to defend it at moments of crisis: this had happened to bring down James II, and it should happen again to remove the overmighty minister of his present days. In response, Dickinson argued, Walpole had attempted to rescue the revolution as a solely Whig achievement. To do this, he had rejected the ancient constitution, and posited a wholly new founding of government by Whigs when William had arrived. Only they had championed the new principles of liberty and replaced an old repressive constitution with something far improved.[5] As Walpole's press organ, the *London Journal,* put it, 'Our modern constitution is infinitely better than the Ancient Constitution', and the situation since the revolution was 'vastly preferable' to any point in the past 'from the Saxons down to that glorious period'.[6]

Dickinson's summary captures the boldness of the Whig vision in the decades after the Hanoverian succession. Few writers would have dismissed the ancient constitution so breezily before. It also suggests a neat pattern: new thinking in opposition circles eventually provoked a reconceptualization among establishment figures. If Jacobites, radical Whigs, and country Tories, saw a novel world after 1688–9 to prove decline after the revolution, their rivals finally represented novelty as a sign of progress and improvement. Yet, whilst this pattern has much to recommend it, this chapter will explore complications which again confuse any neat emergence of new chronologies. It will suggest that elements of a dynamic pro-revolution time sense emerged more swiftly than Dickinson argued, but that this new dynamism came in somewhat different forms and was patchy and ambiguous. There was no easy or early triumph of 'modern' time.

---

[4] The phrase is used in Edward Vallance, *The Glorious Revolution: 1688 England's Fight for Liberty* (London: Abacus, 2006), 9; Mark Goldie, 'John Locke: Icon of Liberty', *History Today*, 54 (2004), 31–6; and elsewhere.

[5] H.T. Dickinson, 'The Eighteenth-Century Debate on the Glorious Revolution', *History*, 61 (1976), 28–45.

[6] *London Journal*, 740 (1 Sept 1733).

5.2 New Williamite Worlds? Toleration and Parliamentary Armies

A large part of the later-eighteenth-century commemoration of 1668–9 as a foundation of freedom centred on its depiction of the revolution as the birth of religious liberty. The 'toleration' act of 1689 had allowed people to worship outside the Church of England and came to be celebrated as the origin of a peculiar and laudable English latitude of faith. By the 1760s, for instance, it was being cited as 'the most just of public laws', and 'certainly of divine origin'.[7] Looking at the very narrow provisions of this measure, this might seem surprising. The act had specifically excluded Catholics and anti-Trinitarians, let alone any non-Christians, from its indulgence; and even for doctrinally orthodox Protestants, it merely suspended the penalties of the laws against Nonconformity (not the law itself), and then only on strict conditions. Yet despite such obvious limitations, a degree of the later excitement about the 1689 toleration began to emerge very soon after it has passed. For example, and as reported in an earlier chapter, movements within English Protestantism in the 1690s soon began to insist that the revolutionary settlement marked a break in the fortunes of the Reformation. A redirection of the established church's evangelical strategy within parishes and the movement to improve national manners were both understood as attempts to reverse the decline of the Reformation in its second age—perhaps even to complete a process of religious renewal that had stalled after the first excitement of Luther's message. These developments claimed William's providential deliverance from Catholicism as their inspiration; but they also depended on conditions after the Toleration Act—and so began that measure's apotheosis.

The renewal of Anglican pastoralism did this by explicitly rejecting coercion as a path to Christian unity. Although leading proponents of the new approach stressed the dissenters' unchanged duty to join the church, they saw toleration as an Anglican escape from long-standing sin. With a civil indulgence on the statute book, the established church could no longer use legal or physical force to bully people back into their fold, and this was significant for two reasons. Firstly, it ensured that Anglicans would not persecute. This saved them from a crime that Burnet and his circle saw as the most heinous breach of Christian charity and which Burnet, certainly, believed was the most characteristic mark of Antichrist.[8] Second, the Toleration Act reorientated the church towards a truly godly strategy for renewal which would be both inherently efficacious and blessed by God. Shorn of the chance to persecute, the church would be left with no weapons but persuasion, example, and pastoral zeal. These were the techniques which had explained the initial success of Protestantism and of the Christian faith

---

[7] William Warburton, *The discourse of grace* (1763), 189–90.   [8] Claydon, 'Latitudinarianism'.

itself; returned to now, they would deliver the faithful from their enemies and perhaps herald the final triumph of Christianity.[9]

The reformation of manners campaign also recognized toleration as a new start. As Craig Rose and other scholars have pointed out, at least some of the energy behind the movement came from an ecumenism that only made sense after the act.[10] Public statements promoted moral policing as an activity that could unite Anglicans and dissenters (since they all agreed what sin was, whatever their position on ceremonies or episcopacy), and some activities were deliberately structured to stress this joint participation. From 1697, for example, the societies that had been set up in London to suppress vice in the city hosted a series of sermons to bolster the cause. These were delivered to mixed congregations, the venue alternating between the Anglican church of St Mary le Bow and the dissenting meeting place in Salters Hall. The denomination of the preachers alternated with these venues, and several stressed the broad range of ecclesiological opinion that was involved.[11] It is true that reformers did not commonly cite the Toleration Act directly as the opportunity for the joint attack on vice. But they often said their efforts involved turning away from failed spiritual coercion. An early history of the societies stressed the need to 'lay aside our unnecessary strifes, and unchristian contentions with one another'; one of their founders thought the cause of virtue had been 'disturbed and interrupted by inconsiderate affectation of uniformity'; and there was complaint that obsession with enforcing the laws against dissent had distracted people from observing those against 'swearing, drunkenness and uncleanness'.[12] Thus, in parallel with Anglican pastoralism (and there was a good deal of overlap in personnel—bishops who pressed for improvement in spiritual care in the parishes also supported the crusade against vice), the movement for reforming manners implied that the 1689 measure had been a considerable step forward.

More widely, the principle of toleration began to bed down as an acknowledged achievement, at least because it had removed the grievances among Protestants that had weakened their movement. As Jeffrey Chambers has pointed out, writers

---

[9] This was the tone of the epistle dedicatory of the manifesto of the strategy, G. Burnet, *Discourse of the pastoral care.*

[10] Craig Rose, 'Providence, Protestant Union and Godly Reformation in the 1690s', *Transactions of the Royal Historical Society*, 6th series, 3 (1993), 151–70; Rose, *England in the 1690s*, ch. 6; T.C. Curtis and W.A. Speck, 'The Societies for Reformation of Manners: A Case Study in the Theory and Practice of Moral Reform', *Literature and History*, 3 (1976), 45–74.

[11] For a selection of ecumenical statements, see Thomas Jekyll, *A sermon preach'd at St Mary le Bow, June 27, 1698, before the societies for reformation of manners,* (1698), preface; *Seasonable advice to the societies for reformation of manners* (1699), 22; Edmund Calamy, *A sermon preach'd before the societies for reformation of manners...Febr. 20, 1698* (1699), preface; John Whitlocke, *A sermon preached to the society for reformation of manners in Nottingham...25th August, 1698* (1699), 43–4.

[12] *An account of the of the societies for reformation of manners,* (2nd edn, 1699), 109; Edward Stephens, *A caveat against flattery* (1689), 33; J[ean] G[ailhard], *Some observations upon the keeping the thirtieth of January* (1694), 45.

from the mid 1690s began to suggest that the political dynamic of dissent had been transformed by the revolution's religious settlement. A group that had tried to subvert English government could now be counted its friend because the new regime had guaranteed its freedom of worship. By this means the Toleration Act began to be viewed as the cornerstone of a new ecclesio-constitutional settlement that had widened the scope of the political nation and removed an opportunity for Catholics to sow strife. Dissenters declared this as they asserted their loyalty to William; Whigs endorsed this view as they savaged Tories for trying to destabilize the new religious accommodation; and a wide variety of Anglicans presented toleration in this way as they explained what would be dangerous about reversing 1689.[13] In some writing on the topic, the sense of a new era was palpable. Daniel Defoe said that, with the Toleration Act, eyes had been 'at last' opened, so the common name of Protestant could be enjoyed by all Englishmen. William Sherlock stated there was no need of a fresh revolution to give the dissenters ease, for they now had all the liberty that they needed.[14]

There was another area in which supporters of the revolution settlement, and of the regime that resulted from it, began to construct a dynamic chronology. This was in the debates of the late 1690s about the standing army. As explained earlier, those who wished to disband William's professional forces at the end of the war had based their case on an evolving plot against English liberties hatched at the revolution, and lamented long-term socio-economic developments which had sapped the martial spirit of the people. Those who wanted to support the king had to counter these arguments, but came up with their own version of changing times to do so. As their arguments unfolded, they not only came to accept that medieval precedents could not bind modern politics, but also began to construct the revolution as a novel settlement, adapted to social transformation.

At the most basic level, pro-army writers started to hint that things had changed, because their opponents surprisingly frequently denied it. As we saw earlier, those hostile to William's military sometimes talked of deep social alterations, but they also made extensive use of classical and other historical examples to prove a professional military would destroy free constitutions. As we saw, the anachronism of this move caused some unease in their own camp, but it proved a gift for their opponents, who savaged the lazy thinking of reaching for distant parallels. Pamphleteers lined up to suggest that history could only be used in political argument if the situation and context were the same. We should consider the 'present circumstances of things', thundered one, and follow 'not what our

---

[13] Jeffrey Chambers, 'Conscience and Allegiance: An Investigation Into the Controversy Over the Oaths of Allegiance and Supremacy During the Reign of William III and II, 1689–1702' PhD Thesis, Trinity College, Dublin, 2016, 186–200.

[14] [Daniel Defoe], *An enquiry into the occasional conformity of dissenters* (1697), 9; William Sherlock, *A second letter to a friend concerning the French invasion* (1692), 29.

ancestors did formerly, but what we ought to do now'.[15] Another said he would forebear quoting historians unless the events they described 'are prov'd to agree with the present conjuncture of affairs in every particular'; whilst a third asserted that 'the same causes will not produce the like effects, unless the same circumstances shall concur'.[16]

Such tactics might look like rhetorical small change. In a political reversal of what happened when the Jacobites faced Williamite precedents, and rejected appeals to the past, the king's supporters in the army controversy were provoked to deny easy lessons from history by their rivals' extensive deployment of them. But a wider consideration of time in the government's arguments suggests supporters of the regime had been moved to think about deeper chronological patterns by the dynamic elements of their opponents' case. In particular, the idea of a collapse of a 'Gothick' balance in society since the end of the Middle Ages received examination and was subverted to a pro-army cause. As was outlined earlier, pamphleteers arguing for disbandment had posited a sociological shift over the past two centuries that had eroded the foundations of liberty. Great military nobles, who once had trimmed to prevent either monarchs or the people becoming dictators, had lost their wealth and status; reinstituting a citizen militia would restore the lost balance as great landowners came to lead it.[17] In response to this argument, pro-government writers did not deny the social shift. Instead they redeployed it. One line was to celebrate, rather than deplore, the end of the 'Gothick' world. Far from medieval nobles preventing tyranny, authors declared, they had established their own in their treatment of their tenants, so their fall was a matter for celebration. One pamphleteer thought the coercion necessary to force ordinary people to serve in a militia would be a greater 'vassalage than the old knight service and all the ancient villanage of England', and thus suggested the Middle Ages had been far less free than the world his readers now enjoyed. Daniel Defoe, in one of his earliest efforts as a political writer, was also sure the last centuries had seen progress, not decline. Under the so-called 'Gothick' 'balance', he claimed, 'the tyranny of the barons was intolerable, the misery and slavery of the common people insupportable, their blood and labour was the absolute will of the lord, and often sacrifice [sic] to their private quarrels'.[18]

More significantly, pro-army writers asserted the irreversibility of the changes their opponents lamented. Even if it had been desirable to restore 'Gothick' society, and its military arrangements, things were now so different that nostalgic, non-army, expedients for national defence were impractical. For one thing,

---

[15] *The case of a standing army fairly and impartially stated* (1698), preface.
[16] *The case of disbanding the army at present* (1698), 2; *A letter to A,B,C,D,E,F* (1697), 4.
[17] See above, ch. 4.5.
[18] *Remarks upon a scurrilous libel called an argument shewing that a standing army...* (1697), 4; [Daniel Defoe], *An argument shewing that a standing army with consent of parliament is not inconsistent with a free government* (1698), 15.

warfare had changed. Technological and strategic advances meant military success now required far more constant experience and training than citizen armies led by great landowners could ever provide. As writer after writer insisted, war was now a professional affair that could not be learned by laymen in occasional chivalric adventures or by drilling on the village green. 'By cunning and contrivance of humane reach and invention', one writer insisted, 'war is become a trade'.[19] Defoe agreed. In former ages, he admitted, there might be no difference between a citizen, a soldier, and a husbandman: but 'tis otherwise now'. 'War', he noted, 'is become a science and arms an employment', and 'the nature of fighting is now changed'.[20] John Somers, arguing for preserving the army from his position at the heart of William's government, made the same point. 'The whole method of war is now such', he argued, 'that disciplined troops must prove a very unequal match to much greater numbers' of those without such training and experience.[21]

Even more profoundly, society had shifted. People were now engaged in an increasingly sophisticated economy based on trade, and this would not allow them to leave business to serve in a militia. The wealth and luxury that had resulted from such commerce had also changed mores, so that everyday civilians were no longer desirous or capable of acting as soldiers. An author who claimed to state the case of a standing army 'fairly and impartially' lamented this in the most dolorous terms. Over the Stuart era, men's spirits had been softened, and a 'luxury unknown to our forefathers' had come into vogue, 'whereby we are degenerated from the old hardiness and fortitude our ancestors were famous for'.[22] Another pointed to the kind of folk who now populated England. They were 'trading people' who 'seldom have the leisure or think it worth their while to neglect their business to trail a pike, or discharge a musket'.[23] Somers, similarly, insisted that the social engineering needed to make a citizen militia effective was deeper than his opponents had ever admitted. Luxury might be eliminated, perhaps, but to recreate the golden age of Sparta, or the Roman republic, and make ordinary people fit to be entrusted with the nation's defence, one would have to go far further and banish all 'wealth and trade'.[24]

In this language, the pro-army writers were probably feeding off a developing sense that England had been undergoing a process of 'improvement': a sense that Paul Slack has explored in the seventeenth century. The obvious commercial boom of the Restoration era, and increasingly accurate economic information, had convinced many of the people of the late Stuart era that they were more

---

[19] *Case of a standing army*, 19.
[20] [Daniel Defoe], *Some reflections on a pamphlet lately published entitled an argument shewing that a standing army…* (1697), 16, 21.
[21] [John Somers], *Letter balancing the necessity of keeping a land force* (1697), 7.
[22] *Case of a standing army*, 8.
[23] *A letter to a foreigner, on the present debates about a standing army* (1698), 8.
[24] [Somers], *Letter balancing,*.10.

prosperous, and their conditions of life more ameliorated, than folk in earlier eras. An emerging discipline of 'political economy' argued that trade and commercial enterprise had grown over the last century, and that this could pay for wars on a much greater scale, using more expensive technologies, if the taxation system were appropriately designed to tap the new wealth.[25] This, of course, was a highly dynamic view of history, even if it only began to touch on debates about 1688–9 in the later 1690s within emerging discussions about the post-revolutionary state. It drove both civic humanist pessimism about a return to the days of landed virtue (and it is notable the Charles Davenant, the country–Tory writer, did much to spread the idea that economic advance was driving cultural and political change) and the Williamite response—which came to insist that rising prosperity meant English people were living in a new world.[26]

If times had changed so much that citizen militias would not work, and if the new wealth meant the 'Gothick' balance was irrecoverable, pro-army pamphleteers suggested that these new times called for new solutions, and it was here that they talked of 1688–9 as a novel settlement that met this challenge. Instead of fearing a professional standing force, the English should look for ways to benefit from the security it gave in a modern world, whilst reducing its threat to liberty; universally, the pro-army campaign saw the solution in the Parliament whose constitutional role had been cemented at the revolution. William's army could not overawe the kingdom, writers insisted, because it was now paid for with the consent of the people via their representatives. They could vote to reduce its size the moment external threats diminished or that they began to worry about its effects on internal politics. The fact that the army was reviewed annually by Parliament was a key point in Somers' pamphlet, and Defoe insisted in the title of one of his works that 'a standing army with consent of parliament is not inconsistent with a free government.'[27] In this way, pro-army writers not only accepted long-term social change in arguing for the inescapability of an army, but underlined the significance of the revolution as a turning point. William's armies were safe, as those of Charles and James had not been, because the king had come as 'the glorious preserver [of]…religion laws and liberties', and because parliament was now the ultimate guarantor that an army would be the servant of the people.[28] As the author of the *Case of disbanding the army* put it, armies were safe for the constitution if they had the 'consent of parliament', and no king could attempt tyranny using one 'under the present settlement' (a phrase that subtly implied a new era had dawned).[29]

---

[25] See Slack, *Invention of Improvement.*
[26] For Davenant, see in particular, [Charles Davenant], *An essay upon the ways and means of supplying the war* (1695).
[27] [Defoe], *Argument shewing that a standing army.*   [28] *Letter to A,B,C,D,E,F*, 3.
[29] *Case of disbanding the army*, 2, 8.

The support for new conditions after 1688–9, seen in the pro-army argument and in some responses to the Toleration Act, suggest that, in some circumstances, those who approved of the revolution could begin to conceive of it as the birth of a new kind of liberty, even in the 1690s. This conclusion is supported by a thorough study of the allegiance controversy by Jeffrey Chambers, whose work on changing attitudes to toleration sits within this wider project. Reading a broader sample of pamphlets than has sometimes been considered by scholars of political thought, Chambers suggested a mid-decade shift away from defending 1688–9 by proving its bare legality to celebrating the benefits it had brought. By the time pamphleteers were denouncing the 1696 assassination plot against William or pressing for abjuration of the exiled Stuarts in the wake of the 1701 death of the duke of Gloucester (the immediate Protestant heir to the throne), those Chambers called 'revolutionists' were doing more than arguing for William's basic legitimacy. For example, loyal addresses to William towards the end of his reign stressed the work he had done in defeating arbitrary rule and allowing good Protestants to worship unmolested, whilst pamphleteers celebrated the guarantees of liberty and exclusion of dangerous Catholics from the throne. By stressing the defeat of monarchical tyranny and popery, the cementing of Parliament's role in the constitution, and the statutory—rather than prerogative—grant of religious freedom, supporters of the post-revolutionary regime suggested liberty had been definitively secured, and this began to hint that 1688–9 had been some kind of new foundation of England.[30]

Yet, as so often in consideration of revolutionary chronologies, this is too simple. It underestimates the hold that static modes of thought retained over William's apologists. In debates about toleration and the army, any emergence of new conceptions of time was hesitant and equivocal. The revolution's emergence as the birth of liberty might have been earlier than in Dickinson's Bolingbrokean formulation, but it was only partial in these early years.

For the toleration debates, this was apparent in a series of time-stilling reactions to the 1689 measure. Although some actors created a sense of a turning point as they worked through the consequences and possibilities of the indulgence, many others denied much had changed. The most obvious example here was the widespread insistence by Anglicans that Christian duty had not shifted in 1689. For most establishment clerics, the act had only been an alteration of civil law. As a slew of publications insisted, it did not absolve anyone of the near-unforgivable sin of schism: it was still a heinous spiritual crime to break the unity of Christ's church by leaving for minor scruples. This point was meat and drink to the emerging 'High Church' party which allied with Tories in a defence of the Church

---

[30] Chambers, 'Conscience and Allegiance', esp. chs 4, 7, 9; for loyal addresses see esp. 352–3.

of England in the 1690s.[31] This faction sometimes even expressed regret that the Toleration Act had passed at all, or that it had gone as far as it had; and some preached against the errors of Nonconformity without even a nod to the changed legal situation.[32] High Churchmen also continued the polemical war against dissent that had raged since the mid-century, and which advanced a time-freezing vision of a puritan conspiracy against true faith that had begun under Edward VI. The very title of one piece, speaking of the *Dissenters new plot*, implied that schismatics never changed their dastardly spots.[33] But 'low' churchmen, who have always been understood as more sympathetic to non-Anglicans, also insisted that toleration had altered little. For them it was an indulgence to end civil injustices and to try to ease some of the divisive passions caused by persecution. It was not a milestone on some great march to spiritual liberty. Gilbert Burnet was a classic low churchman, and an advocate of the Toleration Act, but he constantly repeated that the measure did not absolve dissenters from their former obligation 'by the laws of God and gospel, to maintain the unity of the church.'[34] It merely granted a 'civil impunity' and could not make an 'unjust separation…one whit lawfuller than it was.'[35]

Dissenters, of course, had different reactions to toleration. Yet they too could behave in ways that smoothed over any discontinuity in 1689. For some, the most important duty was to continue to rehearse the reasons for separation from the national church that had been stressed since 1660, and which incorporated criticisms of the establishment that had emerged in Tudor times. For example, Burnet's attacks on schism earned him a rebuke from one Nonconformist writer who insisted on the corruptions of the official church—the substance of which might have been penned at any point over the preceding 120 years.[36] Perhaps more intriguingly, dissenters were confronted by a dilemma after 1689 that had them insisting that their basic position had not changed. The difficulty was that indulgence weakened the Nonconformists' persecution-based identity as true churches. Whilst they had been proscribed, the Protestant conviction that godly Christians were likely to be a persecuted remnant had given them an image of heroic suffering and zealous purity (as some of their rivals had warned).[37]

---

[31] For example, [Thomas Long], *The case of persecution charg'd on the church of England* (1689); Richard Meggot, *A sermon preached before the king and queen at Hampton Court July 14th, 1689* (1689), esp. 27–8; John Norris, *The charge of schism continued* (1691); William Saywell, *The necessity of adhering to the church of England* (1692).

[32] For example, *Brethren in iniquity, or the confederacy of papists with sectaries* (1690); *The Dutch way of toleration most proper for our English dissenters* (1690); Thomas Spark, *A sermon preached at Giulford in Surrey, June the 22nd, 1691* (1691); George Raymond, *A sermon at the primary visitation* (1692).

[33] *A true and impartial narrative of the dissenters new plot* (1690). See also, *The dissenters unmasked* (1691); *A stop to the cause of separation* (1693).

[34] G. Burnet, *Discourse of the pastoral care*, 202.

[35] Gilbert Burnet, *Four discourses delivered to the clergy of the diocese of Sarum* (1694), preface.

[36] *Notes upon the lord bishop of Salisbury's four late discourses* (1695).

[37] Again, Burnet was perceptive: *Discourse of the pastoral care*, 202.

However, this risked evaporating in more tolerant times. As John Spurr has said, this meant Nonconformists now 'had to organize themselves…to sustain a zeal hitherto honed by persecution', and whilst some efforts were made to build structures appropriate to the new liberty, there were other, more backward-looking responses that tried to elide current circumstances with the pre-1689 past.[38] As Alex Walsham has pointed out, the Toleration Act fired the starting gun on a tradition of denominational history in which different brands of dissenters catalogued the sufferings of their forebears in an attempt to recapture the fervour of their first decades.[39] First out of the traps were the heirs of Restoration Presbyterianism, carefully reviewing the hardships and heroism of those of their clan who had been persecuted under Charles II.[40] In such writing it seemed that the freedom granted in 1689 required a mental reversion to a former period, to pretend that little had changed.

Further caution over toleration centres on continuing nostalgia for a united church, even within the movements that were born of the measure. As we saw, a new Anglican pastoralism, and the campaign for reformation of manners, operated in a world created by the 1689 act. However, they were not simply celebrations of it, and they did not necessarily welcome the new religious plurality. It is, in fact, much more useful to view them as compensations for a measure lost at the revolution: namely the comprehension proposals that would have reincorporated the majority of Nonconformists back into the church. This was how Craig Rose read the reformation of manners movement. For participants, combatting vice would give the two sides a forum for cooperation and might, over time, lead to an organic coalescence where sudden, statutory action had failed. The whole movement was soaked in language of ecclesiastical union.[41] And Anglican pastoralism was more than a renewal of clerical virtue (though it was certainly that). As its exponents explained, it was partly aimed at persuading dissenters back into the church; and such evangelism would find more receptive ears in audiences that were no longer persecuted. Ministerial engagement with parishioners would include attempts to reach out to local Nonconformists: a moral, diligent, and active, clergy would impress those who had left the church—especially as they had often done so because dissenting leaders had appeared more authentically Christian than their official rivals. As Burnet stated in the movement's manifesto, if Anglican clergy 'were stricter in our lives, more serious and constant in our labours, and studied more effectually to reform those of our communion, than rail at theirs', then his colleagues would have laid before Nonconformists 'the

---

[38] John Spurr, *English Puritanism, 1603–1689* (Basingstoke: Palgrave, 1998), 149.

[39] Alexandra Walsham, *Charitable Hatred: Tolerance and Intolerance in England 1500–1700* (Manchester: MUP, 2006), 313–14.

[40] See Mathew Sylvester, *Reliquiae Baxteriana* (1696); Edmund Calamy, *An abridgement of Mr Baxter's history* (1702).

[41] Rose, *England in the 1690s*, 201–5.

obligations to love and peace, to unity and concord' and the dissenters themselves might see on 'how slight grounds, they have so long kept up such a wrangling, and made such a rent in the church'.[42]

Even endorsements of the fundamental principle of toleration may have been less impressive than they initially appear. Jeffrey Chambers may point to authors who celebrated the 1689 act as the start of new period of religious liberty, but—read closely—the works he cites often praised it for introducing a new calm and forbearance that might, ultimately, restore a universal church. Henry Compton, the bishop of London, told the clergy of his diocese in 1692 that he welcomed the new legal indulgence, but immediately suggested Nonconformists might now be in a mood to actually listen to the case the church had been putting for uniformity for decades.[43] William Lloyd celebrated toleration, but was sure dissenters recognized the bare freedom of worship they had got was all that could be offered, because they were a small and divided minority: the established church would remain at the privileged heart of the nation's spiritual life.[44] The dissenter Robert Fleming called the 1689 measure a 'beam of hope', but made it clear this was because it created a charitable atmosphere which he hoped would lead to coalescence rather than diversity. Celebrating the understanding the London Congregationalists and Presbyterians reached in the early 1690s, he hoped for a wider 'design of union carried on among good men of all denominations and persuasions'.[45]

And this nostalgia for ecclesiastical unity tended to be expressed in time-freezing and typological language. The point of establishing full Christian communion was less to inaugurate a novel utopia of interdenominational collaboration than to enact timeless ideals of spiritual harmony, to recreate past moments of religious perfection, or to advance the ceaseless struggle of the true church against Antichrist. Thus Simon Patrick preached in favour of comprehension early in 1689, as he and colleagues were drafting the doomed legislation; and, at first sight, his sermon called for a millennially tinged epoch of harmony. Using the Isaiahian text that predicted wolves lying down with lambs and other unlikely creature friendships (11:6), he claimed a radical settling of religious dispute was possible after the revolution. At first glance this looked like a quasi-apocalyptic prediction of new times—but as Patrick dealt with the possible objections of sceptics, it became clearer he saw little real innovation in the years ahead. If English Protestants could find agreement, they would merely be reliving the days of the primitive Christians as described in the post-gospel texts of the New Testament or following the unchanging influence of the Christian faith towards mutual love.[46] Similarly, Burnet's voluminous writing on the need for Protestant harmony

---

[42] G. Burnet, *Discourse of the pastoral care*, 204.

[43] Henry Compton, *The bishop of London's eighth letter to his clergy* (1692), 5–6.

[44] [William Lloyd], *The pretences of the French invasion examined* (1692), 15.

[45] [Robert Fleming], *The rod or the sword* (1694), 70, 73.

[46] Patrick, *A sermon preach'd in the chappel of St James…* (1689).

in the wake of the revolution stressed that it would take the Reformation back to its earliest days. Rather than waste energies and tempt providence with petty squabbles, Protestants could do what the first followers of Luther had done and defeat the popish Babylon with a programme of Christian teaching, example, and evangelism.[47]

Thus reactions to toleration rarely suggested more than reluctant acceptance of a novel religious liberty. More often they involved appeals to recreate a lost world of Christian charity or purity, and on closer inspection, Williamite thought on standing armies also appears less forward facing. For a start, pro-army arguments were not immune to simple appeals to the past (very few seventeenth-century arguments ever were). They could mine history for unabashed precedents, and interestingly, they were drawn into discussion of the seventeenth century, which had been dangerous territory for those insisting on the legitimacy of 1688–9 itself. This happened because anti-army pamphleteers had, naturally, used Oliver Cromwell's military dictatorship as evidence of the threat from a professional military. To counter this, pro-army authors used the English republic as evidence that armies could not, in the end, impose their will on a population. Not only had Cromwell's army ultimately failed to suppress the old English constitution, they insisted, but General Monck's hardened forces had been the very instrument of Charles II's restoration. Once the soldiers had realised how unpopular rule by force had become, they themselves had reintroduced monarchy. One writer even drew a parallel between 1660 and the autumn of 1688, cited as twin instances when English professional forces had rebelled against the tyrants who had called them into being.[48]

But static chronology played a larger role than the seemingly irresistible temptation to use the past as direct exemplar. Running through the insistence that William's army was safe was the assumption that it was acceptable because it was Protestant. Like toleration, parliamentary armed forces were instruments of God in the unending struggle between the false and true churches. Several writers stated this explicitly. Some of the first replies to Trenchard and Moyle's attack on standing armies insisted that their authors had been against a full-time military before 1688–9 because it had been an instrument of a papist power grab, but that the situation was entirely different under Protestant William.[49] Similarly, Defoe refuted Trenchard and Moyles' assertion that tyranny was the same thing under papists and Protestants, using examples to prove the former kind was infinitely worse.[50] More subtly, many pro-army authors raised the spectre of Catholic invasion by

---

[47] See Claydon, 'Latitudinarianism'.

[48] *Some remarks upon a late paper entituled an argument shewing* (1697), 14–15; *Some queries concerning the disbanding of the army* (1698), 9.

[49] *Letter to A,B,C,D,E,F*, 3; *Remarks upon a scurrilous libel*, 5–10; *Case of a standing army*, 7; *Case of disbanding the army*, 3.

[50] [Defoe], *Some reflections on a pamphlet*, 11–12.

reminding readers why William wanted an army, namely to defend the realm against Louis XIV. That king, of course, had been painted as a bigoted persecutor of Protestants through the whole preceding nine years of war propaganda (so his mere mention would set debates about the military in a confessional frame), and some works made the connection openly, especially at the more popular end of the market.[51] Matthew Prior's doggerel verse savaged the Jacobite-inspired opponents of the army: he charged that they wished to undo the war's victories against 'French and Popish Pow'r' by making friends with Louis 'in half an hour'.[52] A series of short, printed queries about disbanding the army included questions about whether Louis had given up his efforts 'for the Propagation of the pretended Catholick Faith', whether the army had not been the greatest security for 'the Protestant religion', and whether abandoning it would not run the risk of being 'invaded and conquered by popery'.[53] Elsewhere, analyses of changes of circumstance that destroyed easy parallels with classical militias or the 'Gothick' balance included the emergence of France as a new kind of threat. Here was a nation grown so powerful that it would take the best efforts of all European nations to control her.[54] Such writing did not always directly include Catholicism in the danger, but it almost certainly lurked implicitly. Images of France in the late seventeenth century were inextricably linked with the horrors of papist persecution; and even secular-seeming discourses centred on the dangers of universal monarchy, and the need to preserve a balance of power to prevent this, were rooted in suspicion of what would happen if a Catholic state became hegemonic.[55]

Such anti-popish confessionalization of the pro-army discourse froze its chronology even as authors insisted times had changed in ways that demanded new kinds of forces. Technology, tactics, and the geopolitical balance of Europe may be shifting, but the fundamental struggle against the false church remained the same. A passage in John Somers' work, which set the agenda for the response to Trenchard and Moyle, exposed the chronological tensions in his whole case. He argued that England had been lucky in the past to escape popery and tyranny, insisted that she should not simply trust such providence again, and concluded that the nation must defend itself in new ways in a new world where all states kept professional armies. So far so dynamic. But Somers past instances of luck came from the classic playlist of static Protestant typology. They were Elizabeth's defeat of the Armada and William's defeat of James, and Somers rehearsed the old

---

[51] Tony Claydon, 'Protestantism, Universal Monarchy and Christendom in William's War Propaganda', in Esther Mijers and David Onnekink, eds, *Redefining William III: The Impact of the King-Stadholder in International Context* (Aldershot: Ashgate, 2007), 125–42; Claydon and Levillain, *Louis XIV Outside In.*

[52] [Matthew Prior], *A new answer to an argument against a standing army* (1697).

[53] *Some queries concerning the disbanding*, 3, 9, 14.

[54] [Somers], *Letter balancing*, 12–13; [Defoe], *Argument shewing that a standing army*, 5; [Defoe], *Some reflections on a pamphlet*, 16–17.

[55] See Claydon, *Europe*, 189–92.

dating coincidence that proved them repeated instances of the great, godly struggle. 'We have had two wonderful eighty-eights', he admitted, 'but we presume too much if we look for a third, without taking care…by what means we shall be saved'.[56] This was a statement hopelessly caught between freeze and flow. God would continue to recognize the English as his favoured instruments in his timeless battle, but only if they adapted to the great processes of military development that had marked the last several hundred years.

5.3 Stuart Declensions

Supporters of William in the 1690s thus inhabited a hybrid chronological world. Dynamism and stasis were interwoven in patterns that were at best complex, at worst incoherent. This will be examined more closely in the conclusion to this book, but Somers' mention of Elizabeth introduces a different Williamite temporality that also mixed a real sense of historical process, with considerable dollops of clock-stilling nostalgia. Somers had lauded the sixteenth-century queen's reign as a moment of past glory that was being relived now. But the moment was sufficiently long ago that much might have happened between the two golden ages. Repeat might thus mean return after prolonged divergence, and so generate a more evolving view of time than simple typology. This notion was key to a set of related lines of thought among Williamites that could simultaneously embrace unchanging verities, whilst analysing change, and recognizing turning points, periods, and processes.

The fastest route to the heart of this vision is through the several histories of England that were written in William's reign to celebrate his accession and rule, and which Kevin Sharpe suggested still await systematic study.[57] Although English print culture had long produced narratives of the national past, there was a burst of these in the decade after the revolution. Their purpose, as explained in prefaces and conclusions, was to recognize the Dutch monarch's huge contribution to England, even if the authors represented a range of political sympathies—albeit with a strong bias towards a Whig worldview. We met some of these works when looking at the allegiance controversy. The examples noted there concentrated upon the fortunes of an ancient constitution through the ages to prove that the revolution was one of its periodic reassertions after the rule of a tyrant. Such books tended to avoid close discussion of the seventeenth century because it was difficult to integrate the civil war, regicide, and republic into their vision.[58] But other writers, particularly those publishing after the initial intensity of the debate about William's legitimacy had burned itself out, did find a way to address the last hundred years.

---

[56] [Somers], *Letter balancing*, 13.   [57] Sharpe, *Rebranding Rule*, 397.
[58] See above, ch. 2.3.

They modified or substituted a timeless national past with an era of decline and crisis that had lasted longer than James II's three years of tyranny. They therefore created a far more structured periodization, and described a more evolutionary process, than simple precedent hunting. Chiming with Somers' hint that England had last seen glory under Elizabeth, they defined an essentially *Stuart* epoch of corruption.

The very titles of some of the works identified the period since the accession of James I as a peculiar one, worthy of study in its own terms. Thus, in 1691, John Phillips combined his separate accounts of early Stuart and Restoration history, which he had published the year before, into a unified coverage of the *State of England during the last four reigns*. Similarly Roger Coke badged his effort a *Secret history of the last four monarchs of Great Britain*. Again, Whig pamphleteer James Welwood outlined *The most material transactions in England in the last hundred years, preceeding the revolution*, but merely summarized the state of the nation in the 1590s, before starting his real narrative with the arrival of the James I.[59] Other works encompassed longer or shorter periods in their coverage, but made clear in prefatory material that the age since 1603 had been significant. John Seller penned a narrative of the whole English past starting with the ancient Britons, but he dedicated it to William, because nobody was a better recipient of a work of history than a man who had 'done such great things for it' in raising the nation from the oblivion it had suffered in 'the late reigns'.[60] An anonymous author covered the eras of James I and Charles I alone, but explained in opening passages that his purpose was to trace the causes of the troubles that had overwhelmed England 'for almost this last century'.[61]

As such remarks suggest, the notable characteristics of the Stuart age that the histories defined were crisis and decline. To establish this, they all began with panegyrics of Queen Elizabeth. For these writers, the Elizabethan era had been a national apogee, witnessing the most glorious heights of military glory, of prosperity and popular content, of artistic achievement, and of a balanced constitution functioning to preserve monarchical honour alongside the people's liberties. Elizabeth was a ruler 'admired by future ages', who was blessed with 'a glorious reign of forty four years'; she was 'the admiration of the people, the love of her subjects,...the happiness of her kingdoms, as well as the glory of her age' and a 'bright occidental star'.[62] All this, of course, built on a cult of Elizabeth that—if it had perhaps been less robust during her actual reign than historians once argued—had

---

[59] [John Phillips], *The secret history of the last four monarchs of Great Britain* (1691); Roger Coke, *A detection of the court and state of England during the last four reigns* (1694); James Welwood, *Memoires of the most material transactions in England for the last hundred years, preceding the revolution* (1700).

[60] Seller, *History of England*, epistle dedicatory.

[61] *Hinc illae lachrymae, or England's miseries set forth in their true light* (1692), preface.

[62] [John Somers], *The true and secret history of the lives and reigns of all the kings and queens of England* (1702), 268–9; *Hinc illae lachrymae*, 16; Michael Sparke, *The truth brought to light, or the history of the first fourteen years of King James I* (1692), 1692 preface to this earlier work.

certainly been constructed in the early Stuart era as people looked back, rosily, to untroubled times.[63] Yet in the Williamite histories, the functions of the Elizabethan age were deeper than this. More than an enduring standard of wise rule and sincere Protestantism against which to contrast current corruptions, the Virgin Queen's reign became the starting point of a coherent periodization that saw a unified era of declension that had lasted from the arrival of the Stuarts to 1688. Thus James Welwood dedicated his history to William, who, he said, had 'restor'd to the English nation that figure they had lost for near an hundred years past'. He made it clear exactly when the loss had started by observing a sudden change at 1603. With Elizabeth's demise, Welwood claimed, 'dyed in great part the glory and fortune of the English nation', and the succeeding reigns 'had served only to render hers the more illustrious'.[64] Similarly Roger Coke talked of Elizabeth as enjoying a hegemony over Europe born of her prudence and resolution, but contrasted this with the disasters brought to the whole continent by catastrophic policies of the 'four kings of the Scottish race'.[65] Slingsby Bethel echoed Welwood as he noted that 'when the queen died, the renoun of England seems to have died with her, and since that time we have gone backward in honour and reputation.'[66]

Importantly, for these historians, the Stuart age that had superseded Elizabeth's imperium had not simply seen an unfortunate run of poor rulers. It had been marred by a coordinated and unfolding process of corruption. Each of the monarchs had had their unique flaws, and each had made their own particular mistakes, but they had also presided over the extended playing out of problems introduced when James headed south to take the English throne. The exact list of charges against James varied in detail, but the scholars were generally agreed he had hankered after an absolute power that had eluded him in his native Scotland; that he had debauched the court with luxury and his dependence on favourites; and that he had been too keen to please, and to ally with, the catholic powers of Europe. The first of these traits had been passed on James's son and grandsons, and this had resulted in their corroding efforts to undermine Parliament. The second had allowed a popish cabal to establish itself at the heart of English government— whence it had not been evicted until 1688. The third had given initially Spain, but rapidly France, far too much influence over England's affairs. This vision unified the whole epoch by tracing developing causes of mischief through the twists and turns of the seventeenth century, but also by ensuring James I was integrated into the pattern—even though his rule had not been marked by the same ructions as

---

[63] For doubts about the reality of the golden age, see John Guy, ed., *The Reign of Elizabeth: Court and Culture in the Last Decade* (Cambridge: CUP, 1995); Julia M. Walker, ed., *Dissing Elizabeth: Negative Representations of Gloriana* (Durham, NC: Duke UP, 1998). For the cult's later construction, see Susan Doran and Thomas Freeman, eds, *The Myth of Elizabeth* (Basingstoke: Palgrave, 2003); Julia M. Walker, *The Elizabethan Icon, 1603–2003* (Basingstoke: Palgrave, 2004), chs. 1–2.

[64] Welwood, *Memoires*, epistle dedicatory, 18.   [65] Coke, *Detection*, preface.

[66] Slingsby Bethel, *The providences of God, observed through several ages* (1691).

those of his next three successors. Although James had left his realm in tolerable calm, the historians were sure he had sowed the seeds of later disaster. As Somers graphically put it, as he introduced the 'dunghill' of the Scots monarch's life, 'a prime Stuart we shall find him'.[67] As another writer caustically observed, James had laid the 'foundations of all our miseries in the late civil wars, of the banishment of the royal family, of the struggles that have been since the restoration'.[68]

From this inauspicious start, the Stuart declension had proceeded as its absolutism, court corruption, and foreign influence had reinforced each other to undermine England's free constitution and godly faith. The reign of Charles I posed some problems for this story because this king's reputation had been polished by the Restoration regime, and (as we explored earlier) readers might be alienated by any attack on this sanctified figure.[69] Some writers coped by absolving the monarch of blame for trends that had been started by his father and were now too powerful to curtail. For Welwood, Charles was a virtuous prince, but one overwhelmed by ministers and counsellors corrupted by arbitrary principles, popery, and France.[70] For the chronicler of *England's miseries* over the last century, Charles was a good Protestant, and a man who would otherwise have tried to work with Parliament, but he was undone by credulous faith in the Catholic faction at court and affection for his French wife.[71] Other writers though, were not so sure; and some found the courage to challenge the cult of the martyred king. Thus Somers insisted there was fault on both sides in the civil war and regicide, as did William Pudsey as he commented on the tensions between Charles and his parliaments.[72] Bolder writers attempted to reverse a generation of royal propaganda with direct assaults on the executed monarch. Slingsby Bethel warned against any sanctification of Charles because he had been contemptuous of Parliament and appeared to have incited the Irish revolt of 1641.[73] John Phillips similarly thought this 'calendared' saint to have been a hypocrite; and the author of a *Short history of the kings of England*, who had denounced most of the nation's rulers as plotting to overthrow its liberties, thought Charles I was the first sovereign to be so open in attempting to implement the oppressive designs of all his ancestors.[74] In these histories, therefore, there was a willingness to think about the 1640s that had been missing in the more immediate cut and thrust of the allegiance controversy pamphlets (in those, writers had feared obscuring their defence of the revolution with any shadow of the regicide). This was possible because the historians had, to a degree, broken with the static and typological approach of the pamphleteers who had discussed

---

[67] [Somers], *True and secret history*, 290.   [68] Sparke, *Truth brought to life*, preface.
[69] See above, ch. 2.3.   [70] Welwood, *Memoires*, 37, 61, 63.
[71] *Hinc illae lachrymae*, 189.
[72] [Somers], *True and secret history*, 393; Pudsey, *Political essay*, 125–8.
[73] Bethel, *Providences of God*, 8–10.
[74] [Phillips], *Secret history of the last four monarchs*, preface; *A short history of the kings of England* (1692), 38–9.

the basic legality of the revolution. The historians could talk about 1649 because they did not treat it as a precedent. Instead, they integrated it into a linear and unfolding narrative of corruption.

The Williamite histories were not much interested in the English republic. Few dedicated more than a few pages to it, partly because many of them were framed as histories of monarchs, but mostly because Cromwell's regime stood outside the processes of decline introduced by James. The Lord Protector's regime might be condemned as illegal, or briefly praised as militarily successful (to throw greater shame on royal rule in the seventeenth century), but the true interest was what was happening to Charles I's sons.[75] Forced into exile in Catholic Europe by the consequences of the first Stuarts' policies, Charles II and James II had fallen further under the influence of absolutism, popery, and France, and this had had consequences that had played out in later decades. It is true that some histories of seventeenth-century corruption began their story in 1660, and so created a shorter 'Restoration' era of decline whose dynamic rested on the debauchery of the second Charles, the popish bigotry of the second James, and the interference of Louis XIV (who, conveniently for the periodization, had taken personal control of French policy in 1661).[76] This absolved the martyred monarch, or the first Stuart, of direct blame, and it gelled with a strand of Anglican Williamite rhetoric which tried to celebrate the Restoration as a return to godly monarchy, but one betrayed by the failings of rulers and subjects in the years that followed.[77] However, most works had a longer coverage that united the two halves of the century, and one writer angrily denied that that the early Stuarts could be excused. John Phillips published his account of 1660 to 1688 in 1690, but followed it up the same year with a volume on 1603 to 1649 because he did not want to leave the impression that problems had begun only with Charles II. 'There are not a few' he reproved, 'who, though they seem to decry the tyranny of the two late kings, yet approve much the same actions of the two that preceded them…not considering that they layd the foundations of the tyranny which the others brought to great perfection.'[78]

Once into the narratives of the post-Restoration regimes, the histories agreed a trajectory in which the degeneration began by James I, reinforced by the hold French ideals and policy came to have over his grandsons, burst out into the wholesale assault on liberty and Protestantism seen after 1685. Some writers thought Charles II had delayed the Franco-popish conspiracy, but only because he was too cowardly and luxurious to risk the political turmoil that would have been caused by too

---

[75] For an example of the dual attitude to Cromwell, see Welwood, *Memoires*, 102–13.

[76] Guy Miege, *A complete history of the late revolution* (1691); R.B., *The history of the last two kings, Charles the Second, and James the Second* (1693); David Jones, *The secret history of Whitehall* (1696).

[77] Tony Claydon, 'Gilbert Burnet: An Ecclesiastical Historian and the Invention of the English Restoration Era', in Peter D. Clarke and Charlotte Methuen, eds, *The Church on Its Past: Studies in Church History 49* (Woodbridge: Boydell, 2013), 181–91.

[78] [John Phillips], *The secret history of the reigns of K. James I and K. Charles I* (1690), preface.

openly advancing the plot. His relative uselessness as a tool of popery and absolutism had merely caused the agents of France and Catholicism to concentrate on capturing his more bigoted brother, thus ensuring that James's promises to rule within the law were revealed as shams within weeks of his coming to the throne, rather than the decades it had taken to expose Charles' insincerity.[79] This, however, had had a paradoxical benefit. James's Catholic tyranny had been so open and alienating that he had united the nation against him. This, along with the heroism of William III and the actions of providence, had ensured the success of the 1688–9 revolution.

The key consequence of this understanding of history for Williamite perceptions of time was to provide a periodization, a sense of evolution, and a perception of 1688–9 as a significant turning point. There had been a clear Stuart age that had been marked by a consistent process of decline, but had been ended by the Dutch invasion. However, and crucially, this perception contained all these chronological dimensions without adopting a fully linear vision of historical change, or abandoning a quasi-typological mindset that sought ideal types in the past. Within this narrative, William's arrival was a restoration. It was a return to the golden age of Elizabeth with which the account had begun. The Stuart age was therefore a clear period with an ongoing internal development, but also an era whose narrative had been reversed and negated with Orange triumph, and so had existed almost out of time. This was most explicit in Slingsby Bethel's coverage of 1688–9. Bethel included a closing panegyric to Elizabeth to establish the now restored standard from which the nation had fallen. Her period of rule could be considered virtually perfect in comparison with that of the next four kings, which was 'chargeable with all that is contrary to these excellences'. Now though, Bethel said, all were 'freed from the grievances of the last four reigns' and must 'hate the remembrance of those times, and never more hanker after the like'.[80] Other writers implied the same sealing of the seventeenth century from the normal run of English history as they lauded William as the saviour of old virtues. For John Phillips, the Dutch king was 'a generous redeemer of the true reformed religion' who had put the English 'in the fair way to recover their pristine glory'.[81] For James Welwood, William had 'restored to the English nation that figure they had lost for near an hundred years past'.[82]

The notion of a Stuart age of corruption had echoes beyond the histories, in other Williamite material—but these too tended to isolate the last century from the normal state of England. An example was the construction of Mary II, within regime propaganda, as a new Elizabeth. Exploiting the fact that there was a queen regnant on the throne (albeit one who only exercised executive powers when her

---

⁷⁹ R.B, *History*, 155; Miege, *A complete history*; *Hinc illae lachrymae*, 190–5.
⁸⁰ Bethel, *Providences of God*, 43–4.   ⁸¹ [Phillips], *Secret history of last four monarchs*, 130.
⁸² Welwood, *Memoires*, epistle dedicatory.

husband was out of the country), poets, preachers, pictorial print makers, and other publicists celebrated parallels that suggested that late-Tudor monarchy had been restored. Perhaps the most sustained example was a broadside verse, published just after Mary's death. This took the form of alternating stanzas in which Elizabeth and Mary praised each other's achievements and was headed by a double portrait of the couple heading to heaven. In sphere after sphere (rescuing church and constitution, defeating universal monarchs and Irish rebellion, and gallantly fending off naval invasion), Mary was shown to have emulated Elizabeth so closely that she could not accept praise from the Tudor ruler. She told Elizabeth she had 'only trod the footsteps you began'.[83] Such sentiments were echoed in other memorial publications for the Stuart queen, which stressed she had been Elizabeth reborn, and in material that had appeared whilst she was still alive that had paired her with her predecessor.[84] A tract that ranted against the dangers of popish rule in 1692 declared that 'in the person of the queen we have a second Queen Elizabeth', whilst Edmund Bohun's sketch of Elizabeth's character recommended that William and Mary take her as their model.[85] Bohun clarified the chronological effects of his advice by saying he was going to describe the Elizabethan epoch to inspire its recreation. By learning lessons from the later sixteenth century he claimed one could avoid the 'calamities' that came in with the vices of the last age and reverse the 'worse times' that had ensued on the great queen's death.[86] This was all graphically underlined by the pictorial frontispiece. In this, William was effectively cuckolded by a dual portrait of Mary and Elizabeth. Here the dead Tudor ruler displaced the king in the standard iconography of the dual monarchy and collapsed the entire seventeenth century by depicting the two queens alive together (Fig. 5.1).

We have already met other visions of a uniquely corrupt Stuart period. Gilbert Burnet's suggestion that the Reformation had unfolded in two contrasting eras became a version of it when he argued the revolution offered a chance to return to the first, successful, stage of the movement. For him, a sixteenth century marked by Protestant expansion had given way to a century of retreat as the godly had fallen out and tried to persecute each other. This was true for Europe as a whole, but it fitted an interpretation of English history, too, as Burnet called for England's Protestants to use William's rule as an opportunity to return to the real priorities of moral reform and Christian charity. The bishop thus created creating a stagnant epoch between periods of spiritual zeal that neatly coincided with the reigns of the

---

[83] *A kind congratulation between Queen Elizabeth and the late Queen Mary II* (1695).

[84] For examples of memorial material, see Gilbert Burnet, *An essay on the late queen* (1695), 150; C.D., *An elegy on the death of the queen* (1695), 7; J.S., *A history of the pious and glorious life and actions of the most glorious Mary* (1695), epistle dedicatory; [Edward Fowler], *A discourse of the great disingenuity and unreasonableness of repining at afflicting providences* (1695), 16–17, 27.

[85] *Chuse which you will: liberty or slavery* (1692), 18; Edmund Bohun, *The character of Queen Elizabeth* (1693), epistle dedicatory and frontispiece.

[86] Bohun, *Character*, preface and 376.

THE

CHARACTER

OF

Queen Elizabeth.

OR,

A Full and Clear Account of Her Policies, and the Methods of Her Government both in Church and State.

Her Virtues and Defects.

Together with

The Characters of Her Principal Ministers of State. And the greatest part of the Affairs and Events that Happened in Her Times.

Collected and Faithfully Represented,

By Edmund Bohun, Esquire.

Semper eadem.

London: Printed for **Ric. Chiswell**; at the *Rose* and *Crown* in St. *Paul's* Church-Yard.   MDCXCIII.

Fig. 5.1 Frontispiece to Edmund Bohun, *The character of Queen Elizabeth* (1693). By kind permission of The Bodleian Libraries, The University of Oxford: Vet. A3 f.168.

first four Stuarts. Williamite writings on political thought shared this chronological patterning. Particularly when countering the Jacobite contention that 1688–9 transgressed traditional Protestant support for rulers, pamphleteers insisted that—in fact—it was the idea of absolute passive obedience that had been the novel interloper. Notions of non-resistance had, writers explained, been introduced by 'Laudian' clerics hoping to gain favour at the courts of the first two Stuart kings and had then run rampant in overcompensation for the horrors of the rebellion of the 1640s.[87] Such writers stressed that an older and true Protestant political philosophy, which had become eclipsed in intervening decades, had guided the actions of Elizabeth. When the godly were oppressed by their rulers in other lands, the Tudor queen had been happy to aid their rebellions, as she had in her interventions in Scotland, France, and the Netherlands.[88] Again, consideration of

---

[87] See, for example, [Long], *Historian unmask'd*, 25; *History of self-defence*, 29.

[88] For this line of argument in the allegiance controversy, see Allix, *Examination of the scruples*, 18–19; Masters, *Case of allegiance*, p. 13; Johnson, *Some reflections*, 3; *Monsieur Jurieau's judgement upon the question of defending our religion* (1689), translator's preface; *A defence of their majesties King William and Queen Mary* (1689), 35–6.

the French threat stressed that the challenge had been seen before. France's plotting might have driven English decline, but this was part of a bid for European dominance, which allowed her to be portrayed as Spain reborn. Pamphlets that analysed the danger from Louis depicted him as the latest universal monarch to try to dominate the continent; they explained the processes by which Versailles had taken over from Madrid as the bigoted bully of international affairs; and they therefore cast the Sun King in the mould of Phillip II, the potential hegemonist who had been thwarted by the martial virtues of the Virgin Queen.[89]

A Stuart age of progressive corruption was thus at the heart of the Williamite vision—at least once supporters of the revolution lifted their eyes from its immediate constitutional justification. In response they modified their static chronology, admitting that a long period had had characteristics somewhat different from the normal run of English history, and detecting linear narratives of development within in. Vices introduced by James I had at first been mild, but had aggravated as left unchecked; the source and style of the threat to England had modified after the first catastrophe of the civil war had sent the Stuart princes into exile amidst French absolutism and popery. Similarly, 1688–9 could be understood as an epoch-defining turning point. William's arrival had excised a political, cultural, and religious tumour that had shaped events for nearly a century, and allowed a moment of wholesale regeneration. Yet, as with writing on toleration and the army, the break was less impressive than at first appears. Overwhelmingly, the vision saw a return to norms that had been corrupted: a setting back of the clock most obvious in claims that there was to be a new Elizabethan age. Linear narrative thus only occurred within the peculiar era of corruption. Now it was over, the task was to uphold the timeless, ancient truths of the Protestant faith and the free, 'Gothick' constitution that Elizabeth had championed. It may be unfair to ask commentators writing so soon after the revolution to discuss any of its unfolding consequences, but those reflecting on the pattern of English history in the seventeenth century never suggested dramatic new directions, causes, or values for the nation in a new age. 1688–9, as those years' date numbers suggested, belonged firmly in epochs that had lasted for millennia. There was no 'Year Zero' in the late Stuart epoch.

[89] Claydon, *Europe*, 152–60.

Conclusion

Time and Revolutions

The Revolution in Time

This book opened with a suggestion about the relationship between proposed changes in senses of time and a possible understanding of the 1688–9 revolution. It asked if a new and dynamic model of chronology might have helped witnesses to William's triumph conceive what had happened as a human-made and radical step forward into a different, and more 'modern', world. The answer has to be broadly, no. Those who saw the collapse of James's regime did sometimes adopt a secular and evolutionary model of time, but they did so very patchily. As we have seen, the rapid events of the prince of Orange's first weeks in England were not unambiguously interpreted as accelerated progress towards a transformed state of the world, and there were swathes of interpretation of the king's ascent to the throne that insisted nothing had altered. Even in the wake of a revolution—and towards the end of most conceptions of the early modern period—the incoming regime was defended as a champion of a remarkably static ancient constitution that dated back to Anglo-Saxon times, and as the salvation of a true church that had been God's instrument on earth since the Fall. These defences were soaked in typological thinking. For those who lived through them, the events of 1688–9 were identical to providential salvations of Protestantism that had occurred over the last century and a half, to medieval depositions of monarchs hundreds of years in the past, or even to divine deliverances of Old Testament Israel millennia ago. This revolution was neither a turning point within a periodized timeline, nor proof of a progressive march of history. People did not, therefore, use a new dynamic chronology to make sense of the political tsunami that had seen, nor did they assume a linear narrative, carrying the nation forward to a different tomorrow, as they processed a torrent of consequent economic, religious, and social change.

In a wider frame, this book has uncovered problems for the whole theory of a shift in chronological perceptions by the later Stuart age. Often, reactions to 1688–9 seem to have reversed the direction of travel within this model, or to have rendered it paradoxical. For example, William's invasion provided a moment of highly accelerated news flow, and of critical individual decision, which might have been expected to produce a richly 'modern' temporality. But in fact the very

The Revolution in Time: Chronology, Modernity, and 1688–1689 in England. Tony Claydon, Oxford University Press (2020). © Tony Claydon.
DOI: 10.1093/oso/9780198817239.001.0001

speed with which things were unfolding disrupted any such experience. There was only limited feeling that a new future was being created in a critical present. As frequently, there was a 'postmodern'-style bewilderment, a directionless rejection of attempts to see patterns in events, or a scripting of experience into familiar plots which shut down the possibility of the new. To take another example: the response of many people to the apparent reconfigurations of their era was to adhere to understandings of time that were considerably less dynamic than had been espoused earlier in the Stuart age. For instance, the version of the ancient constitution clung to by William's supporters was blinder to change than that which had been adopted by early seventeenth-century thinkers, and potentially transformative versions of Protestant history, such as apocalypticism, seemed to play a smaller role in understanding William's arrival than they had in the earlier turmoil of the civil wars. Again, there was paradox in the stance taken by William's opponents. It was not those who needed to defend change after 1688–9 who were most willing to accept that it had occurred. Rather it was those who wished to put the clock back who proved the keenest analysts of changing times (even as they despaired of actually reversing events because they suspected time was irreversible).

Such findings do more than question whether key parts of the posited chronological transformation had occurred in England by the late seventeenth century. They challenge its coherence. The several elements of the supposed new time sense were supposed to have supported one another. For instance, emptying history of its spiritual meaning was supposed to have rendered the present unstable because it could now create a future undetermined by God; abandoning cyclical and typical time should have allowed the perception of periods with unique characteristics; an acceleration of temporal perception would underscore a sense of linear time that broke the hold of the past over human action; and so on. But reactions to 1688–9 have demonstrated that some elements of 'modern' time emerged without others. There was a real sense of acceleration in the autumn of 1688, but no unfolding story. The prevalence of Reformation time questions any notion of secularization, but it was precisely from this Protestant mindset that some of the more developmental understandings of the revolution emerged—though Reformation time was also quintessentially typical. The most radical attempts to deny the relevance of the past to present action emerged in unexpected places: in theological disputes about the meaning of Christ's—surely universally applicable—political teaching, or among Jacobites who were otherwise committed to a timeless and un-negotiable principle of succession. The contradictions of applying a model of chronological change to the revolution have piled up.

From all this we can state our first main conclusion. This is that the people who witnessed the 1688–9 revolution did not make sense of it by a wholesale adoption of 'modern' chronology. They did not move from one set of mutually supporting assumptions about chronology to another, perhaps even more coherent, constellation of ideas that better matched a world that was altering rapidly in the aftermath of regime change. Rather, at the point late in the early modern period which we have been examining, people were constructing time in ways that appear hybrid within any grand theory of temporal modernization. According to exact context and circumstance, folk were seeing chronology as both essentially developmental and essentially static. Given this, we need to change the sort of questions we pose about time-perception at this moment in the late Stuart age. Instead of categorizing chronological awareness according to preset scheme of classification (especially 'modern' or 'pre-modern') or charting how far people had travelled on a journey from one to the other, scholars need to ask how the messy, particular, idiosyncratic, and mixed mindsets of people actually functioned to shape their comprehension of the world.

Of course this risks being a conclusion that explodes its own study. There has been a great deal of exploring 'modern' and 'pre-modern' mental categories in the preceding chapters, which might have been better spent on the consequences of real worldviews. But the opening model has been a powerful one, dominating analysis of chronological awareness, so it has taken some deconstruction. Moreover, the work of challenging the model for 1688–9 has allowed a finer appreciation of exactly how people were constructing time, and has thus provided tools for more precise thinking about how temporal awareness affected their actions. If, for example, the revolutionaries had adopted a 'modern' chronology, they might have been able to think flexibly about political structures, freed from static deference to an ancient constitution, or a belief that English monarchy must play its role in the ceaseless struggle of the true church. That they did not (or could do so only partially) helps to explain their patchy appetite for risk and innovation, and their framing of solutions to match their conservative assumptions. Abandoning the model of a modernizing chronology may only be a first step to knowing what was really going on in seventeenth-century understandings of time, but it is a vital and productive one. The reconsiderations it involves suggest new ways to think about early modern experience.

To start to engage with this alternative agenda, it is useful to outline a second main conclusion of the study. This is that there must be serious questions over presentations of the revolution that have become popular over recent decades. As was outlined in the introduction, a generation of discussion of James's fall has trended towards the idea that it represented a deliberate act of modernization. Charting the substantial changes that occurred with the revolution has, in some cases, spilled over into claims that the people of 1688–9 had conscious plans to transform their country. For some scholars, a new nation of parliamentary liberty, religious freedom, and capitalist economy was a deliberate goal. Yet our examination of chronological awareness is hard to reconcile with this interpretation. Consciously campaigning for modernizing change would surely require a more dynamic sense of how time could work than our evidence suggests was common.

This poses a problem for the current interpretative bent of revolution studies. Yet replacing it is also challenging, because recent scholarship has also highlighted many ways in which William's arrival and rule were genuinely transformative. However their mental furniture was arranged, the English of the last years of the seventeenth century unquestionably recreated their nation. A constitutional settlement that ensconced Parliament as a standing institution of government and placed conditions on who could be monarch, and a Toleration Act which institutionalized spiritual diversity, created a wholly new political and religious situation. William's war with France transformed fiscal, financial, military, and administrative realities, so that by the end of the 1690s, there had been an entire change in the polemic universe. A long-standing rhetoric that had posited popish plot as the explanation for public ills had been replaced by one that worried about state overreach and corruption, about the public virtue of citizens who should resist these evils, and about the very reality of a society rooted in ever-shifting credit. These changes were deep-seated and durable. They fashioned the mould for the parliamentary-imperial society of Georgian and Victorian Britain; and they were never reversed, as so many of the initially more radical changes of the 1640s and '50s were at the Restoration. One can argue, as Jonathan Scott has done, that the later parts of seventeenth century were essential a reply of its early decades, with battles fought over the same issues, but, as he suggested, the world after the revolution became entirely different.[1]

This disjunction between the real, rapid, and deep changes in politics and society, and the conservative, static, and past-dominated chronologies of those who accepted the changes, is the analytic challenge that remains in interpreting 1688–9. It suggests transformation took place without chronological assumptions that assumed alteration was natural. Before turning to the wider implications of this study for ideas about time in the early modern West, this conclusion will make some suggestions about how to transcend this tension. Rather than simply noting that chronological awareness in William's reign was not entirely keeping up with other political, infrastructural, and cultural shifts, we will sketch ways in which, perhaps, the temporal perceptions we have traced may have worked to facilitate change, even though they did not always recognize (let alone welcome) it.

One obvious way this may have happened is through psychological reassurance. When people witness huge alterations in their world, even when they are effecting these, it can be comforting to pretend that nothing much is happening. Similarly, the wholly novel can sometimes only be made comprehensible by imagining that, in fact, it is time-honoured and familiar. These sorts of coping mechanisms were clearly in play as witnesses to 1688–9 scripted events into already-known narratives, or as bewilderment at William's triumph was rapidly

---

[1] Jonathan Scott, *England's Troubles: Seventeenth English Political Instability in European Context* (Cambridge: CUP, 2000).

repackaged into vehement insistence that this had happened before. Something first thought unique in its unexpectedness, or one too strange to understand, soon became a familiar reiteration: the latest instance of God's deliverance of the true religion, or yet another reassertion of ancient liberty. The zeal with which people clung to such typological readings of 1688–9, and the depth of their insistence that this was an exact replay of history, is perhaps an indication of how radically transformative they sensed their situation actually was. It may, indeed, have been the reassurance of the timeless that allowed them to accept, even advance, the wholesale remodelling of their world.

And the insistence on typology probably did more than prevent psychological breakdown. It provided a programme for immediate action during William's invasion, and one that proved remarkably successful in steadying society, and allowing new solutions to be found, in the midst of a disruptive revolution. It therefore allowed the rapid and reasonably stable establishment of the new regime that would soon cause such dramatic change. Clearly a comprehensive settlement was needed urgently in the early weeks of 1689, when so many old structures were in abeyance, and there was huge potential for conflict. The radical-Whig to high-Tory spectrum encompassed a vast variety of possible political and ecclesiastical futures, even amongst those who were glad to see James gone. But in this situation, a belief that the past should be the guide, and that Englishmen had surmounted exactly these challenges before, focused minds on where answers to the predicament would lie. Despite the huge uncertainty, and deep tensions, there was astonishing consensus on two issues—agreements that perhaps prevented any new civil war. First, immediately upon meeting, the convention unanimously resolved that Catholics must in future be excluded from the actual exercise of sovereignty. This effectively stymied Tory attempts to preserve some role for the exiled king and forced acceptance of William as monarch (debate would largely be limited to exactly why he was so). Second, within days of excluding Catholics from power, all shades of opinion were collaborating on a definitive statement of the customary rights that they thought English law granted the legislature and individuals against excesses of royal power. These responses presupposed a settlement that would contain change within familiar institutions such as monarchy, Parliament, and a reformed official church. Of course, at one level, these responses were simply reactions to James's absolutist Catholicism. But they were not the only possible responses. Rather, they were solutions shaped by the temporal modes that had been adopted to make sense of the revolution. What was done had to gel with the conviction that the ancient constitution had just reasserted itself and that God had once again saved his true faith as it had been embodied in Protestant monarchy.

Static chronology may thus have prevented political breakdown in 1688–9, and so—in a sense—made possible the rapid developments that came after. But the frozen sense of time might also, paradoxically, have encouraged alterations as radical as any allowed by belief in a progressive and accelerated process of history. The chronological senses we have explored might have denied that deep transformation could happen, but they were not necessarily conservative or quietist. They could demand action, and so create an unstable present with possibilities of remodelling the future, even though they failed to provide any real mental framework to support historical development. They did this, first, because a typological view of the universe recognized temporary diversions from necessary norms, and second, because the timeless states of static chronologies were not always ones of eventless harmony, but might instead be marked by ceaseless conflicts in which people were required to engage. In these closely related dimensions, there was considerable dynamism at the heart of 'pre'-modern mentality.

The urgent need for action within typology is obvious as soon as one reflects what the key precedents used after William's arrival actually were. When people leapt over centuries to find analogies with their own situation, they did not pick examples at random from a homogenous past. Rather, they sought instances where timeless structures had been temporarily perverted, and argued that people now needed to emulate those who had defended these structures before. Usually, the precedents were described as restorations. They were moments when the correct state of the world, the one whose continuing legitimacy allowed the appeal to history, was reimposed after a diversion. Precedents were such things as the defeat of tyrants to re-establish ancient liberties, or the providential failure of threats to the true church. The diversions were usually short lived (otherwise they would open up disturbing epochs of history that did not prove the unbroken validity of the principle to be restored), but they had demanded urgent action to reverse. People who believed in millennia of *stasis*, could thus also believe in the pressing need to recast situations in which they found themselves. Those who rebelled against their king in the autumn of 1688 did so buoyed by the sense that earlier perversions of the cosmos had been corrected by popular mobilization and divine providence. This could create the sense of a critical present moment seen, for example, in Lord Delamer's appeal to his tenants to rally to William's side.

And the precedents could also be conceived as points in a ceaseless struggle which had involved dynamic choices by individuals. The constant and legitimating state of the world might not be a 'correct' one which people must work to restore, but rather a timeless Manichean conflict that pitted good against evil. This was most obvious in Protestant depictions of false and true churches which had fought through all ages since Adam's, but there were constitutional versions in which the principles of parliamentary consent and private liberties had been barriers to a restless royal power that always strove for dominance. In such conceptualizations, precedents *could* be drawn randomly from any point in the past, because time's fractal nature meant every moment was a microcosm of all history. But this internecine past taught that life would always demand action, often very radical. Lauding William as a reborn David pitched him into that earlier figure's struggle with God's enemies and aligned him with everyone else who had, in any time, struggled for righteousness. Talk of the Baron's Wars cast the prince of Orange as the latest in an unbroken line of champions who had fought for liberty and to block the ever encroaching forces of tyrannous power. Both visions demanded vigorous popular support for a man who came to overthrow a king.

Static chronology could thus push people to extraordinary positions over the winter of 1688–9. But the restorative action, and the timeless conflict, at the heart of this kind of temporal awareness continued to generate innovation though the rest of William's reign. Beyond the constitutional settlement, the most far-reaching effects of the era were probably the abandonment of a strictly confessional state (with the Toleration Act, the absolute identity of church and commonwealth, which had been an ideal since Tudor times, ceased) and the far-reaching socio-economic developments rooted in the war with France. Although, as we saw, both generated some sense of chronological dynamism, both can also be explained as workings of largely undevelopmental philosophies.

Our survey of arguments over toleration did not reveal any great advance for new, 'liberal' notions of religious freedom. Almost everyone involved believed in the traditional ideal of a united church, encompassing all believers. Toleration was accepted, not for its own sake, but as the only way to end the sin of persecution and to turn people from fruitless doctrinal coercion towards a truly Christian life. In making these arguments, commentators used both restorative precedent and timeless struggle. They cited moments in history at which God's people had returned to his message of peace between the faithful. They focused on the era of primitive Christianity (presented as a time of mutual charity, responding to Christ's revelation of the underlying meaning of God's earlier messages to mankind) and the early Reformation (presented as a rebirth of primitive Christianity). They also advocated religious forbearance as the duty of those caught in the cosmic controversy. As the Bible, Foxe, and the history of popery proved, the false church's chief weapon (indeed its most easily identifiable characteristic) had been persecution, and had been in all eras. Abandoning coercion was thus to declare one's most passionate allegiance to true faith; and—moreover—it would be the most effective strategy in the battle. Christians united in mutual love would be stronger against the armies of the Antichrist, and heaven would favour them as reward for their fidelity to the principle of charity. The vision of ceaseless warfare could also recognize superficial shifts in circumstance. The fundamental struggle could never alter, but any struggle could change in detail as each blow was struck, and different tactics might be needed at different times. Those who argued that Protestantism had weakened since the sixteenth century, and so could no longer afford internal divisions, were speaking within this mode.[2]

---

[2] See above, ch. 3.2

The story was similar for the battle with Louis XIV. There has not been space in this volume to outline in detail why the English were so committed to their campaign against Louis that they were prepared to remodel their nation in its interests (that has been major part of this author's earlier researches). But the short version is that they thought the French monarch was the reincarnation of earlier Catholic hegemons, such as Charles V or Philip II, and that he represented that latest incarnation of the eternal forces of tyranny, bigotry, deceit, ambition, and error that had challenged true religion throughout its history.[3] Within these assumptions, restorative precedent, and timeless conflict, became the ideology for transformative war. Restorative precedent was used when William's rolling back of the popish universal monarch was compared with England's earlier heroics. Elizabeth I was the most obvious candidate here, hence the frequent comparisons between 1588 and 1688. Timeless conflict was invoked as Louis was cast as an enemy of Christianity. War propaganda portrayed the French king as a man incapable of keeping faith with Christians, as a cruel and brutal suppressor of all Christian churches, as a foe of Christendom (as evidenced in his alliance with the Ottomans), and as a man driven by hellish ambition towards global domination. All this allowed William's cheerleaders to label Louis as the Antichrist, as the Beast of Revelation, or as a Turk (that figure identified as the Antichrist whenever Islam made advances). English society was thus remodelled on the altar of typological warfare. The English state fought not only Louis, but a series of identical opponents scattered through history and the never-sleeping forces of evil.

Thus, England did not become a 'modern' society at the end of the seventeenth century because it adopted a progressive chronology that allowed folk to plan a new world. Rather it modernized, at least to some extent, precisely because it had not altered in its thinking about time. It was a static view of history that provided the psychological, political, and constitutional stability that permitted the broad and far-reaching innovations of William's reign, and it was typological mindsets that shaped radical programmes as they applied precedents and timeless conflicts to the present. Over the years, it is true, England became such a different place that a more linear, periodized, and accelerated views of history were adopted to describe what had happened. But even here, an important dynamic was the rhetorical response to conservative forces that had developed a progressive narrative in order to demand that it be reversed.

A Revolution in Time?

The revolution, then, will not fit a neat pattern of chronological modernization, but, of course, this has implications for the whole notion of a shift in chronological

---

[3] See Tony Claydon, *William III and the Godly Revolution*; Claydon, 'Protestantism, Universal Monarchy'.

awareness in the West in the early modern centuries. Most importantly, it must question the speed, completeness, neatness—and even the existence—of the grand theories of changes in temporal perception with which this book started.

As has been stressed, one of the strongest impressions to emerge from this study of late-seventeenth-century temporality has been its hybridity. Picking a point in time which many scholars have argued was already exhibiting a 'modern' sense of chronology, we instead found a highly mixed picture. People could certainly express empty, periodized, developmental, and linear views of how chronology worked, but they could also insist on providentially full, static, typological, and cyclical ones. Sometimes their position could seem incoherent or self-contradictory (for instance, those in the immediate throes of the events of William's invasion saw those events as at once chaotic and highly scripted; and speakers in the 1689 convention could insist on timeless axioms from an ancient constitution and insist that *salus populi* removed the need for detailed precedent). Sometimes they seemed to hold several models of how time worked in their heads simultaneously and to swop between them according to their immediate needs (for example, opponents of the standing army could, within a single paragraph, both draw directly lessons from Roman history and insist the world had changed profoundly since the classical age, whilst Protestant preachers could use both providentially unfolding, and the typological, dimensions of their faith to excite audiences with the significance of William's arrival). Temporal perceptions in the aftermath of the revolution were thus more complex, and perhaps had offered greater freedom of choice, than any simple notion of the arrival of a neatly packaged modernity might imply.

And it seems likely that this hybridity was a feature of many early modern European societies, and at many other moments, beyond the crisis of late-seventeenth-century England. This study has no space to examine other situations in detail as comparisons, but work by other scholars has begun to find parallels to the chronological variety of the late-Stuart realm.[4] Moreover, there are good grounds to think people in early modern Europe had particular reasons to adopt a hybrid view of time. They lived in societies where the predominant mode of political and social legitimation was traditional (current structures were explained and justified primarily through their time-honoured continuity), but also in societies challenged by novel religious conflicts after the Reformation, by significant technological developments, and by political revolutions that upended long established regimes. All these demanded more fluid conceptions of how history worked than traditional authority could provide. More importantly, these were

---

[4] See, for example, Paul Glennie and Nigel Thrift, *Shaping the Day: A History of Timekeeping in England and Wales, 1300–1800* (Oxford: OUP, 2009), 8; Judith Pollmann, *Memory in Early Modern Europe* (Oxford: OUP, 2017), ch. 2; Alexander Nagle and Christopher S. Wood, *Anachronic Renaissance* (New York: Zone, 2010).

profoundly Christian societies. In the early modern era, Christianity still determined understanding of the cosmos, and the internal disputes of the faith set political agendas—both within states, and in international relations. Yet, as was explained in chapter three, Christianity had a profoundly equivocal chronology. It insisted that truth was timeless and eternal, and that it emerged equally at all points of history, in its symmetrical and fractal pattern. But Christianity also insisted that truth unfolded in a great story told through the ages. Moments in real time (the Fall, the Atonement) had transformed the world; moments in the future would do so again—and adherents of the faith had a duty to act in time to prepare for these great upheavals. No culture so deeply influenced by such a set of beliefs was likely to have a simple temporal model. The shattered and contradictory chronologies we have been exploring for 1688–9 were therefore almost certainly symptoms of a much wider phenomenon.

So, understandings of William's arrival were hybrid, and it is probable that study of many other points in early modern European history would reveal that witnesses were similarly inconsistent in their comprehension of time. This raises deep questions for the grand narrative of temporal change. It obviously demonstrates that even by a point quite late in the suggested process of chronological transformation, people were holding on to static conceptions of time. But maybe more worryingly, it troubles the evidential base of the theory. The problem with the likely hybridity of chronological awareness through the early modern centuries is that mixed sets of data can—by conscious or unconscious selection—support any argument about change or continuity one wishes to make. If one wanted to confirm the grand theory of chronological transformation, one could certainly find instances of people thinking in 'modern' terms at the end of a period, and in a pre-modern way before that. But one could just as easily disprove the theory by selecting other instances. One could even, perhaps, construct the case that 'modern' thought came before pre-modern. In this book we have seen people on the cusp of the eighteenth century believing they were in the same position as medieval parliamentarians or Hebrew prophets. Assuming people in the late Middle Ages also had a hybrid temporality, they could no doubt think in 'modern' terms: sometimes believing in periodized historical development (for instance, espousing ideas of progressive spiritual ages, especially in millenarian movements), or that time was an empty resource to be filled with their own actions (as in the conceptions of merchant and labour time, examined some while ago by Jacques Le Goff).[5] Scholars may therefore need to be far more cautious in claiming grand

---

[5] The classic study of late medieval millenarianism is Norman Cohn, *The Pursuit of the Millennium* (rev. edn, Oxford: OUP, 1970); for merchant and labour time in the later medieval period, see Jaques Le Goff, *Time, Work and Culture in the Middle Ages*, trans. Arther Goldhammer (Chicago: University of Chicago Press, 1980), chs 2–3.

transformations. Apparent shifts may be optical illusions, created by picking particular illustrations from a very diverse range of evidence.

Of course, a universal hybridity in time perception does not automatically mean there were no 'modernizing' tendencies over the early modern centuries. New temporalities may have become more common, more characteristic, or more influential, even as older ones lingered in certain areas of the collective *psyche*. But the strong persistence of static and typical time in 1690s England (at a point late in the broad period, and in a country which was otherwise undergoing very rapid change), argues against this happening in any fast or wholesale way. It not only suggests any shift was slow and patchy, but also that it was never a 'zero sum' game. Any 'modern' ideas that were adopted did not have to displace 'pre-modern' ones; rather, developmental time might have emerged or have been strengthened to run alongside a still vigorous static time, and to enhance the range of chronological choices. In addition, the fact that some of the dominant ideas used to discuss 1688–9 were *less* progressive than versions deployed earlier in the century suggests any changes need not have run smoothly in one direction. In the earlier Stuart era, commentators had been happy to argue the English constitution evolved over centuries—sometimes with major discontinuities—or to assert that apocalyptic was working out its final transformation of the cosmos. By William's era, however, circumstances had encouraged people back to far more static positions. If temporal perceptions were altering, therefore, they may have taken almost as many steps 'back' as 'forward'.

Does all this doubt about temporal transformation leave any real concept of 'modern' attitudes to time? Perhaps. There does seem to be a set of attitudes that hang together conceptually and may have been adopted by people. Believing that time is empty, periodized, progressive, atypical, and has been moved forward ever faster by an unstable and human-shaped present, is a coherent view that was sometimes adopted by people, and 'modern' may not be a wholly inappropriate label for this cosmology. It does seem to have been powerful in the West in the nineteenth and twentieth centuries: it was certainly prominent in many historiographies, political positions, and assertions about processes of human development in that era. Yet for all the usefulness of the concept of 'modern' time as an analytic term, it has strict limitations. We can only use it if we remain aware that there was no very clear, or inevitable, or irreversible movement towards people thinking about time in this way. This study has shown that 'modern' chronology was nowhere near triumphant as late as the dawn of the eighteenth century. Commentary on postmodernism has suggested it has lost any grip it had in the last few decades. It was almost certainly never absolutely hegemonic even in the nineteenth and twentieth centuries, and the likely hybridity of time awareness in all periods suggests at least elements of it may have been available as an option from the earliest eras of Western history. We should, therefore, adopt the same attitude to the examination of chronology generally that we earlier recommended for examining the witnesses of 1688–9. Instead of plotting where people are on a journey from a traditional worldview to a more 'modern' one, we should examine how they actually thought about time in all its complexity and perhaps its incoherence. In this analysis we can perhaps use 'modern' to label certain types of reaction—but we must not assume these prove people had started a trajectory, let alone a self-conscious one, to a novel worldview. Instead we must think about why they adopted these particular models of times to talk about the particular things they were talking about: what roles they performed in that particular moment, why they were chosen above other models that were always potentially available.

Such a conclusion spoils any neat account of cultural transformation. We are positing a constant babble of chronologies, which may well drown out any clear signal that attitudes were changing. Movement towards a more 'modern' sense of time was so partial, erratic, and reversible that it may be impossible to assert it was happening at all. Yet if this makes the story harder to tell, it may make it far more interesting. For example, and as we have seen, close study of William's triumph in England has opened us up to the paradoxical dynamism that may have been latent in static worldviews. Political, social, and cultural modernity have arrived without temporal modernity—indeed may have come precisely because other ways of thinking about time were working out their consequences. In the convention of January 1689, John Dolben may have leapt back 400 years to rescue his fellow statesmen from their inability to process the enormity of what had just happened to them. But when he did so, he unleashed a true revolution. A deep, unvarying past accelerated an unrecognizable future: change, like the truth, is rarely pure, and never simple.

Select Bibliography

Later printings of manuscript material

E.S. De Beer, ed., *The Diary of John Evelyn*, 6 vols (Oxford: OUP, 1955)

George Agar Ellis, ed., *The Ellis Correspondence*, 2 vols (1892)

Anchitell Grey, *Debates in the House of Commons from 1667 to 1694*, 10 vols (1769)

HMC, *The manuscripts of the Duke of Rutland preserved at Belvoir Castle* (1889)

HMC, *The manuscripts of the House of Lords 1689–1690* (1889)

HMC, *The manuscripts of S.H. Le Fleming* (1890)

HMC, *The manuscripts of the Duke of Beaufort* (1891)

HMC, *The manuscripts of the Duke of Portland preserved at Welbeck Abbey*, vol. III (1893)

HMC *The manuscripts of Lord Kenyon*, (1894)

HMC, *The manuscripts of the Earl of Buckingham, the Earl of Lindsey etc.* (1895)

HMC, *The manuscripts of the Earl of Dartmouth*, vol. III (1896)

HMC, *The manuscripts of the late Reginald Rawden Hastings* (London: HMSO, 1930)

Henry Horwitz, ed., *The Parliamentary Diary of Narcissus Luttrell, 1691–93* (Oxford: OUP, 1972)

David Lewis Jones, ed., *A Parliamentary History of the Glorious Revolution* (London: HMSO, 1988)

Russell J. Kerr and Ida Coffin Duncan, eds, *The Portledge papers* (London: Cape, 1928)

The letters of Lady Rachel Russell (7th edn, 1809)

Stephen Taylor, ed., *The entring book of Roger Morrice*, vol.4: *1687–1689* (Woodbridge, Boydell, 2007)

Printed Primary Sources

Allegiance vindicated, or the takers of the new oath of allegiance to K William and Q Mary justified (1690)

'An answer to the desertion discussed', in *A complete collection of papers in twelve parts* (1689)

[Peter Allix], *An examination of the scruples of those who refuse the oaths of allegiance* (1689)

[Peter Allix], *Reflections upon the opinions of some moderate divines* (1689)

[William Anderton], *Remarks upon the present confederacy* (1693)

[Francis Atterbury], *Letter to a convocation man* (1696)

William Atwood, *The fundamental constitution of English government* (1690)

William Atwood, *Proposals for printing the fundamental constitution of the English government* (1690)

R.B., *The history of the last two kings, Charles the Second, and James the Second* (1693)

Nathaniel Bacon, *An historical and political discourse of the laws & government of England from the first times…collected from some manuscript notes of John Selden* (1689)

Slingsby Bethel, *The providences of God, observed through several ages* (1691)

Thomas Beverley, *The late great revolution, argued according to Revelation 17* (1689)

[Edmund Bohun], *The doctrine of non-resistance and passive obedience* (1689)

[Edmund Bohun], History of the desertion (1689)

Edmund Bohun, *The character of Queen Elizabeth* (1693)

R[ichard] B[ooker], *Satisfaction tendered to all that pretend conscience for nonsubmission* [1689]

[Robert Brady], *An enquiry into the remarkable instances of history and parliamentary records* [1690?]

A brief account of the nullity of King James's title (1689)

A brief vindication of the parliamentary proceedings against James II (1689)

Thomas Browne, *The case of allegiance due to the king in possession* (1690)

Gilbert Burnet, *The history of the reformation...the first part* (1679)

Gilbert Burnet, *A sermon preached before the House of Commons, 31 January, 1688/9* (1689)

Gilbert Burnet, *A sermon preached in the chappel of St James before his highness the prince of Orange, 23 December, 1688* (1689)

Gilbert Burnet, *A sermon preach'd before the queen at White-hall, on the 16th day of July* (1690)

Gilbert Burnet, *A sermon preache'd at Whitehall before the king and queen on 29th April, 1691* (1691)

Gilbert Burnet, *A discourse of the pastoral care* (1692)

Gilbert Burnet, *Some sermons preached on several occasions* (1713)

Gilbert Burnet, *A vindication of the ordinations of the church of England* (1688)

Thomas Burnet, *The theory of the earth...the last two books* (1690)

Lilly Butler, *A sermon preached at St. Mary-le-Bow, before the Lord Mayor, Court of Aldermen and citizens of London* (1691)

Thomas Cary, *A sermon preached in the parish-church of St. Philip and Jacob, in the city of Bristol* (1691)

The case of a standing army fairly and impartially stated (1698)

The case of disbanding the army at present (1698)

The case of the people of England in their present circumstances (1689)

The character of Thomas Merkes, bishop of Carlise (1689)

Roger Coke, *A detection of the court and state of England during the last four reigns* (1694)

[Jeremy Collier], *Animadversions upon the modern explanation of II Henry 7 cap.1* (1689)

[Jeremy Collier], *The desertion discuss'd in a letter to a country gentleman* (1689)

[Jeremy Collier], *Vindiciae juris regii* (1689)

A complete collection of papers in twelve parts, relating to the great revolution (1689)

[Charles Davenant], *The true picture of a modern Whig* (1701)

[Charles Davenant], *Tom Double returned out of the country* (1702)

The debate at large between the Lords and Commons at the free conference (2nd edn, corrected, 1710)

[Daniel Defoe], *The advantages of the present settlement* (1689)

[Daniel Defoe], *Reflections upon the late great revolution* (1689)

[Daniel Defoe], *An enquiry into the occasional conformity of dissenters* (1697)

[Daniel Defoe], *Some reflections on a pamphlet lately published entitled and argument shewing that a standing army...* (1697)

[Daniel Defoe], *An argument shewing that a standing army with consent of parliament is not inconsistent with a free government* (1698)

[Henry Dodwell], *Concerning the case of taking the new oaths of fealty and allegiance* [1689]

The Dutch design anatomized (1689)

[Robert Ferguson], *A letter to Mr Secretary Trenchard* (1694)

[Robert Ferguson], *Whether the parliament be not in law dissolved* (1695)

[Andrew Fletcher], *A discourse concerning militias and standing armies* (1697)

A form of prayer and thanksgiving to almighty God for having made…the prince of Orange the glorious instrument of this great deliverance (1689)

A fourth collection of papers relating the present juncture of affairs in England (1688)

A friendly debate between Dr Kingsman, a dis-satisfied clergy-man and Gratianus Trimmer (1689)

[Francis Fulwood], *Agreement betwixt the present and the former government* (1689)

[Francis Fulwood], *Obedience due to the present king* (1689)

[Samuel Grascome], *Two letters written to the author of a pamphlet entituled Solomon and Abiathar* (1692)

[Samuel Grascome], *New court-contrivances* (1693)

George Halley, *A sermon preached in the cathedral and metropolitical church of St Peter of York…fourteenth of February, 1688/9* (1689)

[George Hickes], *A letter to the author of a late paper* (1689)

[George Hickes], *An apology for the new separation* (1691)

Hinc illae lachrymae, or England's miseries set forth in their true light (1692)

The history of self-defence in requital to the history of passive obedience (1689)

The history of the most illustrious William, prince of Orange (1688)

An honest Commoner's speech (1694)

Robert Howard, *The history of the reigns of Edward and Richard II* (1690)

[Robert Jenkin], *The title of a usurper after a thorough settlement examined* (1690)

Samuel Johnson, *Some reflections on the history of passive obedience* (1689)

Samuel Johnson, *Remarks upon Dr. Sherlock's book, intituled, The case of allegiance* (1690)

Samuel Johnson, *An argument proving that the abrogation of King James…was according to the constitution of the English government* (1692)

[Samuel Johnson], *A confutation of a late pamphlet* (1698)

[Nathaniel Johnston] *The dear bargain* (1689)

Pierre Jurieu, *The reflections of the reverend and learned monsieur Jurieu* (1689)

Benjamin Keach, *Antichrist stormed* (1689)

[White Kennett], *A dialogue between two friends occasioned by the late revolution of affairs* (1689)

[John Kettlewell], *The duty of allegiance settled on its true grounds* (1691)

The late honourable convention proved a legal parliament (1689)

[Charlwood Lawton], *The Jacobite principles vindicated* (1693)

[Charlwood Lawton], *A short state of our condition* (1693)

[Charlwood Lawton], *Some paradoxes presented as a new-years-gift* (1693)

A letter from a loyal member of the church of England to a relenting abdicator (1689)

A letter from Oxford concerning Mr Samuel Johnson's late book (1693)

A letter to A,B,C,D,E,F (1697)

A letter to a dissenting clergyman of the church of England concerning the oaths of allegiance (1690)

A letter to a member of parliament concerning guards and garrisons (1699)

William Lloyd, *A discourse of God's ways of disposing of kingdoms* (1691)

[Thomas Long], *The historian unmask'd* (1689)

[Thomas Long], *Resolution of certain quearies concerning submission to the present government* (1689)

Samuel Masters, *The case of allegiance in our present circumstances consider'd* (1689)

Guy Miege, *A complete history of the late revolution* (1691)

James Montgomery, *Great Britain's just complaint* (1692)

[Walter Moyle], *A second part of an argument shewing that a standing army is inconsistent with a free government* (1697)

The muses farewell to popery and slavery (1688)

The new oath of allegiance justified from the original constitution (1689)

Observations upon the late revolution in England (1689)

[Thomas Orme], *The late prints for the standing army* (1698)

Simon Patrick, *A sermon preach'd in the chappel of St James…20 January* (1689)

Samuel Peck, *Jericho's downfall: in a sermon preached upon January 31 1688/9* (1689)

The people of England's grievances offered to be enquired into (1693)

[John Phillips], *The secret history of the last four monarchs of Great Britain* (1691)

Popish treaties not to be rely'd on (1688)

Prayers to be used in all cathedral, collegiate and parochial churches…during this time of public apprehensions from the danger of invasion (1688)

The present case stated: or the oaths of allegiance and supremacy (1689)

The price of the abdication (1693)

William Pudsey, *A political essay, or summary review of the kings and government of England* (1698)

Remarks upon a scurrilous libel called an argument shewing that a standing army (1697)

A remonstrance and protestation of all the good Protestants of this kingdom (1689)

A review of Dr Sherlock's case (1691)

[John Richardson], *Providence and precept* (1691)

Henry Sacheverell, *The perils of false brethren, both in church and state, set forth in a sermon preached before the right honourable, the lord mayor* (1709)

The sad estate of the kingdom (1689)

[Abednego Seller], *The history of passive obedience since the reformation* (1689)

John Seller, *The history of England* (1696)

A sermon preach'd in a country church, February 14, 1688 (1689)

William Sherlock, *The case of allegiance due to sovereign powers* (1691)

William Sherlock, *A sermon preached at White-Hall, before the Queen, on the 17th of June, 1691* (1691)

John Sleidan, *The general history of the reformation of the church from the errors and corruptions of the church of Rome*, trans. Edmund Bohun (1689)

Some considerations touching succession and allegiance (1689)

Some reflections upon his highness the prince of Orange's declaration (1688)

Some queries concerning the disbanding of the army (1698)

[John Somers], *Letter balancing the necessity of keeping a land force* (1697)

[John Somers], *The true and secret history of the lives and reigns of all the kings and queens of England* (1702)

Thomas Spark, *A sermon preached at Giulford in Surrey, June the 22nd, 1691* (1691)

A supplement to the muses farewell to popery and slavery (1690)

William Talbot, *A sermon preached at the cathedral church of Worcester…September 16, 1691* (1691)

John Tillotson, *A sermon preache'd at Lincoln's Inn Chappel, on the 31st of January, 1688* (1689)

John Tillotson, *A sermon preached at White-hall before the Queen on the monthly fast-day, September 16th 1691* (1691)

[John Toland], *The militia reformed* (1698)

[John Trenchard], *A letter from the author of the argument against a standing army* (1698)

[John Trenchard], *A short history of standing armies* (1698)

[John Trenchard and Walter Moyle], *An argument shewing that a standing army in time of peace is inconsistent with a free government* (1697)

James Tyrell, *Bibliotheque politica* (1694)

A Vindication of those who have taken the new oath of allegiance to King William and Queen Mary (1689)

[Thomas Wagstaff], *A letter out of Lancashire to a friend in the country* (1694)

William Wake, *A brief history of several plots* (1692)

James Welwood, *A vindication of the present great revolution* (1689)

James Welwood, *Memoires of the most material transactions in England for the last hundred years, preceeding the revolution* (1700)

[Daniel Whitby], *A letter from a city minister* (1689)

[Daniel Whitby], *An historical account of some things relating to the nature of the English government* (1690)

Secondary Works

Benedict Anderson, *Imagined Communities* (rev. edn, London: Verso, 1991)

Robert Beddard, *A Kingdom Without a King* (Oxford: Phaidon, 1988)

Marshall Berman, *All That Is Solid Melts into Air: The Experience of Modernity* (New York: Simon and Schuster, 1982)

Etinenne Bourdon, 'Temporalities and History in the Renaissance', *Journal of Early Modern Studies*, 6 (2017), 39–60

Glenn Burgess, *The Politics of the Ancient Constitution* (Basingstoke: Longman, 1992)

Jeffrey Chambers, 'Conscience and Allegiance: An Investigation Into the Controversy Over the Oaths of Allegiance and Supremacy During the Reign of William III and II, 1689–1702', PhD Thesis, Trinity College, Dublin, 2016

Paul Christianson, 'Royal and Parliamentary Voices on the Ancient Constitution, 1604–1621', in Linda Levy Peck, ed., *The Mental World of the Jacobean Court* (Cambridge: CUP, 1991), 71–98

Tony Claydon, *William III and the Godly Revolution* (Cambridge: CUP, 1996)

Tony Claydon, 'William III's *Declaration of Reasons* and the Glorious Revolution', *Historical Journal*, 39:1 (1996), 87–108

Tony Claydon, *Europe and the Making of England* (Cambridge: CUP, 2007)

Tony Claydon, 'Protestantism, Universal Monarchy and Christendom in William's War Propaganda', in Esther Mijers and David Onnekink, eds, *Redefining William III: The Impact of the King-Stadholder in International Context* (Aldershot Ashgate, 2007), 125–42

Tony Claydon, 'Latitudinarianism and Apocalyptic History in the Worldview of Gilbert Burnet, 1643–1715', *Historical Journal*, 51 (2008), 577–97

Tony Claydon, 'The Sermon Culture of the Glorious Revolution', in Peter McCullough, Hugh Adlington, and Emma Rhatigan, eds, *The Oxford Handbook of the Early Modern Sermon* (Oxford: OUP, 2011), 480–494

Tony Claydon, 'Daily News and the Construction of Time in Late Stuart England, 1695–1713', *Journal of British Studies*, 53 (2013), 55–7

Tony Claydon and Charles-Edouard Levillain, eds, *Louis XIV Outside In: Images of the Sun King Beyond France, 1661–1715* (Aldershot: Ashgate, 2016)

David Cressy, *Bonfires and Bells: National Memory and the Protestant Calendar in Elizabethan and Stuart England* (Berkeley: Weidenfeld and Nicolson, 1989)

252 SELECT BIBLIOGRAPHY

Brendan Dooley, ed., *The Dissemination of News and the Emergence of Contemporaneity in Early Modern Europe* (Farnham: Ashgate, 2010)

Arthur B. Ferguson, *Clio Unbound: Perception of the Social and Cultural Past in Renaissance England* (Durham, NC: Duke UP, 1979)

Peter Fritzche, *Stranded in the Present: Modern Time and the Melancholy of History* (Cambridge, MA: Harvard UP, 2004)

Northrop Frye, *The Great Code: The Bible and Literature* (New York: Houghton, 1981)

Noelle Gallagher, *Historical Literatures: Writing About the Past, 1660–1760* (Manchester: MUP, 2012)

Samuel Garland, 'News in Late Seventeenth-Century Britain', PhD Dissertation, Bangor University, 2016

Mark Goldie, 'The Revolution of 1689 and the Structure of Political Argument', *Bulletin of Research in the Humanities*, 83 (1980), 473–564

Mark Goldie, *Roger Morrice and the Puritan Whigs* (Woodbridge: Boyell, 2007)

Mark Goldie and Clare Jackson, 'Williamite Tyranny and the Whig Jacobites', in Esther Mijers and David Onnekink, eds, *Redefining William III: The Impact of the King-Stadholder in International Context* (Aldershot: Ashgate, 2007), 177–200

Achsah Guibbory, *The Map of Time: Seventeenth-Century English Literature and Ideas of Pattern in History* (Urbana, IL: Illinois UP 1986)

Timothy Hampton, *Writing from History: The Rhetoric of Exemplarity in Renaissance Literature* (Ithaca: Cornell UP, 1990)

Tim Harris, *London Crowds in the Reign of Charles II* (Cambridge: CUP, 1987)

Christopher Hill, 'The Norman Yoke' in *The Intellectual Origins of the English Revolution Revisited* (Oxford: OUP, 1997), 361–5

Geoffrey S. Holmes, *The Trial of Dr Sacheverell* (London: Eyre Methuen, 1973)

Lynn Hunt, *Measuring Time, Making History* (Budapest: Central European UP, 2007)

Ronald Hutton, *The Rise and Fall of Merry England* (Oxford: OUP, 1994)

Robert Ingram, *Reformation Without End: Religion Politics and the Past in Post-Revolutionary England* (MUP, 2018)

Warren Johnston, 'Revelation and the Revolution of 1688–9', *Historical Journal*, 48:2 (2005), 351–89

Anthony Kemp, *The Estrangement of the Past* (Oxford: OUP, 1991)

J.P. Kenyon, *Revolution Principles: The Politics of Party, 1689–1720* (Cambridge: CUP, 1977)

Reinhart Koselleck, *Futures Past: On the Semantics of Historical Time*, trans. Keith Tribe (New York: Columbia UP, 2004)

Peter Laslett, 'The English Revolution and Locke's Two Treaties of Government', *Cambridge Historical Journal*, 12:1 (1956), 40–55

Karl Löwith, *Meaning in History* (Chicago: Chicago UP, 1949)

Frank E. Manuel, *Shapes of Philosophical History* (Stanford: Stanford UP, 1965)

James McConnel, 'The 1688 Landing of William III at Torbay: Numerical Dates and Temporal Understanding in Early Modern England', *Journal of Modern History*, 84:3 (2012), 539–71

Natalie Mears, Alasdair Raffe, Stephen Taylor, and Philip Williamson, eds, *National Prayers: Special Worship Since the Reformation*, vol. I (Woodbridge: Boyell, 2013)

Paul Monod, *Jacobitism and the English People, 1688–1788* (Cambridge: CUP, 1989)

Robert Nisbet, *The History of the Idea of Progress* (New York: Basic Books, 1980)

C.A. Patrides, *The Grand Design of God: The Literary Form of the Christian View of History* (London: Routledge, 1972)

Steve Pincus, *1688: The First Modern Revolution* (New Haven: Yale UP, 2009)

J.G.A. Pocock, *The Ancient Constitution and the Feudal Law* (Cambridge: CUP, 1957)

J.G.A. Pocock, *The Machiavellian Moment* (Princeton: Princeton UP, 1975)

J.G.A. Pocock, 'Civic Humanism and Its Role in Anglo-American Thought', in *Politics, Language and Time* (Chicago: Chicago UP, 1989), 80–103

Robert Poole, *Time's Alteration: Calendar Reform in Early Modern England* (London: UCL Press, 1998)

Craig Rose, *England in the 1690s* (Oxford: Blackwell, 1999)

J.L. Russell, 'Time in Christian Thought', in J.T. Fraser, ed., *The Voices of Time* (Amhurst: University of Massachusetts Press, 1981) 59–77

Zachary Sayre Schiffman, *The Birth of the Past* (Baltimore: Johns Hopkins UP, 2011)

Kevin Sharpe, *Image Wars: Promoting Kings and Commonwealths in England, 1603–1660* (New Haven: Yale UP, 2010)

Kevin Sharpe, *Rebranding Rule: The Restoration and Revolution Monarchy, 1660–1714* (New Haven: Yale UP, 2013)

Paul Slack, *The Invention of Improvement: Information and Material Progress in Seventeenth Century England* (Oxford: OUP, 2015)

C. John Sommerville, *The News Revolution in England* (Oxford: OUP, 1996)

Charles Taylor, *A Secular Age* (Cambridge, MA: Harvard UP, 2007)

Keith Thomas, *Religion and the Decline of Magic* (London: Wiedenfield and Nicolson, 1971)

Philip Turetzky, *Time* (London: Routledge, 1988)

Ernest Lee Tuveson, *Millennium and Utopia: A Study in the Background of the Idea of Progress* (New York: Harper and Row, 1949)

David Vincent, *Literacy and Popular Culture* (Cambridge: CUP, 1989)

Alexandra Walsham, *Providence in Early Modern England* (Oxford: OUP, 1991)

Corrine C Weston, 'England: Ancient Constitution and Common Law', in J.H. Burns and Mark Goldie, eds, *The Cambridge History of Political Thought* (Cambridge: CUP, 1991), 374–411

G.J. Whitrow, *Time in History: The Evolution of Our General Awareness of Time* (Oxford: OUP, 1988)

Donald J. Wilcox, *The Measure of Times Past: Pre-Newtonian Chronologies and the Rhetoric of Relative Time* (Chicago: Chicago UP, 1987)

Daniel R. Woolf, *Reading History in Early Modern England* (Cambridge: CUP, 2000)

Daniel R. Woolf, 'News, History and the Construction of the Present in Early Modern England', in Brendan Dooley and Sabrina. A Baron, eds, *The Politics of Information in Early Modern Europe* (London: Routledge, 2002), 80–118

Daniel R. Woolf, 'From Histories to the Historical: Five Transitions in Thinking About the Past, 1500–1700', *Huntington Library Quarterly*, 68 (2005), 33–70

Index

For the benefit of digital users, indexed terms that span two pages (e.g., 52–53) may, on occasion, appear on only one of those pages.

The manufacturer's authorised representative in the EU for product safety is Oxford University Press España S.A. of el Parque Empresarial San Fernando de Henares, Avenida de Castilla, 2 – 28830 Madrid (www.oup.es/en or product. safety@oup.com). OUP España S.A. also acts as importer into Spain of products made by the manufacturer.

www.ingramcontent.com/pod-product-compliance
Ingram Content Group UK Ltd.
Pitfield, Milton Keynes, MK11 3LW, UK
UKHW021841070726
473043UK00014B/149